new interchange

English for international communication

Jack C. Richards

with Jonathan Hull and Susan Proctor

teacher's edition

1

New Interchange Teacher's Edition
revision prepared by Susan Proctor.

CAMBRIDGE
UNIVERSITY PRESS

81996

PUBLISHED BY THE PRESS SYNDICATE OF THE UNIVERSITY OF CAMBRIDGE
The Pitt Building, Trumpington Street, Cambridge, United Kingdom

CAMBRIDGE UNIVERSITY PRESS
The Edinburgh Building, Cambridge CB2 2RU, UK
40 West 20th Street, New York, NY 10011–4211, USA
477 Williamstown Road, Port Melbourne, VIC 3207, Australia
Ruiz de Alarcón 13, 28014 Madrid, Spain
Dock House, The Waterfront, Cape Town 8001, South Africa

http://www.cambridge.org

First published 1997
6th printing 2003

New Interchange Teacher's Edition 1 has been developed from *Interchange* Teacher's Manual 1,
first published by Cambridge University Press in 1990.

Printed in the United States of America

Typeface New Century Schoolbook   *System* QuarkXPress®   [AH]

A catalog record for this book is available from the British Library

ISBN 0 521 62881 4 Student's Book 1
ISBN 0 521 62880 6 Student's Book 1A
ISBN 0 521 62879 2 Student's Book 1B
ISBN 0 521 62878 4 Workbook 1
ISBN 0 521 62877 6 Workbook 1A
ISBN 0 521 62876 8 Workbook 1B
ISBN 0 521 62875 X Teacher's Edition 1
ISBN 0 521 62874 1 Teacher's Manual 1
ISBN 0 521 62873 3 Class Audio Cassettes 1
ISBN 0 521 62871 7 Student's Audio Cassette 1A
ISBN 0 521 62869 5 Student's Audio Cassette 1B
ISBN 0 521 62872 5 Class Audio CDs 1
ISBN 0 521 62870 9 Student's Audio CD 1A
ISBN 0 521 62868 7 Student's Audio CD 1B
ISBN 0 521 95019 8 Audio Sampler 1–3
ISBN 0 521 77381 4 Lab Guide 1
ISBN 0 521 77380 6 Lab Cassettes 1

Also available
ISBN 0 521 62867 9 Video 1 (NTSC)
ISBN 0 521 62866 0 Video 1 (PAL)
ISBN 0 521 62865 2 Video 1 (SECAM)
ISBN 0 521 62864 4 Video Activity Book 1
ISBN 0 521 62863 6 Video Teacher's Guide 1
ISBN 0 521 91481 7 Video Sampler Intro–3
ISBN 0 521 62667 6 CD-ROM (PC format)
ISBN 0 521 62666 8 CD-ROM (Mac format)
ISBN 0 521 77381 4 Lab Guide 1
ISBN 0 521 77380 6 Lab Cassettes 1
ISBN 0 521 80575 9 Teacher-Training Video with
                  Video Manual
ISBN 0 521 62882 2 New Interchange/Passages
                  Placement and Evaluation Package

Book design, art direction, and layout services: Adventure House, NYC
Illustrators: Adventure House, Barbara Griffel, Randy Jones, Mark Kaufman, Kevin Spaulding,
Sam Viviano; Jack DeGraffenried, Daisy de Puthod *(Tests)*
Photo researcher: Sylvia P. Bloch

Contents

Introduction

THE NEW EDITION

New Interchange is a revision of *Interchange*, one of the world's most successful and popular English courses. *New Interchange* incorporates many improvements suggested by teachers and students from around the world. Some major changes include many new Conversations, Snapshots, and Readings; more extensive Grammar Focus models and activities; a greater variety and amount of listening materials; extensive changes to the **Teacher's Edition** and **Workbook**; and additions to the **Video.**

New Interchange is a multi-level course in English as a second or foreign language for young adults and adults. The course covers the four skills of listening, speaking, reading, and writing, as well as improving pronunciation and building vocabulary. Particular emphasis is placed on listening and speaking. The primary goal of the course is to teach communicative competence, that is, the ability to communicate in English according to the situation, purpose, and roles of the participants. The language used in *New Interchange* is American English; however, the course reflects the fact that English is the major language of international communication and is not limited to any one country, region, or culture. This level is for beginners and takes students from the beginning to low-intermediate level.

This level builds on the foundations for accurate and fluent communication already established in the prior level by extending grammatical, lexical, and functional skills. Because the syllabus covered in this Student's Book reviews language features taught at the prior level, students who have not previously used *New Interchange* can successfully study at this level.

COURSE LENGTH

Each full level of *New Interchange* contains between 70 and 120 hours of class instruction time. For classes where more time is available, the Teacher's Edition gives detailed suggestions for Optional Activities to extend each unit. Where less time is available, the amount of time spent on Interchange Activities, Reading, Writing, Optional Activities, and the Workbook can be reduced.

Each split edition contains approximately 35 to 60 hours of classroom material. The Student's Book, Workbook, and Student's Audio Cassettes or CDs are available in split editions.

COURSE COMPONENTS

The **Student's Book** contains 16 six-page units, each divided into two topical/functional "cycles," as well as four review units. At the back of the book are 16 communication tasks, called "Interchange Activities," and summaries of grammar and vocabulary taught in each unit.

The full-color **Teacher's Edition** features detailed teaching instructions directly across from the Student's Book pages, along with audio scripts, cultural notes, answer keys, and optional activities. At the back of the Teacher's Edition are instructions for Interchange Activities, an Optional Activities Index, a Workbook Answer Key, and four photocopiable Achievement Tests with audio scripts and answer keys.

The **Workbook** provides a variety of reading, writing, and spelling exercises to reinforce the grammar and vocabulary taught in the Student's Book. Each six-page unit follows the same teaching sequence as the Student's Book; some exercises recycle teaching points from previous units in the context of the new topic. The Workbook can be used for classwork or homework.

The **Class Audio Program**, available on cassette or CD, is intended for classroom use. The Conversations, Grammar Focus models, Pronunciation exercises, and Listening activities in the Student's Book are all recorded naturally with a variety of native and some nonnative accents. Recorded exercises are indicated with the symbol ▣◉.

The **Student's Audio Program** provides opportunities for self-study. It contains recordings of all Student's Book exercises marked with the symbol ▣◉, except for the Listening tasks, which are intended only for classroom use. These tasks appear exclusively on the Class Audio Program and are indicated by the symbol ▣ CLASS AUDIO ONLY ▶.

The **Video** offers entertaining dramatic or documentary sequences that review and extend language learned in each unit of the Student's Book. The **Video Activity Book** contains comprehension, conversation, and language practice activities, and the **Video Teacher's Guide** provides instructional support, answer keys, and photocopiable transcripts of the video sequences.

The **CD-ROM**, appropriate for home or laboratory use, offers a wealth of additional practice. Each of the 16 units is based on a sequence from the Video. Four tests help students monitor their progress.

The **Placement Test** helps determine the most appropriate level of *New Interchange* for incoming students. A booklet contains the four-skills test on photocopiable pages, as well as instructions for test administration and scoring. A cassette accompanies the listening section of the test.

The **Lab Cassettes** provide self-study activities in the areas of grammar, vocabulary, pronunciation, listening, and functional use of English. The **Lab Guide** contains photocopiable pages that guide students through the activities.

The **Teacher-Training Video** offers clear guidance for teaching each section of the Student's Book and professional development activities appropriate for individual or group use.

APPROACH AND METHODOLOGY

New Interchange teaches students to use English for everyday situations and purposes related to school, social life, work, and leisure. The underlying philosophy is that learning a second or foreign language is more rewarding, meaningful, and effective when the language is used for authentic communication. Throughout *New Interchange,* students are presented with natural and useful language. In addition, students have the opportunity to personalize the language they learn, make use of their own knowledge and experiences, and express their ideas and opinions.

Adult and International Content

New Interchange deals with contemporary topics that are of high interest and relevance to both students and teachers. The topics have been selected for their interest to both homogeneous and heterogeneous classes.

Integrated Syllabus

New Interchange has an integrated, multi-skills syllabus that links topics, communicative functions, and grammar. Grammar – seen as an essential component of second and foreign language proficiency and competence – is always presented communicatively, with controlled accuracy-based activities leading to fluency-based communicative practice. In this way, there is a link between grammatical form and communicative function. The syllabus is carefully graded, with a gradual progression of teaching items.

Enjoyable and Useful Learning Activities

A variety of interesting and enjoyable activities provide thorough individual student practice and enable learners to apply the language they learn. The course also makes extensive use of information-gap tasks; role plays; and pair, group, and whole class activities. Task-based and information-sharing activities provide a maximum amount of student-generated communication. These variations in learning activities allow for a change of pace within lessons while also making the course ideal for both large and small classes, as *New Interchange* gives students a greater amount of individual practice and interaction with others in the classroom.

Focus on Productive and Receptive Skills

In *New Interchange*, both production and comprehension form the basis of language learning. Students' productive skills are developed through speaking and writing tasks, and their receptive skills are developed through listening and reading. The course teaches students to understand language that is at a higher level than they can produce, and this prepares them to make the transition from the classroom to the real world.

Teacher's and Learners' Roles

The teacher's role in *New Interchange* is to present and model new learning items; however, during pair work, group work, and role play activities, the teacher's role is that of a facilitator. Here the teacher's primary function is to prepare students for an activity and then let them complete it using their own language resources. During this phase, the teacher gives minimum informal feedback to students but also encourages maximum student participation.

The learners' role in *New Interchange* is to participate actively and creatively in learning, using both the materials they study in the course and their own knowledge and language resources. Students are treated as intelligent adults with ideas and opinions of their own. Students learn through interacting with others in pair, group, or whole class activities and draw both on previous learning as well as their own communicative skills.

Teacher-friendly and Student-friendly Presentation

New Interchange is easy to follow, with clearly identified teaching points, carefully organized and sequenced units, comfortable pacing, and a variety of stimulating and enjoyable learning tasks.

■ SYLLABUS

Grammar The course has a graded grammar syllabus that contains the essential grammar, tenses, and structures needed for a basic level of language proficiency. The grammar points are introduced in communicative contexts (in each Conversation, in Grammar Focus exercises, and in example dialogs included in activities throughout the rest of a cycle) and through grammar summaries (the Grammar Focus models, which are presented in easy-to-read boxes) that illustrate the meaning and usage of each item.

Functions A functional syllabus parallels the grammar syllabus in the course. Each unit presents several key functions (e.g., introducing oneself, asking for personal information, greeting people) that are linked to the grammar points and topics of the two cycles in each unit. Student's Book 1 presents about 55 essential functions, which provide a communicative base for beginner students and which enable them to participate in simple communication on a wide variety of topics.

Topics The course deals with topics that are of interest to learners of various ethnic and cultural backgrounds. Information is presented that can serve as a basis for cross-cultural comparison and that both students and the teacher will find stimulating and enjoyable. The topics have been selected for their interest to students of both genders in homogeneous and heterogeneous classes.

Listening The course reflects current understanding of the nature of listening comprehension in second and foreign language learning. Two kinds of listening skills are taught: *Top-down processing skills* require students to use background knowledge, the situation, context, and topic to arrive at comprehension through using key words and predicting; *bottom-up processing skills* require students to decode individual words in the message to derive meaning. Both of these skills are used in listening for gist, listening for details, and inferring meaning from context.

Speaking Speaking skills are a central focus of *New Interchange.* Many elements in the syllabus (grammar, functions, topics, listening, pronunciation, vocabulary) provide solid support for oral communication. Speaking activities in the course focus on conversational fluency, such as the ability to open and close conversations in English, introduce and develop conversational topics, take turns in conversations, use communication strategies and clarification requests, and understand

and use a variety of idiomatic expressions. In addition, a range of useful conversational expressions is taught and practiced.

Reading The course treats reading as an important way of developing receptive language and vocabulary. At the same time, the reading passages provide stimulating adult content that both students and the teacher will enjoy. The readings demonstrate a variety of text types – newspaper and magazine articles, surveys, letters, and interviews – and develop the reading skills of guessing words from context, skimming, scanning, and making inferences, as well as reading for pleasure and for information. This approach also develops both top-down and bottom-up processing skills in reading.

Writing Writing activities in *New Interchange* focus on various forms of writing: descriptions, narratives, postcards, reviews. Writing is sometimes used as a basis for other activities, such as games and information-sharing activities. The teaching notes for each unit give helpful suggestions on how to present writing activities in order to focus on the process of writing: through brainstorming and collecting information about a topic; planning, drafting or writing multiple drafts; revising; and editing.

Pronunciation Level One treats pronunciation as an integral part of oral proficiency. The pronunciation exercises focus on important features of spoken English, including stress, rhythm, intonation, reductions, and linking sounds.

Vocabulary Vocabulary plays a key role in *New Interchange.* Student's Book 1 teaches a productive vocabulary of about 1,200 words, including vocabulary reviews from *Intro.* Vocabulary is introduced in two main ways: Productive vocabulary is presented through a wide variety of vocabulary exercises and through speaking and grammar activities; receptive vocabulary is introduced through reading and listening exercises.

■ UNIT STRUCTURE AND ORGANIZATION

Although the sequencing of exercise types varies throughout *New Interchange,* a typical unit presents two main topics and functions with related exercises. The exercises in each unit are grouped into two sections; these are referred to as "Cycle 1" and "Cycle 2" in the teaching notes.

A cycle is a self-contained sequence of exercises that usually consists of the introduction of a new topic through a Snapshot or Word Power exercise; a Conversation that introduces the new grammar structure; a Grammar Focus that provides controlled practice, which is usually followed by freer communicative grammar practice; Pair Work, Group Work, Role Play exercises, or Class Activities that provide fluency practice on a specific teaching point; and a Listening exercise.

Also, in each unit there are a Pronunciation exercise, a Writing activity, and an Interchange Activity note. (This note refers students to the unit's communicative activity, which is presented at the back of the Student's Book.) Finally, there is an interesting Reading exercise that always ends Cycle 2 in each unit.

The exercise types listed in the chart below are used throughout the course.

EXERCISE TITLE	PURPOSE
Snapshot	These exercises contain interesting, real-world information that introduces the topic of a unit or cycle. They also build receptive and productive vocabulary. The information in the Snapshot is presented in a graphic form, which makes it easy to read. Follow-up questions encourage discussion of the Snapshot material and personalize the topic.
Word Power	The Word Power activities develop students' vocabulary as related to the unit or cycle topic through a variety of interesting tasks, such as word maps and collocation exercises. These activities are usually followed by oral or written practice that helpsstudents understand how to use the vocabulary in context.
Conversation	Conversation exercises introduce new grammar points and functions in each cycle. They present the grammar in a situational and communicative context and also serve as models for conversational expressions and for speaking tasks.
Grammar Focus	These exercises present summaries of new grammar items followed by controlled and freer communicative practice of the grammar. These freer activities often havestudents use the grammar in a personal context.
Pair Work **Role Play** **Group Work** **Class Activity**	These oral fluency exercises provide more personalized practice of the new teaching points and increase the opportunity for meaningful individual student practice.
Pronunciation	These exercises practice important pronunciation features – such as stress, rhythm, intonation, reductions, and blending – that are usually found in the Conversation or Grammar Focus exercises.
Listening	The listening activities develop a wide variety of receptive skills, including listening for gist, listening for details, and inferring meaning from context. Charts or graphics often accompany these task-based exercises to lend support to students.
Writing	The Writing exercises include practical writing tasks that extend and reinforce the topic and grammar of the unit or cycle and help develop students' compositional skills. These exercises are often task-based (e.g., writing a postcard, describing a person).
Reading	Reading exercises develop reading skills as well as receptive language and vocabulary. The reading passages use various types of texts adapted from authentic sources. Pre-reading and post-reading questions use the topic of the reading as a springboard to discussion.
Interchange Activities	These information-sharing and role-playing activities provide a communicative extension to the unit. These exercises are a central part of the course and allow students to extend and personalize what they have practiced and learned in each unit.

■ REVIEW UNITS, UNIT SUMMARIES, AND TESTS

Review Units These occur after every four units and contain exercises that review the teaching points from the four preceding units. They are mainly speaking exercises, including one listening activity, that review grammar, vocabulary, conversational functions and expressions, and listening. They can also be used as informal criterion reference tests of students' oral production and listening skills.

Unit Summaries These are at the end of the Student's Book and contain a summary of the key productive vocabulary used in each unit, together with functional expressions and grammar extensions. The Key Vocabulary lists the productive vocabulary used in the Conversations, Word Power, pair, group, whole class, and role play activities.

Tests There are four tests, one for use after every four units of the Student's Book. The tests enable the teacher to evaluate students' progress in the course and to decide if any areas of the course need further review. The tests are on pages T-153–T-168 in this Teacher's Edition; all tests may be photocopied for class use. Complete information on administering and scoring the tests, as well as the answer keys, is located at the back of this book.

■ GENERAL GUIDELINES FOR TEACHING *NEW INTERCHANGE*

New Interchange follows a multi-skills syllabus in which each component of the course is linked. For example, a vocabulary-building exercise can serve as the basis for a speaking task; a role play activity may lead into a listening task or vice versa; or a grammar exercise prepares students for a functional activity.

The following general guidelines can be used when teaching the course.

Teaching Vocabulary

Vocabulary is a key element in *New Interchange* because a wide productive vocabulary is essential in learning a second or foreign language. Before presenting any exercise, it is helpful to determine which words are needed in order to complete the task and which are not essential – not all new vocabulary needs presentation in advance. Students should recognize that in most language-learning situations, they will encounter vocabulary they do not know; however, they do not need to understand every word. In addition, students need to understand that when they encounter an unknown word, they can often guess its meaning from the situation or context.

Where it is necessary to pre-teach new vocabulary, the following strategies may be helpful:

■ Ask students to look at the context in which a word is used and to try to find any clues to its meaning. Encourage students to guess the meaning of a new word by first looking at all the other words surrounding it and then considering the general meaning of the phrase or sentence in which it is located. Encourage students to ask themselves: How does this new word fit into this general idea or the context here?

■ Where necessary, provide the meanings of words through definitions, mime, synonyms, antonyms, examples, or translation. It is not necessary to give long explanations as the majority of adult students will already understand the concept of the new word (or know the equivalent word) in their native language.

■ In general, discourage the use of dictionaries during class time, except where it is suggested in the teacher's notes within an exercise.

■ After teaching a unit, ask students to review the Unit Summary (at the back of the Student's Book) to check how many of the words and their meanings they can remember.

■ Encourage students to keep a vocabulary notebook (or a special section of their English class notebook) and to write down new words as they learn them.

Teaching Grammar

Correct use of grammar is an essential aspect of communicative competence. In *New Interchange*, grammatical accuracy is an integral part of proficiency, but it is always a means to an end rather than an end in itself. It is important to remember that second language learners do not usually develop grammatical proficiency by studying rules. They generally acquire new grammar by using the language in situations where it is needed. This means that grammar should always be practiced communicatively. However, language learning also involves testing out hypotheses about how the language works. Therefore, in developing these hypotheses, some students will rely more on grammatical explanations than others.

In the Grammar Focus exercises, the information in the color boxes should be used to explain new grammar points. Give additional examples and explanations, if necessary, to clarify the grammar, but avoid turning any lesson into a grammar class. Lead students into the practice activities for the new grammar points as quickly as possible. Then use the students' performance on these activities to decide if further clarification or grammar work is needed. Whenever this is the case, remember that there are many additional grammar exercises in the Workbook that can be used as a follow-up.

Teaching Listening Skills

The Listening exercises are designed to bridge the gap between the classroom and the real world. While most of these exercises have the heading "Listening," there are also some that act as an extension in the

Conversations, the Word Power activities, or fluency activities.

When teaching listening, it is important to remind students that in most listening situations the aim is *not* to remember the specific words or phrases used but to extract the main ideas or information. To help students do this, the Listening exercises usually contain a task that enables students to identify a purpose for listening which, in turn, encourages them to ignore language that is not related to that purpose. When presenting an exercise, it is also important to prepare students for the task through pre-listening activities. These include asking questions about the topic, asking students to make predictions, and making use of the context provided by the pictures and the situation.

Teaching Speaking Skills

A number of different kinds of activities focus on speaking skills in the course: Conversations, pair work, role plays, group work, and whole class activities, including the Interchange Activities. Each of these activities involves different learning arrangements in the class.

In doing these types of speaking activities, the following guidelines are important:

- Set up pairs or groups so that students of different ability levels and different native languages can work together. This arrangement will encourage students to help and learn from one another.

- Vary the pair or group arrangements so that students do not always work with the same classmates.

- Discourage use of the students' native languages when doing an activity by continually encouraging students to use as much English as possible in class.

Giving Feedback It is important to give clear feedback on students' performances, but feedback should not inhibit students' attempts to communicate with one another. Accuracy in speaking a new language takes a long time to accomplish in second language learning, and both student and teacher need to realize this fact. Also, some aspects of language will be more difficult than others – depending on the students' levels of proficiency and/or first languages. Immediate results are not always apparent. Assess which aspects of the students' performances are worth drawing attention to at any particular time in their language development.

It is better to give occasional but focused feedback on one thing at a time than to overwhelm a student with too much information. There will be many opportunities to give individual feedback when students are working in pairs or groups. During these activities, walk around the class and discreetly listen in to what the students are doing and how they are getting along with the task. Then either take

notes on any problems the students seem to be having in order to share them later with the whole class, or decide to give immediate feedback to the pair or group on any difficulties they might be experiencing with grammar, pronunciation, and vocabulary. Students often prefer this type of "private" or personalized feedback to feedback given in front of the whole class. This is also an opportunity to determine if additional practice work is needed before the class goes on to the next exercise.

Conversations These exercises can be used for both listening and speaking practice. They usually require students to work with a partner. Since the Conversation exercises model conversational expressions and pronunciation, and present new teaching items, accurate repetition of the Conversations on the audio program is important. However, students should not be asked to memorize these conversations verbatim.

When students practice Conversations, teach them to use the "Look Up and Say" technique: A student looks at the line of the dialog that he or she needs to say next, and then looks up and says the line while maintaining eye contact with a partner. This encourages students to avoid a "readinglike" pronunciation and intonation when practicing Conversation exercises together.

Pair Work The course makes extensive use of pair work activities. These give students a chance for individual practice and maximize the amount of speaking practice they get in each class. However, some students may be unfamiliar with pair work tasks and may not think that they can learn from their classmates. If so, remind students that practicing with a partner is a useful way of improving their fluency in English because it gives them more opportunities to speak English in class.

Role Plays These exercises are important for developing fluency and are also fun. They focus on the creative use of language and require students to draw on their own personal language resources to complete a task or to improvise and keep a conversation going.

Group Work and Class Activities The course also makes frequent use of group work and whole class activities. In the group work activities, students usually work in groups of three to six. Often one student is the group secretary and takes notes to report back to the class later. In the class activities, however, the whole class is involved (e.g., completing a survey, gathering information, sharing facts or ideas previously learned in a group work activity).

Teaching Reading Skills

The approach for teaching reading in *New Interchange* is similar to that used for teaching listening. The purpose for reading determines the strategy the students should use, such as reading the passage for main ideas (skimming), looking quickly for specific information in the passage (scanning), reading more slowly for detailed understanding, reading for the author's attitude or tone, or reading to identify a sequence of events. It is important not to present each reading exercise as if it always requires the same approach (e.g., 100 percent comprehension of the passage). When students are doing a reading exercise, check that they are using appropriate reading strategies. For example:

■ Students should read silently and not subvocalize (pronounce words or move their lips while reading).

■ Students should read only with their eyes and not use a pencil or finger to follow each sentence they are reading.

■ Students should not use their dictionaries to look up every new word they encounter in a reading passage.

To encourage student interaction in the class, many reading passages can be done as pair work, group work, or whole class activities. In addition, reading activities can be assigned for homework if class time is short.

Teaching Writing Skills

The Writing exercises present models of different kinds of writing, but it is important to use these models simply as a springboard for the students' writing rather than as a basis for copying. Most of the writing tasks can be completed by a sequence of activities that focus on the writing process.

Pre-writing Phase Through discussion of the topic, reading of the model composition or the example of the beginning of one, brainstorming on the topic, or interviews, students generate ideas and collect information related to the topic, and then make notes.

Free Writing Students use their ideas, information, and notes to plan their compositions. During this phase, students write freely on the topic. The focus here is on organizing their ideas – not yet on having to worry about perfecting grammar and spelling.

Drafting Students now write a first complete draft in sentence and paragraph form, but again without worrying too much about spelling, grammar, or punctuation.

Revising In pair or small group feedback sessions, students read their own or a classmate's composition. Then they ask questions for clarification, or they can give suggestions for what additional information might be included. After this type of feedback session, each student works alone again to reorganize, revise, and rewrite his or her draft.

Editing Students, working alone or in pairs, check their second drafts for accuracy. This time, they concentrate first on checking that their ideas are clearly organized and that they have included enough details. When content and organization seem fine to them, students then focus their attention on correcting grammar, spelling, and punctuation.

Final phase Students write, word process, or type a clean third (and final) draft to hand in for comments, or they can put their compositions up on a classroom bulletin board for others to read.

■ TESTING STUDENTS' PROGRESS

The following testing procedures are suggested for use with *New Interchange*.

Using the Tests in the Teacher's Edition

Four tests are contained in the Teacher's Edition (see pages T-153–T-168) to assess students' learning. There is one test to be used after every four units. These are progress tests (also known as criterion reference tests, which only test what students have actually studied, learned, and practiced in a unit or in a set of units). These tests assess students' learning of grammar, conversational expressions, productive vocabulary, and listening skills. (For testing students' oral performance, see the following section – "Using Tests Prepared by the Teacher.") The tests draw on each set of four units as a whole. Only items actively presented and practiced in the Student's Book are tested. Each test takes approximately 45–60 minutes to complete in class; this includes one listening test item that has been included in the audio program. A satisfactory rate of learning should lead to accuracy of 80 percent and above. If students score lower than this, the teacher may wish to reteach some sections of the units, give additional supplementary exercises, or assign extra homework exercises. In addition to using these tests, the teacher can also informally check students' oral and written progress at the end of each unit.

Using Tests Prepared by the Teacher

It is also possible to check students' progress at the end of each unit using teacher-prepared tests. When developing such tests, it is important to keep the following principles in mind.

■ The main goal of *New Interchange* is communicative competence. Therefore, test items should reflect use of language in communicative contexts rather than in isolation.

■ Test items should closely mirror the kind of practice activities used within a unit, i.e., test only what has been taught and test it in a format similar to that in which it was originally presented.

■ Distinguish items that were presented receptively (i.e., listening and reading activities) from those that were presented productively (i.e., speaking and writing activities) in the class. Then focus on testing productively only the language that students have practiced productively.

Here are some examples of acceptable types of test items for any unit in *New Interchange*.

1. Asking follow-up questions on a particular topic to keep the conversation going or to get more information.

2. Completing missing parts of a conversation while focusing on the grammar, vocabulary, or expressions in the unit.

3. Providing suitable conversational expressions for various purposes or functions (e.g., opening a conversation, expressing apologies).

4. Selecting an item from two or three choices (e.g., choosing an appropriate pronoun or adverb in a sentence).

5. Completing a sentence with the suitable grammatical form or the correct word.

6. Reordering scrambled sentences using the correct word order.

7. Choosing the correct word or phrase to complete a sentence.

8. Supplying missing words in a passage either by selecting from choices given in a list or in parentheses, or by using the cloze technique (the random removal of words from a text, such as every verb or every tenth word).

9. Completing a short writing task similar to one presented in the unit.

10. Answering questions or supplying information following a model provided in the unit.

11. Reading a sentence aloud with correct pronunciation.

12. Reading a passage similar to one in the unit and completing questions or a simple task based on it.

Other useful information on oral testing techniques can be found in *Testing Spoken Language* by Nic Underhill (Cambridge University Press, 1987).

HOW TO TEACH A TYPICAL UNIT IN *NEW INTERCHANGE*

The unit-by-unit teacher's notes in the Teacher's Edition gives detailed suggestions for teaching each exercise in each unit. However, on a more general basis, the following procedures can be used to teach *New Interchange*.

Beginning a New Unit

- Introduce the topic of the unit by asking questions and eliciting information from the students related to the theme or topic.

- Then explain and write on the board what the students will study in the unit. Mention the main topics, functions, grammar, and pronunciation as presented in the Plan of Student's Book 1 (in the front of the Student's Book and Teacher's Edition).

Teaching the Exercises in a Unit

Present and teach each exercise within a unit (preferably in the order given in the Student's Book), while using the following general guidelines.

Snapshot

- Books closed. Introduce the topic by asking questions about it. Also, use these questions to elicit or present the key vocabulary of the Snapshot and to ask for students' opinions on the topic they are going to read about.

- Books open. Lead the students through the information in the Snapshot. Go over any problems of comprehension as they arise.

- Students can complete the tasks and talk or think about the questions individually, in pairs, in groups, or as part of a whole class activity.

- Students compare answers with a partner, in groups, or as a class.

- As an alternative, ask students to look over the Snapshot for homework using a dictionary. Tell them to write answers to the tasks or the questions. Later in class, students can compare answers with a partner or partners.

Word Power

- Introduce and model the pronunciation of the new words listed in the exercise.

- Explain the task and model how to do it.

- Students complete the task individually or in pairs, using a dictionary only if absolutely necessary.

- Students compare answers. At this time, encourage students to check their dictionaries if necessary.

- Check students' answers.

Conversation

- **Optional:** Books open. Students cover the conversation. Use the picture to set the scene.

- Books closed. Before presenting the conversation, explain the situation (e.g., which people are talking together, where they are). Then write a few general listening comprehension questions on the board, which are based on the conversation. Students use them to focus their listening.

- Play the conversation on the audio program or read it aloud to the class. Students listen for answers to the questions on the board. Then check students' answers.

- Books open. Play the audio program or read the conversation again. Students only listen.

- Present the conversation line by line, pausing (the audio program, if used again) after each sentence. As a class, students repeat each line to practice pronunciation, intonation, and stress. Then present and explain any new vocabulary and idiomatic expressions.

- Students practice the conversation in pairs, using the "Look Up and Say" technique (described on page ix of this Teacher's Edition.)

- **Optional:** Ask for volunteers to act out the conversation in front of the class, using their own words. Elicit and give helpful feedback on their performance by pointing out what was good and what, if anything, could be improved.

Grammar Focus

- Use the audio program to present the example sentences and forms in the boxes.
- Give students additional examples to illustrate the grammar point where necessary. If appropriate, practice the language in the boxes by conducting an individual or whole class drill.
- If helpful, model how to do the first item in the task. Then students complete the rest of the task. In addition, an exercise can often be completed orally as a whole class activity before students complete it individually or in pairs. If necessary, students can write the answers on a separate piece of paper instead of in their textbooks.
- Students compare answers in pairs or groups.
- To check students' answers and to give feedback, call on students to read their answers aloud; alternatively, elicit answers around the class from volunteers.

Pair Work

- Divide the class into pairs. If there is an odd number of students, form one set of three.
- Explain the task and model it with one or two students. Call on a pair of students to do the task as a further model if necessary.
- Set an appropriate time limit. It may be useful to write it on the board, like this:
  Pair work = 5 minutes
  or *Pair work: Start at 9:20. Finish at 9:25.*
- Students practice in pairs. Move around the class and give help as needed.
- **Optional:** Students change partners and do the task again.
- **Optional:** Call on pairs of students or volunteer pairs to do the activity in front of the class. Elicit and give helpful feedback on their performance.

Group Work

- Divide the class into small groups of three or four, or larger groups of five or six, whichever seems more appropriate for the task.
- Explain the task and model it with several students.
- Set a time limit.
- Students practice in groups. Move around the class and give help as needed.
- **Optional:** Students form new groups and try the task again.

Role Play

- Divide the class into pairs or groups, as necessary. Assign the roles to the students.
- Explain each role and clarify the cues.
- Model each role with several students in the class while showing how to use the cues. Encourage students to be creative and to use their own language resources. Tell them not to look at each other's cues or information.
- Set a time limit.
- Students do the role play. Go around the class and give help as needed.
- If time allows, students change roles and do the role play again.
- **Optional:** Call on students or ask for volunteers to act out the role play in front of the class. Elicit and give helpful feedback.

Pronunciation

- Use the audio program to introduce the pronunciation point.
- Play the audio program again. Students practice by repeating the words or sentences.
- If helpful, give additional examples for students to practice by writing them on the board and then modeling each one.
- When doing other tasks in the unit (e.g., during the Conversation, Pair Work, Group Work, Role Play, and Interchange Activity), remind students of the pronunciation point.

Listening

- **Optional:** Books open. Use the picture, if available, to set the scene.
- Books closed. Set the scene and explain the situation.
- Play the audio program. Students listen for general comprehension. Point out any key vocabulary that is essential for the task.
- Books open. Explain the task. Remind students that they don't have to understand everything on the recording.
- Play the audio program once or twice more. Students listen and complete the task.
- Students compare answers in pairs or groups.
- Check students' answers.

Writing

- Explain the task and go over the model composition.
- Through brainstorming, elicit key vocabulary and additional language students might need. It may be helpful to write this on the board for Ss to copy into their notebooks.
- Students use their brainstorming notes to write rough drafts of their compositions. They should not worry about grammar, spelling, or punctuation at this stage.
- Students get feedback on the content and organization of their drafts from other classmates while they work in pairs or small groups, and from the teacher whenever possible. Students then revise their drafts.
- **Optional:** This writing process of composing, getting feedback, and revising can be done several times if needed and if time allows.
- Students prepare another draft. (The second,

third, or final draft can be done for homework if necessary.) At this time, students check carefully for content, organization, grammar, vocabulary, punctuation, and spelling.

- **Optional:** In pairs or groups, students exchange compositions and read them. Alternatively, students put their compositions on the bulletin board for everyone to read.

Reading

- Before students read the passage, use the pre-reading question(s) to introduce the topic of the passage and to help establish the students' background knowledge.
- Preview the vocabulary and pre-teach only key words that students might not be able to guess or infer from context. Encourage students to guess the meanings of words using context clues.
- Explain the task.
- Students read the passage silently. Discourage students from using a pencil or finger to point at the text or words. Also, try to prevent them from subvocalizing (pronouncing words silently, usually while moving their lips) while reading the passage.
- Then students go on to the task and do it either individually or in pairs, whichever is more appropriate.
- Students compare answers in pairs or groups.
- Check students' answers.
- Ask the discussion questions given, general follow-up discussion questions on the topic, or other specific questions to find out students' personal reaction to the passage and topic.

Interchange Activities

- Where necessary and appropriate for the task, divide the class into pairs or groups and assign the students their roles (A, B, C, etc.) and their corresponding page numbers.
- Model the activity with one or more students. Encourage students to be creative and to have fun. They should focus on communication, not on grammar. Also, they should not refer back to the unit once they have begun the activity.
- Students do the task. Go around the class and give help as needed.
- Where appropriate, call on pairs or groups to do the activity in front of the class. As usual, elicit and give some helpful feedback on each performance.
- **Optional:** Use an audio tape recorder or a video camera to record the students' performances. Then play them back to the class and discuss their merits.

Unit Summaries

Students can study the Unit Summary in two ways.

- Assign a Unit Summary for homework – before the teacher presents a new unit in class – so that students can familiarize themselves with the vocabulary and expressions that will be studied and used in the unit.
- Alternatively, have students use the Unit Summary as a review activity after each unit has been taught (e.g., for a homework assignment, as a quick check or self-test, or as a study guide for a class test).

Workbook

Preview each unit of the Workbook exercises before introducing the unit, or part of a unit, in class. Note that the Workbook exercises present teaching points in the same sequence as the exercises in a unit in the Student's Book, but the Workbook exercises are more integrative, often combining vocabulary and teaching points from two or more exercises in the Student's Book into one activity. In addition, most units contain "review exercises" that recycle teaching points from earlier units in the context of the new topic. The Workbook can be used in a number of ways.

- After students complete a Student's Book exercise, assign a Workbook exercise that has the same teaching point. Students can complete it in class individually, in pairs or in groups, or as a homework assignment.
- After several Student's Book exercises have been completed, assign appropriate Workbook exercises to be done as homework.
- After completing one cycle of a unit in the Student's Book (see how each unit is divided by checking the teacher's notes), assign the designated Workbook exercises included in the teacher's notes at the end of each cycle.
- At the end of a unit, have students do all the corresponding unit's Workbook exercises as an in-class review or for homework.

■ FROM THE AUTHORS

We hope you enjoy teaching *New Interchange* and using the exercises and activities in it. We have confidence that this course will be interesting, innovative, and useful to you, the teacher, and to your students who want to learn English as a second or foreign language. We would be most happy to receive any comments that you or your students might like to share with us.

Best wishes,
Jack C. Richards
Jonathan Hull
Susan Proctor

Spelling Differences Between American and British English

Words in Book 1 that have a different spelling in British English:

American spelling	*British spelling*
center	centre
check (noun)	cheque (noun)
color	colour
favorite	favourite
flavor	flavour
glamorous	glamourous
harbor	harbour
humor	humour
jail	gaol
jewelry	jewellery
kilometer	kilometre
labor	labour
liter	litre
neighbor	neighbour
neighborhood	neighbourhood
program	programme
theater	theatre

Phonetic Symbols

iy	(sh**ee**p)	ʊ	(b**oo**k)	k	(**k**ey)	w	(**w**indow)
ɪ	(sh**i**p)	uw	(b**oo**t)	g	(**g**irl)	y	(**y**ellow)
ɛ	(y**e**s)	ay	(f**i**ne)	s	(**s**un)	h	(**h**ow)
ey	(tr**ai**n)	ɔy	(b**oy**)	z	(**z**oo)	θ	(**th**ink)
æ	(h**a**t)	aw	(h**ou**se)	ʃ	(**sh**oe)	ð	(**the** fea**th**er)
ʌ	(c**u**p)	ɜr	(w**or**d)	ʒ	(televi**si**on)	m	(**m**outh)
ə	(**a** banana)	p	(**p**en)	tʃ	(**ch**air)	n	(**n**ose)
ər	(lett**er**)	b	(**b**aby)	dʒ	(**j**oke)	ŋ	(ri**ng**)
ɑ	(f**a**ther)	t	(**t**ie)	f	(**f**an)	l	(**l**etter)
ɔ	(b**a**ll)	d	(**d**oor)	v	(**v**an)	r	(**r**ain)
ow	(n**o**)						

Authors' Acknowledgments

A great number of people contributed to the development of *New Interchange*. Particular thanks are owed to the following:

The **reviewers** using the first edition of *Interchange* in the following schools and institutes – the insights and suggestions of these teachers and their students have helped define the content and format of the new edition: Jorge Haber Resque, **Centro Cultural Brasil-Estados Unidos (CCBEU),** Belém, Brazil; Lynne Roecklein, **Gifu University,** Japan; Mary Oliveira and Montserrat M. Djmal, **Instituto Brasil-Estados Unidos (IBEU),** Rio de Janeiro, Brazil; Liliana Baltra, **Instituto Chileno Norte-Americano,** Santiago de Chile; Blanca Arazi and the teachers at **Instituto Cultural Argentino Norteamericano (ICANA),** Buenos Aires, Argentina; Mike Millin and Kelley Seymour, **James English School,** Japan; Matilde Legorreta, **Kratos, S.A. de C.V.,** Mexico D.F.; Peg Donner, Ricia Doren, and Andrew Sachar, **Rancho Santiago College Centennial Education Center,** Santa Ana, California, USA; James Hale, **Sundai ELS,** Japan; Christopher Lynch, **Sunshine College,** Tokyo, Japan; Valerie Benson, **Suzugamine Women's College,** Hiroshima, Japan; Michael Barnes, **Tokyu Be Seminar,** Japan; Claude Arnaud and Paul Chris McVay, **Toyo Women's College,** Tokyo, Japan; Maria Emilia Rey Silva, **UCBEU,** São Paulo, Brazil; Lilia Ortega Sepulveda, **Unidad Lomoa Hermosa,** Mexico D.F.; Eric Bray, **Kyoto YMCA English School,** Kyoto, Japan; John Pak, **Yokohama YMCA English School,** Yokohama, Japan; and the many teachers around the world who responded to the *Interchange* questionnaire.

The **editorial** and **production** team: Suzette André, Sylvia P. Bloch, John Borrelli, Mary Carson, Natalie Nordby Chen, Karen Davy, Randee Falk, Andrew Gitzy, Pauline Ireland, Penny Laporte, Kathy Niemczyk, Kathleen Schultz, Rosie Stamp, and Mary Vaughn.

And Cambridge University Press **staff** and **advisors**: Carlos Barbisan, Kate Cory-Wright, Riitta da Costa, Peter Davison, Peter Donovan, Cecilia Gómez, Colin Hayes, Thares Keeree, Jinsook Kim, Koen Van Landeghem, Carine Mitchell, Sabina Sahni, Helen Sandiford, Dan Schulte, Ian Sutherland, Chris White, and Ellen Zlotnick.

Plan of the Book

Title/Topics	Functions	Grammar
Please call me Chuck. Introductions and greetings; names and titles; countries and nationalities	Introducing yourself; introducing someone; checking information; asking about someone; exchanging personal information	Wh-questions and statements with *be*; yes/no questions and short answers with *be*; contractions; subject pronouns; possessive adjectives
How do you spend your day? Occupations, workplaces, and school; daily schedules; clock time	Describing work and school; asking for and giving opinions; talking about daily schedules	Simple present Wh-questions and statements; time expressions: *at, in, on, around, until, before, after, early,* and *late*
How much is it? Spending habits, shopping, and prices; clothing and personal items; colors and materials	Talking about prices; giving opinions; talking about preferences; making comparisons; buying and selling things	Demonstratives: *this, that, these, those; one* and *ones*; questions: *how much* and *which*; comparisons with adjectives
Do you like jazz? Music, movies, TV programs; entertainers; invitations and excuses; dates and times	Talking about likes and dislikes; giving opinions; making invitations and excuses	Simple present yes/no and Wh-questions with *do*; question: *what kind*; object pronouns; modal verb *would*; verb + *to* + verb
Tell me about your family. Families and family life	Talking about families and family members; exchanging information about the present; describing family life	Present continuous yes/no and Wh-questions, statements, and short answers; determiners: *all, nearly all, most, many, a lot of, some, not many, a few,* and *few*
How often do you exercise? Sports and exercise; routines	Asking about and describing routines and exercise; talking about frequency; talking about abilities	Adverbs of frequency: *always, almost always, usually, often, sometimes, seldom, hardly ever, almost never, never*; questions with *how: how often, how much time, how long, how well, how good*; short answers
We had a great time! Free-time and weekend activities; vacations	Talking about past events; giving opinions about past experiences; talking about vacations	Past tense yes/no and Wh-questions, statements, and short answers with regular and irregular verbs; past tense of *be*
How do you like the neighborhood? Stores and places in a city; neighborhoods; houses and apartments	Asking about and describing locations of places; asking about and describing neighborhoods; asking about quantities	*There is/there are; one, any, some*; prepositions of place; questions: *how much* and *how many*; countable and uncountable nouns

Listening/Pronunciation	Writing/Reading	Interchange Activity
Recognizing formal and informal names; listening for personal information Intonation of clarification questions	Writing questions requesting personal information "Meeting and Greeting Customs": Reading about greeting customs	"Getting to know you": Collecting personal information from classmates
Listening to descriptions of jobs and daily schedules Unstressed words	Writing a description of an occupation "The Daily Grind": Reading about students with part-time work	"Common ground": Finding similarities in classmates' daily schedules
Listening to people shopping; listening for items, prices, and opinions Linked sounds	Writing a comparison of prices in different countries "Shop Till You Drop": Reading about different kinds of shopping	"Swap meet": Buying and selling things
Identifying musical styles; listening for likes and dislikes; listening to invitations Question intonation	Writing invitations and excuses "The Sound of Music": Reading about musicians from around the world	"What an invitation! What an excuse!": Making up unusual invitations and excuses
Listening for family relationships; listening to information about families and family life Blending with *does*	Writing a description of family life "The Changing Family": Reading about an American family	"Family facts": Finding out information about classmates' families and family members
Listening to people talk about free-time activities; listening to routines; listening to descriptions of sports participation Sentence stress	Writing a description of favorite activities "Smart Moves": Reading about fitness for the brain	"Fitness quiz": Interviewing about fitness habits
Listening to descriptions and opinions of past events and vacations Reduced forms of *did you*	Writing a postcard "Vacation Postcards": Reading about different kinds of vacations	"Vacation photos": Telling a story using pictures
Listening for locations of places; listening to descriptions of places in neighborhoods Reduced forms of *there is* and *there are*	Writing a description of a home "City Scenes": Reading about neighborhood life in cities around the world	"Neighborhood survey": Comparing two neighborhoods

Title/Topics	Functions	Grammar

Listening/Pronunciation	Writing/Reading	Interchange Activity
		PAGES IC-12 and IC-14 UNIT 9
Listening to descriptions of people; identifying people Contrastive stress	Writing a description of someone "Hip-Hop Fashions": Reading about clothing styles	"Find the differences": Comparing two pictures of a party
		PAGE IC-13 UNIT 10
Listening for time and place of an event; listening to descriptions of events Pronunciation of *have*	Writing a description of an unusual activity "Taking the Risk": Reading about unusual or dangerous sports	"Lifestyles survey": Finding out about a classmate's lifestyle
		PAGE IC-15 UNIT 11
Listening to descriptions of cities and hometowns; listening for incorrect information Pronunciation of *can't* and *shouldn't*	Writing a description of an interesting city "Famous Cities": Reading about cities around the world	"City guide": Creating a city guide
		PAGE IC-16 UNIT 12
Listening to advice; listening to requests in a drugstore Reduced form of *to*	Writing about a home remedy "Grandma Knows Best!": Reading about home remedies	"Talk radio": Giving advice to callers on a radio program
		REVIEW OF UNITS 9-12
		PAGES IC-17 and IC-18 UNIT 13
Listening to people make dinner plans; listening to restaurant orders Stress in responses	Writing a restaurant review "To Tip or Not to Tip?": Reading about tipping customs	"Are you ready to order?": Ordering a meal in a restaurant
		PAGE IC-19 UNIT 14
Listening to a TV game show; listening for information about a country Intonation in questions of choice	Writing about an interesting or beautiful place "Things You Can Do to Help the Environment": Reading about the environment	"How much do you know?": Taking a quiz on general knowledge
		PAGE IC-20 UNIT 15
Listening for information about invitations; receiving telephone messages Reduced forms of *could you* and *would you*	Writing a request to give a message "Ways to Keep Phone Calls Short": Reading about telephone manners	"What are you going to do?": Finding out about classmates' weekend plans
		PAGE IC-21 UNIT 16
Listening to descriptions of changes; listening to hopes for the future Reduced form of *to*	Writing about future plans "The Future Looks Bright": Reading about the plans of three successful students	"Unfold your future!": Planning a possible future
		REVIEW OF UNITS 13-16
		UNIT SUMMARIES
		APPENDIX

1 Please call me Chuck.

1 CONVERSATION *Introducing yourself*

🎧 Listen and practice.

Elizabeth: Hello, I'm Elizabeth Mandel.
Chuck: Hi! My name is Charles Chang.
But please call me Chuck.
Elizabeth: Nice to meet you, Chuck.
You can call me Liz.
Chuck: OK. And what's your last
name again?
Elizabeth: Mandel.

2 CHECKING INFORMATION

A 🎧 Match the questions in column A with the responses in column B.
Listen and check. Then practice with a partner. Give your own information.

A

1. How do you pronounce your last name? ....
2. Excuse me, what's your first name again? ....
3. How do you spell your last name? ....
4. What do people call you? ....

B

a. C-H-A-N-G.
b. It's Mandel, with the accent on "del."
c. Well, everyone calls me Chuck.
d. Oh, it's Amy.

B *Group work* Make a list of names and nicknames for your group.
Introduce yourself with your full name. Use the expressions above.

A: Hi! I'm Joseph Block. Please call me Joe.
B: OK, Joe. And what's your last name again?
A: It's Block.

1 Please call me Chuck.

Cycle 1, Exercises 1–5

1 CONVERSATION *Introducing yourself*

🔊 This exercise presents conversational expressions used for self-introductions and introduces the verb *be*.

■ Books open. Tell the class to look at the picture. Then ask some pre-listening questions like these:

Where are these people?
Do they know each other?
What's the man's name?
What are the two women's names?

■ Play the audio program several times. Ss only listen. Explain any unfamiliar words and expressions, such as:

Hello = Hi (more informal); Good morning/afternoon/evening (more formal)
But please call me . . . ./You can call me . . . . = My first name is . . . , but everyone uses my nickname, ...
last name = family name or surname (first name = given name)

■ Introduce the "Look Up and Say" technique, a helpful method for Ss to use whenever they practice conversations printed in the text: Ss briefly look at a sentence on the page and then look up at their partner and say the sentence by relying on their short-term memory.

■ Model how to use this technique to practice this conversation. Also, encourage Ss to "act out" their parts by using gestures and displaying emotions whenever appropriate (e.g., here, Ss could shake hands and smile while practicing).

■ Play the audio program again, stopping after each sentence. Ss listen while looking at the sentence and then look up and say it aloud.

■ Divide the class into pairs to practice the conversation. Walk around the class and give help as needed.

■ **Optional:** Books closed. Ask for volunteer pairs to stand up and act out the dialog. For a more challenging task, have Ss use their real names instead of those used in the dialog.

2 CHECKING INFORMATION

This exercise practices ways to clarify or check information about people's names, using rising intonation with Wh-questions.

A 🔊

■ Individually or in pairs, Ss match the questions and responses. Play the audio program once and then elicit Ss' answers to check them.

Answers

1. b	2. d	3. a	4. c

■ Model how to use rising intonation with Wh-questions to clarify or check information. Ss repeat. Tell the class to ask you each question while you demonstrate how to answer, using your real first and last names.

■ **Optional:** Review the letters of the alphabet to help Ss spell their names.

■ Pairs practice for several minutes using their own names. Go around the class and give help as needed.

B *Group work*

■ Explain the task and any new vocabulary:

nickname = a name used informally instead of a person's given name (e.g., Liz for Elizabeth, Red for a person with red hair, Mac for Michael MacNeil)
full name = a person's legal name, including the first, middle (sometimes optional), and last names (e.g., John Fitzgerald Kennedy)

■ Model the A/B dialog with several Ss and try to extend it by using expressions from part A.

■ Ss form small groups and practice introducing themselves.

Optional activity: *The name game*

Time: 10 minutes. Ss may enjoy this as an icebreaker on their first or second day of class. Decide if Ss should use only first names or both first and last names while playing the game.

1. The class sits or stands in a circle.
2. Use something small, like a tennis ball or a paper ball. Say your name and throw the ball to a S.
3. This S quickly says his or her name and throws the ball to another S.
4. Continue until all Ss have participated.

■ **Optional:** Play the game again, this time with Ss saying the name of the person they are throwing the ball to.

3 NAMES AND TITLES

This exercise clarifies the use of titles with names in English and anticipates the common problem of Ss' misusing a title with a first name (e.g., Mr. Dave, Miss Sharon).

A

■ Explain that people in the United States and Canada use first names more often than titles and last names. In situations where people see each other regularly (e.g., at work, in an English class), they usually use first names.

■ **Optional:** In a heterogeneous class, ask how titles and names are used in the Ss' native languages as compared with English.

■ Write your own first and last names on the board with the correct title. Tell the class which name and form – formal (with a title) or informal – you prefer them to use.

■ Read aloud the information on addressing someone formally and informally while using the art as an example. Show the differences by pointing out certain Ss and using their full names with appropriate titles (e.g., She's Ms. Maria Cruz. That's Mr. Kenji Sato.) and by pointing to other Ss and using their first names or nicknames (e.g., This is Mila. He's Joe.).

■ Pronounce and explain the titles in the box: Mr. /'mɪstər/, Ms. /mɪz/, Miss /mɪs/, and Mrs. /'mɪsɪz/. Go over the checklist to clarify "Single" and "Married" usage. Point out that a title is used with a full name (i.e., first and last names) or with just the family, or last, name – but never with just a first name.

■ **Optional:** Explain the titles Dr. /'dɑktər/ and Professor /prə'fɛsər/.

■ To help Ss say what they would like to be called in class, write these expressions on the board for them to use:

Please call me . . . .
My name is . . . , but please call me . . . .
Everyone calls me . . . .

Call on Ss to identify others in the class. Ask "Who is this/that?" or "What's his/her name?"

Optional: Ask for one or two volunteers to name everyone in class. Do the same during the next few classes.

B

■ Read the instructions aloud. Play the audio program once. Ss only listen.

Audio script

1. CHUCK: Good afternoon.
   WOMAN: Good afternoon, Mr. Chang. Please sit down.
2. CHUCK: Good morning.
   WOMAN: Hello, Chuck. Nice to see you.
3. MAN: Hello, Liz.
   LIZ: Hi. How are you?
4. LIZ: Hi, I'm Elizabeth Mandel.
   MAN: It's nice to meet you, Ms. Mandel.
5. MAN: Carol, this is Ms. Kim.
   WOMAN: Pleased to meet you, Ms. Kim.
   AMY: Nice to meet you, too.
6. AMY: Hi! How are you?
   MAN: Oh, hi, Amy. I'm fine.

■ Explain the task and write *F* for "Formal" and *I* for "Informal" on the board. Play the audio program again while Ss write their answers.

■ Elicit answers around the class to check them.

Answers

1. F	2. I	3. I	4. F	5. F	6. I

---

4 CONVERSATION Introducing someone

This exercise includes conversational expressions used for introductions and presents Wh-questions and the verb *be*.

A

■ Ask Ss to cover the dialog and look at the picture. Ask a few pre-listening questions:

Where are these people?
What are they doing?

■ Books closed. Play the audio program. Ss listen.

■ Check comprehension by asking a few simple questions like:

What is Paulo's friend's first name? (Tom)
Where are Paulo's parents from? (Rio/
  Rio de Janeiro/Brazil)

■ Books open. Play the audio program again.
  Explain any new vocabulary:

father/Dad = a male parent
mother/Mom = a female parent
parents = a mother and a father
Where are you from in . . . (country)? = In which city
  or state do you live (in your country)?

■ Ss practice the conversations in groups of four.

B *Group work*

■ Ss form small groups. Use the A/B dialog with one group to model the activity. Set a time limit of about four minutes for Ss to practice making introductions.

Optional activity: *Scrambled letters*

■ See page T-146.

3 NAMES AND TITLES

A Use a title with a last name to address someone formally.

	Titles	Single	Married
males:	Mr.	✓	✓
females:	Ms.	✓	✓
	Miss	✓	☐
	Mrs.	☐	✓

Use a first name or nickname without a title to address someone informally.

B 🔊 Listen to people talk to Chuck Chang, Elizabeth Mandel, and Amy Kim. Do they address them formally (**F**) or informally (**I**)?

1. .... 2. .... 3. .... 4. .... 5. .... 6. ....

---

4 CONVERSATION *Introducing someone*

A 🔊 Listen and practice.

Tom: Paulo, who is that over there?
Paulo: Oh, that's my father! And that's my mother with him.
Tom: I'd like to meet them.

Paulo: Mom and Dad, this is Tom Hayes. Tom, these are my parents.
Tom: Pleased to meet you, Mr. and Mrs. Tavares.
Mrs. Tavares: Nice to meet you, Tom.
Paulo: My parents are here from Brazil. They're on vacation.
Tom: Oh, where are you from in Brazil?
Mr. Tavares: We're from Rio.

B *Group work* Take turns introducing a partner to others.

A: Juan, this is Maria. She's from Argentina.
B: Hi, Maria.

3

5 *GRAMMAR FOCUS*

Wh-questions and statements with be

		Contractions	Subject pronouns	Possessive adjectives
What's your name?	My name **is** Chuck.	I am = I'm	I	my
Where are you from?	I'm from Taiwan.	You are = You're	you	your
		He is = He's	he	his
Who is that?	His name **is** Tom.	She is = She's	she	her
What's her name?	Her name **is** Amy.	It is = It's	it	its
Where is she from?	She's from Korea.	We are = We're	we	our
		They are = They're	you	your
Where are you from?	We're from the United States.		they	their
		What is = What's		
Who are they?	They're Amy's parents.			
What are their names?	Their names **are** Mr. and Mrs. Kim.			
Where are they from?	They're from Korea.			

For a list of countries and nationalities, see the appendix at the back of the book.

A Complete this conversation. Then compare with a partner.

Yoko: Rich, who are the two women
over there?
Rich: Oh, ... names are Lisa
and Kate.

Rich: Hi, Kate. This .... Yoko.
.... from Japan.
Yoko: Hello. Nice to meet you.
Kate: Good to meet you, Yoko.
Lisa: And .... name .... Lisa.
Yoko: Hi, Lisa.
Rich: Lisa and Kate .... from Canada.
Yoko: Oh? Where .... you from in Canada?
Kate: .... from Toronto.

B Complete these questions.
Then practice with a partner.

1. A: *Who*.... *is*......... that?
   B: That's Rich.

2. A: .... he from?
   B: He's from Los Angeles.

3. A: .... his last name?
   B: It's Brown.

4. A: .... the two students over there?
   B: Their names are Lisa and Kate.

5. A: .... they from?
   B: They're from Canada.

C *Group work* Write five questions about your classmates.
Then take turns asking and answering your questions.

Who is she?
Where is Su Hee from?

5 *GRAMMAR FOCUS* *Wh-questions and statements with* **be**

This grammar focus shows how Wh-questions, statements, and contractions are formed with the verb *be*. It also presents subject pronouns (e.g., *I, he*) and possessive adjectives (e.g., *my, his*).

■ First, use the audio program to present the questions and statements in the first box. Then play the audio program again, pausing between each exchange. Ss repeat.

■ **Optional:** Play the audio program again, but this time divide the class into two groups: One group repeats the questions and the other group repeats the responses. Switch roles for even more practice.

■ Review the function of a pronoun: It takes the place of a noun. Point out that subject pronouns (e.g., *he, she*) usually take the place of names (e.g., *Tom, Amy*). Write these examples on the board:

Tom is from the U.S. = He is from the U.S.
Amy is my friend.   = She is my friend.

■ Next, play the audio program to model the contractions, or reduced forms, of *be* (e.g., *I'm, It's, What's*). Ss repeat. Explain that reduced forms are commonly used in conversation; full forms are often used in writing.

■ Play the audio program to present the pronouns and adjectives in the last box. Clarify the differences between subject pronouns and possessive adjectives by writing examples on the board:

I am Chuck.   *My name is Chuck.*
You are Amy.   *Your name is Amy.*
We are from Brazil.   *Our family is from Brazil.*

Point out that *you're/your* and *they're/their* are pronounced the same but spelled differently.

■ **Optional:** Let Ss work in pairs to make up additional examples. Check their sentences and have some Ss write the better ones on the board.

■ Finally, show how possessive adjectives can take the place of possessive nouns. Give these examples:

Tom is Amy's friend.   *Tom is her friend.*
They are Paulo's parents. *They are his parents.*

Elicit a few additional examples.

A

■ Encourage Ss to use contractions when possible in this task. Ss fill in the missing words individually and then form pairs to compare their answers. Elicit responses to check answers.

Answers

> YOKO: Rich, who are the two women over there?
> RICH: Oh, **their** names are Lisa and Kate.
> RICH: Hi, Kate. This **is** Yoko. **She's** from Japan.
> YOKO: Hello. Nice to meet you.
> KATE: Good to meet you, Yoko.
> LISA: And **my** name **is** Lisa.
> YOKO: Hi, Lisa.
> RICH: Lisa and Kate **are** from Canada.
> YOKO: Oh? Where **are** you from in Canada?
> KATE: **We're** from Toronto.

■ Ss practice the conversation in groups of four.

B

■ Since there are two blanks to fill in for each question, tell Ss to use the Wh-word with the full form of *be*. Ss first work alone to finish the task and then form pairs to check answers.

Answers

> 1. **Who is** that?
> 2. **Where is** he from?
> 3. **What is** his last name?
> 4. **Who are** the two students over there?
> 5. **Where are** they from?

C *Group work*

■ Explain the task and go over the model Wh-questions. Then elicit a few additional questions and write them on the board as examples.

■ Ss first work alone to write down five Wh-questions. Walk around the class and check Ss' questions.

■ Ss form small groups and take turns asking their questions and giving real responses. Write a time limit of about ten minutes on the board for this activity.

■ Walk around the class and give help wherever needed. Also, note any common grammatical problems that groups might be experiencing. When time is up, clarify any problems with the whole class.

Optional activity: *Lots of languages*

■ See page T-146.

 Workbook

For homework, assign Exercises 1–6 on pages 1–3 in the Workbook. Check Ss' answers during the next class. (Answers can be found on page T-175 of the Workbook Answer Key in this Teacher's Edition.)

6 SNAPSHOT Greetings from around the world

This text presents different types of gestures used when greeting people in various parts of the world.

- Books closed. Go around the class and shake hands with each S while saying "Hello," "Hi," or "Good morning/afternoon/evening." If you get any weak, "dead fish" handshakes, model again how to gently but firmly press someone's hand.

- Have the class stand up and practice greeting one another while shaking hands.

- Books open. Ss look over the pictures and phrases that describe different types of greetings.

- Pronounce the new vocabulary and, if necessary, explain the new words by acting out each gesture.

- **Optional:** In a heterogeneous class, ask what kinds of gestures are used as greetings in the Ss' countries. Ask for volunteers to stand up and show the class how the greeting is properly done.

- Hold a short class discussion to answer the two questions given here. Alternatively, have Ss work in pairs or small groups to do the task.

- Check Ss' answers to the first question by taking a class survey, asking, e.g., "Do people shake hands in your country?"

- Check answers to the second question by asking "In which country do people greet each other with . . . (e.g., a bow)?"

Possible answers

> *(second question)*
> a handshake (Canada, Peru, England)
> a bow (Korea, Japan, Indonesia)
> a kiss on the cheek (Brazil, France, Italy)
> a hug (the United States, Denmark, Egypt)
> a pat on the back (Greece, Russia, Mexico)

7 CONVERSATION Asking about someone

This conversation contains the grammar points presented in Exercise 8. (In the dialog, the present continuous in "Oh, are you studying English?" is used only as an expression; Ss will study this structure in Unit 5.)

A 🔊

- Books closed. Present the target function by inviting two Ss to come up to the front of the class. Then introduce them and encourage each to ask questions about the other.

- Play the first part of the audio program. Ss listen. Ask a few simple comprehension questions to check Ss' understanding:

  Who are friends? (Sarah and Tom; Tom and Paulo)
  Is Paulo from Brazil? (Yes.)
  Is he a student? (Yes.)
  Are Paulo and Tom in the same class? (No.)
  Are they on the same baseball team? (No. They're on the same volleyball team.)

- Books open. Play the audio program again while Ss listen; allow them to read along if they wish. Then use the picture to help present the conversation. Explain these words and expressions:

How's everything? (informal) = How are you?
Not bad./Pretty good, thanks. (informal) = I'm fine, thank you.
engineering = the science or profession of planning, designing, and building machines, roads, bridges, etc.
team = a group of people who work, play, or act together; here, a group that plays volleyball

- Ss practice the conversation in groups of three.

B 🔊

- Books closed. Tell Ss not to worry about understanding every word; they only need to understand the gist of what is said.

- Play the second part of the audio program once or twice.

Audio script

> PAULO: Are you from the United States, Sarah?
> SARAH: *(laughing)* No, I'm not. I'm from Australia.
> PAULO: And what are you studying?
> SARAH: I'm studying engineering, too. In fact, I think we're in the same class!
> PAULO: Say, I think you're right!

- Books open. Tell Ss to listen for the answer to the question. Play the audio program again. Check answers.

Answer

> She's from Australia.

6 *SNAPSHOT*

Greetings from Around the World

a handshake

a bow

a kiss on the cheek

a hug

a pat on the back

Source: Brigham Young University,
Center for International Studies

Talk about these questions.

Which greetings are typical in your country?
Can you name a country for each greeting?

7 *CONVERSATION* *Asking about someone*

A 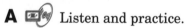 Listen and practice.

Sarah: Hi, Tom. How's everything?
  Tom: Not bad. How are you?
Sarah: Pretty good, thanks.

  Tom: Sarah, this is Paulo. He's from Brazil.
Sarah: Hello, Paulo. Are you on vacation?
Paulo: No, I'm not. I'm a student here.
Sarah: Oh, are you studying English?
Paulo: Well, yes, I am. And engineering, too.
Sarah: Are you and Tom in the same class?
Paulo: No, we aren't. But we're on the same
       volleyball team.

B 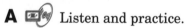 Listen to the rest of the conversation.

Where is Sarah from?

8 GRAMMAR FOCUS

Yes/No questions and short answers with be

Are you on vacation?	No, I**'m not**. I**'m** a student.
Are you a student?	Yes, I **am**.
Is Sarah from the United States?	No, she **isn't**. (No, she**'s not**.) She**'s** from Australia.
Is Sarah from Australia?	Yes, she **is**.
Are you and Tom in the same class?	No, we **aren't**. (No, we**'re not**.) We**'re** on the same volleyball team.
Are you and Tom on the volleyball team?	Yes, we **are**.
Are Mr. and Mrs. Tavares American?	No, they **aren't**. (No, they**'re not**.) They**'re** Brazilian.
Are Mr. and Mrs. Tavares Brazilian?	Yes, they **are**.

A Complete these conversations. Then practice with a partner.

1. A: .... you from the United States?
   B: Yes, I .... from Chicago.

2. A: .... Rosa in English 101?
   B: No, she .... in English 102.

3. A: .... you and Monique from France?
   B: Yes, we .... from Paris.

B *Pair work* Read the conversations in Exercises 4 and 7 again. Then answer these questions. For questions you answer "no," give the correct information.

1. Are Tom and Paulo on the baseball team? ....
2. Are Mr. and Mrs. Tavares on vacation? ....
3. Are Mr. and Mrs. Tavares from Mexico? ....
4. Is Paulo from Brazil? ....
5. Is Paulo on vacation? ....

C *Group work* Write five questions about your classmates. Then take turns asking and answering your questions.

> *Are Maria and Su Hee friends?*

Getting to know you
Find out about your classmates. Turn to page IC-2.

9 LISTENING

   Listen to these conversations and complete the information about each person.

First name	Last name	Where from?	Studying?
1. *Joe*	....	*the United States*	....
2.	*Vera*	....	*engineering*
3. *Min Ho*	*Kim*	....	....

6

8 GRAMMAR FOCUS Yes/No questions and short answers with be

This grammar focus shows how yes/no questions and short answers are formed with *be*.

- Play the audio program. Ss repeat.
- Model the correct stress patterns for short answers (e.g., "No, I'm **not**."). Point out that the verb in "Yes, I am" in a short answer cannot be reduced to the contraction *I'm*.
- Explain how yes/no questions are formed from statements: by inverting the subject and *be*. Write some examples on the board. Elicit additional simple statements with *be* and ask other Ss to form questions from them.
- Ask similar questions with *be* about Ss in the class. Allow Ss to answer with a short "Yes," but encourage them to give the correct information for "No" responses.

A

- Ss do the task individually and then compare answers with a partner. Check Ss' answers.

Answers

1. A: **Are** you from the United States?
   B: Yes, I **am**. **I'm** from Chicago.
2. A: **Is** Rosa in English 101?
   B: No, she **isn't/'s not**. **She's** in English 102.
3. A: **Are** you and Monique from France?
   B: Yes, we **are**. **We're** from Paris.

- Pairs practice the conversations.

B Pair work

- Explain the task. Ss work in pairs to write answers and then take turns asking and answering the questions.
- Check answers around the class.

Answers

1. No, they aren't/they're not. They're on the volleyball team.
2. Yes, they are.
3. No, they aren't/they're not. They're from Brazil.
4. Yes, he is.
5. No, he isn't/he's not. He's a student.

C Group work

- Go over the task and the example question. Ss form small groups. Tell them to first write their questions individually and then to take turns asking and answering their questions.

Optional activity: *Who am I?*

- See page T-146.

 INTERCHANGE 1 Getting to know you

See page T-106 in this Teacher's Edition for notes.

9 LISTENING

This exercise practices listening for specific information about people.

- Go over the task and the information in the chart. To help Ss develop a pre-listening schema, ask a few questions like these:

   In number 1, where is Joe from?
   What do you think his last name is?

- Play the audio program once or twice. Ss complete the chart. Check Ss' answers.

Audio script

1. MAN: Joe, this is my friend Linda Tanaka. We're in the same English class.
   JOE: Hi, Linda. I'm Joseph Miller. Everyone calls me Joe.
   LINDA: Nice to meet you, Joe. And what's your last name again?
   JOE: It's Miller. M-I-L-L-E-R.
   LINDA: Where are you from, Joe?
   JOE: I'm from here, the United States – originally from Chicago.
   LINDA: What are you studying here?
   JOE: Chemistry.
   LINDA: Oh, chemistry. That sounds interesting.

2. CLERK: OK, Ms. Vera. Let me just check this information. Is your first name spelled E-L-L-E-N?
   ELENA: No, it's not. My first name is Elena. It's spelled E-L-E-N-A.
   CLERK: OK. Thanks. And you're from Chile, correct?
   ELENA: No, I'm not from Chile. I'm from Mexico.
   CLERK: Oh, sorry. Mexico. But you *are* studying English, right?
   ELENA: No, I'm not. I'm studying engineering.
   CLERK: Engineering. OK. Got it.

3. MAN: Say, are you In Sook Kim?
   IN SOOK: Yes, that's right.
   MAN: Is your brother Min Ho Kim?
   IN SOOK: Yes, he is!
   MAN: Tell me, is Min Ho still here at the university?
   IN SOOK: No, he's not. Min Ho is at home in Korea.
   MAN: Oh, he's in Korea! Is he in school there?
   IN SOOK: Yes. He's studying English at Seoul University this semester.

Answers

First name	Last name	Where from?	Studying?
1. Joe	**Miller**	the U.S.	**chemistry**
2. **Elena**	Vera	**Mexico**	engineering
3. Min Ho	Kim	**Korea**	**English**

10 *READING* *Meeting and greeting customs*

In this text, students explore the topic of meeting and greeting customs around the world; they also practice scanning for specific information.

■ **Optional:** Bring a world map to class to help Ss identify the countries being discussed here.

■ Books closed. Write the names of the five countries on the board: *Chile, Finland, the Philippines, Korea, the United States.* Make sure the class knows where these countries are located.

■ **Optional:** Does the class know the nationality of each country here? If they don't, write this information on the board and have Ss take notes:

Country	Adjective	Person (People)
Chile	*Chilean*	*Chilean(s)*
Finland	*Finnish*	*Finn(s)*
the Philippines	*Philippine*	*Filipino(s)*
Korea	*Korean*	*Korean(s)*
the United States	*American*	*American(s)*

■ Ask the pre-reading question as a topic warm-up. If possible, follow up by asking for more specific information from the class, like this:

How do you (e.g., two male/female Ss from the same country) greet each other in . . . ?
Do you know how Filipinos greet one another?

■ **Optional:** Allow Ss to take turns asking similar questions around the class or in groups.

■ Books open. While Ss read the information about each country, encourage them to circle or highlight any words whose meanings they can't guess from the context of the article.

■ When Ss finish, elicit any words that they still don't know. Explain the words or ask Ss to check their dictionaries. Here are a few examples:

Chile
usually = almost always, generally
sometimes = now and then, but not very often
kiss = to touch with the lips as a sign of love or as a greeting
cheek = either side of the face below the eye
"kiss the air" = to put one's lips near, but not touching, another person's cheek
male = a boy or man
female = a girl or woman
Finland
firm = steady and strong
close friends = friends who like or love each other very much

The Philippines
everyday = common
Korea
slightly = a little bit
The United States
often = many times
situations = positions or conditions at the moment

A

■ Go over the task and read each statement in the chart aloud. Ss scan the text and check the names of the correct country or countries for each statement. Check answers around the class.

Answers

	Chile	Finland	the Philippines	Korea	the U.S.
1.		✓	✓		
2.				✓	
3.	✓				
4.	✓	✓	✓		✓
5.	✓	✓			✓
6.				✓	

B *Pair work*

■ Read the instructions aloud and model the task with one or two Ss, like this:

T: Carlos, how do two male friends greet each other in your country, Mexico?
S1: Well, they sometimes shake hands or hug each other.
T: And Noriko, how do a male and a female friend greet each other in Japan?
S2: They bow or sometimes just nod their heads.

■ Ss work in pairs to do the task. Encourage Ss to stand up to perform the gesture or style of greeting. After a few minutes, ask volunteers to demonstrate for the rest of the class some of the greetings they discussed.

Optional activity: *Crossword puzzle*

■ See page T-146.

 *Workbook*

Assign Exercises 7–12 on pages 4–6 for Ss to complete for homework or allow them to work with partners at the end of the hour or at the beginning of the next class. When they finish, elicit Ss' answers around the class. (Answers can be found on page T-175 of the Workbook Answer Key in this Teacher's Edition.)

10 *READING*

Meeting and Greeting Customs

How do you think the people in these countries greet each other?

There are many different greeting customs around the world. Here are some.

Chile

People usually shake hands when they meet for the first time. When two women first meet, they sometimes give one kiss on the cheek. (They actually "kiss the air.") Women also greet both male and female friends with a kiss. Chilean men give their friends warm *abrazos* (hugs) or sometimes kiss women on the cheek.

Finland

Finns greet each other with a firm handshake. Hugs and kisses are only for close friends and family.

The Philippines

The everyday greeting for friends is a handshake for both men and women. Men sometimes pat each other on the back.

Korea

Men bow slightly and shake hands to greet each other. Women do not usually shake hands. To address someone with his or her full name, the family name comes first, then the first name.

The United States

People shake hands when they are first introduced. Friends and family members often hug or kiss on the cheek when they see each other. In these situations, men often kiss women but not other men.

A According to the article, in which country or countries are the following true? Check (✓) the correct boxes.

	Chile	Finland	the Philippines	Korea	the U.S.
1. People shake hands every time they meet.	☐	☐	☐	☐	☐
2. Women do not shake hands.	☐	☐	☐	☐	☐
3. Women kiss at the first meeting.	☐	☐	☐	☐	☐
4. Men hug or pat each other on the back.	☐	☐	☐	☐	☐
5. Women kiss male friends.	☐	☐	☐	☐	☐
6. The family name comes first.	☐	☐	☐	☐	☐

B *Pair work* How do these people greet each other in your country?

1. two male friends
2. a male and female friend
3. two strangers
4. two female friends

2 How do you spend your day?

Work and School Days

	Brazil	the United Kingdom	South Korea	the United States
Average number of working hours per week	44	44	48	40
Average number of paid vacation days per year	20–21	27	20	12
Number of national holidays	10	8	10	11
Number of school days per year	182	192	222	178
Hours of instruction in school per day	4.5	5	4.5	5.5

Information compiled from *The New York Times*, *Digest of Educational Statistics*, and interviews.

Talk about these questions.

Which country would you like to work in? Why?
Where would you like to be a student? Why?

2 WORD POWER *Jobs*

A Complete the word map with jobs from the list.

architect
receptionist
company director
flight attendant
supervisor
engineer
salesperson
secretary
professor
sales manager
security guard
word processor

Professionals
architect

Service occupations
flight attendant

Jobs

Management positions
company director

Office work
receptionist

B Add two more jobs to each category. Then compare with a partner.

2 How do you spend your day?

This unit teaches Ss how to talk about their jobs, schools, and daily routines. It also introduces simple present Wh-questions and statements, and time expressions including prepositions.

Cycle 1, Exercises 1–6

1 SNAPSHOT Work and school days

This exercise introduces the themes of time spent at work and school, and numbers of holidays and vacation days.

- Books closed. Introduce the topic of how people spend time in various countries by brainstorming with the class, like this:

1. Write and circle the word *TIME* on the board.

2. Ask the class to help you think of some words that relate to "time." If there are no suggestions after a few seconds, start adding some words like these to the board – *hours, days, years* – and explain them, if necessary, as each one is added. Continue writing the Ss' words and your own until there are no more suggestions or the board is full. (*Note:* When brainstorming, no words should be considered wrong or inappropriate. Free word association is the key to effective brainstorming.)

- Books open. Present any new vocabulary (e.g., *average number* vs. *number per day/week/year; working hours;*

national holidays) and give some examples. If you prefer, have Ss read the Snapshot on their own with their dictionaries.

- Model how to read decimal points (e.g., 4.5 = "four point five").

- **Optional:** Ask some Wh-questions so Ss can practice scanning the chart for numbers:

  What is the average number of working hours per week in the United Kingdom? (44)
  Which two countries have ten national holidays? (Brazil and South Korea)

- Ss do the task by reading each question and then writing the country's name and their reason for choosing it. Go around the class and give help as needed.

- Ss form pairs to compare answers. Check Ss' answers and write on the board the names of the countries and reasons mentioned most often.

2 WORD POWER Jobs

This exercise presents the vocabulary of jobs and ways to categorize jobs.

A

- Ask Ss to look through the vocabulary list. Pronounce and explain any new words, including the category titles in the chart, but take care not to give away a category that a word may belong to. Alternatively, have Ss check their dictionaries.

- Ss complete the word map individually.

B

- Ss write two more examples for each category. Then have Ss work in pairs to compare answers.

- Elicit answers around the class and write them on the board under the appropriate categories. Tell Ss to use this information to add any additional jobs to their own charts.

Answers *(extra examples in boldface)*

Professionals	*Service occupations*
architect	flight attendant
engineer	salesperson
professor	security guard
lawyer	**waiter/waitress**
doctor	**hairstylist**
Management positions	*Office work*
company director	receptionist
supervisor	secretary
sales manager	word processor
president	**mailroom clerk**
CEO (chief executive officer)	**departmental assistant**

Optional activity: *What's his/her job?*

- See page T-147.

3 WORK AND WORKPLACES

This controlled practice develops Ss' ability to write simple present sentences describing people's jobs.

A

■ Use the pictures and gestures to explain any new words in columns A, B, and C, like this:

What kind of job is this in picture number 1? (She's a salesperson.)
What's the name of a big airline? (United)
What's another way to say someone "cares for patients"? (He or she helps sick people.)

Try not to reveal the relationships among the words and phrases in the three lists.

■ **Optional:** Ask Ss to suggest a category title for each column (e.g., A = Job titles; B = Workplaces and companies; C = Job descriptions).

■ Describe the task by going over the example: the circled and connected items in A, B, and C. Have Ss work alone to match the rest.

B *Pair work*

■ To model the activity, read aloud the example description. You may want to ask a volunteer to read the next set of sentences. Then Ss form pairs to compare their answers orally.

Answers

> She's a salesperson. She works in a department store. She sells clothes.
> He's a chef. He works in a restaurant. He cooks food.
> He's a flight attendant. He works for an airline. He serves passengers.
> She's a carpenter. She works for a construction company. She builds houses.
> He's a receptionist. He works in an office. He answers the phone.
> She's a nurse. She works in a hospital. She cares for patients.

■ **Optional:** Ss use the information to write their own sentences. Have Ss write descriptions of five of the jobs listed in Exercise 2 on page 8.

Optional activity: *Scrambled letters*

■ See page T-146.

4 CONVERSATION *Describing work*

This conversation introduces simple present statements and Wh-questions.

A 🔊

■ Books closed. Set the focus by writing these questions on the board:

What's Andrea's job? (She's a [tour] guide.)
Is it interesting? (Yes, it is.)
Is the man a student? (Yes, he is.)
Where does he work? (He works in a fast-food restaurant/at Hamburger Heaven.)

■ Ask Ss to listen for the answers to the questions on the board. Play the audio program several times. Then check Ss' answers. Ask for any additional information students may have heard.

■ Books open. Present the conversation line by line. If necessary, explain any new words and expressions like these:

> **Oh, really?** = an exclamation used to express interest or surprise
> **guide** = a person whose job is to show a place or an area to visitors
> **tours** = visits to places or areas
> **That sounds . . . !** = I think that's . . . !

■ Play the audio program again, pausing after each line. Ss repeat. Model the stress in "Where do you **work**, Andrea?" and "What do you **do** there?"

■ Ss practice the conversation in pairs. Remind them to use the "Look Up and Say" technique. (*Note:* This is described in Unit 1, Exercise 1, of this Teacher's Edition.)

B 🔊

■ Read aloud the two questions. Play the audio program for part B once or twice. Ss listen for the answers.

Audio script

> ANDREA: What do you do, exactly? Do you make hamburgers?
> JASON: No, I don't. I just take orders.
> ANDREA: And what's it like there? Do you like your job?
> JASON: Sure. It's fun! And I get free hamburgers, too!

■ Elicit answers around the class.

Answers

> 1. He takes orders.
> 2. He likes his job because it's fun. He gets free hamburgers, too.

3 WORK AND WORKPLACES

A Look at the pictures. Match the information in columns A, B, and C.

A	B	C
a salesperson	for an airline	builds houses
a chef	in a restaurant	cares for patients
a flight attendant	for a construction company	answers the phone
a carpenter	in a hospital	cooks food
a receptionist	in a department store	serves passengers
a nurse	in an office	sells clothes

B *Pair work* Take turns describing each person's job.

"She's a salesperson. She works in a department store. She sells clothes."

4 CONVERSATION Describing work

A 🔊 Listen and practice.

Jason: Where do you work, Andrea?
Andrea: I work for Thomas Cook Travel.
Jason: Oh, really? What do you do there?
Andrea: I'm a guide. I take people on tours to countries in South America, like Peru.
Jason: That sounds interesting!
Andrea: Yes, it's a great job. I love it. And what do you do?
Jason: I'm a student, and I have a part-time job, too.
Andrea: Oh? Where do you work?
Jason: In a fast-food restaurant.
Andrea: Which restaurant?
Jason: Hamburger Heaven.

B 🔊 Listen to the rest of the conversation.

1. What does Jason do, exactly?
2. How does he like his job?

5 *GRAMMAR FOCUS*

Simple present Wh-questions and statements 📼

What do you **do**?	I'm a student, and I **have** a part-time job.	*I/You*	*He/She*
Where do you **work**?	I **work** at/in a restaurant.	work	works
Where do you **go** to school?	I **go** to the University of Texas.	take	takes
How do you **like** your school?	I **like** it very much.	study	studies
		teach	teaches
Where does Andrea **work**?	She **works** for Thomas Cook Travel.	do	does
What does she **do**?	She's a guide. She **takes** people on tours.	go	goes
Where does Jason **go** to school?	He **goes** to New York University.	have	has
How does he **like** it?	He **loves** it.		

A Complete these conversations. Then practice with a partner.

1. A: What .... you .... ?
   B: I'm a student. I study business.
   A: And .... do you .... to school?
   B: I .... to Jefferson College.
   A: .... do you like your classes?
   B: I .... them a lot.

2. A: What .... Kanya do?
   B: She's a teacher. She .... mathematics
      at a school in Bangkok.
   A: And what about Somsak? Where .... he work?
   B: He .... for an electronics company.
   A: .... does he do, exactly?
   B: He's a salesman. He .... computer equipment.

B *Pair work* What do you know about these jobs? Complete the chart.
Then write sentences describing each job, using *he* or *she*.

A doctor	A travel agent	A police officer
▪ *works in a hospital*	▪	▪ ....
▪ *has an office*	▪	▪ ....
▪ *works long hours*	▪	▪ ....
▪ *cares for patients*	▪	▪ ....

A doctor works in a hospital. She has an office, too. . . .

C *Group work* Ask your classmates questions about work and school.

A: What do you do, Aki?
B: I'm a student.
C: Where do you go to school?
B: . . .

5 GRAMMAR FOCUS *Simple present Wh-questions and statements*

This grammar focus practices simple present Wh-questions (with the auxiliary verb *do*) and statements using pronouns *I, you, she,* and *he.* It also shows how the prepositions *at, in, to,* and *for* are used. Prepositions are a difficult part of English grammar, and there are many exceptions to usage rules for them. However, at this level, simply refer Ss to the Unit Summary for Unit 2 on page S-3 of the Student's Book.

■ Use the audio program to present the questions and statements in the first box. Ss repeat.

■ Explain how *do* is used to form Wh-questions in the simple present: *do* (with *I, you, we, they*) or *does* (with *he, she, it*) + subject (pronoun or noun) + simple form of the verb. Point out that the main verb in the question is always in its simple form: It has no final *-s.* Write this information on the board:

Statement	Question
I <u>work</u> in an office.	Where <u>do</u> you <u>work</u>?
He <u>works</u> in an office.	Where <u>does</u> he <u>work</u>?

■ Model the reduced form of *do* in questions (e.g., "What 'dya' do?" /wʌt dyə duw/, "Where 'dya' work?" /wɛr dyə wərk/; also model the stress in questions (e.g., "**What** do you **do**?" or "**Where** does she **work**?"). Point out that prepositions and articles (*a, an, the*) are almost always unstressed.

■ Use the audio program to present the pronouns and their simple present verb forms in the chart. Make sure Ss understand the need to add an *-s* to verbs with the third person pronouns *he* and *she* (and *it*). Point out the regular verbs *work* and *take,* the spelling changes in *study – studies* and *teach – teaches,* and the irregular verb forms *do – does, go – goes,* and *have – has.*

■ Ask the first four Wh-questions from the box around the class. Ss answer using real information about themselves if they can.

A

■ Ss complete the conversations individually and then compare answers with a partner.

■ Check answers and explain any new words before pairs practice the conversations.

Answers

1. A: What **do** you **do**?
   B: I'm a student. I study business.
   A: And **where** do you **go** to school?
   B: I **go** to Jefferson College.
   A: **How** do you like your classes?
   B: I **like** them a lot.
2. A: What **does** Kanya do?
   B: She's a teacher. She **teaches** mathematics at a school in Bangkok.
   A: And what about Somsak? Where **does** he work?
   B: He **works** for an electronics company.
   A: **What** does he do, exactly?
   B: He's a salesman. He **sells** computer equipment.

B *Pair work*

■ Explain the task: Pairs work together to complete the chart; then they write a short paragraph (three to four sentences) to describe each job in the chart. Check Ss' answers around the class.

Possible answers *(in sentence form)*

A doctor works in a hospital. She has an office, too. She works long hours. She cares for patients.
A travel agent works for a travel agency. He takes trips, too. He makes reservations and writes airline tickets for customers.
A police officer works outside and patrols the city in a police car. She has a partner. She writes traffic tickets, too.

C *Group work*

■ Present the A/B/C model dialog with the help of several Ss. Alternatively, call on volunteers to talk about the kind of work they do or other schools they go to. Then Ss spend about five minutes doing the activity in groups.

Optional activity: *Game – What's the question?*

■ See page T-147.

 Workbook

Assign Exercises 1–5 on pages 7–9 in the Workbook for about ten minutes of in-class work; Ss can complete the rest for homework. In the next class, elicit responses to check answers. (Answers can be found on page T-176 of the Workbook Answer Key in this Teacher's Edition.)

6 *WRITING*

This exercise gives Ss an opportunity to write a short description of what they do.

- **Optional:** Part A of the activity can be assigned for homework. If it is, ask Ss not to write their names on their compositions.

A

- Have Ss read the model composition and then write a short description about themselves. Encourage them to give as much information as they can. Remind Ss not to write their names on their compositions.

- **Optional:** Give an additional model by writing a paragraph on the board about yourself or another person Ss know.

- As Ss write their compositions, move around the class and help as necessary. (*Note:* It is not necessary to correct every error here.)

B *Group work*

- Ss work in groups to pass around their compositions, read one another's (either silently or aloud – as each group decides), and then try to guess who wrote each one.

- **Optional:** Each group votes on the most interesting composition. Then one member (but not the author) reads it aloud to the class, and the others try to guess who wrote it.

Cycle 2, Exercises 7–11

7 *CONVERSATION* *Daily schedules*

This conversation introduces the topic of daily schedules and routines, and uses time expressions with adverbs and prepositional phrases.

A 🔊

- Books closed. Introduce the topic of daily schedules, times, and routines by asking several Ss these questions:

  What do you do on weekdays? on weekends?
  What time do you . . . (get up, eat breakfast, go to sleep)?

- Set the scene and play the audio program once or twice. Ask some comprehension questions like these:

  When does Helen get up? (She gets up around ten.)
  When does she get home? (She gets home around midnight.)
  What does she do? (She's a TV announcer.)

- Books open. Go over the conversation line by line and explain any new vocabulary. Then Ss practice the conversation in pairs.

B 🔊

- Go over the questions and tell Ss to take notes as they listen. Play the second part of the audio program several times.

Audio script

> HELEN: And you, Daniel? What's your day like?
> DANIEL: Well, right now I'm in school, so I just have a part-time job. But I'm pretty busy. I get up early, around six A.M. Then I work from seven until nine. I go to school and study until four P.M. Then I work again from five until seven.
> HELEN: So what do you do?
> DANIEL: (*laughs*) I'm a dog walker.
> HELEN: A what? What's that?
> DANIEL: A dog walker. I take people's dogs for walks. It's great, and it keeps me in shape, too!

- Elicit answers around the class to check Ss' comprehension.

Answers

> 1. He gets up around six A.M., goes to work at seven, and studies until four P.M.
> 2. He's a dog walker.

---

8 *PRONUNCIATION* *Unstressed words*

This exercise focuses on unstressed words – in particular, prepositions – and also emphasizes how key words are stressed in sentences. The sentences illustrate the need for a stress-timed rhythm in English.

A 🔊

- Books open. Play the audio program several times. Ss listen and repeat. Show them how to clap their hands together on each stressed beat.

B *Pair work*

- Replay the audio program for part A in Exercise 7 or read the conversation aloud while clapping or tapping on the desk each time a word or syllable is stressed. Show Ss how to add accent marks to the text to help them remember which words are stressed.

- Pairs practice the conversation again.

6 WRITING

A Write a description of what you do. Don't write your name on the paper.

> I'm a student. I go to McGill University in Canada.
> I'm a freshman. I study computer science. I work
> part time at a radio station, too. I'm a disc jockey.
> I play music. I love my job!

B *Group work* Pass your descriptions around the group. Can you guess who wrote each description?

7 CONVERSATION Daily schedules

A 🔊 Listen and practice.

Daniel: How do you spend your day, Helen?
Helen: Well, on weekdays I get up around ten. Then I read the paper for an hour and have lunch at about noon.
Daniel: Really? What time do you go to work?
Helen: I start work at three.
Daniel: And when do you get home at night?
Helen: I get home pretty late, around midnight.
Daniel: So what do you do, exactly?
Helen: I'm a TV announcer. Don't you recognize me? I do the weather report on KNTV!
Daniel: Gee, I'm sorry. I don't watch TV.

B 🔊 Listen to Daniel describe how he spends his day.

1. What time does he get up? start work? study until?
2. What does he do?

8 PRONUNCIATION Unstressed words

A 🔊 Listen and practice. The prepositions in these sentences (*around, for,* and *at*) are not stressed.

I get **úp** around **tén.**
I read the **pá**per for an **hóur.**
I have **lúnch** at about **nóon.**

B *Pair work* Practice the conversation in Exercise 7 again. Be careful not to stress prepositions.

9 GRAMMAR FOCUS

Time expressions

I get up	**at** 7:00	**in** the morning	**on** weekdays.
I go to bed	**around** ten	**in** the evening	**on** weeknights.
I leave work	**early**	**in** the afternoon	**on** weekends.
I get home	**late**	**at** night	**on** Fridays.
I stay up	**until** midnight	**on** Saturdays.	
I wake up	**before/after** noon	**on** Sundays.	

Ways to express clock time
7:00
seven o'clock
seven
7:00 in the morning = 7:00 A.M.
7:00 in the evening = 7:00 P.M.

A Complete these sentences with time expressions.

1. I get up .... six .... the morning
   .... weekdays.
2. I go to bed .... midnight .... weeknights.
3. I start work .... 11:30 .... night.
4. I arrive at work .... Mondays,
   .... 7:00 A.M.
5. I have lunch .... three .... the afternoon
   .... weekdays.
6. I stay up .... weekends.
7. I have a little snack .... 9:00 .... the evening.
8. I sleep .... noon .... Sundays.

B Rewrite the sentences above so that they are true for you.
Then compare with a partner.

C *Pair work* Take turns asking and answering these questions.

1. What days do you get up early? late?
2. What are two things you do before 8:00 in the morning?
3. What are three things you do on Saturday mornings?
4. How late do you stay up on Saturday nights?
5. What is something you do only on Sundays?

interchange 2

Common ground
Take a survey. Compare
your schedule with your
classmates' schedules.
Turn to page IC-3.

10 LISTENING

A Listen to Rodney, Tina, and Ellen talk about
their daily schedules. Complete the chart.

	Job	Gets up at . . .	Gets home at . . .	Goes to bed at . . .
Rodney	....	....	....	....
Tina	....	....	....	....
Ellen	....	....	....	....

B *Class activity* Who do you think has the best daily schedule? Why?

9 GRAMMAR FOCUS *Time expressions*

This grammar focus presents adverbs and prepositional phrases to express time.

- Use the audio program to present the sentences and phrases in the boxes. Ss listen and repeat.
- Use a clock or draw a clock face on the board and mime the time expressions to clarify them (e.g., I get up at seven.). Explain any new words.
- On the board, write these rules for time expressions:

Prepositional phrase		*Usage rule*
at/around/until/ before/after 7:00	=	*at/around/until/before/ after + clock time; also + "noon" and "midnight"*
in the morning/ afternoon/evening	=	*in the + main portions of day (except "night")*
at night	=	*at + "night"*
on Friday(s)	=	*on + day(s) of the week*

- Tell Ss that *early* and *late* are adverbs. Explain that adverbs describe the action of a verb, usually by telling when or how. Illustrate the point by writing these sentences and questions on the board; Ss should be able to supply the correct adverbs as answers:

I leave work early.	*When do I leave work?*
I get home late.	*When do I get home?*

A

- Go over the task. Ss fill in the blanks. Elicit answers and explain any new vocabulary.

Answers

1. I get up **at/around/before** six **in** the morning **on** weekdays.
2. I go to bed **around/at/before/after** midnight **on** weeknights.
3. I start work **at** 11:30 **at** night.
4. I arrive at work **early on** Mondays, **at/before/around** 7:00 A.M.
5. I have lunch **at/around** three **in** the afternoon **on** weekdays.
6. I stay up **late on** weekends.
7. I have a little snack **around/at** 9:00 **in** the evening.
8. I sleep **until** noon **on** Sundays.

B

- Model the task with a S and rewrite one or two sentences on the board. Ss first work alone; then they compare sentences with a partner.

C *Pair work*

- To model the task, let Ss ask you the five questions. Alternatively, have volunteers ask each other.

 INTERCHANGE 2 Common ground

See page T-107 in this Teacher's Edition for notes.

10 LISTENING

This exercise practices listening for specific information about people's daily schedules.

A

- Go over the task and the chart. Play the audio program several times. Ss fill in the chart. Check Ss' answers.

Audio script

TINA: What do you do, Rodney?
RODNEY: I'm a chef.
TINA: Hey, that's great! So what are your work hours like?
RODNEY: They're OK. I work in the afternoons and evenings. I get up around nine A.M., and I work from eleven A.M. until ten P.M. I get home fairly late, about eleven P.M. And I'm usually in bed by one in the morning. And what do you do, Tina?
TINA: Well, I'm an office manager. It's a regular nine-to-five office job, so I get up at seven A.M. and get home around six P.M. That's OK, though, because I like to go out at night. I go to bed around midnight on weekdays.
RODNEY: What about you, Ellen?
ELLEN: Well, my job is a bit different – I'm a flight attendant. I start work at six in the morning, so I have to get up before five A.M.
TINA: Wow! That's too early for me!
ELLEN: Then I often have long flights, so I don't get home until nine o'clock at night. But I always go straight to bed – around ten.

Answers

	Job	*Gets up at . . .*	*Gets home at . . .*	*Goes to bed at . . .*
Rodney	chef	9 A.M.	11 P.M.	1 A.M.
Tina	office manager	7 A.M.	6 P.M.	midnight
Ellen	flight attendant	5 A.M.	9 P.M.	10 P.M.

B *Class activity*

- Elicit Ss' responses and take a class vote.

Optional activity: *True or false?*

- See page T-53.

11 READING   *The daily grind*

This text explores the reasons some students have part-time jobs; Ss also practice scanning for specific information and making inferences.

■ Books closed. Introduce the topic by asking questions like these around the class:

Do you have a job?
Do you work part time or full time?
What do you do, exactly?

■ Books open. Read the pre-reading questions aloud. Then write the following on the board:

STUDENT + JOB = Good idea? or Bad idea?

Elicit some comments and write a few of the Ss' ideas on the board under the appropriate heading. What is the general consensus?

■ Tell Ss to read the three passages straight through once. Encourage Ss to guess new words through context; however, if they still can't figure out some meanings, tell them to circle, underline, or highlight the words. Then either explain any unfamiliar vocabulary or allow Ss to check their dictionaries.

A

■ Explain this scanning task: Ss look through the text for specific information needed to complete the chart. Let Ss know that they may need to make some inferences, i.e., "educated guesses." You may also want to point out that two of the items have more than one answer.

■ Check answers around the class.

Answers

	Brandon	Lauren	Erica
1. To earn money for college	✓		✓
2. To buy nice clothes		✓	
3. To go out on the weekend	✓	✓	
4. To pay for a car		✓	
5. To get job experience			✓

B *Pair work*

■ Introduce this as a fun activity with interesting questions for partners to debate and figure out. Questions 2 and 3 require a bit of simple addition and multiplication. Go around the class and give help as requested or needed.

Answers

1. Ss' answers will vary.
2. Brandon works 16 hours a week (maybe fewer, depending on whether or not he is given a lunch break), Lauren 20, and Erica 15.
3. Brandon earns $88, Lauren $135, and Erica $123.75 per week.
4. Ss' answers will vary.

Workbook

Assign Exercises 6–11 on pages 10–12. At the start of the next class, allow Ss a few minutes to compare answers in pairs or small groups before checking their responses. (Answers can be found on page T-176 of the Workbook Answer Key in this Teacher's Edition.)

Optional activities

1 *Classified ads*

Time: 15 minutes. Many Ss enjoy being intellectually challenged in class. This categorizing activity is not only fun but also mentally stimulating.

Preparation: Make photocopies of job ads from an English-language newspaper and bring them to class. Alternatively, ask Ss to bring in a classified section from an English-language newspaper that includes employment opportunities.

■ Ss work in groups of four. Make sure that each group has either photocopies of job ads or their own classified section of the newspaper to work with.

■ Explain the task: Ss choose some jobs in the ads to classify into various categories that they think up together. To model the activity, read a few of the job ads and then write those job titles on the board. Elicit appropriate category examples for each one and write them on the board, too, like this:

Jobs		Possible job categories
secretary	=	an indoor job; an office job
lifeguard	=	an outdoor job; a service job
airline pilot	=	a job that requires English
tour guide	=	an exciting job; not a 9:00–5:00 job
office worker	=	a boring job; a white-collar job
police officer	=	a dangerous job; a difficult job
actor	=	a glamorous job; a fun job

■ Groups do the task and then take turns reporting their classifications to the class.

2 *Game – Word Bingo*

■ See page T-33.

11 *READING*

The Daily Grind

Is it a good idea for a student to have a job? Why or why not?

Brandon Smith

I'm a junior in high school, and I have a part-time job in a restaurant. I bus dishes on Saturdays and Sundays from 8:00 until 4:00. I earn $5.50 an hour. It isn't much money, but I save almost every penny! I want to go to a good university, and the cost goes up every year. Of course, I spend some money when I go out on Saturday nights.

Lauren Russell

I'm a senior in high school. I have a job as a cashier in a grocery store. The job pays well – about $6.75 an hour. I work every weeknight after school from 4:00 until 8:00. I don't have time for homework, and my grades aren't very good this year. But I have to work, or I can't buy nice clothes and I can't go out on Saturday nights. Also, a car costs a lot of money.

Erica Davis

I'm a freshman in college. College is very expensive, so I work in a law office for three hours every weekday afternoon. I make photocopies, file papers, and sort mail for $8.25 an hour. The job gives me good experience because I want to be a lawyer someday. But I don't want to work every semester. I need time to study.

A Read the article. Why do these students work? Check (✓) the correct boxes.

	Brandon	Lauren	Erica
1. To earn money for college	☐	☐	☐
2. To buy nice clothes	☐	☐	☐
3. To go out on the weekend	☐	☐	☐
4. To pay for a car	☐	☐	☐
5. To get job experience	☐	☐	☐

B *Pair work* Talk about these questions.

1. Look at the reasons why each student works. Who has good reasons to work? Who doesn't, in your opinion?
2. How many hours a week does each student work?
3. How much money does each student earn per week?
4. What are the advantages and disadvantages of part-time work for students?

3 How much is it?

1 SNAPSHOT

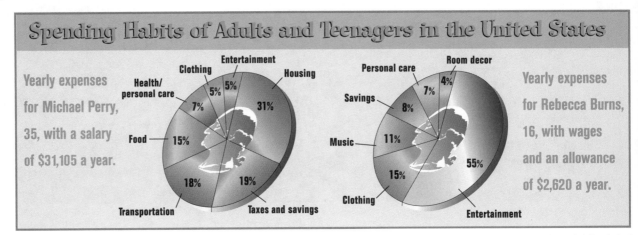

Spending Habits of Adults and Teenagers in the United States

Yearly expenses for Michael Perry, 35, with a salary of $31,105 a year.

Clothing 5%
Entertainment 5%
Health/personal care 7%
Housing 31%
Food 15%
Transportation 18%
Taxes and savings 19%

Yearly expenses for Rebecca Burns, 16, with wages and an allowance of $2,620 a year.

Personal care 7%
Room decor 4%
Savings 8%
Music 11%
Clothing 15%
Entertainment 55%

Portraits based on information from the *Statistical Abstract of the U.S.* and the Rand Youth Poll.

Talk about these questions.

How does Michael Perry spend most of his money?
How does Rebecca Burns spend most of her money?
How do their spending habits compare?
How do you spend your money? Make two lists: things you have to buy and things you like to buy.

2 CONVERSATION Prices

A Listen and practice.

Steve: Oh, look at those earrings, Maria. They're perfect for you.
Maria: These red ones? I'm not sure.
Steve: No, the yellow ones.
Maria: Oh, these? Hmm. Yellow isn't a good color for me.
Steve: Well, that necklace isn't bad.
Maria: Which one?
Steve: That blue one right there. How much is it?
Maria: It's $42! That's expensive!
Steve: Hey, let me get it for you. It's your birthday present.

CLASS AUDIO ONLY ▶ **B** Listen to the rest of the conversation.

1. What else do they buy?
2. Who pays for it?

14

3 How much is it?

This unit helps Ss talk about money, especially with regard to shopping. It introduces How much . . . ? with demonstratives this/that/ these/those and the pronouns one/ones. Ways of expressing preferences and making comparisons with adjectives are also presented.

Cycle 1, Exercises 1–6

1 SNAPSHOT *Spending habits of adults and teenagers in the United States*

This exercise introduces the theme of annual expenses and spending habits of a typical adult and teenager.

■ Books closed. Introduce the topic by writing *YEARLY EXPENSES* on the board. Then brainstorm with the class. Ask Ss to suggest some typical products and services that people buy or have to pay for each year (e.g., rent, car insurance, food, CDs, books, clothes). Write Ss' ideas on the board. Then ask the class to choose the five most important items. Can Ss suggest how much someone might spend yearly on those five items, or can they rank the items from 1 (the most expensive) to 5?

Optional: Use the brainstorming map on the board to include the concept of percentages based on yearly expenses. Choose five of the most important items and ask the class to suggest a realistic percentage (e.g., 5%, 10%, 25%) that an average person might spend yearly on each one.

■ Books open. Present any new vocabulary (e.g., *housing, entertainment, taxes, savings, room decor*) or ask Ss to use their dictionaries. Model the pronunciation of each word. Ss repeat.

■ Ss work individually to look at the information and then answer the questions. For the last question, tell Ss to write the names of five or so products or services on each of their two lists; they do not have to write down percentage estimates for these expenses.

■ Have Ss compare responses in pairs or in groups. Alternatively, elicit answers around the class.

Possible answers

> Michael Perry spends most of his money on housing (31% = $9,643).
> Rebecca Burns spends most of her money on entertainment (55% = $1,441).
> Michael spends only 5% ($1,555) of his yearly expenses on entertainment, but Rebecca spends over half, 55% ($1,441). Rebecca also spends more on clothing (15%) than Michael does (5%).
> *Last question:* Ss' answers will vary.

■ **Optional:** Take a class poll: For the last question, find out which three products and services Ss listed the most often and write them on the board.

2 CONVERSATION *Prices*

This exercise introduces demonstratives (*this, that, these, those*) and the pronouns *one/ones,* and reviews some colors used within the context of shopping.

A 🎧

■ Books open. To set the scene, refer Ss to the picture. Ask them where the people are and what they are doing.

■ Books closed. Write these questions on the board and ask Ss to listen for the answers:

> *Does Maria like the yellow earrings?* (No.)
> *How much is the blue necklace?* (It's $42.)
> *Does the man buy the necklace for Maria?*
>   *Why or why not?* (Yes. It's her birthday present.)

■ Play the first part of the audio program once or twice. Check Ss' answers to the questions on the board.

■ Books open. Present the conversation line by line. Explain any new vocabulary – for example:

I'm not sure. = I don't (really) know.
Hmm. = a sound made to express doubt
isn't bad = is OK/all right
Hey = an interjection used to call attention to someone or something or to express interest, surprise, etc.

let me . . . = I'd like to . . .
get = buy

■ Ss practice the conversation in pairs. Remind them to use the "Look Up and Say" technique.

B 🎧

■ Set the scene: Maria and Steve are going to look at something else in the department store. Go over the two questions and then play the second part of the audio program. Check Ss' answers.

Audio script

> MARIA: Steve, come and look at this tie. What do you think?
> STEVE: It's a nice tie, but look at the price – $25!
> MARIA: Oh, that's not bad. And I want you to have it. Let me get it for you.
> STEVE: OK. Sure!

Answers

> 1. They buy a tie.
> 2. Maria pays for it.

3 *GRAMMAR FOCUS* Demonstratives; one, ones

🔊 This exercise presents demonstrative adjectives *(this/that, these/those)*, the pronouns *one/ones*, colors, and prices.

- Use the audio program to present the questions and statements in the boxes. Ss repeat.

- Explain the difference between *this/that* and *these/those* in this way: Use *this* or *these* to refer to any object or objects (e.g., a pen, books) close to you; use *that* and *those* for any object or objects further away. Make sure Ss understand that *this/that* are used with single items and *these/those* with plural items or things that have two parts (e.g., earrings, glasses, jeans).

- Tell Ss that the pronoun *one* replaces a singular noun (e.g., *necklace*) and that *ones* replaces a plural noun (e.g., *earrings*). Point out that *one* is used after *this/that* but *ones* is almost never used after *these/those*.

- Use the audio program to model the pronunciation of dollar prices. Ss repeat.

- Call on Ss to take turns asking questions with "How much is/are . . . ?" about things pictured in this unit or in the classroom; others respond with real or made-up prices.

- Use the color chart and the audio program to present the new vocabulary. Encourage Ss to ask and answer questions about the colors of objects in class.

- Explain that Ss should use the pictures to complete the two conversations. Ss do the task individually and then compare answers with a partner.

- Before eliciting Ss' answers, explain this new expression:

Are you kidding? (informal) = Is that true, or are you joking? (said when someone is very surprised)

Answers

1. A: Excuse me. How much **are those** jeans?
   B: Which **ones**? Do you mean **these**?
   A: No, the light blue **ones**.
   B: Oh, **they're** $59.95.
   A: Almost sixty dollars! Are you kidding?
2. A: I like **that** backpack over there. How much **is** it?
   B: Which **one**? Each backpack has a different price.
   A: **That** red **one**.
   B: It's $98.50. But **this** green **one** is only $45.
   A: OK. Let me look at it.

- Pairs practice the conversations.

Optional activities

1 *Game – Colorful things around us*

Time: 10–15 minutes. This activity involves identifying the colors of objects in the classroom.

- On the board, write the names of the twelve colors from the color chart. Then brainstorm with the class and try to come up with additional names of colors in English that the Ss already know. Add these to the list on the board.

- Using the total number of colors on the board, divide the class into small groups, assigning one or two colors to each group.

- Explain the game: Each group looks around the classroom and makes a list of the names of objects that have their assigned color(s). The group that finds the most objects in five minutes is the winner.

- When time is up, groups report their findings to the class, like this:

  T: Group 1, how many things did you find?
  S1: We found six red things in the classroom.
  T: What are they?
  S1: Well, Sabrina's skirt is red.
  S2: And your pen has red ink.
  S3: There are red stripes in the U.S. flag.
  S4: And . . .

2 *How much do you think it is?*

Time: 10 minutes. This activity practices guessing and discussing the prices of clothing and accessories.

Preparation: Bring pictures of clothing and accessories from mail-order catalogs or from newspaper and magazine ads. Remove or cover up the prices, but keep a record of them. (This activity works best if the items pictured are rather expensive or overpriced.)

- Ss form groups (or pairs). Give different pictures to each group or make photocopies of one set of pictures and pass copies out to each group. Ss try to guess the price of each item.

- When groups have finished, elicit prices for each item and write them on the board. Take a quick class vote of raised hands to determine which price Ss think is the best or most correct. Then give the actual price.

3 GRAMMAR FOCUS

Demonstratives; one, ones

| How much is **this** necklace? **this one**? | How much is **that** necklace? **that one**? | Which **one**? | The blue **one**. | It's $42. |
| How much are **these** earrings? **these**? | How much are **those** earrings? **those**? | Which **ones**? | The yellow **ones**. | They're $18. |

Prices
$42 = forty-two dollars
$59.95 = fifty-nine ninety-five
or fifty-nine dollars and
ninety-five cents

Colors

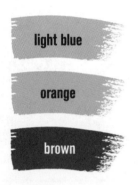  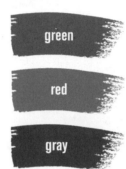 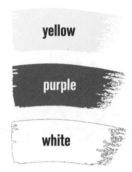

light blue	dark blue	green	yellow
orange	pink	red	purple
brown	black	gray	white

Look at the pictures and complete these conversations.
Then practice with a partner.

1. A: Excuse me. How much
      .... jeans?
   B: Which .... ? Do you mean .... ?
   A: No, the light blue ....
   B: Oh, ... $59.95.
   A: Almost sixty dollars! Are you kidding?

2. A: I like .... backpack over there.
      How much .... it?
   B: Which .... ? Each backpack has a
      different price.
   A: .... red ....
   B: It's $98.50. But .... green
      .... is only $45.
   A: OK. Let me look at it.

4 THAT'S EXPENSIVE!

Pair work Ask and answer questions about these products.
For help with numbers, see the appendix at the back of the book.

Computers	Jeans	Athletic Shoes	Watches
$5,456	$16.99	$21.89	$6.99
$1,696	$54.39	$79.95	$124.50

A: How much is the computer?
B: Which one?
A: The small one./This one.
B: It's $5,456.
A: That's expensive!

useful expressions
That's cheap.
That's reasonable.
That's OK/not bad.
That's expensive.

5 LISTENING

  Listen to Tim and Sandra shopping, and complete the chart.

CLASS AUDIO ONLY

Item	Price	Do they buy it?		Reason
		Yes	No	
1. Rollerblades	....	☐	☐	....
2. cap	....	☐	☐	....
3. sunglasses	....	☐	☐	....

6 PRONUNCIATION *Linked sounds*

A Listen and practice. Final consonants are often
linked to the vowels that follow them.

A: How much are these pants?
B: They're forty-eight dollars.

A: And how much is this sweater?
B: It's thirty-seven dollars.

B *Pair work* Ask and answer four questions about
prices in this unit. Pay attention to the linked sounds.

interchange 3

Swap meet
See what kinds of deals
you can make as a buyer
and a seller. Turn to
pages IC-4
and IC-5.

4 *THAT'S EXPENSIVE!*

This is a fluency activity that reviews the language used in Exercises 1–3.

Pair work

- Pronounce the names of the pictured items and model the various ways prices can be pronounced, like this:

  T: This is a laptop computer. It's $5,456 (five thousand four hundred [and] fifty-six dollars). These jeans are $16.99 (sixteen dollars and ninety-nine cents *or* sixteen ninety-nine).

- If necessary, clarify the four useful expressions, explaining that they are ranked according to price – from least expensive to most expensive.

- Model the A/B dialog with one or two Ss. Remind Ss to make all the necessary changes for the plural objects and to use appropriate expressions from the box.

- In pairs, Ss take turns asking and answering questions about the eight products. Go around the class and give help as needed.

5 *LISTENING*

This exercise practices listening for prices and the reasons for buying or not buying things.

- Ask Ss what each item in the chart might cost in your city and write some of the prices on the board. Make sure Ss understand the adverb *too* (which occurs twice on the audio program as a reason for not buying something). Refer Ss back to Exercise 3 on page 15, like this:

  T: How much are the jeans in the first conversation?
  S1: $59.95.
  T: Does he buy them?
  S2: No.
  T: Why not?
  S3: They're expensive.
  T: Yes. They're *too* expensive.

- Set the scene by going over the instructions. Play the audio program once or twice. Ss complete the chart.

Audio script

1. TIM: Look at these! Rollerblades! I really want a pair.
   SANDRA: But they're pretty expensive. They're $165!
   TIM: Oh, yeah. You're right. A hundred and sixty-five dollars *is* too expensive.

2. TIM: Here's a great cap for you!
   SANDRA: That one? Hmm. Is it expensive?
   TIM: Not really. It's only $9.95.
   SANDRA: Nine ninety-five is very reasonable. I think I'll take it.
3. SANDRA: What do you think of those sunglasses? They're only $16.
   TIM: They're nice. Try them on.
   SANDRA: Oh, no. I think they're too big.
   TIM: You're right. They *are* too big.

- Check Ss' answers around the class.

Answers

Item	Price	Do they buy it?	Reason
1. Rollerblades	$ 165.00	No	too expensive
2. cap	$ 9.95	Yes	very reasonable
3. sunglasses	$ 16.00	No	too big

6 *PRONUNCIATION* *Linked sounds*

This exercise practices linking a final consonant sound with the initial vowel sound that follows it.

A

- Explain the notion of "linked sounds": The final consonant of a word is linked, or attached, to the vowel sound that starts the word that follows it.

- Write the first question on the board and mark the linked sounds as you say them. Ss repeat.

- Play the audio program. Ss practice the questions and responses using linked sounds.

B *Pair work*

- In pairs, Ss take turns asking four questions with "How much is/are . . . ?" about any items in this unit that are pictured with a price (see pages 14–16).

 INTERCHANGE 3 Swap meet

See pages T-108 and T-109 in this Teacher's Edition for notes.

 Workbook

Assign Exercises 1–5 on pages 13–15 in the Workbook for homework. Elicit Ss' answers at the beginning of the next class. (Answers can be found on page T-177 of the Workbook Answer Key in this Teacher's Edition.)

7 WORD POWER Materials

This exercise presents adjectives describing what clothing and accessories are made of.

A *Pair work*

- Model the pronunciation of the listed items.
- Tell Ss to work in pairs to match each item with the correct picture and then to write the words on the blank below each picture. Check answers.

Answers

1. a plastic bracelet	5. leather gloves
2. a gold ring	6. a cotton shirt
3. a silk scarf	7. silver earrings
4. polyester pants	8. rubber boots

- Have a quick brainstorming session on other types of materials that things can be made of. Write Ss' suggestions on the board. Then pairs can use dictionaries to make their own lists for each of the eight items. Elicit Ss' ideas.

Possible answers

scarf, pants, and shirt: cotton, wool, silk, linen, polyester, rayon, nylon, knit, satin

gloves: leather, rubber, plastic, suede, cotton, lace, wool knit, polyester
boots: leather, rubber, plastic, suede
bracelet, ring, and earrings: plastic, gold, silver, copper, brass, glass, jade, diamond, pearl, ruby, emerald

B *Class activity*

- Model the task by talking about what you are wearing or things you have with you in class. Write some example sentences like these on the board:

  I'm wearing . . . (e.g., a cotton shirt, wool slacks).
  I have . . . (e.g., a silver pen, a leather wallet).

- Go over the example sentences. Then elicit the Ss' own responses around the class.

- **Optional:** For extra practice, have Ss compose four sentences about what they are wearing – items that others can see. Tell them not to write their name on their paper. Collect the descriptions and mix them up. Then give one to each S, who reads it aloud while others try to guess who it is about.

Optional activity: *Game – Tic-Tac-Toe*

- See page T-147.

8 CONVERSATION Shopping

This exercise introduces expressing preferences and making comparisons.

A

- **Optional:** To introduce comparative forms (more fully practiced in Exercise 9), ask Ss to compare two similar objects in the classroom (e.g., backpacks, dictionaries, pens), like this:

  T: *(holding up two different-sized dictionaries)* Which dictionary is bigger?
  S: The red one.
  T: *(writing on board)* The red dictionary is bigger than the black one.

- Books closed. Set the scene by telling Ss to listen to two friends who are shopping. Ask them to listen for answers to these questions:

  What are they shopping for? (Jackets)
  How much is the leather one? (It's $499.)
  Does the woman buy it? (No.)

- Play the audio program. Ss listen and suggest answers.

- Books open. Play the audio program again. Explain any new words and expressions, such as:

  like better = prefer
  try it on = put something on to see if it fits
  But thank you anyway. = a polite refusal

- Ss practice the conversation in groups of three.

B

- Go over the questions, explaining that *What does Sue think of it?* means "What's Sue's opinion of it?" Also mention that Anne speaks first.

- Play the audio program.

Audio script

ANNE: Wow! That jacket is really expensive! I don't want to spend that much money.
SUE: Oh, look. There are some things on sale over there.
ANNE: Oooh, you're right! These T-shirts are really nice. And they're cheap, too. I like this one with the bird on it.
SUE: That *is* nice! And the colors are really pretty.
ANNE: Great! I'll take it.

- Elicit answers from volunteers.

Answers

1. Anne buys a T-shirt with a bird on it.
2. Sue thinks it's nice and the colors are really pretty.

7 WORD POWER Materials

A *Pair work* Identify these things. Use the words from the list.
What other materials are these things sometimes made of? Make a list.

a **cotton** shirt   **leather** gloves   a **plastic** bracelet   a **silk** scarf
a **gold** ring   **polyester** pants   **rubber** boots   **silver** earrings

1. ....   2. ....   3. ....   4. ....

5. ....   6. ....   7. ....   8. ....

B *Class activity* Which of the materials can you find in your classroom?

"Juan has a leather bag."

8 CONVERSATION Shopping

A Listen and practice.

Anne: Look! These jackets are nice.
      Which one do you like better?
 Sue: I like the wool one better.
Anne: Really? Why?
 Sue: It looks warmer.
Anne: Well, I prefer the leather one.
      It's more attractive than the wool one.
 Sue: Hmm. There's no price tag.
Anne: Excuse me. How much is this jacket?
Clerk: It's $499. Would you like to try it on?
Anne: Oh, no. That's OK! But thank you anyway.
Clerk: You're welcome.

B Listen to the rest of the conversation.

1. What does Anne buy?
2. What does Sue think of it?

17

9 GRAMMAR FOCUS

Preferences; comparisons with adjectives 🔊

Which one do you **prefer**? I **prefer** the leather one. Which one do you **like better/more**? I **like** the leather one **better/more**.	That one is **nicer than** the wool one. This one is **cheaper than** . . . . The leather jacket is **prettier than** . . . . It looks **bigger than** . . . . It's **more attractive than**	nice → nicer cheap → cheaper pretty → prettier big → bigger good → better

For more information on comparatives, see the appendix at the back of the book.

A Complete these conversations. Then practice with a partner.

| polyester tie | silk tie | medium shirt | large shirt | leather boots | rubber boots |

1. A: Which tie is .... , the orange one or the blue one? (pretty)
   B: Well, the blue one is silk. And silk is .... polyester. (nice)

2. A: Is this green shirt .... that yellow one? (large)
   B: No, the yellow one is .... It's a large. The green one is a medium. (big)

3. A: Which are .... , the brown boots or the black ones? (cheap)
   B: The brown ones are leather. And leather is .... rubber. (expensive)

B *Pair work* Compare the items above with a partner. Give your own opinions.

A: Which tie do you like better?
B: I like the orange one better. The design is nicer.

useful expressions

The color is prettier.
The design is nicer.
The style is more attractive.
The material is better.

10 WRITING

How much do these items cost in your country? Fill in the chart.
Then compare the prices in your country with the prices in the U.S.

	Cost in my country	Cost in the U.S.
gasoline	....	$ 1.10/gallon
a compact disc	....	$ 12.99
a haircut	....	$ 23.00
a pair of jeans	....	$ 34.00

Many things are more expensive in my country than in the United States. For example, a liter of gas is about $.66. In the U.S. it's cheaper. It's about $1.10 per gallon. . . .

9 GRAMMAR FOCUS — Preferences; comparisons with adjectives

This grammar focus introduces ways to express preferences and make comparisons. Several ways to compare things are presented: (1) talking about one's preferences using a Wh-question with *prefer* (e.g., Which one do you prefer?) and with *like* + adverb (e.g., Which one do you like better/more?), and (2) making comparisons using adjectives (e.g., The leather jacket is prettier/more attractive than the wool one.) with two different patterns – adjective + *-er* + *than* + noun and *more* + adjective + *than* + noun.

Refer Ss to the Unit Summary for Unit 3 on page S-4 of the Student's Book. Then share with the class these guidelines for making comparisons with adjectives:

1. For one-syllable adjectives, add *-er* (or just *-r* if the adjective ends in *e*): *nice – nicer*; *cheap – cheaper*.
2. For one- or two-syllable adjectives ending in *y*, change *y* to *i* and add *-er*: *pretty – prettier*.
3. For adjectives ending in a single vowel + consonant, double the final consonant and add *-er*: *big – bigger*.
4. For other adjectives of two or more syllables, add *more*: *attractive – more attractive*.
5. For the irregular comparative form of *good*, use *better*.

- Use the audio program to present the questions, statements, and adjective forms in the boxes. Ss repeat.
- Point out that *than* always comes after the adjective. Also explain that in comparisons with *more*, the adjective is usually stressed (e.g., It's more at**trac**tive than the wool one.).
- **Optional:** Ask more questions about Ss' clothing and other things they have in class. Use additional adjectives (e.g., *larger, smaller, older, warmer, greener, more useful, more beautiful*). (*Note:* See the list of adjectives in the appendix at the back of the book.) Ss respond using comparatives.

A

- The pictures above each conversation illustrate the difference between the two objects being compared. Tell Ss to look at each picture and the adjectives in parentheses before filling in the blanks.

- Explain that the phrases *a small/a medium/a large/an extra large* are often used for clothing sizes.
- Ss compare answers in pairs. Then check answers around the class.

Answers

1. A: Which tie is **prettier**, the orange one or the blue one?
   B: Well, the blue one is silk. And silk is **nicer than** polyester.
2. A: Is this green shirt **larger than** that yellow one?
   B: No, the yellow one is **bigger**. It's a large. The green one is a medium.
3. A: Which are **cheaper**, the brown boots or the black ones?
   B: The brown ones are leather. And leather is **more expensive than** rubber.

- In pairs, Ss practice the conversations.
- **Optional:** Introduce adjectival order: Write the phrases *blue silk tie* and *brown leather boots* on the board. Ask Ss if they can figure out the rule for the order of these two kinds of adjectives. (Answer: Color comes before material.)

B Pair work

- Tell the class to look again at the pictures in part A. Then model the A/B dialog in part B and show how to use the useful expressions in the box. Pairs practice giving their own opinions. Encourage them to compare other similar objects pictured in this unit or found in the classroom.
- **Optional:** Did Ss come up with any other "useful" expressions? If so, ask for volunteers to write them on the board. Check for spelling and grammatical accuracy; the other Ss copy the expressions into their vocabulary notebooks.

Optional activity: *Guess the word*
- See page T-86.

---

10 WRITING

This exercise practices comparing U.S. prices with prices in the Ss' home countries.

- Go over the task and the items in the chart. Read the model aloud. (*Note:* If Ss aren't sure what each item costs in their countries, they can make up realistic prices.) Ss fill in the chart.
- Ss can draft their short paragraphs in class or as a homework assignment.

- Ss work in pairs and read each other's draft together. They can help double-check grammar, particularly any comparisons with adjectives.
- **Optional:** Ss may want to recopy or retype their paragraphs before handing in a final draft for comments.

11 READING Shop till you drop

In this text, Ss explore the different kinds of shopping available in the United States; they also practice scanning for facts and key words, and making inferences.

■ Books closed. To introduce the reading, write the opening question and this brainstorming topic on the board: *KINDS OF SHOPPING IN MY COUNTRY*. Ss work individually to make a brainstorming map and then share ideas in small groups. Elicit Ss' examples of how, when, and where they shop in their countries. Write that information on the board.

A

■ Books open. Ss should be able to read these paragraphs and answer the questions in both exercises without using their dictionaries. It may be a good idea, however, to ask Ss to underline, circle, or highlight any word whose meaning they can't guess from its context in a sentence. Then elicit and explain any new vocabulary:

Catalog shopping
music club = a mail-order company from which members order music (cassettes, CDs) at discount prices
Television shopping
QVC = "Quality, Value, and Convenience"
Computer shopping
households = homes
posters = pictures, often reproductions of original paintings or photographs and printed on large sheets of paper, which can be framed or pinned to a wall or board

■ Ss complete the chart individually and then compare answers in pairs or small groups. Check answers around the class.

Answers

1. T
2. F – The Home Shopping Network is the name of a television shopping channel.
3. F – About 37% of American households have personal computers.

B Pair work

■ Go over questions 1 and 2 and the eight kinds of shopping listed. Explain any new vocabulary (e.g., *discount stores; secondhand or thrift stores; mall*). Ss work individually to think about their answers and then check the boxes.

■ Ss form pairs or groups. Tell them to take turns asking and answering the questions. Walk around the class and give help as needed.

■ **Optional:** Take a quick class survey to find out which are the three most popular kinds of shopping among the Ss. This can be done simply through a show of hands.

 Workbook

Assign Exercises 6–10 on pages 16–18 for Ss to do in class or for homework. In the next class, have Ss work with partners to compare their work. Answer any questions Ss may have, particularly ones that result from differences in their responses. (Answers can be found on page T-177 of the Workbook Answer Key in this Teacher's Edition.)

Optional activities

1 Car for sale

Time: 10–15 minutes. This creative and fun activity practices writing a description of a car.

Preparation: Cut out color magazine pictures of cars or other vehicles. (If the picture appears in an ad, cut out any text that accompanies it.) Plan to divide the class into small groups; each group needs one picture.

■ Explain the activity: In groups, Ss write an ad for the car in the picture, using their own information. Write these cues on the board and explain or model how to use them with an extra picture of a car:

Information needed for a car ad
Model/Type of vehicle:
Year:
Miles/Kilometers:
Color:
Condition (excellent, good, fair, etc.):
Price:
Special features:
Person to contact:
Phone:

■ Groups use the cues to prepare their ads. Go around the class and give help as needed.

■ Groups take turns reading their ads to the class. The others ask questions to get more information. Are there any "serious" buyers?

■ Hold a brief class discussion: Which vehicle would Ss most like to buy? Why?

2 Crossword puzzle

■ See page T-146.

3 Game – Word Bingo

■ See page T-33.

11 READING

Shop Till You Drop

Look at the pictures of different kinds of shopping in the United States. What kind of shopping can you do in your country?

Catalog Shopping

People in the United States often shop from catalogs. There are special catalogs for almost every need – including clothing, furniture, health and beauty products, and things for the kitchen. People also order about 40% of their music from music club catalogs. Customers say that music stores are too noisy.

Television Shopping

Television shopping began in 1986. About 5% to 8% of the American public now shops by television. Some popular shopping channels are the Home Shopping Network and QVC. Customers say that television shopping is easier than shopping in a store. How do they buy things? They make a phone call and charge the item to their credit card. And TV shopping channels are on late at night, so people can "go shopping" anytime.

Computer Shopping

Is computer shopping the way of the future? About 37% of American households now have personal computers. And shopping by computer (or "shopping on-line") is interesting to more people every day. Already, shoppers can use their computers to order many different products, such as computer products, flowers, food, T-shirts, and posters. And new on-line shopping services appear every day. Soon people may be able to shop for anything, anytime, anywhere in the world.

A Read the article. Check (✓) True or False. For the false statements, give the correct information.

	True	False
1. About 60% of music in the United States is sold through music stores.	☐	☐
2. The Home Shopping Network is the name of a computer shopping service.	☐	☐
3. About 37% of American households do their shopping through the computer.	☐	☐

B *Pair work* Talk about these questions.

1. Do you like shopping? How often do you usually shop?
2. What kinds of shopping do you like? Check (✓) the appropriate boxes.

☐ shopping at discount stores
☐ television shopping
☐ shopping at department stores

☐ shopping at small stores
☐ catalog shopping
☐ shopping at secondhand or thrift stores

☐ computer shopping
☐ shopping at a mall

4 Do you like jazz?

SNAPSHOT

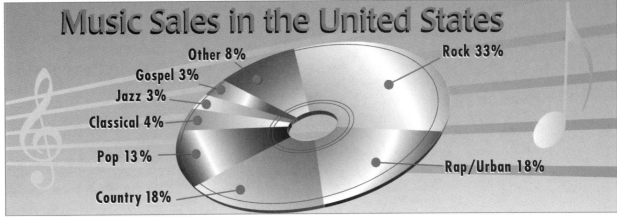

Music Sales in the United States

Other 8%
Gospel 3%
Jazz 3%
Classical 4%
Pop 13%
Country 18%
Rock 33%
Rap/Urban 18%

Source: The Recording Industry Association of America

Talk about these questions.

Which of these kinds of music do people in your country listen to?
What other kinds of music do people in your country like?

Listen and number the musical styles from 1 to 8 as you hear them.

| .... classical | .... gospel | .... New Age | .... rap |
| .... country | .... jazz | .... pop | .... rock |

---

2 WORD POWER Entertainment

A Complete the chart with words from the list.

classical	salsa
game shows	science fiction
horror films	soap operas
jazz	talk shows
news	thrillers
pop	westerns

B Add three more words to each category. Then compare with a partner.

C Number the items in each list from 1 (you like it the most) to 7 (you like it the least).

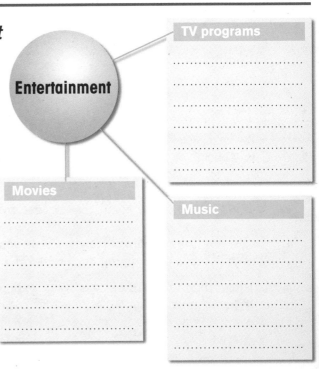

TV programs

Entertainment

Movies

Music

Do you like jazz?

This unit teaches Ss how to talk about the topics of entertainment and personal likes and dislikes, and how to make invitations. It presents yes/no questions with do, object pronouns, the modal would, and verb + to + verb constructions.

Cycle 1, Exercises 1–7

1 SNAPSHOT *Music sales in the United States*

This exercise introduces the theme of music and presents the vocabulary for various types of music currently popular in the United States.

- Books closed. To introduce the topic, tell the class about some of your favorite kinds of music. Then ask some general questions about Ss' preferences in music and write their responses on the board:

  Do you like music? What kind?
  Which group/singer do you like best?
  What kinds of music do you think Americans buy?

- Books open. Ss look over the information. Explain any new vocabulary:

  country (and western) = a style of popular music based on the white folk music of the western and southern U.S.
  gospel = a style of religious music originally performed by African Americans
  rap/urban = a type of rhythmic talking, spoken to music

- **Optional:** Brainstorm with the class on additional types of music that might represent "Other = 8%" in the Snapshot (e.g., religious or choir music, reggae, ethnic music like Irish ballads or African chants).

- Ss work in pairs, small groups, or as a whole class to answer the questions.

- Before playing the audio program, read aloud the types of musical styles listed. Then play the audio program while Ss listen and number the musical styles in the order they are heard.

Audio script

- Ss will hear snippets of eight different musical styles, played in this order:

1. pop	5. rap
2. gospel	6. country
3. classical	7. rock
4. jazz	8. New Age

- Have students compare answers in pairs. Then check responses around the class.

Answers

3 classical	2 gospel	8 New Age	5 rap
6 country	4 jazz	1 pop	7 rock

- **Optional:** What kind of music does the class like best? Take a poll. Also, ask Ss to bring tapes or CDs to class and play a few examples of their favorite music for the rest of the class.

2 WORD POWER *Entertainment*

This exercise presents vocabulary related to various types of entertainment – movies, music, and TV programs – that Ss will use in this unit.

A

- Model the pronunciation of the words in the list. Ss repeat.

- Explain the task. Allow Ss to use their dictionaries to classify the words. Walk around the class and give help as requested or needed.

B

- Ss add three additional words to each category, using dictionaries if they wish. Then elicit Ss' answers around the class.

Answers *(extra examples in boldface)*

Movies	*TV programs*	*Music*
horror films	game shows	classical
science fiction	news	jazz

Movies	*TV programs*	*Music*
thrillers	soap operas	pop
westerns	talk shows	salsa
adventure	**cartoons**	**reggae**
comedies	**documentaries**	**opera**
musicals	**sports events**	**heavy metal**

C

- Explain the task: Ss look over the seven types of movies they have listed in the "Movies" column and write *1* next to the type they like the most, *2* next to the one they like second best, and so on. They do the same for the items listed under "TV programs" and "Music."

- Have Ss form small groups to compare their rankings.

- **Optional:** Take a class survey to find out which types of entertainment were the top three items in each category.

Optional activity: *Scrambled letters*

- See page T-146.

3 CONVERSATION *Likes and dislikes*

This conversation introduces yes/no questions with *do* for talking about likes and dislikes.

A 🔊

- Books closed. Ask a few pre-listening questions to help Ss focus on the topic being discussed here – people's likes and dislikes of music and musicians:

  Who likes jazz? What about rock?
  Is anyone a fan of . . . (musician/group)?
  I love . . . (singer/group), but I can't stand . . . .
     How about you?

- Set the scene: Two friends are talking about music. Play the audio program. Ss listen. Then ask a few general comprehension questions:

  Does Tom like jazz? (No.)
  What does Wynton Marsalis play? (He plays
     the trumpet.)
  What kind of group is The Cranberries? (They're a
     rock group.)
  Does Liz like them? (No. She can't stand them.)

- Books open. Refer to the pictures and present the conversation line by line. Explain that *I can't stand . . . !* is an idiom that means "I hate or strongly dislike . . . ."

- Model the blend in "Do you . . . ?" /dəyə/ and the pronunciation of *them* /ðəm/ in "Do you like them?" (which is unstressed here).

- Ss practice the conversation in pairs.

B 🔊

- Read over the questions to direct the Ss' listening. Be sure the class understands the meaning of *favorite*. Then play the second part of the audio program once or twice.

Audio script

> TOM: What about singers, Liz? Who do you like?
> LIZ: Oh, I like lots of different ones. I guess my favorite singer is Whitney Houston.
> TOM: Whitney Houston? You must be kidding!
> LIZ: Why? Don't you like her?
> TOM: No, I don't. I guess her voice is OK, but I don't like her songs.

- Allow Ss to compare answers with several classmates sitting nearby. Then check answers around the class.

Answers

> 1. Whitney Houston.
> 2. No, he doesn't. Her voice is OK, but he doesn't like her songs.

4 GRAMMAR FOCUS *Yes/No and Wh-questions with do*

🔊 This grammar focus presents yes/no questions with *do,* reviews Wh-questions with *do,* and introduces object pronouns (e.g., *me, you, him*).

- Use the audio program to present the questions and responses in the box along with the object pronouns. Play the audio program again, this time pausing it for Ss to repeat.

- Point out that a singular noun (e.g., *jazz*) takes a singular object pronoun (e.g., *it*) and a plural noun (e.g., *The Cranberries, R.E.M.*) takes a plural object pronoun (e.g., *them*).

- Review how *do* is used to form Wh-questions with simple form verbs. (See Unit 2, Exercise 5, page T-10, in this Teacher's Edition.) Then explain that yes/no questions with *do* follow the same rules. Write these examples on the board and go over them:

Question	*Statement*
Do you like jazz?	*Yes, I do.*
Does he play the piano?	*No, he doesn't.*
Do they like R.E.M.?	*Yes, they do.*

- Elicit a few more examples and write them on the board. Let Ss take turns asking similar Wh- and yes/no questions with *do* around the class.

- Ss complete the conversations individually or in pairs. Check answers around the class before pairs practice together.

Answers

> 1. A: **Do** you like horror films?
>   B: No, I **don't** like **them** very much. I like comedies.
>   A: How about Lisa and Brian? **Do** they like
>   horror films?
>   B: Well, I think Brian **does**. Why don't you ask **him**?
> 2. A: **Do** you like the singer Bonnie Raitt?
>   B: Yes, I **do**. I really like **her** a lot.
>   A: What **kind** of music **does** she sing?
>   B: She's a rock singer.
>   A: **Does** she sing country music, too?
>   B: I don't know. I have her new CD. Let's listen to **it**.

Optional activity: *Likes and dislikes*

- See page T-148.

3 CONVERSATION *Likes and dislikes*

A Listen and practice.

Wynton Marsalis

The Cranberries

Liz: Do you like jazz, Tom?
Tom: No, I don't like it very much. Do you?
Liz: Well, yes, I do. I'm a real fan of
    Wynton Marsalis.
Tom: Oh, does he play the piano?
Liz: No, he doesn't! He plays the trumpet.
    So, what kind of music do you like?
Tom: I like rock a lot.
Liz: Who's your favorite group?
Tom: The Cranberries. I love their music.
    How about you? Do you like them?
Liz: No, I don't. I can't stand them!

B Listen to the rest of the conversation.

1. Who is Liz's favorite singer?
2. Does Tom like that singer? Why or why not?

4 GRAMMAR FOCUS

Yes/No and Wh-questions with do

Do you **like** jazz?	**What kind of** music **do** you **like**?	*Object pronouns*
Yes, I **do**. I like it a lot.	I like rock a lot.	me
No, I **don't** like it very much.		you (singular)
		him
Does he **play** the piano?	**What does** he **play**?	her
Yes, he **does**.	He plays the trumpet.	it
No, he **doesn't**.		us
		you (plural)
Do they **like** The Cranberries?	**Who do** they **like**?	them
Yes, they **do**. They love them.	They like R.E.M.	
No, they **don't** like them very much.		

Complete these conversations. Then practice with a partner.

1. A: .... you like horror films?
   B: No, I .... like .... very much. I like comedies.
   A: How about Lisa and Brian? .... they like horror films?
   B: Well, I think Brian .... Why don't you ask .... ?

2. A: .... you like the singer Bonnie Raitt?
   B: Yes, I .... I really like .... a lot.
   A: What .... of music .... she sing?
   B: She's a rock singer.
   A: .... she sing country music, too?
   B: I don't know. I have her new CD. Let's listen to ....

5 PRONUNCIATION Question intonation

A 📀 Listen and practice. Yes/No questions usually have rising intonation. Wh-questions usually have falling intonation.

Do you like movies? ⤴   What kind of movies do you like? ⤵

Do you like pop music? ⤴   What kind of music do you like? ⤵

B Practice these questions.

Do you like TV? What programs do you like?
Do you like music videos? What videos do you like?

6 ENTERTAINMENT SURVEY

A *Group work* Write five questions about entertainment and entertainers. Then ask and answer your questions in groups.

Do you like . . . ?
     (pop music, TV, movies, plays)
What kinds of . . . do you like?
     (music, movies, TV programs)
What do you think of . . . ?
     (*Star Trek*, horror films,
     gospel music)

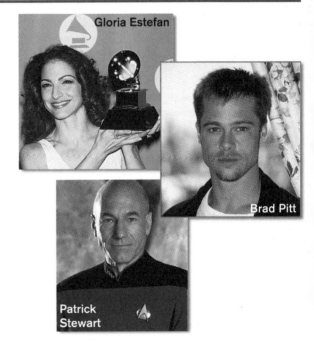

Gloria Estefan

Brad Pitt

Patrick Stewart

B *Group work* Complete this information about your group.

Our Group Favorites	
What's your favorite kind of . . . ?	**Who's your favorite . . . ?**
music:	singer: ....
movie:	actor: ....
TV program:	actress: ....

C *Class activity* Read your group's list to the class. Then find out the class favorites.

useful expressions
Our favorite . . . is . . . .
We all like . . . .
We don't agree on . . . .
We can't stand . . . .

5 *PRONUNCIATION* *Question intonation*

This exercise introduces intonation patterns used with yes/no and Wh-questions with *do*.

A 🔊

- Books closed. Explain that "intonation" is the musical pitch of the voice, which rises and falls throughout a sentence in English.

- Books open. Play the first part of the audio program or model the intonation patterns in the questions. Point out that yes/no questions usually end with rising intonation and Wh-questions usually end with falling intonation.

- Play the audio program again. Ss repeat each question.

B

- In pairs or small groups, Ss practice the four questions, using rising and falling intonation.

- **Optional:** Ss look back at Exercise 3 on page 21. Tell them to mark the rising or falling intonation patterns above the questions in the conversation. Then have pairs practice the conversation again, this time paying special attention to correct question intonation.

6 *ENTERTAINMENT SURVEY*

This is an open-ended follow-up activity to Exercises 3–5 in this unit. The focus is on getting the Ss to express themselves using their own information, with an emphasis on fluency – not necessarily accuracy.

A *Group work*

The first part of this three-part exercise is a free discussion on entertainment and entertainers.

(*Note:* In a heterogeneous class with Ss from many different countries, tell them to talk about entertainers and types of entertainment well known in the country in which the class is being held, not in the Ss' own countries. This will ensure that Ss won't have difficulty answering questions about less well known entertainers or ones not internationally famous that perhaps only one S knows something about.)

- Have Ss look at the photos. Ask them if they know who these people are by showing how to use the question stems provided:

  Do you like Gloria Estefan?
  What kinds of movies do you like?
  What do you think of the TV program *Star Trek*?

> **Gloria Estefan** = a Cuban American pop musician
> **Brad Pitt** = an American movie star
> ***Star Trek*** = a popular science fiction TV series created in 1966 and still running more than thirty years later; Patrick Stewart is a star of a recent version of the program

- Ss first work individually to write down five questions to ask one another. Then they form groups and take turns asking their questions. Set a time limit of about five to seven minutes for this part of the activity.

- Walk around the class and observe how Ss are responding. You might want to encourage them to give longer, more elaborate responses. If that's the case, stop the group work and model exchanges like this with one or two groups:

  S1: Do you like pop music?
  T: Um, not really, but I love classical music.
  S2: Oh, really? Who's your favorite composer?
  T: Mozart. I love his music! How about you?
  S3: Well, I prefer Bach. And what about . . . ?

B *Group work*

- Explain that groups need to come to a consensus *before* they complete their charts. Go around the class and give help as needed.

C *Class activity*

- Present the useful expressions in the box. Groups take turns reporting their information while the group secretary writes their results on the board. After all reports have been given, a quick tabulation of the results should easily determine the class favorites.

- **Optional:** Books closed. Ss take turns asking one another questions about people in entertainment. Encourage a lively give-and-take of information; Ss should ask and answer quickly, without pausing. Start the activity by addressing one S:

  T: Who's your favorite American actor, Kei?
  S1: Tom Hanks, I guess.
  T: Oh, really? I like him, too. Now it's your turn to ask someone a similar question.

  A more challenging way to do this is not to allow any S to repeat a question that has already been asked.

Optional activity: *Who am I?*

- See page T-146.

7 LISTENING *TV game show*

This exercise practices listening for likes and dislikes. The task is based on a popular American TV game show called *The Dating Game.*

A

- Books closed. Set the scene: Linda is on a game show called *Who's My Date?* She's going to choose to have a date with either Bill, John, or Tony – based on interests they share with her.
- Play the audio program once. Ss only listen.

Audio script

> HOSTESS: (*music and clapping*) Welcome to *Who's My Date?* Today, Linda is going to meet Bill, John, and Tony. So, let's start with the first question . . . on music. Bill, what kind of music do you like?
> BILL: Oh, classical music.
> HOSTESS: Classical. OK. And how about you, John?
> JOHN: Well, I like jazz.
> HOSTESS: And you, Tony?
> TONY: My favorite music is rock.
> HOSTESS: How about you, Linda?
> LINDA: Well, I like pop music. I don't like jazz or classical music very much. (*clapping*)
> HOSTESS: OK. Now let's talk about movies. Bill, what kind of movies do you like?
> BILL: I like thrillers.
> HOSTESS: And how about you, John?
> JOHN: Oh, I like westerns.
> HOSTESS: Westerns are good. And how about you, Tony?
> TONY: I love horror films.
> HOSTESS: And what about you, Linda?
> LINDA: I really like horror films, too. (*audience laughs*)
> HOSTESS: And now for question number three. Let's talk about TV programs. Bill, what kind of TV programs do you like?
> BILL: Well, I like to watch TV news programs.
> HOSTESS: John?
> JOHN: Uh, well, you know, I really like TV talk shows.
> HOSTESS: And Tony, how about you?
> TONY: I like TV game shows a lot.
> HOSTESS: And Linda, what do you like?
> LINDA: Well, I like TV talk shows *and* game shows. (*clapping/buzzer sounds*)
> HOSTESS: OK! Time is up! Now who's the best date for Linda?

- Books open. Point out that Ss need to write only one- or two-word answers.
- Play the audio program again while Ss do the task. Use the pause button, where necessary, to give Ss time to write their answers.
- Have students compare answers in pairs. Then check answers around the class.

Answers

	Music	Movies	TV programs
Bill	classical	thrillers	news programs
John	jazz	westerns	talk shows
Tony	rock	horror films	game shows
Linda	pop	horror films	talk shows and game shows

B *Class activity*

- Elicit Ss' opinions around the class.

Possible answer

> Tony. (They both like horror films and game shows, and Linda never disagrees with what he likes. However, she disagrees with both Bill and John on music, i.e., she doesn't like classical or jazz. *Note:* If Ss think Bill or John is a better date for Linda, find out why.)

 Workbook

Assign Exercises 1–8 on pages 19–22 in the Workbook. Ss compare answers in groups at the beginning of the next class. Check Ss' answers. (Answers can be found on page T-178 of the Workbook Answer Key in this Teacher's Edition.)

Cycle 2, Exercises 8–12

8 CONVERSATION *Invitations*

This exercise introduces making and accepting invitations; it also presents the grammatical structure verb + *to* + verb and the modal *would.*

- Books open. Ss look at the picture while listening to the audio program. Then model the stress in "Would you **like** to **go**?" and "**That** sounds **fine.**" Pairs practice the conversation.
- **Optional:** Review telling time. Write the following

times on the board. Draw a clock face and add these times while pronouncing each expression. Ss repeat.

1:00	=	one o'clock
2:05	=	five after two/two-oh-five
3:15	=	a quarter after three/three-fifteen
4:20	=	twenty after four/four-twenty
5:30	=	five-thirty
6:45	=	a quarter to seven/six forty-five

7 LISTENING TV game show

A  Listen to four people playing *Who's My Date?* Three men want to invite Linda on a date. What kinds of things do they like? What kinds of things does Linda like?

	Music	Movies	TV programs
Bill	*classical*	......	......
John	......	......	......
Tony	......	......	......
Linda	......	......	......

B *Class activity* Who do you think is the best date for Linda?

8 CONVERSATION Invitations

 Listen and practice.

Dave: I have tickets to *The Phantom of the Opera* on Friday night. Would you like to go?
Susan: Thanks. I'd love to. What time is the show?
Dave: It's at 8:00.
Susan: That sounds great. So, do you want to have dinner at 6:00?
Dave: Uh, I'd like to, but I have to work late.
Susan: Oh, that's OK. Let's just meet at the theater before the show, around 7:30.
Dave: That sounds fine.

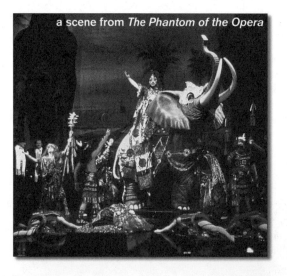

a scene from *The Phantom of the Opera*

9 GRAMMAR FOCUS

Would; verb + to + verb

Would you like to go out on Saturday night?	Would you like to see a movie?	Contraction
Yes, I would.	I'd like to, but I have to work late.	I would = I'd
Yes, I'd love to. Thanks.	I'd like to, but I need to save money.	
Yes, I'd really like to go.	I'd like to, but I want to visit my parents.	

A Respond to these invitations. Then practice with a partner.

1. A: I have tickets to the baseball game on Saturday. Would you like to go?
   B: ....

2. A: Would you like to come over for dinner tonight?
   B: ....

3. A: Would you like to go to the gym with me on Friday night?
   B: ....

4. A: There's a great movie on TV tonight. Would you like to watch it with me?
   B: ....

B *Pair work* Think of three different things you would like to do. Then invite a partner to do them with you. Ask and answer follow-up questions like these:

When is it?   What time does it start?
Where is it?   What time should I/we . . . ?

10 LISTENING

CLASS AUDIO ONLY ▶ 🔊 Listen to three people inviting friends to events and activities. Complete the chart. Do the friends accept the invitations?

	Event/Activity	Day	Time	Accept?	
				Yes	No
1. Jake and Paula	....	....	....	☐	☐
2. Lucy and Chris	....	....	....	☐	☐
3. Rich and Ed	....	....	....	☐	☐

11 WRITING

See Interchange 4 for the writing assignment.

interchange 4

What an invitation! What an excuse!

Make up unusual invitations and funny excuses. Turn to page IC-6.

9 GRAMMAR FOCUS Would; *verb + to + verb*

This grammar focus practices using the modal *would* with the structure verb + *to* + verb (e.g., Would you like to go . . . ?) for polite invitations. It introduces how to accept and refuse invitations, too. The conjunction *but* is also practiced; Ss learn how to use it to connect two independent clauses in contrastive statements.

■ Use the audio program to present the questions and responses as well as the contraction *I'd*. Ss practice. Point out that this modal expression is more polite than "Do you want to . . . ?" when inviting someone to do something.

■ Explain that the conjunction *but* combines two independent clauses (i.e., two complete sentences) and is used to express a difference or to introduce an added statement.

■ Give additional practice with "*Would you like to + verb . . . ?*" like this:

T: *(writing on board)* Would you like to . . . ? *(then saying cue)* . . . go skating today? Al?

AL: Would you like to go skating today, Sue?

SUE: Yes, I'd love to. Thanks.

T: *(saying another cue)* see a movie later?

SUE: May, would you like to see a movie later?

MAY: I'd like to, but I . . . .

A

■ Ss write responses to the invitations and compare with a partner before practicing together. Go around the room and spot-check written answers (they will vary). If common problems exist, make a note of them and stop the pair practice in order to go over any general difficulties with the whole class. Then have pairs resume the practice.

B *Pair work*

■ Go over the task and model the four questions. Then Ss think of three real or imaginary things they would like to invite someone to do. Tell pairs to begin with "Would you like to . . . ?"

Optional activity: *Let's go!*

■ See page T-148.

10 LISTENING

This exercise practices listening for specific information and making inferences.

■ Books closed. Set the scene: Ss will hear three different conversations in which people are inviting their friends to do something with them. Play the audio program once. Find out what kinds of information Ss heard and understood.

■ Books open. Explain the task. Then play the audio program again and have Ss do the task.

Audio script

1. JAKE: Hey, Paula, would you like to see a movie on Wednesday?
   PAULA: Maybe. What time?
   JAKE: How about the nine o'clock show? I'm not free before then.
   PAULA: Nine o'clock? Oh, sorry, Jake. That's too late for me. I have to get up early on weekdays.

2. LUCY: Chris, there's a very good jazz pianist playing downtown. Would you like to go?
   CHRIS: A jazz pianist! I'd love to go! When is the show?
   LUCY: It's on Thursday at 8:30.
   CHRIS: Thursday at 8:30. That's perfect. Thanks a lot, Lucy.

3. RICH: Hey, Ed, do you want to play baseball on Saturday?
   ED: Yeah. That would be great, Rich. What time on Saturday?
   RICH: How about two P.M.?
   ED: Two is fine.

■ Check Ss' answers around the class.

Answers

	Event/ Activity	Day	Time	Accept?
1. Jake & Paula	movie	Wed.	9:00 P.M.	No
2. Lucy & Chris	jazz pianist	Thur.	8:30 P.M.	Yes
3. Rich & Ed	baseball	Sat.	2:00 P.M.	Yes

11 WRITING

This exercise practices writing creative invitations to fictional "social" events and funny or clever responses to them. In this unit, the writing exercise appears in parts A and B of Interchange 4, which also has a follow-up communicative activity in part C.

 INTERCHANGE 4 What an invitation! What an excuse!

See page T-110 in this Teacher's Edition for notes.

12 READING *The sound of music*

In this text, Ss read about three musicians from three different countries; they also practice scanning for ideas and facts.

- Books closed. Write the initial discussion question on the board. Explain that *traditional,* here, describes a form of music that people in a particular country or area have passed down from generation to generation.

- Stimulate a short class discussion on traditional, folk, and other ethnic kinds of music that are still popular in the Ss' countries, like this:

  T: People say that rock and jazz are both traditional kinds of music in the U.S., but what about another country, like Spain?
  S1: Spain has classical guitar music.
  T: That's right!
  S2: Well, flamenco is still popular in Spain.
  T: Yes. Well, what about your country?
  S2: Well, we have old folk music called . . . .

- **Optional:** Brainstorm on the topic of "Musical instruments." Write the topic and Ss' suggestions on the board. Can Ss classify those instruments into appropriate categories (e.g., strings; brass; woodwinds; percussion; electric/electronic or amplified)?

A

- Books open. Point out the pictures of the three musicians and pronounce their names: Caetano Veloso /kay'tɑnow vɛ'lowsow/, Bonnie Raitt /'bɑniy reyt/, and Cui Jian /tsey dʒiyɑn/. Then allow Ss several minutes to read the passages. Again, remind Ss to try to guess from context any words they are unsure of.

- Elicit and explain any new vocabulary:

Introduction
popular = well liked by many people
Latin America = Mexico and the Spanish- or Portuguese-speaking countries of South and Central America
blend = mix together
Caetano Veloso
is still = continues to be
Bahia . . . is strongly influenced by African culture. = African culture has had an important effect on Bahia.
excellent = very good
canvas = the material that artists paint pictures on
Bonnie Raitt
rough = not smooth, gentle, or delicate
Cui Jian
growth = the act of getting bigger
however = but
feelings = joy, sorrow, love, etc.

- Ss complete the chart individually, in pairs, or in small groups. Check their answers.

Answers

	Nationality	*Types of music he/she blends*
1. Caetano Veloso	Brazilian	rock with Bahia region
2. Bonnie Raitt	American	rock with country and blues
3. Cui Jian	Chinese	jazz and rap with Chinese

B *Pair work*

- Go over all four questions and allow pairs to find and discuss the answers.

Answers

1. They blend their country's music with popular sounds.
2. He makes them like a painter paints his canvas.
3. She has a strong, rough voice.
4. He wants it to express the feelings of Chinese young people.

Optional activities

1 *Game – Word Bingo*

- See page T-33.

2 *Crossword puzzle*

- See page T-146.

 Workbook

Tell Ss to do Exercises 9–12 on pages 23–24 for homework. At the beginning of the next class, assign an exercise to each group so they can compare answers. Walk around and give help as needed. Then groups take turns being the "teacher" at the front of the class; i.e., they elicit and check other Ss' responses to their exercise. (Answers can be found on page T-178 of the Workbook Answer Key in this Teacher's Edition.)

12 *READING*

The Sound of Music

What are some traditional kinds of music in your country?

Do you like popular music from Latin America, the United States, or Asia? Many musicians from around the world blend their country's music with popular sounds.

Caetano Veloso

After thirty years, Caetano Veloso is still one of Brazil's most important musicians. He mixes rock with the music of the Bahia region. Bahia is a state of Brazil that is strongly influenced by African culture. Caetano Veloso is an excellent songwriter and poet. He says of his music, "I make my records like a painter paints his canvas."

Bonnie Raitt

Bonnie Raitt is an American singer, songwriter, and guitarist. Her music blends rock with country and the blues. The blues is a kind of folk music that is often sad. It is usually about love and the problems of life. Bonnie Raitt's strong, rough voice is perfect for singing country and the blues.

Cui Jian

Cui Jian [pronounced "tsay jyan"] is a very important musician in the growth of rock music in China. Western styles, like jazz and rap, clearly influence his music. However, his music is very Chinese in its instruments and sounds. Cui Jian says his music expresses the feelings of Chinese young people.

A Read about the three musicians. Complete the chart.

	Nationality	Types of music he/she blends
1. Caetano Veloso	....	....
2. Bonnie Raitt	....	....
3. Cui Jian	....	....

B *Pair work* Talk about these questions.

1. What do these three musicians have in common?
2. How does Caetano Veloso make his records?
3. Why is Bonnie Raitt's voice good for country and blues music?
4. What does Cui Jian want his music to express?

Review of Units 1-4

1 GETTING TO KNOW YOU

Pair work You are talking to someone at school.
Have a conversation.

A: Hi. How are you?
B: . . .
A: By the way, my name is . . . .
B: How do you pronounce your name again?
A: . . . Where are you from?
B: . . .
A: Are you a student here?
B: . . . And how about you? What do you do?
A: . . .
B: Oh, really? And where are you from?
A: . . .
B: Well, nice talking to you. . . .

2 WHAT'S THE QUESTION?

Look at these answers. Write the questions.
Then compare with a partner.

1. No, Teresa and I aren't in the same class. She's in the morning class.

2. My sister? She goes to the University of Toronto.

3. I get up before 11:00 A.M. on Sundays.

4. No, my teacher isn't American. She's Canadian.

5. Rock music is OK, but I like jazz better.

6. I leave home at 6:30 in the evening on weekdays.

7. A video? Sure, I'd love to watch one with you.

8. The red sweater is nicer than the purple one.

Review of Units 1-4

1 GETTING TO KNOW YOU

This exercise reviews Wh- and yes/no questions and statements with *be*, and making self-introductions.

Pair work

■ Read the situation aloud and refer Ss to the picture. Explain that in this conversational practice, Ss should pretend that they don't know their partner.

■ Model how to use the dialog cues with one or two Ss. Then demonstrate how Ss can form their responses, like this:

A: Hi. How are you?
B: **Fine, thanks.**
A: By the way, my name is **Mary Gibbs.**
B: How do you pronounce your name again?
A: **Mary Gibbs.** Where are you from?
B: **I'm from Osaka, Japan.**
A: Are you a student here?
B: **Yes, I am. I go to Riverside Community College.** And how about you? What do you do?

A: **Oh, I work for an advertising agency. I'm a graphic artist.**
B: Oh, really? And where are you from?
A: **I'm from California.**
B: Well, nice talking to you, **Mary. I hope to see you again.**

■ Ss try the conversation in pairs. Remind them to use the "Look Up and Say" technique when using the dialog cues. Also, encourage Ss to use appropriate body language and gestures and to keep the conversation going by asking more questions and giving each other additional information. Go around the class and give help, especially when there seems to be a communication breakdown.

■ **Optional:** Books closed. Pairs perform their conversations in front of the class. Offer some comments on what was good (particularly, what sounded natural in English conversation). Can the rest of the class give some helpful hints on anything that could be improved?

2 WHAT'S THE QUESTION?

This exercise reviews question formation and other grammar structures presented in Units 1–4.

■ Read the instructions aloud. Point out that there may be more than one correct question for each answer. Remind Ss that responses with "Yes" or "No" at the beginning almost always need yes/no questions with *be* or *do* and that others usually need Wh-questions.

■ Model the task with the class, like this:

T: *(reading response 1 aloud)* "No, Teresa and I aren't in the same class. She's in the morning class." What's the question?
S1: Are you and Teresa in the same class?
T: That's right! Good! Can anyone ask another yes/no question?
S2: Is Teresa in your class?
T: Fine! Yes, that's a good question, too.

■ Ss do the task individually and write down eight questions. Give Ss help as needed.

■ Ss compare answers in pairs. Check Ss' answers.

Answers

1. Are you and Teresa in the same class?/Is Teresa in your class?
2. Where does your sister go to school?
3. What time do you get up on Sundays?
4. Is your teacher American?

5. Do you like rock music?
6. When do you leave home on weekdays?
7. Would you like to watch a video with me?
8. Which sweater is nicer?/Which sweater do you like better/more?/Which sweater do you prefer?

Optional activity: *Class telephone list*

Time: 10–15 minutes. This useful activity involves spelling names and writing down phone numbers.

■ Tell the Ss that they are going to make a class phone list, which might be helpful to have if they need to call a classmate to check on a homework assignment or something they missed because of an absence. Write this example on the board:

English Class Telephone List

First name	Last name	Phone number
Pedro	Garcia	(310) 632-0573
Yoko	Morita	(213) 845-9921

■ Model or elicit the kinds of questions Ss need to ask and write them on the board, like this:

What's your first/last name? How do you spell it?
What's your telephone number?

■ Ss get up and go around the class to get the information to make their own phone lists.

3 ROLE PLAY *In a department store*

This is a fluency activity that reviews the language used to talk about the prices of things; it focuses on demonstratives and the pronouns *one/ones*.

Pair work

■ Read the instructions and use the picture to help explain the activity and the situation.

■ Model the role play with one or two Ss.

■ Have Ss form pairs. Tell them to choose several personal items to put on their desks to use during the role play.

■ Pairs do the role play. Set a time limit of about five minutes. Go around the class to monitor Ss' conversations. It's best not to explicitly correct errors, but help if Ss are having serious difficulties.

■ Ss change roles and do the activity again. Encourage them to put new items on their desks to use if they wish.

■ **Optional:** Ask one or two pairs to act out their role play in front of the class. Then give helpful comments on their performance; you may also wish to elicit feedback from the rest of class.

4 LISTENING

In this exercise, Ss practice listening for questions and choosing correct responses to them.

■ Books closed. Set the scene: People are talking at a party. Play the audio program straight through once. Ss only listen.

Audio script

1. Do you leave home early to get to work?
2. How do you spend Sundays?
3. How much is a laptop computer?
4. Are you a student here?
5. So, what kind of music do you like?
6. Would you like to see a movie on Friday night?

■ Books open. Explain how to do the task and give Ss a few minutes to look over the response choices before playing the audio program again. This time, pause after each question to give Ss time to check the correct answer.

■ Pairs compare their answers. Check Ss' answers.

Answers

1. Yes, very early. Before 7:00 A.M.
2. Oh, I just stay in and work around the house.
3. A good laptop computer costs over $2,000.
4. Actually, I work here.
5. Almost any kind except classical.
6. Thanks, I'd love to. What time?

5 TV AND RADIO

This exercise reviews asking Wh- and yes/no questions and responding with short statements.

A Pair work

■ Explain that the task in this part involves talking about TV. Then model the activity with one or two Ss, trying to elaborate on your responses, like this:

S: When do you usually watch TV?
T: Let me see. I guess I watch TV only about two or three times a week. Usually just on weekends.
S: Oh, really? What kinds of programs do you prefer?
T: Well, my favorite program is *Masterpiece Theater* on Sunday evenings at nine o'clock. It's on PBS (the Public Broadcasting System), and it's always a wonderful show. And what about you? When do you usually watch TV?
S: Well, I usually watch it . . . .

■ Ss do the task in pairs. Go around the class and give help as needed.

B Pair work

■ Explain that Ss should change partners and use the questions to talk about radio. Model the activity, if necessary. Then have the new pairs practice.

■ **Optional:** Take a class poll to find out about Ss' TV and radio interests and habits.

Alternative presentation

■ Ss work in groups of four and use the questions in both parts A and B to have one lively discussion about TV and radio. Set a time limit of about ten minutes.

Optional activity: *Game – Hangman*

■ See page T-64.

Test 1

See page T-152 in this Teacher's Edition for general instructions on using the tests. Test 1 covers Units 1–4. Photocopy the test (pages T-153–T-156) and distribute a copy to each S. Allow 45–60 minutes for the test. Listening material for the tests is at the end of the Class Audio Program. The Test Audio Scripts and Answer Key start on page T-169 of this book.

3 *ROLE PLAY* *In a department store*

Pair work Put items "for sale" on your desk or a table – notebooks, watches, or bags. Use items of different colors.

Student A: You are a clerk. Answer the customer's questions.

Student B: You are a customer. Ask about the price of each item. Say if you want to buy it.

A: Can I help you?
B: Yes. I like that . . . . How much . . . ?
A: Which one(s)?
B: . . .

Change roles and try the role play again.

4 *LISTENING*

Listen to people asking questions at a party. Check (✓) the best response.

1. ☐ I work in an office.
   ☐ Yes, very early. Before 7:00 A.M.

2. ☐ Not very much.
   ☐ Oh, I just stay in and work around the house.

3. ☐ Yes, I have a laptop.
   ☐ A good laptop computer costs over $2,000.

4. ☐ Yes, I'm from Italy.
   ☐ Actually, I work here.

5. ☐ Almost any kind except classical.
   ☐ No, I don't play the piano.

6. ☐ Thanks, I'd love to. What time?
   ☐ It's on at the Varsity Theater.

5 *TV AND RADIO*

A *Pair work* Take turns asking and answering these questions.

TV

When do you usually watch TV?
What kinds of programs do you prefer?
What's your favorite channel?
What's your favorite program?
What time is it on?
Do you watch . . . (name of program)?

B *Pair work* Change partners. Take turns asking and answering these questions.

Radio

When do you listen to the radio?
What kinds of programs do you listen to?
Do you listen to programs in English?

What's your favorite radio station?
Who are your favorite singers and groups?
What's your favorite radio program?

5 Tell me about your family.

1 WORD POWER The family

A Look at Sam's family tree. How are these people related to him? Add these words to the family tree.

cousin
father
grandmother
niece
sister-in-law
uncle
wife

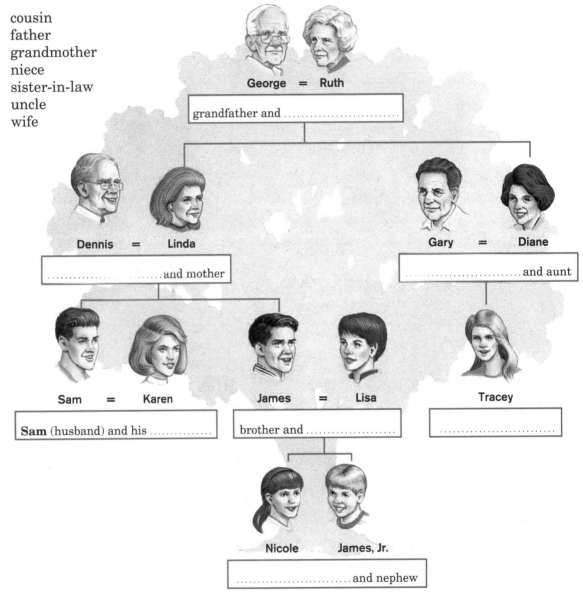

George = Ruth

grandfather and ....

Dennis = Linda

.... and mother

Gary = Diane

.... and aunt

Sam = Karen

Sam (husband) and his ....

James = Lisa

brother and ....

Tracey

....

Nicole   James, Jr.

.... and nephew

B *Pair work* Draw your family tree. Then take turns talking about your families. Ask follow-up questions to get more information.

For a single person:	*For a married person:*	*Follow-up questions:*
There are 6 in my family.	There are 4 in my family.	Where do/does your . . . live?
I have 2 sisters and a brother.	We have a daughter and a son.	What do/does your . . . do?

28

5 Tell me about your family.

This unit introduces the theme of families and family life. It practices the present continuous in questions and in statements, and presents the use of determiners.

Cycle 1, Exercises 1–5

1 WORD POWER The family

This exercise presents the vocabulary needed to talk about family members. Ss will use these terms throughout the unit.

A

■ Go over the instructions. Read aloud each word in the list and on the family tree. Ss repeat. Explain that the symbol = means "marries" when used in a family tree. Point out and model the pronunciation of these words: the voiced /z/ in *cousin* /'kʌzən/, the dropped /d/ in *grandmother* /'græn(d)ˌmʌðər/ and *grandfather* /'græn(d)ˌfɑðər/, and the correct pronunciation of *niece* /niys/ and *nephew* /'nefyuw/. Also model the correct position of the tongue for the /ð/ in *mother* /'mʌðər/ and *father* /'fɑðər/, i.e., the tip of the tongue lightly touches the back of the top teeth. Have Ss practice saying each one.

■ Ss complete the task individually or in pairs without using their dictionaries. Then have Ss compare choices in pairs or small groups. Elicit answers around the class.

Answers

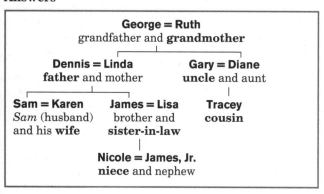

```
                    George = Ruth
              grandfather and grandmother
              ┌──────────────┴──────────────┐
        Dennis = Linda              Gary = Diane
        father and mother           uncle and aunt
    ┌────────┴────────┐                    │
Sam = Karen      James = Lisa         Tracey
Sam (husband)    brother and          cousin
and his wife     sister-in-law
                      │
              Nicole = James, Jr.
              niece and nephew
```

B Pair work

■ Ss first work individually to draw their family tree. Unmarried Ss should include their immediate family members (e.g., grandparents, mother, father, brothers, sisters); married Ss, however, may wish to describe the members of their own families (e.g., wife or husband, children, grandchildren).

■ Present the sentences to use for a single or a married person and the follow-up questions. Model the task by drawing your own (or someone else's) family tree and then talking about the various members. Answer any questions Ss may have about additional vocabulary (e.g., *great-grandmother, stepfather, divorced, remarried*).

■ Ask questions around the class, like this:

T: Tell us about your family, Ana.
S1: Well, there are six in my family. I have . . . .
T: And where does your grandmother live?
S1: She lives in . . . .
T: Really? And, Keiko, what about your family?

■ Encourage Ss to use the follow-up questions and additional ones of their own to find out more information about their partner's family.

■ **Optional:** Ask pairs to share with the class the most interesting piece of information they learned about each other.

Optional activities

1 *People in the news*

Time: 15 minutes. In this communication activity, each group chooses an interesting or a famous person who has been in the news recently. The group must pool their information on the person. One S in each group acts as secretary and takes notes. Ss start like this: "Let's talk about . . . ." or "Well, how about discussing . . . ?"

■ Group secretaries use their notes to tell the class about the person that they discussed.

2 *Game – Twenty questions*

Time: 10 minutes. In this popular game, Ss practice asking yes/no questions in the simple present tense while trying to guess the names of famous living people.

■ Ss form groups. Explain the game: One S thinks of a famous person and then answers the group's questions with "Yes" or "No" about that person. The winner is either the S who correctly guesses the name of the person or the S who answers twenty questions before anyone in the group correctly guesses the name.

3 *Scrambled letters*

■ See page T-146.

4 *Guess the word*

■ See page T-86.

2 LISTENING Hollywood families

This listening focuses on key information.

- Tell Ss to look at the photos of the six famous people. Do Ss know anything about them? (*Note:* All six people here are famous American movie actors.)

- Play the audio program. Ss only listen.

- Read aloud the six names to help Ss focus their listening. Then play the audio program again. Ss listen and write down the family relationships.

Audio script

1. A: *(newspaper unfolding)* Oh! Here's an article about my favorite movie star, Warren Beatty. Say, do you know who his sister is? It's Shirley MacLaine!
   B: I don't think I know her.
   A: Sure you do! She's a movie star, too.
   B: Well, do you know who Warren Beatty's wife is?
   A: Yes. It says right here – Annette Bening.
   B: Yeah, that's right.

2. A: I'm reading a really interesting book about Charlie Sheen.
   B: Oh, I love his movies.
   A: Yeah, me, too. They're usually very funny. His father is Martin Sheen, you know.
   B: Oh, sure. They're in that movie together. What's it called?
   A: Do you mean *Wall Street*?
   B: Yeah, that's the one.
   A: Well, I really prefer his comedies – like *Men at Work*!
   B: Uh-huh. Charlie Sheen's brother is in that movie. What's his name again?
   A: Uh, Emilio Estevez.

- Have Ss compare answers in pairs. Then check answers around the class.

Answers

> 1. sister, wife
> 2. father, brother

3 CONVERSATION Asking about families

This exercise introduces the first grammar point of the unit – the present continuous.

A

- Books closed. Set the scene: Rita is asking about Sue's family. Write some focus questions on the board like these:

  Does Sue have a sister? (Yes, she does.)
  Who lives in Seattle? (Sue's sister)
  Where is her brother this month? (He's in Argentina.)
  Is he a lawyer? (No. He's a painter.)

- Play the first part of the audio program once or twice. Check Ss' answers to the questions on the board.

- Books open. Play the audio program again. Then present the conversation line by line. Use the art, where possible, to explain any new vocabulary:

  Washington, D.C. = the capital and center of the U.S. government
  top secret = hidden or known to only a few people
  Wow! = an informal exclamation used to show surprise and sometimes pleasure

- Ss practice the conversation in pairs.

B

- Go over the two questions. Play the second part of the audio program once or twice.

Audio script

> SUE: What about your parents, Rita? Where do they live?
> RITA: They live in Texas.
> SUE: Oh, where in Texas?
> RITA: In Austin. It's a small city, but it's very nice.
> SUE: And are they still working?
> RITA: Oh, yes. My mother is teaching at the university there, and my father is an architect.

- Allow Ss to compare answers with several classmates sitting nearby. Then check answers around the class.

Answers

> 1. Rita's parents live in Austin, Texas.
> 2. Her mother is teaching at the university there, and her father is an architect.

4 PRONUNCIATION Blending with does

This exercise focuses on the reduction and blending of consonants with *does*.

- Play the two conversations once or twice. Point out the phonetic transcriptions above the reduced consonant

blendings in the questions with *does*. Then model each one and have Ss repeat.

- In pairs, Ss practice the reduced and blended forms.

2 *LISTENING* *Hollywood families*

Listen to two conversations about famous people. How are the people related?

1.

Warren
Beatty

Shirley
MacLaine

Annette
Bening

2.

Charlie
Sheen

Martin
Sheen

Emilio
Estevez

....

3 *CONVERSATION* *Asking about families*

A Listen and practice.

Rita: Tell me about your brother and sister, Sue.
Sue: Well, my sister is a lawyer.
Rita: Really? Does she live here in Seattle?
Sue: Yes, she does. But she's working in
      Washington, D.C., right now.
      Her job is top secret.
Rita: Wow! And what does your brother do?
Sue: He's a painter. He's working in Argentina
      this month. He has an exhibition there.
Rita: What an interesting family!

B Listen to the rest of the conversation.

1. Where do Rita's parents live?
2. What do they do?

4 *PRONUNCIATION* *Blending with does*

 Listen and practice. Notice the blending of **does** with other words.

1. A: My brother is married.
    [dəziy]
   B: **Does he** have any children?
   A: Yes, he does.
    [wədəziy]
   B: **What does he** do?
   A: He's a painter.

2. A: My sister lives in Seattle.
    [dəʃiy]
   B: **Does she** live with you?
   A: No, she doesn't.
    [wədəʃiy]
   B: **What does she** do?
   A: She's a lawyer.

29

5 GRAMMAR FOCUS

Present continuous

Are you **living** at home now?	Yes, I **am**./No, I'**m not**.	*Some verbs generally not used*
Is she still **working** in Seattle?	Yes, she **is**./No, she **isn't**.	*in the present continuous*
Are they **going** to college this year?	Yes, they **are**./No, they **aren't**.	have
		know
Where **are** you **working** this month?	I'**m working** in Japan.	like
What **is** she **doing** these days?	She'**s teaching** at a university.	love
Who **are** they **visiting** this week?	They'**re visiting** their parents.	want

A Complete these conversations using the present tense or the present continuous. Then practice with a partner.

1. A: Is anyone in your family looking for a job?
   B: Yes, my sister is. She .... (work) part time in a restaurant now, but she .... (look) for a job in a theater company. She .... (love) acting.

2. A: What is your brother doing these days?
   B: He .... (go) to college this semester. He .... (like) it a lot. He .... (study) mathematics.

3. A: Where do your parents live?
   B: They .... (live) in Chicago most of the time, but they .... (stay) in Florida this winter. They .... (have) a house there.

B *Pair work* Take turns asking the questions in part A or similar questions of your own. Give your own information when answering.

C *Group work* Take turns. Ask each student about his or her family. Then ask follow-up questions to get more information.

Topics to ask about
traveling
living abroad
taking a class
moving to a new home
going to college or high school
studying a foreign language
looking for a job

A: Is anyone in your family traveling right now?
B: Yes, my father is.
C: Where is he?
B: He's in Bangkok.
D: What's he doing there?
B: . . .

interchange 5

Family facts
Find out some interesting facts about your classmates' families. Turn to page IC-7.

5 *GRAMMAR FOCUS* *Present continuous*

This grammar focus practices the present continuous. The present continuous is used to describe the following:

1. incomplete actions or events (e.g., They're *visiting* their parents [right now]. = They're there for only a few days, but they have to go home on Friday.)

2. events that are true at the moment of speaking, or "momentary" actions (e.g., I'm *working* in Japan [right now]. = I don't always work in Japan because I usually work in Seattle.)

However, events that are permanent or unchanging (i.e., states or habits) are described with the simple present (e.g., I *live* in Seattle. She *teaches* English.).

■ Use the audio program to present the questions and statements in the box. Point out that *be* in present continuous statements is normally reduced, or contracted, in conversation (e.g., I'm *working* in Japan. She's *teaching* at a university.).

■ Explain the contrast between the simple present (permanent or unchanging states or habits) and the present continuous by writing some examples on the board. Elicit additional contrast sets around the class:

Simple present	Present continuous
I <u>watch</u> TV every night.	I'm <u>watching</u> my favorite TV program right now.
She <u>works</u> at a bank downtown.	She's <u>working</u> at a branch office in the suburbs this month.

■ Use the audio program to go over the verbs in the box that are generally not used in the present continuous; give some examples like these:

Incorrect: He's ~~knowing~~ the answer.
Correct: He <u>knows</u> the answer.

■ Ask some follow-up yes/no and Wh-questions about Ss in the class like these:

Are you living alone right now?
Is Anton taking English 101 this semester?
Are Juan and Saul working these days?
What are you studying right now?
Where is Katrina living this year?

A

■ Ss complete the conversations individually. Then check responses around the class.

Answers

1. A: Is anyone in your family looking for a job?
   B: Yes, my sister is. She**'s working** part time in a restaurant now, but she**'s looking** for a job in a theater company. She **loves** acting.

2. A: What is your brother doing these days?
   B: He**'s going** to college this semester. He **likes** it a lot. He**'s studying** mathematics.

3. A: Where do your parents live?
   B: They **live** in Chicago most of the time, but they**'re staying** in Florida this winter. They **have** a house there.

■ Ss practice the conversations in pairs.

B *Pair work*

■ Model the task, demonstrating how Ss should change the focus of the questions to fit their partner's family members – for example:

T: Is anyone in your family looking for a job, Ty?
S1: Yes, my brother is.
T: Oh? What kind of job is he looking for?
S1: He's trying to get a job in computer programming.
T: And do you have a sister?
S1: Yes, I do.
T: What is your sister doing these days?
S1: Well, she's going to NYU. She's studying art.

■ Ss work in pairs and do the task. Walk around the class and give help as needed.

C *Group work*

■ Model the dialog with several Ss and go over the "Topics to ask about" in the box that Ss can use in this free communication activity. Group members take turns asking and answering questions about their families.

■ **Optional:** Have Ss share with the rest of the class the most interesting fact or facts they learned about their classmates.

 INTERCHANGE 5 Family facts

See page T-111 in this Teacher's Edition for notes.

 Workbook

Assign Exercises 1–5 on pages 25–27 in the Workbook for end-of-class work or for homework. Ss compare answers in pairs or groups when all exercises have been completed. (Answers can be found on page T-179 of the Workbook Answer Key in this Teacher's Edition.)

Optional activities

1 *Game – What's the question?*
■ See page T-147.

2 *Guess who!*
■ See page T-148.

3 *Who am I?*
■ See page T-146.

6 SNAPSHOT *Facts about families in the United States*

This chart extends the unit topic by providing information for cross-cultural comparisons.

- Books closed. Write some of the Snapshot topics on the board: *children with working parents, single parents, marriage and divorce,* and *the elderly.* Then conduct a quick class discussion by asking questions like these:

  Do you think many American mothers with small children work?

  Do marriages in the U.S. often end in divorce?

  Do parents in the U.S. sometimes live with their adult children?

- Before Ss read the Snapshot individually, explain any new words and expressions like these:

> **single parent** = a divorced or an unmarried person who takes care of his/her child or children; also, *single mother, single father*
>
> **the elderly** = older people

- Books open. Ss read the information in the chart and answer the four questions. (*Note:* Tell the class to answer the first question personally. Point out that the last two questions refer to Ss' own countries.)

Alternative presentation

- Have Ss read the Snapshot by themselves and use their dictionaries to check any new words.

- Let volunteers read the questions aloud; then have them call on other Ss to give responses.

7 CONVERSATION *Describing family life*

This exercise introduces the use of determiners (e.g., *all, few*), especially for discussing facts.

A 🔊

- Books closed. Set the scene: Two friends, Ryan (American) and Soo Mi (Korean), are talking.

- Write some general comprehension questions on the board to help Ss focus their listening:

  What are the two people talking about?
  (Marriage in the U.S. and in Korea)
  Do many people get divorced in Korea?
  (No, most Korean couples stay together.)
  Do women in Korea usually work after they get married?
  (No, a lot of women stay home and take care of their families. But some work.)

- Ask Ss to listen for the answers to the questions on the board. Play the audio program once or twice.

- Have Ss form groups to discuss answers. Check responses.

- Books open. Refer Ss to the picture and ask:

  What is Ryan doing? (He's showing Soo Mi a headline in the newspaper.)
  Where do "50% of All Marriages End in Divorce"? (In the U.S.)

- Play the audio program again. Tell Ss to read along if they wish.

- Go over the conversation line by line and explain any new vocabulary. Then Ss practice the conversation in pairs.

B 🔊

- Read the question aloud. Tell Ss to take notes as they listen. Play the second part of the audio program.

Audio script

> RYAN: Families sure are different in the United States.
> SOO MI: Well, there are more divorces, but what else is different?
> RYAN: Well, I think people get married younger.
> SOO MI: Oh? How much younger?
> RYAN: Well, I think some people get married before the age of 20.
> SOO MI: Really? What else?
> RYAN: Hmm. A lot of women work after they get married. And I think most women who have babies go back to work fairly soon, too.

- Have Ss form small groups to compare answers. Walk around the class and give help as needed.

- Check responses around the class by writing *Families in the U.S.* on the board and circling it. Then one S from each group writes two of their agreed-upon "facts" on the board. Tell the class that any "fact" can appear only once. (*Note:* This will induce groups to work quickly together while also encouraging a little friendly class competition.)

Possible answers

> Ryan says that U.S. families are different from Korean families in several ways:
> 1. People in the U.S. get married younger – some before the age of 20.
> 2. A lot of women work after they get married.
> 3. Most women who have babies go back to work fairly soon.

6 *SNAPSHOT*

Facts About Families in the United States

Children

57% of children under six have two parents who work or a single parent who works.

63% of women with children work.

50% of working women return to work within a year of having a baby.

Marriage

50% of marriages end in divorce.

80% of divorced people remarry; more than 50% divorce again.

Elderly

20% to 30% of the population now cares for an elderly relative, or will within five years.

Source: The Family and Medical Leave Act

Talk about these questions.

Which of these facts surprises you?
Do women with children usually work in your country?
Do people often get divorced?
Do elderly people generally live with relatives?

7 *CONVERSATION* *Describing family life*

A Listen and practice.

Ryan: Look at this headline, Soo Mi.
Soo Mi: Wow! So many people in the United States get divorced!
Ryan: Is it the same in Korea?
Soo Mi: I don't think so. In Korea, some marriages break up, but most couples stay together.
Ryan: Do people get married young?
Soo Mi: Not really. Very few people get married before the age of 20.
Ryan: Hmm. Do women usually work after they get married?
Soo Mi: No, a lot of women stay home and take care of their families. But some work.

B Listen to the rest of the conversation.

What does Ryan say about families in the United States? Write down two things.

8 GRAMMAR FOCUS

Determiners

100%	All Nearly all Most	women with children work.
	Many A lot of Some	women stay home after they get married.
	Not many A few Few	couples stay together.
0%	No one	gets married before the age of 20.

A Rewrite these sentences using determiners. Then compare with a partner.

1. In Australia, 87% of married couples have children.

....

2. Six percent of 20- to 24-year-olds in the United States are divorced.

....

3. Thirty-five percent of the people in Germany live alone.

....

4. In China, 50% of women get married by the age of 22.

....

B *Pair work* Rewrite the sentences in part A so that they are about your country. Then discuss your information with a partner.

> *In my country, only some married couples have children.*

useful expressions

Is that right?
Do you think so? I think . . . .
I don't agree.
I don't think so.
It's different in my country.

9 WRITING

A Write about families in your country. Use some of your ideas from Exercise 8.

> *In my country, most people get married by the age of 30. Not many women work after they get married. Grandparents, parents, and children often live in the same house. . . .*

B *Group work* Take turns reading your compositions. Then answer any questions from the group.

8 *GRAMMAR FOCUS* Determiners

This exercise practices determiners (also known as quantity determiners, quantifiers, quantity words, and expressions of quantity).

A determiner is a word or phrase that goes in front of a noun to show how the noun is being used. A determiner usually shows the quantity of the noun being referred to. When we want to be precise about quantities, we can use a number; however, in everyday conversations that include statements of fact, determiners are often used instead.

The determiners presented here are used with plural nouns (e.g., most *women,* a few *couples*) to indicate the approximate number of a particular group in a certain country. Note that the pronoun *no one* is introduced here to express "0%"; the use of *no one* (or *nobody*) is more common than *no* + plural noun (e.g., no women).

- Use the audio program to present the sentences in the box. Ss repeat. Point out how the determiners are presented in the graded scale:

$$100\% = all$$
$$80\%–99\% \text{ (approx.)} = nearly\ all,\ most$$
$$36\%–79\% \text{ (approx.)} = many,\ a\ lot\ of,\ some$$
$$1\%–35\% \text{ (approx.)} = not\ many,\ a\ few,\ few$$
$$0\% = no\ one$$

- Make it clear that these determiners can all be used with plural nouns to express facts not distorted by the speaker's or writer's opinions (e.g., I can't say that *all* American couples stay together, but I can say that *a lot of* couples do.).

A

- Explain the task: Ss choose a suitable determiner from the box to use as a substitute for the given percentage + *of* and then rewrite each sentence using that determiner. Encourage Ss to focus on the meaning of each sentence and to choose a determiner based on their own view of the facts. To model the task, choose a fact from the Snapshot on page 31 and write a set of example sentences on the board, like this:

In the U.S., 50% of marriages end in divorce. = In the U.S., many /a lot of marriages end in divorce.

- Point out that more than one determiner is possible for each sentence. Also explain that the percentage given in one fact may seem low in one context but high in another, and vice versa.

- After Ss work individually to complete the exercise, have them compare answers in pairs. Then elicit answers around the class.

Possible answers

1. In Australia, **nearly all/most** married couples have children.
2. **Not many/A few/Few** 20- to 24-year-olds in the United States are divorced.
3. **Some/Many** (of the) people in Germany live alone.
4. In China, **many/a lot of/some** women get married by the age of 22.

B *Pair work*

- To explain the task, read aloud the example and compare it with the first sentence in part A. Then Ss write sentences individually. Go around the class and give help as needed.

- Before Ss compare sentences in pairs, present the useful expressions in the box. Point out that the last four expressions here are used when we disagree with someone.

- **Optional:** Ask for volunteers to write some of their sentences on the board.

- **Optional:** In a heterogeneous class, collect the Ss' sentences and read some to the class without revealing the name of the country or of the S who wrote the sentences. Ss guess which country each fact is about.

Optional activity: *Game – Tic-Tac-Toe*

- See page T-147.

9 *WRITING*

This exercise practices writing descriptions of typical families in the Ss' countries.

A

- Read aloud the example and call attention to the picture. Can Ss guess which country is being described here? (Answer: Korea)

- Have Ss first brainstorm individually about typical families in their own countries. Then tell Ss to use their brainstorming maps (and their sentences from part B in Exercise 8) to write a first draft. Encourage them to concentrate on writing as much as they can in sentence

form without worrying too much about spelling or grammar.

- Have Ss read over their drafts and revise them. Help Ss by asking "Can you add any more details or information? What do you need to change or delete?"

- After Ss finish revising their drafts for content, tell them to carefully check their grammar and spelling.

B *Group work*

- In groups, Ss take turns reading their compositions aloud and answering any questions.

10 READING The changing family

This text presents cultural information on a modern American family; in the exercise, Ss practice scanning for main ideas.

■ Books closed. Ask some questions like these to stimulate a class discussion on how families are changing:

How are families today different from families fifty years ago?

Back then, did both parents usually work outside the home? What about now?

Fifty years ago, what things did children usually do after school? What about these days?

■ Books open. Read the pre-reading question aloud and elicit responses around the class.

■ **Optional:** Write some interesting responses on the board. After Ss read the article, the class looks again at the ideas on the board.

A

■ Go over the task. Then either have Ss read the passage silently or read it aloud to them. Encourage Ss to underline, circle, or highlight any words whose meanings they can't guess from context.

■ After Ss read the passage, write the following questions on the board. Tell Ss to write them down in their notebooks and to use them whenever they ask about new vocabulary:

What does . . . mean?
How do you define . . . ?
What's the definition for . . . ?

■ Elicit Ss' questions about any new words they marked. Write each word on the board and ask if anyone can explain it or give another word (a synonym) for it. Or have a "class challenge" to see who can look up each word the fastest in the dictionary. Be sure to explain any words that the class wasn't able to define, such as:

> **after-school program** = an activity or a class for children to go to at the end of the school day
> **pick . . . up** = to go and get . . .
> **chores** = regular, necessary but boring jobs (e.g., housework, laundry)

■ Ss complete the chart individually. Tell them to scan the text to find various types of problems to include in the chart.

■ Check Ss' answers around the class.

Possible answers

	Problems
1. Steve	has to help Judy with the housework; doesn't enjoy it
2. Judy	feels tired and too busy; worries about the children
3. Steve and Judy	don't have a lot of free time together

B *Pair work*

■ Read over the questions and explain the task. Ss work in pairs and take turns suggesting problems and solutions for question 1 and answers for 2.

Optional: Pairs report their ideas to the class.

Answers

> 1. Ss' answers will vary.
> 2. Josh and Emily are benefiting from Judy's working. Ben is not.

 Workbook

Tell Ss to do Exercises 6–10 on pages 28–30 in the Workbook or assign them as homework. Have Ss work in small groups to compare answers. Elicit responses around the class. (Answers can be found on page T-179 of the Workbook Answer Key in this Teacher's Edition.)

Optional activity: *Game – Word Bingo*

Time: 10–15 minutes. This activity reviews vocabulary and spelling, and practices listening for and writing down key words. It can easily be used with any unit.

■ Make up a list of 24 words from Unit 5. Then show Ss how to make a Bingo card on an 8 ½" × 11" sheet of paper with 25 spaces on it, like this:

B	I	N	G	O
		FREE		

■ Dictate the words from your list: First, say the word and spell it. Then use it in a sentence, like this:

T: *Family.* F-A-M-I-L-Y. There are three in my *family.*

■ Ss listen and write down each word inside a box in random order on their Bingo cards.

■ One by one, randomly call out the words from your list. Ss find each word on their card and circle it. (*Note:* Check the word off on your own list so that no words are repeated. This will also help when checking a S's card later, after he or she gets "Bingo.")

■ The first S to get five circled words in a row in any direction (including the "Free" space) shouts "Bingo!" Ask the S to read aloud the five circled words. Check them against the original list. If all the words are correct, that S is the winner.

10 *READING*

The Changing Family

What kinds of problems do parents have in your country?

Now that Judy is working, Steve has to help her more with the housework. He doesn't enjoy it, however.

Judy loves her work, but she feels tired and too busy. She also worries about the children. Judy has to work on Saturdays, so Steve and Judy don't have a lot of free time together.

American families are changing. One important change is that most married women now work outside the home. What happens when both parents work? Read about the Morales family.

Judy and Steve Morales have three children: Josh, 12; Ben, 9; and Emily, 6. Steve is a computer programmer. This year, Judy is working again as a hospital administrator. The family needs the money, and Judy likes her job. Everything is going well, but there are also some problems.

Emily is having a great time in her after-school program. When Judy comes to pick her up, she doesn't want to leave.

Unfortunately, Ben's school doesn't have an after-school program. Right now, he's spending most afternoons by himself in front of the TV.

Josh is enjoying his new freedom after school. He's playing his music louder and spending more time on the phone. He's also doing a few household chores.

A Read the article. What are Steve's and Judy's problems? Complete the chart.

Problems	
1. Steve	....
2. Judy	....
3. Steve and Judy	....

B *Pair work* Talk about these questions.

1. Which of the problems above do you think is the most serious?
   Offer some solutions for that problem.
2. Which of the children are benefiting from Judy's working?
   Which one is not?

6 How often do you exercise?

1 SNAPSHOT

	MALES	FEMALES
Top six sports and fitness activities for teenagers in the United States	1. Football 2. Basketball 3. Weight training 4. Jogging 5. Bicycling 6. Swimming	1. Swimming 2. Basketball 3. Bicycling 4. Aerobics 5. Jogging 6. Regular fitness program

Source: *America's Youth in the 1990s;* George H. Gallup International Institute

Talk about these questions.

Do males and females in your country enjoy any of these sports or activities?
Do you enjoy any of these or other sports or activities? Which ones?

2 WORD POWER Sports and exercise

A *Pair work* Which of these activities are popular with the following age groups? Check (✓) the activities. Then compare with a partner.

	Children	Teens	Young adults	Middle-aged people	Older people
aerobics	☐	☐	☐	☐	☐
baseball	☐	☐	☐	☐	☐
bicycling	☐	☐	☐	☐	☐
Rollerblading	☐	☐	☐	☐	☐
soccer	☐	☐	☐	☐	☐
swimming	☐	☐	☐	☐	☐
tennis	☐	☐	☐	☐	☐
weight training	☐	☐	☐	☐	☐
yoga	☐	☐	☐	☐	☐

A: I think aerobics are popular with teens.
B: And with young adults.

B *Pair work* Which of the activities above are used with *do, go,* or *play?*

do aerobics .... go bicycling .... play baseball ....
....
....

How often do you exercise?

This unit introduces the topics of sports, exercise, fitness routines, and leisure activities. It also presents adverbs of frequency, questions with how, *and short answers.*

Cycle 1, Exercises 1–8

1 SNAPSHOT *Top six sports and fitness activities for teenagers in the U.S.*

This text introduces the theme of sports and fitness.

- Books closed. Introduce the topic of sports and fitness by asking how much time the Ss spend each day or week doing certain activities (e.g., playing a sport, jogging).

- Books open. Read aloud the headings and the name of each sport. Have Ss repeat. Make sure Ss know that the reference here is to American football, not to soccer.

- Have Ss skim through the list of sports and activities individually. Tell them to highlight any new words and

then to check their dictionaries. Alternatively, explain (or mime the action of) any new words or expressions:

weight training = exercises that use heavy metal equipment to shape the body and muscles
aerobics = lively exercises (often performed to music)
regular fitness program = a daily or weekly exercise routine that a person does to keep healthy and fit

- As a class, group, or pair activity, Ss use the questions to have a short discussion.

2 WORD POWER *Sports and exercise*

This task presents additional vocabulary for Ss to use when talking about sports and exercise.

A *Pair work*

(*Note:* This task can be done in several ways: Ss can consider which activities are "generally" popular with certain age groups worldwide, or they can limit these age groups to people in their own countries.)

- Go over the instructions. Then point to each word and picture, and model the correct pronunciation. Ss repeat. Explain (or mime the action of) any new words:

Rollerblading = similar to roller-skating, but the wheels on Rollerblades are set in a straight line under each shoe (See the picture in Exercise 3 on page 35.)
yoga = a system of Hindu (East Indian) exercises to help control the body and mind, including meditation, deep breathing, and various postures
middle-aged = from about 40 to 65 years old

- Ss work individually to complete the task.

- Model the example A/B dialog with several volunteers. Then Ss work in pairs to compare answers by having similar conversations.

- Check answers around the class.

Possible answers

	Children	Teens	Young adults	Middle-aged people	Older people
aerobics		✓	✓	✓	
baseball	✓	✓	✓		
bicycling	✓	✓	✓	✓	
Rollerblading	✓	✓	✓		
soccer	✓	✓	✓		
swimming	✓	✓	✓	✓	✓
tennis	✓	✓	✓	✓	✓
weight training		✓	✓	✓	✓
yoga		✓	✓	✓	✓

B *Pair work*

This is a collocation task where Ss decide which verbs are used with particular activities.

- Go over the three examples to show how some of the activities listed in part A are used with the specific verbs given here.

- Ss form pairs to work together to complete the task. You may want Ss to use their dictionaries; otherwise, they can just make educated guesses.

- Elicit answers around the class.

Answers

do aerobics	go bicycling	play baseball
do weight training	**go Rollerblading**	**play soccer**
do yoga	**go swimming**	**play tennis**

- **Optional:** Ask Ss to work in pairs or small groups to form some "rules" for these collocations. Write this question on the board:

  What are the "rules" for using do, go, *and* play*?*

- After Ss have made up their rules, ask two pairs or groups to work together to "test" their rules using the vocabulary on page 34 and any additional sports or activities they can think of.

Possible answers

do + an activity involving martial arts or individual types of exercises
go + an activity ending in *-ing* (exception: *do* + *weight training*)
play + a sport played with a ball (exception: *go* + *bowling*)

3 CONVERSATION *Describing routines*

This exercise introduces adverbs of frequency (e.g., *almost always, often, five times a week*).

A 🔊

- Use the picture to set the scene.
- Books closed. Play the audio program once or twice. Ss only listen. Then ask some questions like these:

  Does Paul lift weights? (Yes, he does.)
  Does the woman often go Rollerblading? (No. Paul does – about five times a week.)
  Is the woman in good shape? (No. She's a real couch potato.)
  What does the woman do in her free time? (She watches TV.)

- If Ss have difficulty answering the questions, play the audio program again.
- Books open. Present the conversation line by line. Explain that a "couch potato" is a person who watches a lot of TV and does not have an active lifestyle.
- Ss practice the conversation in pairs.

B 🔊

- Read aloud the question that Ss need to focus their listening on. Then play the second part of the audio program once or twice.

Audio script

> MARIE: So, what else do you like to do, Paul?
> PAUL: Well, I like video games a lot. I play them every day. It drives my mom crazy!
> MARIE: Hey, I play video games all the time, too.
> PAUL: Well, listen, I have some great new games. Why don't we play some after class today?
> MARIE: OK!

- Check Ss' answers around the class.

Answer

> He plays video games.

4 GRAMMAR FOCUS *Adverbs of frequency*

🔊 This grammar focus introduces and practices questions with *How often . . . ?*, yes/no questions with *ever*, and adverbs of frequency.

- Use the audio program to present the *How often . . . ?* question and responses in the box on the left. Model the correct pronunciation of *usually,* which has three syllables /ˈyuwdʒəliy/. Explain that while we commonly say "once" (not "one time") and "twice" (not "two times"), we do say "three times," "four times," and so on.
- Elicit additional sentences, like this:

  T: How often do you usually exercise? *(giving cue)*
    Every day.
  S1: I (usually) exercise every day.
  S2: I do aerobics every day.
  T: *(giving cue)* Once a week.
  S3: I go jogging once a week.

- Now play the rest of the audio program to present the *Do you ever . . . ?* question and responses and the grading of the adverbs.
- Explain that the normal position for adverbs of frequency is before the main verb (e.g., I *almost always* watch TV after dinner.). Point out that *sometimes* can also begin a sentence (e.g., *Sometimes* I watch TV before bed.). With the verb *be,* however, adverbs of frequency usually come after the verb (e.g., He is *never* on time.).
- Ask the question *"Do you ever . . . ?"* with various activities (e.g., do aerobics, go Rollerblading, play tennis) and cue adverbs (e.g., *always, often, sometimes*) to elicit additional sentences.

A

- Go over the instructions. Show Ss how to use a caret symbol (∧) to indicate the place a word is inserted and then to write the adverb above it. Alternatively, tell Ss to write out the sentences on a sheet of paper or in their notebooks. To make the task even more challenging, have the Ss cover the grammar box.
- In pairs, Ss compare answers. Then check answers around the class.

Answers

> 1. A: What do you **usually** do on Saturday mornings?
>   B: Nothing much. I **almost always** sleep until noon.
> 2. A: Do you **ever** go bicycling?
>   B: Yeah, I **often** go bicycling on Saturdays.
> 3. A: How often do you **usually** play sports?
>   B: Well, I play tennis **twice a week**.
> 4. A: What do you **usually** do after class?
>   B: I go out with my classmates **about three times a week**.
> 5. A: How often do you **usually** exercise?
>   B: I **seldom** exercise.

- Have students work in pairs to practice asking and answering the five questions.

B *Pair work*

- Pairs take turns asking and answering the questions in part A, this time responding with their own information.

3 CONVERSATION *Describing routines*

A Listen and practice.

Marie: You're really fit, Paul. Do you exercise very much?
Paul: Well, I almost always get up very early, and I lift weights for an hour.
Marie: You're kidding!
Paul: No. And then I often go Rollerblading.
Marie: Wow! How often do you exercise like that?
Paul: About five times a week. What about you?
Marie: Oh, I hardly ever exercise. I usually just watch TV in my free time. I guess I'm a real couch potato!

CLASS AUDIO ONLY ▶ **B** 🔊 Listen to the rest of the conversation.

What else does Paul do in his free time?

4 GRAMMAR FOCUS

Adverbs of frequency 🔊

How often do you **usually** exercise?	Do you **ever** watch television in the evening?	100% **always**
I lift weights **every day.**	Yes, I **almost always** watch TV after dinner.	**almost always**
I go jogging about **once a week.**	I **sometimes** watch TV before bed.	**usually**
I play basketball **twice a month.**	**Sometimes** I watch TV before bed.*	**often**
I exercise about **three times a year.**	I **seldom** watch TV in the evening.	**sometimes**
I don't exercise **very often/very much.**	No, I **never** watch TV.	**seldom**
		hardly ever
		almost never
	*Sometimes *can begin a sentence.*	0% **never**

A Put the adverbs in the correct place. Then practice with a partner.

1. A: What do you do on Saturday mornings? (usually)
   B: Nothing much. I sleep until noon. (almost always)

2. A: Do you go bicycling? (ever)
   B: Yeah, I go bicycling on Saturdays. (often)

3. A: How often do you play sports? (usually)
   B: Well, I play tennis. (twice a week)

4. A: What do you do after class? (usually)
   B: I go out with my classmates. (about three times a week)

5. A: How often do you exercise? (usually)
   B: I exercise. (seldom)

B *Pair work* Take turns asking the questions in part A. Give your own information when answering.

5 PRONUNCIATION *Sentence stress*

A Listen to the syllables stressed in each sentence. Notice that the adverbs of frequency are stressed. Then practice the sentences.

I hardly éver do yóga in the mórning.
I óften go Róllerblading on Sáturdays.
I almost álways play ténnis on wéekends.

B *Pair work* Write four sentences about yourself using adverbs of frequency. Then take turns saying the sentences using the correct stress.

6 FITNESS POLL

A *Group work* Take a poll in your group. One person takes notes. Take turns asking each person these questions.

1. Do you have a regular fitness program? How often do you exercise?

2. Do you ever go to a gym? How often do you go? What do you do there?

3. Do you play any sports? How often do you play?

4. How often do you take long walks? Where do you go?

5. What else do you do to keep fit?

B *Group work* Study the results of the poll. Who in your group has a good fitness program?

7 LISTENING

CLASS AUDIO ONLY

 Listen to what Ted, Wanda, and Kim like to do in the evening. Complete the chart.

	Favorite activity	How often?
Ted		
Wanda		
Kim		

5 *PRONUNCIATION* *Sentence stress*

This exercise introduces the use of sentence stress, which gives a natural rhythm to spoken English.

The rhythm of spoken English is determined by the occurrence of stressed syllables. Stressed syllables occur at more or less equal intervals in English. The other syllables in a sentence are reduced or blended to accommodate the regular beat of the stressed syllables. This contrasts with many other languages where syllables receive more or less the same stress. Ss should aim for a stress-timed rhythm, rather than a syllable-timed rhythm as in languages such as French, Spanish, and Japanese.

A

- Use the audio program to present the sentences. Ss repeat. Point out the stressed syllables, i.e., those that appear in bold type with stress marks (ʹ) above them.

Explain that we stress the most important words or syllables in an English sentence.

- Demonstrate the regularity of stressed rhythm in English by keeping the beat: Clap your hands or tap on the desk three times while reading each sentence aloud. Then do it again and have the class keep the beat with you.

B *Pair work*

- Go over the task: Ss first work individually to write four sentences about themselves that use adverbs of frequency; Ss then form pairs to take turns saying their sentences using the correct stress. Encourage both partners to "keep the beat" by clapping or tapping on each stressed syllable. Go around the class and give help as needed.

6 *FITNESS POLL*

This is a fluency activity that reviews asking "How often . . . ?" and "Do you (ever) . . . ?" and responding with adverbs of frequency.

A *Group work*

- Go over the task and point out the need to choose a group secretary to take notes. Then read each question aloud and have Ss repeat.

- Ss form groups of four to five and choose a secretary. Then they take turns asking one another the questions in the chart. Go around the class and give help as needed. Make sure the secretaries are taking clear notes.

B *Group work*

- Group members look over the secretary's notes and vote on who has a good (or the best) fitness program.

- Group secretaries report their findings to the rest of the class.

7 *LISTENING*

This exercise practices listening for key words and phrases.

- Books closed. To introduce the topic of this listening task, ask questions around the class, like this:

  T: What do you usually do in the evening, Papo?
  S1: Well, I usually do my homework and then watch TV before bed.
  T: Do you ever exercise in the evening, Kim?
  S2: Yes, I often work out at the Y.
  T: Really? How often do you work out there?
  S2: Oh, about twice a week.

- Set the scene by reading aloud the instructions. Play the audio program once. Ss only listen.

Audio script

WANDA: So, what do you usually do in the evening, Ted?
TED: I exercise a lot. I like to go jogging after work.
KIM: Yeah? How often do you go jogging?
TED: About four or five times a week.
WANDA: Well, I guess you're in great shape.
TED: Thanks!
KIM: You're in great shape, too, Wanda!

WANDA: Oh, thanks, Kim. I usually go to the gym and work out in the evenings. I love it! And I meet a lot of my friends there.
TED: How often do you go?
WANDA: About three times a week, I guess. What about you, Kim? Do you ever work out in the evenings?
KIM: No, I don't exercise very much. I almost always practice my guitar after work. I practice for a couple of hours every night.
TED: Gee, you must be pretty good!

- Books open. Play the audio program again. Ss complete the chart and then compare answers in pairs.

- To check Ss' answers, play the audio program again, pausing it after the information for each answer is given.

Answers

	Favorite activity	*How often?*
Ted	jogging	about 4–5 times a week
Wanda	working out	about 3 times a week
Kim	practicing the guitar	a couple of hours every night

8 *WRITING* Favorite activities

This exercise practices writing descriptions of favorite activities and routines, using adverbs of frequency and the simple present tense.

A

■ Explain the task by referring to the pictures while reading the example paragraph aloud.

■ Encourage Ss to spend about five minutes brainstorming about activities that they usually do each week. Then they can organize the information in their brainstorming maps and use it to write a first draft of their compositions.

B *Group work*

■ Ss form small groups and read their paragraphs aloud to one another. After answering questions from their

group, Ss revise their drafts to include any additional information that group members asked them about.

■ **Optional:** Ask each group to select the most interesting composition. Then have one group member read the composition aloud to the class. This class activity could also become a guessing game if the other groups don't know who the writers of the selected compositions are.

 *Workbook*

Ss complete Exercises 1–7 on pages 31–34 in the Workbook either in class or for homework. When they finish, check responses around the class. (Answers can be found on page T-180 of the Workbook Answer Key in this Teacher's Edition.)

Cycle 2, Exercises 9–12

9 *CONVERSATION* Describing exercise

This exercise introduces additional Wh-questions that deal with frequency (e.g., How often . . . ?) and with ability (How well . . . ?).

■ Books closed. Introduce the common use of questions with *How . . . ?* by asking a few questions like these around the class:

T: What sport do you regularly do, Teresa?
S1: I go swimming at the pool on campus.
T: That's great! So, how often do you swim?
S1: Oh, about three times a week.
T: Wow! And Sam, how well do you swim?
S2: OK, I guess, but I don't swim very often.

■ Now write some questions on the board like these and ask Ss to listen for the answers:

Where does Keith work out? (He works out at a gym.)
How often does he exercise? (Every day after work)
What types of exercise does he do? (He does aerobics, and he plays racquetball.)

■ Play the audio program once or twice. Check Ss' answers to the questions on the board.

■ Books open. Play the audio program again. Explain these words and expressions, if necessary:

fitness freak = a person who really enjoys exercising to stay in good shape
racquetball = a game similar to tennis, but played by two people hitting a ball against a wall in a small room
No problem. = Don't worry about it.
I won't play hard. = said by a good player to someone who doesn't play as well to show that he/she won't make the usual effort to win

■ Ss practice the conversation in pairs.

■ **Optional:** Books closed. Ss practice the conversation again, this time using only their own words (i.e., they don't need to memorize or use exactly the same language as in the conversation).

Optional activity: *In my free time*

Time: 15 minutes. This activity practices the simple present tense with adverbs of frequency. Ss try to identify classmates by finding out what they do in their free time.

■ Write these cues on the board:

What I like to do in my free time
I like . . . (sports, music, TV, videos).
I . . . every day.
I usually/often/sometimes . . . in the evening.
I . . . on Saturday/Sunday.
For my summer vacation, I usually . . . .

■ Ask Ss to use the cues to write a total of five sentences about themselves – each sentence on a separate index card or small piece of paper (e.g., 3" × 5"). Tell Ss not to write their names on their papers. Collect the papers, mix them up, and then give one to each S.

■ Explain the activity: Ss ask one another questions based on the information they have in the description on the piece of paper. When they find the person who fits the description, they write the S's name on it and keep it. Then they get another description. Whoever finds the most people is the winner.

■ Elicit the kinds of questions Ss could ask and write some of them on the board for them to use as models.

■ Set a time limit of about ten minutes. Ss move around the class asking questions and matching Ss with descriptions. When time is up, find out who made the most matches.

8 *WRITING* Favorite activities

A Write about your favorite activities.

> *I love to exercise. I usually work out every day. I get up early in the morning and go running for about an hour. Then I often go to the gym and do aerobics. Sometimes I go for a walk in the afternoon. About once a week, I play basketball.*

B *Group work* Take turns reading your compositions. Then answer any questions from the group.

9 *CONVERSATION* Describing exercise

 Listen and practice.

Rod: You're in great shape, Keith.
Do you work out at a gym?
Keith: Yeah, I do. I guess I'm a real fitness freak.
Rod: So, how often do you work out?
Keith: Well, I do aerobics every day after work.
And then I play racquetball.
Rod: Say, I like racquetball, too.
Keith: Oh, do you want to play sometime?
Rod: Uh, . . . how well do you play?
Keith: Pretty well, I guess.
Rod: Well, all right. But I'm not very good.
Keith: No problem, Rod. I won't play too hard.

10 LISTENING

Listen to John, Anne, and Phil discuss sports and exercise. Which one is a couch potato? a fitness freak? a sports fanatic?

a couch potato

a fitness freak

a sports fanatic

1. ....

2. ....

3. ....

11 GRAMMAR FOCUS

interchange 6

Fitness quiz
Find out how fit you are. Turn to page IC-8.

Questions with how; short answers

How often do you work out?	Twice a week. Not very often.
How much time do you spend at the gym? **How long** do you spend working out?	Around two hours a day. I don't work out.
How well do you play racquetball?	Pretty well. About average, I guess. Not very well.
How good are you at sports?	I'm pretty good at sports. I guess I'm OK. Not too good.

A Complete these questions. Practice with a partner. Then write four more questions.

1. A: .... at volleyball?
   B: I guess I'm pretty good.

2. A: .... swim?
   B: Not very well, but I'd like to learn to swim better.

3. A: .... watch sports?
   B: Pretty often. About three or four times a week.

4. A: .... spend exercising?
   B: I spend about an hour every day.

B Group work Take turns asking the questions in part A and your own questions. Give your own information when answering.

Who in your group is a couch potato? a fitness freak? a sports fanatic?

10 LISTENING

This exercise practices making inferences.

- Books closed. Set the scene by telling Ss that they are going to listen to three people – John, Anne, and Phil – discussing sports and exercise. Write the three speakers' names on the board and then play the audio program once. Ss only listen.

Audio script

ANNE: How good are you at sports, John?
JOHN: Are you kidding? I'm terrible! But I love to watch sports. I go to football or baseball games all the time. And I buy three or four different sports magazines every week.
ANNE: Wow!
PHIL: Do you like sports, Anne?
ANNE: Oh, yes. I like to exercise. But I don't watch sports very much, and I never buy sports magazines.
PHIL: How much time do you spend exercising?
ANNE: Well, I guess I exercise about two or three hours a day. I do aerobics three times a week, and the other days I go swimming. It makes me feel good.

PHIL: That's great!
JOHN: And what about you, Phil?
PHIL: Oh, I'm too lazy to play sports – I really hate exercising! And I almost never go to any sporting events. In my free time, I like to sit with my feet up and watch my favorite TV shows.

- Ask Ss to share whatever specific information they remember hearing during the discussion, and write it in note form on the board.

- Books open. Go over the task and read the questions aloud. Use the pictures to explain the three types of people.

- Play the audio program again once or twice. Ss complete the task and then compare answers with a partner.

- Elicit answers around the class.

Answers

1. Phil	2. Anne	3. John

11 GRAMMAR FOCUS Questions with how; short answers

This exercise focuses on asking additional questions with *how* and responding with short answers.

- Use the audio program to present each question-and-answer set. Explain any new vocabulary that Ss find difficult.

- Make sure Ss know the difference between *well* and *good*: *well* is an adverb and describes verbs; *good* is an adjective and describes nouns. Ask several yes/no questions like these around the class:

T: Are you a good swimmer, Ali?
S1: Yes, I am.
T: Sara, does Ali swim well?
S2: Yes, he does.

- Start a question-and-answer practice around the class, like this:

T: Antonio, how often do you work out?
S1: Mmm, not very often. How much time do you spend studying every day, Chang?
S2: About three hours a day. Jenny, how well do you play tennis?
S3: About average, I guess.

A

- Present the task.

- Ss first work individually to complete the four questions. Check answers before pairs practice together.

Answers

1. **How good are you** at volleyball?
2. **How well do you** swim?
3. **How often do you** watch sports?
4. **How much time do you** spend exercising?

- Ss work individually or in pairs to write four more *How . . . ?* questions. Walk around the class and give help as needed.

B Group work

- Explain the task by reading the instructions aloud. Tell pairs from part A to separate and to form new groups of four Ss each. Then Ss take turns asking their own four questions along with the other four questions in part A while giving real answers. After about five minutes, ask each group to share their findings, like this:

S: In our group, Charlie says he's a couch potato, Sara and Han are both fitness freaks, and I'm really a sports fanatic.

Optional activities

1 *Game – What's the question?*

- See page T-147.

2 *Question and answer*

- See page T-148.

 INTERCHANGE 6 Fitness quiz

See page T-112 in this Teacher's Edition for notes.

12 READING Smart moves

In this article, Ss read about some of the things that exercise does for the body and brain; they also practice scanning, identifying details, and making inferences.

- Books closed. Brainstorm with the class on how exercise helps people. Write some of the Ss' responses on the board, like this:

How does exercise help you?
Exercise . . .
  makes you fit.
  can improve your body.
  helps you relax.

- Books open. Read aloud the pre-reading task. Have Ss read each statement in part A and decide individually or in pairs if it is true or not.

- Take a quick class vote (through a show of hands) to see which statements Ss think are generally true.

- Tell Ss to read the passage silently and to mark any words whose meanings they can't guess from context. Encourage Ss to use their dictionaries to check the meanings of any difficult words.

- Elicit and explain any expressions that Ss still don't understand – for example:

lifts the spirit = makes a person feel happier
builds confidence = makes a person believe in him/herself

Alternative presentation

- Assign the reading for homework. Tell Ss to check their dictionaries for any words that they aren't sure about.

A Pair work

- Go over the instructions. Ss form pairs and work together to decide on and check the statements that are true, this time based on information given in the article. Then they scan the passage again and underline any words or phrases that helped them determine which statements are true.

- Check Ss' answers around the class.

Answers *(helpful information in parentheses)*

1. ✓ (lifts the spirit)
2. ✓ (builds confidence)
3. ✓ (makes the bones, muscles, heart, and lungs stronger)
4. –
5. ✓ (helps you learn new things)
6. ✓ (helps you . . . remember old information better)
7. –
8. ✓ (walking four to five miles . . . five times a week helps you live longer)

B Pair work

- Go over the three questions. Make sure Ss know that *benefits* means "helpful things, advantages."

- Decide if Ss should work again with their same partners or switch to new partners for variety. As pairs discuss answers to the questions, walk around the class and note any problems the Ss are having, particularly with grammar or using new vocabulary correctly. When Ss finish their discussions, go over any problems with the whole class.

- As a class activity, read each question aloud and ask pairs to volunteer their responses.

 Workbook

Assign Exercises 8–11 on pages 35–36 in the Workbook for in-class work or as homework. When they finish, have Ss work in pairs to compare answers. Then check answers around the class. (Answers can be found on page T-180 of the Workbook Answer Key in this Teacher's Edition.)

Optional activities

1 *Game – Questions . . . and more questions*

Time: 10–15 minutes. This activity reviews talking about routines and abilities using adverbs of frequency and questions with *how* and *do*.

Preparation: Each S will need five blank cards (e.g., index cards, paper from a small note pad).

- Divide the class into two teams – A and B (or into four groups designated as teams A, B, C, and D). Each S writes five statements describing his or her routine. Tell Ss to write one sentence on each card and to use an adverb of frequency in each sentence (e.g., I *usually* stay home on my day off./I work out *five times a week*.).

- Collect Ss' cards and put them in a pile facedown.

- Team A starts. One S takes a card and reads the statement to a S on Team B (e.g., "I go jogging twice a week."). That S on Team B tries to make a question from the statement (e.g., "How often do you usually go jogging?" or "How much time do you spend jogging?" or "Do you ever go jogging?").

- Ss on both teams (or all four teams) decide if the question is correct. If it is, Team B gets a point. If it isn't, Team A gets a turn to make a question for the statement. If that question is correct, Team A gets the point instead.

- Keep a record of the team scores on the board. The team with the most points is the winner.

2 *Game – Word Bingo*

- See page T-33.

3 *Crossword puzzle*

- See page T-146.

12 *READING*

Smart
Moves

Look at the statements in part A below. Which do you think are true?

It won't surprise fitness freaks to learn that aerobic exercise does more than raise the heart rate: It lifts the spirit and builds confidence. But many brain researchers believe that something else happens, too. Just as exercise makes the bones, muscles, heart, and lungs stronger, researchers think that it also strengthens important parts of the brain.

Research suggests that aerobic exercise helps you learn new things and remember old information better. Aerobic exercise sends more blood to the brain and it also feeds the brain with substances that develop new nerve connections. If the exercise has complicated movements like dance steps or basketball moves, the brain produces even more nerve connections – the more connections, the better the brain can process all kinds of information.

Scientists still don't fully understand the relationship between exercise and brain power. For the moment, people just have to trust that exercise is helping them to learn or remember. Scientific research clearly shows, however, that three or more workouts a week are good for you. A study in the *Journal of the American Medical Association,* for example, shows that walking four to five miles (6.5 to 8 km) an hour for 45 minutes five times a week helps you live longer. So don't be a couch potato. Get out there and do something!

A *Pair work* According to the article, which of these statements are probably true? Check (✓) the statements. What information helped you determine this? Underline the information in the article.

Exercise . . .

1. makes you feel happier. ☐
2. makes you feel more self-confident. ☐
3. strengthens the body. ☐
4. can increase your height. ☐

5. can help you learn things better. ☐
6. helps you remember things better. ☐
7. gives you better eyesight. ☐
8. helps you live longer. ☐

B *Pair work* Talk about these questions. Explain your answers.

1. Do you think that exercise helps people to learn and remember better?
2. Can you think of other benefits from exercise?
3. What benefits are most important to you?

7 We had a great time!

1 SNAPSHOT

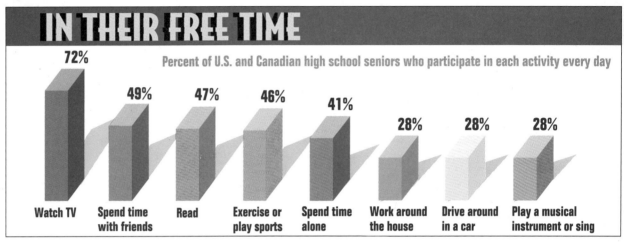

IN THEIR FREE TIME

Percent of U.S. and Canadian high school seniors who participate in each activity every day

72% Watch TV
49% Spend time with friends
47% Read
46% Exercise or play sports
41% Spend time alone
28% Work around the house
28% Drive around in a car
28% Play a musical instrument or sing

Source: University of Michigan, Institute for Social Research

Complete these tasks and talk about them.

Which of these activities do you do every day?
List three other activities you like to do almost every day.
Put the activities you do in order: from the most interesting to the least interesting.

2 CONVERSATION *The weekend*

A Listen and practice.

Chris: So, what did you do this weekend, Kate?
Kate: Oh, Diane and I went for a drive in the country on Saturday.
Chris: That sounds nice. Where did you go?
Kate: We drove to the lake and had a picnic. We had a great time! How about you? Did you do anything special?
Chris: Not really. I just worked on my car all day.
Kate: That old thing! Why don't you just buy a new one?
Chris: But then what would I do every weekend?

CLASS AUDIO ONLY ▶ **B** Listen to Kate talk about her activities on Sunday.

1. What did she do?
2. Where did she go?

40

We had a great time!

This unit practices describing daily, weekend, and leisure activities as well as vacations. It introduces the past tense in Wh- and yes/no questions and statements with regular and irregular verbs.

Cycle 1, Exercises 1–7

1 SNAPSHOT *In their free time*

This graph introduces the theme of leisure time; it also presents useful verbs for talking about daily activities.

- Books closed. Introduce the theme of leisure or free-time activities by brainstorming with the Ss on which activities they usually do after school or work every day. Write Ss' suggestions on the board, like this:

Daily leisure activities

exercise	study and do homework
watch TV	meet friends for coffee
read	listen to music

- Books open. Ss read over the information in the graph; if necessary, explain any new words or expressions:

> **free time** = the time when you aren't working or doing other duties
> **high school seniors** = students in the last year (twelfth grade) of high school or secondary school in the U.S. and Canada; most are 17–18 years old
> **work around the house** = do household chores
> **drive around** = drive in a car for the fun of it, usually not going anywhere specific

- Go over the three tasks. For the third task, explain how to rank the activities: Ss write *1* for the most interesting activity to *8* for the least interesting.

- Allow Ss to work individually for a few minutes to complete the tasks. Go around the class and give help as needed.

- As a pair or group activity, Ss take turns reading the questions and sharing their answers.

- Check Ss' answers like this:

First question: Take a class poll by eliciting responses through a show of hands on which activities Ss do every day.

Second question: Tell pairs or groups to look over their lists again and to vote on the three most popular activities they like to do almost every day; one S from each pair or group writes their three choices on the board.

Third question: Ask pairs or groups to share their top three choices for the most interesting and least interesting activities in the graph.

2 CONVERSATION *The weekend*

This exercise introduces the past tense of regular and irregular verbs through a conversation about the weekend.

(*Note:* If possible, Exercises 2–6 should be scheduled near the start of the week: After the past tense has been presented and practiced in Exercise 3, Ss will be given the chance to talk about their own weekends in Exercise 6.)

A 🔊

- Books closed. Set the scene: Chris and Kate are talking about their weekends. Ask Ss to listen to what each person did. Ss don't need to take notes.

- Play the audio program. Then ask Ss to name some of the activities that Chris and Kate talked about. Write any correct responses on the board.

- Books open. Play the audio program again once or twice. Ss listen and look at the pictures or read along if they wish. Then go over the conversation line by line. Explain any new vocabulary (e.g., *in the country, lake*).

(*Note:* The modal *would* is used in the last line of the dialog only as part of an expression. In the last two lines, Kate makes a suggestion ("Why don't you just . . . ?"). Chris's response is intended to be humorous, implying that he works on his car because he has nothing else to do – not because it's old and in need of repairs.

B 🔊

- Read the two questions aloud to help Ss focus their listening. Play the second part of the audio program once or twice.

Audio script

> KATE: Did you do anything on Sunday, Chris?
> CHRIS: No, I just stayed home all day. What about you, Kate? What did you do?
> KATE: I met some friends.
> CHRIS: Oh, where did you go?
> KATE: We went to a great outdoor concert. Then we had dinner out and went dancing.
> CHRIS: It sounds like you had a busy weekend!
> KATE: Yeah, I guess I did.

- Have Ss compare answers in small groups. Then check answers around the class.

Answers

> 1. She met some friends.
> 2. She went to a (great outdoor) concert, had dinner out, and went dancing.

3 GRAMMAR FOCUS *Past tense*

🔊 This grammar focus practices the past tense in questions and statements with regular and irregular verbs.

■ Use the audio program to present the questions, statements, and verb forms in the boxes. Point out the difference between regular and irregular verbs in English:

1. Explain that many verbs have regular past forms that end in *-ed*. Go over the regular verbs in the right-hand box. Write additional examples on the board to illustrate how to change the simple form to the past tense – *play/play**ed**, enjoy/enjoy**ed**, dance/danc**ed***. Present the pronunciation rules for regular past forms in the appendix in the Student's Book.

2. Explain that some verbs have irregular past forms that need to be memorized. Again, ask Ss to look at the appendix, this time going over the list of irregular verb past forms. Tell Ss to refer to this list whenever they need to.

■ Explain the use of the auxiliary verb *did* in the past tense (e.g., *Did* you do/go . . . ? Yes, I *did.*/What *did* you do . . . ?/Where *did* you go . . . ?). Give other examples, write them on the board, and mark stress patterns over the words, using different colored chalk or by inserting accent marks – for example:

Q: *Did you **play** any **sports** on **Sa**turday?*
A: *Yes, I **did**. I **played ten**nis with my **friend**.*
Q: ***What** did you **eat** for **break**fast?*
A: *I **had** some **ce**real and **toast**.*
Q: ***Where** did you **go yes**terday?*
A: *I **came** to **school**.*

■ Play the audio program again, this time pausing it after each question and response; Ss repeat to practice stress-timed intonation once more.

A

■ Go over the task: Ss complete the conversation individually and then compare answers with a partner.

Check answers around the class before pairs practice the conversations together.

Answers

1. A: **Did** you **go** out on Friday night?
   B: No, I **didn't**. I **invited** friends over, and I **cooked** dinner for them.
2. A: How **did** you **spend** your last birthday?
   B: I **had** a party. Everyone **enjoyed** it, but the neighbors **complained** about the noise.
3. A: What **did** you **do** last night?
   B: I **went** to the new Tom Cruise film. I **loved** it!
4. A: **Did** you **do** anything special over the weekend?
   B: Yes, I **did**. I **went** shopping. Unfortunately, I **spent** all my money. Now I'm broke!

Alternative presentation

■ Go through the task orally with the class by calling on volunteers to read their completed sentences aloud.

B *Pair work*

■ Model how to respond to the four questions in part A by having Ss ask you the questions and then giving detailed responses like these:

S1: Did you go out on Friday night?
T: No, I didn't. I stayed home and watched a video. I saw *Star Wars* again, and it was still really good.
S2: How did you spend your last birthday?
T: Oh, my whole family took me out to dinner. We had delicious Chinese food at a new restaurant downtown. We had a great time!

■ Before pairs begin the practice, explain that if a S feels a question is too personal, he or she may just make up an answer or respond with "I'd rather not say."

Optional activity: *Game – Tic-Tac-Toe*

■ See page T-147.

4 PRONUNCIATION *Reduced forms of* did you

This exercise presents the reduced form and blending of *did* with the pronoun *you,* a normal feature of colloquial spoken English. It is more important to be able to recognize (i.e., hear) reductions than to produce them. Therefore, don't force Ss to produce reductions if they have too much trouble or think it sounds strange.

A 🔊

■ Play the audio program. Point out the reduced forms and ask Ss to practice saying the sentences using the reductions. Call on individual Ss around the class to check their use of the reduced forms. Then model the

pronunciation again, followed by the whole class repeating each time.

B *Pair work*

■ Go over the instructions: This time, Ss practice asking the questions in the grammar box in Exercise 3. Remind Ss again that they don't have to give true answers if they don't want to; encourage them, however, to give detailed answers whenever possible and to ask follow-up questions to get more information.

■ Walk around the class and give feedback on individual Ss' pronunciation and use of reductions.

3 GRAMMAR FOCUS

Past tense 💿

Did you **stay** home on Sunday?	Yes, I **did**. I **watched** a football game on TV. No, I **didn't**. I **invited** friends out to dinner.	*Regular verbs* invite → invit**ed** work → work**ed** stay → stay**ed** study → stud**ied**
What **did** you **do** on Saturday?	I **worked** on my car. I **stayed** home and **studied**.	
Did you **do** anything special?	Yes, I **did**. I **drove** to the lake. No, I **didn't**. I **had** to baby-sit.	*Irregular verbs* drive → **drove** go → **went** have → **had**
Where **did** you **go** on Sunday?	I **saw** a good movie. I **went** to a concert.	see → **saw** spend → **spent**

For a list of irregular past forms and pronunciation rules for
regular past forms, see the appendix at the back of the book.

A Complete these conversations. Then practice with a partner.

1. A: .... you .... (go) out on Friday night?
   B: No, I .... I .... (invite) friends over,
   and I .... (cook) dinner for them.

2. A: How .... you .... (spend) your last birthday?
   B: I .... (have) a party. Everyone .... (enjoy) it,
   but the neighbors .... (complain) about the noise.

3. A: What .... you .... (do) last night?
   B: I .... (go) to the new Tom Cruise film.
   I .... (love) it!

4. A: .... you .... (do) anything special over the weekend?
   B: Yes, I .... I .... (go) shopping. Unfortunately,
   I .... (spend) all my money. Now I'm broke!

B *Pair work* Take turns asking the questions in part A.
Give your own information when answering.

4 PRONUNCIATION *Reduced forms of* did you

A 💿 Listen and practice. Notice how **did you** is reduced in
the following questions.

[dɪdʒə]
Did you have a good time?

[wədɪdʒə]
What did you do last night?

B *Pair work* Practice the questions in the grammar box in Exercise 3.
Pay attention to the pronunciation of **did you**.

5 WORD POWER Collocation

A Find two other words or phrases from the list that are usually paired with each verb.

an art exhibition	a vacation	a party	a trip	shopping
a lot of fun	the dishes	dancing	a play	the laundry

did	*housework*		
went	*swimming*		
had	*a good time*		
saw	*a movie*		
took	*a day off*		

B Write five sentences using words from the list.

I saw a movie last weekend.

6 ANY QUESTIONS?

Group work Take turns. One student makes a statement about the weekend. Other students ask questions. Each student answers at least four questions.

A: I went dancing on Saturday night.
B: **Where** did you go?
A: To the Rock-it Club.
C: **Who** did you go with?
A: I went with my brother.
D: **What time** did you go?
A: We went at around 10:00.
E: **How** did you like it?
A: . . .

7 LISTENING

A Listen to John and Laura describe what they did last night. Check (✓) the correct information about each person.

B Listen to the conversation again. What did each person do? Take notes. Then take turns telling their stories to a partner.

	John	Laura
had a boring time	☐	☐
had a good time	☐	☐
met someone interesting	☐	☐
got home late	☐	☐

5 WORD POWER Collocation

This exercise practices making collocations, also known as "word partners."

A

■ Explain the task by presenting the verbs and the examples given in the chart. Then pronounce the words and phrases listed above it. Ss repeat. Explain any new vocabulary (e.g., *the dishes, the laundry*).

■ Ss work individually to match each verb with two more words or phrases. (*Note:* If Ss find this task very difficult, you may wish to allow them to use their dictionaries.) When Ss finish, have them compare answers with a partner.

■ Check answers around the class.

Answers

did	housework	**the dishes**	**the laundry**
went	swimming	**dancing**	**shopping**
had	a good time	**a lot of fun**	**a party**
saw	a movie	**an art exhibition**	**a play**
took	a day off	**a vacation**	**a trip**

B

■ Present the task and read the example sentence aloud. Ss do the task individually. Then Ss form small groups, taking turns reading their five sentences aloud.

6 ANY QUESTIONS?

This is a fluency activity that provides practice with the past tense as well as practice in an essential conversational skill: showing interest in what someone is saying by asking follow-up questions in a lively manner.

(*Note:* This type of activity could be practiced regularly to promote conversational fluency.)

Group work

■ Model the task by asking a S to make a statement about something he or she did on the weekend. Then model how to ask follow-up questions, like this:

S1: I went for a drive on Sunday.
T: Where did you go?
S1: I went to the mountains.
T: Did you have a good time?
S1: Yes, I did.

Ss repeat the follow-up questions. Elicit other questions until at least four have been asked.

■ Model the example dialog with four Ss. Then Ss form groups and try the activity. Since this is a fluency activity, give help only if it is really needed.

7 LISTENING

This exercise practices making inferences and listening for key words to get the gist of a conversation.

A

■ Read aloud the instructions to set the scene. Then play the audio program once. Ss only listen.

Audio script

LAURA: So, what did you do last night, John?
JOHN: Uh, I went to my boss's house for dinner.
LAURA: Really? How was it?
JOHN: Oh, the food was OK, but the people weren't very interesting. They talked about football all night, and I hate football. Then we watched some boring sports videos. I didn't get home until after midnight.
LAURA: Well, that doesn't sound like much fun. Gee, I had a great time last night! I went to a party and met an old school friend of mine. We haven't seen each other for years, so we had lots to talk about. We stayed at the party all night!
JOHN: Hmm, it sounds like you had a much better time than I did.
LAURA: Yeah. I guess you're right!

■ Play the audio program again. This time, Ss check the correct information in the chart.

■ Have Ss compare answers with a partner.
■ Check answers around the class.

Answers

	John	Laura
had a boring time	✓	
had a good time		✓
met someone interesting		✓
got home late	✓	✓

B

■ Read the instructions aloud. Make sure Ss understand that this is a note-taking task. Explain that they will need to use their notes for the story-telling activity.

■ Play the audio program again. Then Ss form pairs and use their notes to retell the stories.

 **Workbook**

Ss complete Exercises 1–6 on pages 37–39 in the Workbook for end-of-class work or for homework. (Answers can be found on page T-181 of the Workbook Answer Key in this Teacher's Edition.)

8 CONVERSATION On vacation

🔊 This conversation presents the past tense of *be* in questions and statements.

■ Books closed. Set the scene: Two friends are talking about a vacation. Write these focus questions on the board:

Where did Celia go? (She went to the United States.)
How long was she there? (About three weeks)
How was the weather? (OK most of the time, but it snowed a lot in Chicago)
What was the best thing about her trip? (She liked Nashville the best.)

(*Note:* Chicago is in Illinois, a midwestern state; the Midwest is often referred to as "the most American region in the U.S.," and Chicago has been called the most American city. Nashville is the capital of Tennessee,

located in the southeastern part of the U.S.; it is the center of country music and the home of the famous Grand Ole Opry theater and many country music stars.)

■ Play the audio program. Elicit Ss' answers to the questions on the board.

■ Books open. Play the audio program again as Ss look at the pictures and the dialog. Then go over the conversation line by line and explain any words or expressions that the Ss still don't understand.

■ Ss practice the conversation in pairs.

■ **Optional:** Ask for volunteers to come up to the front of the class and try the conversation again without looking at their books. Encourage them to use their own words to keep the conversation going.

9 GRAMMAR FOCUS Past tense of be

🔊 This grammar focus practices the past tense of *be* in questions and statements.

■ Use the audio program to present the questions, statements, and contractions. Point out that *was not* becomes *wasn't* in its contracted form and that *were not* becomes *weren't*.

■ Play the audio program again, pausing after each question, statement, and contraction to give Ss time to repeat.

■ Present the past tense of *be* by conjugating the verb on the board, like this:

Singular	*Plural*
I was	we were
you were	you were
he/she/it was	they were

Then point to one of the forms and call on a S to make up a question with it. That S then asks another S in the class to respond, like this:

T: (*pointing to* you were *singular*) Joong, please make a question with this and ask another student your question.
S1: Were you out late last night, Andy?
S2: No, I wasn't. Were you at the game last Saturday, Dick?
S3: Yes, I was.
T: (*pointing to* he was) Kelly.
S4: Was he at the game last Saturday, Hui?
T: (*pointing to* they)
S5: Yes, he was. Luiz, were Gloria and Paolo in class yesterday?
S6: No, they weren't.

■ Do a similar practice with "How long . . . ?" and "How . . . ?" by giving cues and having Ss make up additional questions to ask others around the class.

■ Allow Ss to work alone or in pairs to complete the task. Check Ss' answers before they practice the conversations.

Answers

1. A: How long **were** your parents in Europe?
   B: They **were** there for a month.
   A: **Were** they in London the whole time?
   B: No, they **weren't.** They also went to Paris and Madrid.

2. A: **Were** you away last weekend?
   B: Yes, I **was.** I **was** in San Francisco.
   A: How **was** it?
   B: It **was** great!
   A: How **was** the weather?
   B: Oh, it **was** foggy and cool as usual.

3. A: I **was** in Istanbul last summer.
   B: Really? How long **were** you there?
   A: For six weeks.
   B: **Were** you there on business or on vacation?
   A: I **was** there on business.

(*Note:* Istanbul is a seaport in northwestern Turkey.)

Alternative presentation

■ Go through the task orally with the class by calling on individual Ss to read aloud and complete one sentence each in the conversations.

■ **Optional:** Pairs change partners. This time, tell them to cover the conversations and look at the pictures for cues while practicing similar conversations together.

Optional activity: *Game – Twenty questions*

■ See page T-28.

8 CONVERSATION *On vacation*

🔊 Listen and practice.

Mike: Hi, Celia! How was your trip to the
United States?
Celia: It was terrific. I really enjoyed it.
Mike: Great. How long were you away?
Celia: I was there for about three weeks.
Mike: That's a long time! Was the
weather OK?
Celia: Yes, most of the time. But it snowed
a lot in Chicago.
Mike: So, what was the best thing about
your trip?
Celia: Oh, that's difficult to say. But I guess
I liked Nashville the best.

9 GRAMMAR FOCUS

Past tense of be 🔊

Were you away last week?	Yes, I **was**.
Was your brother away . . . ?	No, he **wasn't**.
Were you and your sister away . . . ?	Yes, we **were**.
Were your parents away . . . ?	No, they **weren't**.
How long **were** you away?	I **was** away for three weeks.
How **was** your vacation?	It **was** terrific!

Contractions
was not = wasn't
were not = weren't

Complete these conversations. Then practice with a partner.

1. A: How long .... your parents in Europe?
   B: They .... there for a month.
   A: .... they in London the whole time?
   B: No, they .... They also went to Paris
   and Madrid.

2. A: .... you away last weekend?
   B: Yes, I .... I .... in San Francisco.
   A: How .... it?
   B: It .... great!
   A: How .... the weather?
   B: Oh, it .... foggy and cool as usual.

3. A: I .... in Istanbul last summer.
   B: Really? How long .... you there?
   A: For six weeks.
   B: .... you there on business or on vacation?
   A: I .... there on business.

10 VACATIONS

A *Group work* Take turns talking about vacations.
Ask these questions and others of your own.

Where did you spend your last vacation?
How long were you away?
Were you with your family?
What did you do there?

How was the weather? the food?
Did you buy anything?
Do you want to go there again?

interchange 7

Vacation photos

Use the vacation photos
to tell a story. Student A
turns to page IC-9.
Student B turns
to page IC-10.

B *Class activity* Who in your group had the most
interesting vacation? Tell the class who and why.

11 LISTENING

CLASS
AUDIO
ONLY

Listen to Jason and Barbara talk about their vacations.
Complete the chart.

	Vacation place	Enjoyed it?		Reason(s)
		Yes	**No**	
Jason	....	☐	☐	....
Barbara	....	☐	☐	....

12 WRITING

A Read this postcard.

Dear Richard,
Greetings from Acapulco! I'm having a
great time! Yesterday I went on a tour
of the city, and today I went shopping.
I bought some beautiful jewelry. Oh,
and last night, I heard some Mariachi
singers on the street. They were terrific.
That's all for now.

Love,
Kathy

B *Pair work* Write a postcard to a partner about your last vacation
or an interesting place you visited recently. Then exchange postcards.

10 VACATIONS

This open-ended fluency activity is a follow-up to Exercises 3, 6, and 9. The purpose here is to get Ss to give as much information as they can about a real vacation they have taken.

A Group work

- Go over the instructions and questions. Have Ss repeat each question.

- With the class, do some quick brainstorming on the words *weather* and *food* and write their responses on the board for the groups to use, like this:

	Weather	**Food**
adjectives(with be) =	*rainy, sunny, cool, warm, hot, dry, humid, wet, OK, nice, good, bad, horrible*	*good, delicious, bad, terrible, fine, terrific, spicy, bland, unusual*
verbs =	*rain, snow*	*cook, eat, buy*

- Model the task by talking about a vacation you have taken. Encourage Ss to ask appropriate questions from among those given in the text as well as some of their own.

- Ss work in small groups and take turns talking about their vacations. Go around the class and give help wherever needed.

B Class activity

- Groups vote on whose vacation was the most interesting and then tell the class about it. Encourage others to ask questions to show interest and to get more information.

 INTERCHANGE 7 Vacation photos

See pages T-114 and T-115 in this Teacher's Edition for notes.

Optional activity: *Chain story – A terrible day!*

- See page T-149.

11 LISTENING

This exercise practices listening for key words and reasons.

- Books closed. Set the scene: Two friends, Jason and Barbara, are talking about their vacations. Play the audio program once. Ss only listen.

Audio script

> BARBARA: Jason! Hi! Welcome back. You were away last week, right?
> JASON: Yeah, I was on vacation.
> BARBARA: Where did you go?
> JASON: I went to San Francisco.
> BARBARA: Nice! How was it?
> JASON: Oh, I loved it!
> BARBARA: What did you like most about it?
> JASON: Well, San Francisco is such a beautiful place. And the weather was actually pretty nice!
> BARBARA: Well, that sounds more exciting than my last vacation.
> JASON: What did you do, Barbara?
> BARBARA: I just stayed home. I couldn't afford to take a trip anywhere.

> JASON: Oh, that's too bad.
> BARBARA: Oh, not really. I actually enjoyed my vacation. I went to the gym every day, and I lost three pounds!
> JASON: Well, that's great. Good for you!

- Books open. Explain the task: Ss write down key words and phrases in the chart. Point out that Ss don't have to write full sentences for the "Reason(s)." Play the audio program again once or twice. Ss complete the chart.

- Have Ss compare answers in pairs or groups. Then check answers around the class.

Answers

	Vacation place	*Enjoyed it?*	*Reason(s)*
Jason	San Francisco	Yes	beautiful place; weather nice
Barbara	home	Yes	went to gym every day; lost 3 pounds

12 WRITING

This exercise practices reading and then writing a short narrative on a postcard while using the past tense.

A

- Have Ss read the example postcard silently. Use the picture to help explain some of the new vocabulary.

B Pair work

- Go over the task. Tell Ss to use the questions in Exercise 10 to help make notes on the topic.

- Point out some ways to end a postcard (e.g., Take care./Wish you were here./See you soon.) and write them on the board.

- Ss use their notes to write first drafts. Walk around the class and check Ss' work. Then Ss revise their drafts.

- Pairs (preferably those Ss who did not work together in Exercise 10) exchange and read each other's postcards.

13 READING *Vacation postcards*

This exercise presents descriptions of three interesting vacations; it also provides practice in scanning for main ideas and making inferences.

- Have Ss cover the writing on the postcards and look only at the three pictures of vacation places – Egypt, Hawaii, and Alaska. Ask the pre-reading question "What do you think each person did on his or her vacation?" and elicit ideas around the class.

Alternative presentation

- This reading exercise could be assigned for homework. If it is, encourage Ss to use their dictionaries at home to check the meanings of any words whose meanings they can't guess from context.

- **Optional:** Have any Ss taken a vacation to any of these three places? If so, ask them to take the "hot seat" in the front of the class and answer any questions the other Ss may have.

A

- Go over the task. Remind Ss to try to guess the meanings of any words they don't know and to circle any others they can't guess from context. Then Ss read the three postcards and check the true statements in the chart.

- Have Ss compare answers in pairs or small groups. Also, encourage Ss to ask their partners for the meanings of any words they circled.

- Check any vocabulary that Ss still can't guess or simply don't understand – for example:

Margaret's postcard
desert = land covered with sand or rocks, where there is very little rain and not many plants
dig in . . . ruins = carefully remove earth from buried objects that belonged to people who lived long ago

Sue's postcard
spa = a place where people go to get healthier by doing exercises, eating nutritious food, and so on
Koloa = a town on Hawaii's northernmost island of Kauai
meditated = gave attention to only one thing, either as a religious activity or as a way of becoming calm and relaxed
vegetarian food = vegetables, grains, and fruit (no meat, fish, or dairy products)
snorkeling = a water sport that involves swimming while looking at the bottom of the ocean through a mask and breathing through an air tube

Kevin's postcard
the Arctic National Wildlife Refuge = a large area in northern Alaska where animals are given special protection from humans and other environmental dangers
hiked = walked a long distance
rafts = small rubber or plastic boats filled with air
the Arctic Ocean = an ocean north of North America, Asia, and the Arctic Circle
Anchorage = a seaport town in southern Alaska

- Check Ss' answers around the class.

Answers

1. –	2. ✓	3. –	4. ✓	5. –	6. –

- **Optional:** Have Ss work in groups to correct the information in the false statements.

B *Group work*

- Ss form groups and take turns asking and answering each question. Go around the class and give help as needed.

- To check answers, have groups share their responses with the rest of the class.

Answers

1. Margaret
2. Kevin
3. Sue
4. Ss' answers will vary.

Optional activities

1 *Vacation snapshots and souvenirs*

Preparation: Ask Ss to bring real vacation photos along with any other things that they have from a trip (e.g., guidebooks, brochures, souvenirs) to share with others in the class.

- Ss form small groups. Then they take turns sharing their photos and other souvenirs while telling one another about their vacations.

2 *Game – Word Bingo*
- See page T-33.

3 *Crossword puzzle*
- See page T-146.

4 *Picture story*
- See page T-65.

 Workbook

Tell Ss to do Exercises 7–11 on pages 40–42 in the Workbook or assign them as homework. Have Ss work in small groups to compare answers. Elicit responses around the class. (Answers can be found on page T-181 of the Workbook Answer Key in this Teacher's Edition.)

13 *READING* Vacation postcards

Look at the pictures. What do you think each person did on his or her vacation?

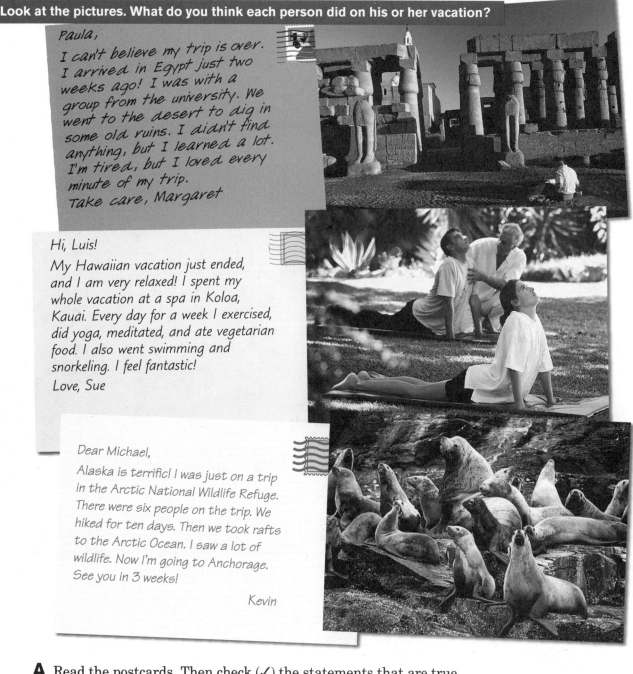

Paula,
I can't believe my trip is over. I arrived in Egypt just two weeks ago! I was with a group from the university. We went to the desert to dig in some old ruins. I didn't find anything, but I learned a lot. I'm tired, but I loved every minute of my trip.
Take care, Margaret

Hi, Luis!
My Hawaiian vacation just ended, and I am very relaxed! I spent my whole vacation at a spa in Koloa, Kauai. Every day for a week I exercised, did yoga, meditated, and ate vegetarian food. I also went swimming and snorkeling. I feel fantastic!
Love, Sue

Dear Michael,
Alaska is terrific! I was just on a trip in the Arctic National Wildlife Refuge. There were six people on the trip. We hiked for ten days. Then we took rafts to the Arctic Ocean. I saw a lot of wildlife. Now I'm going to Anchorage. See you in 3 weeks!
Kevin

A Read the postcards. Then check (✓) the statements that are true.

☐ 1. Margaret had a very relaxing vacation.
☐ 2. Margaret enjoyed her vacation.
☐ 3. Sue was in Hawaii for two weeks.
☐ 4. Sue got a lot of exercise.
☐ 5. Kevin spent his vacation alone.
☐ 6. Kevin's vacation is over.

B *Group work* Talk about these questions. Explain your answers.

1. Which person learned a lot on vacation?
2. Who had a vacation that was full of adventure?
3. Who had a very relaxing vacation?
4. Which vacation sounds the most interesting to you?

8 How do you like the neighborhood?

1 WORD POWER Places

A Match the words and the definitions. Then practice asking the questions with a partner.

What's a . . . ?

1. barber shop ....
2. laundromat ....
3. library ....
4. stationery store ....
5. travel agency ....
6. grocery store ....
7. theater ....

It's a place where you . . .

a. wash and dry clothes.
b. buy food.
c. buy cards and paper.
d. get a haircut.
e. see a movie or play.
f. make reservations for a trip.
g. borrow books.

B *Pair work* Write definitions for these places.

bank	coffee shop	drugstore	gym	post office
bookstore	dance club	gas station	hotel	restaurant

> *It's a place where you keep your money. (bank)*

C *Group work* Read your definitions in groups. Can others guess what each place is?

2 CONVERSATION The neighborhood

Listen and practice.

Jack: Excuse me. I'm your new neighbor, Jack. I just moved in.
Woman: Oh. Yes?
Jack: I'm looking for a grocery store. Are there any around here?
Woman: Yes, there are some on Pine Street.
Jack: OK. And is there a laundromat near here?
Woman: Well, I think there's one across from the shopping center.
Jack: Thank you.
Woman: By the way, there's a barber shop in the shopping center, too.
Jack: A barber shop?

46

How do you like the neighborhood?

This unit introduces language used to talk about places. It presents several grammar points: there is/there are, prepositions for describing locations, and uncountable and countable nouns with how much and how many.

Cycle 1, Exercises 1–6

1 WORD POWER Places

This exercise presents useful vocabulary related to neighborhood places.

A

(*Note:* It is not necessary to pre-teach the vocabulary here since the task itself enables Ss to learn the new words by themselves.)

- Model how to do the task by matching the first item on the list, i.e., "1. barber shop" with "d. get a haircut." Write the answer *d* on the blank next to "barber shop."
- Have Ss work individually to complete the task.
- Before pairs take turns asking the questions, check Ss' answers around the class. Do this by modeling the correct pronunciation for each word and the stress in each question and answer. Ask Ss to repeat for additional practice in using correct pronunciation with stress-timed intonation, like this:

  Q: **What's** a **bar**ber shop?
  A: It's a **place** where you **get** a **hair**cut.

Answers

1. d	2. a	3. g	4. c	5. f	6. b	7. e

- In pairs, Ss practice asking the questions.

B *Pair work*

- Model the pronunciation of the ten place names.
- Present the example definition for *bank:* "It's a place where you keep your money." Then elicit additional possible definitions from the class and write the better ones on the board.

- Ss work in pairs and write a definition for each place. If they aren't sure about the definition, tell them to make an educated guess. (*Note:* The task will be more challenging if Ss don't use their dictionaries.)
- Check Ss' answers. Write the best definitions on the board.

Possible answers

> *bank:* It's a place where you keep your money.
> *bookstore:* It's a place where you buy books and magazines.
> *coffee shop:* It's a place where you have coffee, juice, soft drinks, and snacks, or eat an informal/inexpensive meal.
> *dance club:* It's a place where you dance to live music or to CDs.
> *drugstore:* It's a place where you buy medicine and toiletries.
> *gas station:* It's a place where you get gas for your car.
> *gym:* It's a place where you work out/exercise and play sports.
> *hotel:* It's a place where you stay overnight away from home.
> *post office:* It's a place where you buy stamps and mail letters and packages.
> *restaurant:* It's a place where you eat a full/formal meal.

C *Group work*

- Write the following structure and question on the board for Ss to use in this follow-up activity:

  It's a place where you . . . . What is it?

- Model the task with the whole class. Have two or three pairs from part B form new groups of four or six. Then pairs take turns reading their definitions.

2 CONVERSATION The neighborhood

This exercise presents questions and responses with *there is/there are* in the context of talking about locations of places in a neighborhood.

- Books closed. As a topic warm-up, write this question on the board:

  When you move into a new neighborhood, what kinds of things do you need to ask about?

  Then ask the question to elicit Ss' suggestions and write them on the board.
- Tell the class to listen to someone who just moved into a new neighborhood. Play the audio program once.

- Find out which key words or phrases Ss heard on the audio program; write them on one side of the board. Ask the class to compare these words with the others that they had suggested earlier.
- Books open. Tell Ss to look at the picture as they listen to the audio program again.
- Present the conversation line by line. Ask Ss why the woman tells Jack about the barber shop. If they don't know, tell them to look again at the picture for a clue. (Answer: She thinks he needs a haircut.)
- Ss practice the conversation in pairs.

T-46

3 GRAMMAR FOCUS There is, there are; one, any, some

🔊 This grammar focus practices the structures *there is/there are* with the pronoun *one* and the determiners *any* and *some*. Also presented are prepositions for giving locations (e.g., *on, next to, across from*).

This is the first full presentation of *there is/there are* in questions and statements. These structures function as empty subjects. It might be helpful to point out the equivalence between sentences like these:

Statement with a singular noun
Structure: The . . . is . . . . = There is a . . . .
Examples: The laundromat is across from the shopping center. = There is a laundromat across from the shopping center.
Question: Is there a . . . ?
Response: Yes, there is./No, there isn't.

Statement with a plural noun
Structure: The . . . are . . . . = There are . . . .
Examples: The grocery stores are on Pine Street. = There are grocery stores on Pine Street.
Question: Are there any . . . ?
Response: Yes, there are./No, there aren't.

■ Use the audio program to present the language in the boxes. Point out that *one* replaces the singular noun phrase *a laundromat* and that *some* replaces the plural noun *grocery stores*. Explain that *any* is used with questions and negatives (i.e., indefinite) and that *some* is used with affirmative statements (i.e., definite). Also remind Ss that *but* is used to signal contrasting information.

■ Use the audio program again, this time pausing it to let Ss practice the questions and responses in the box. Ask about other places in your neighborhood or city to elicit answers with "There is a . . . ," "There is one . . . ," and "There are some . . . ." Use some of the places listed in the Word Power exercise on page 46 – for example:

Is there a barber shop near here?
Is there a theater around here?
Are there any bookstores near here?
Are there any restaurants around here?

■ Present the prepositions in the box and model their pronunciation. Ss repeat. Explain how these words are used for giving locations by pointing to some places on the map in part A of this grammar focus. Also, give some example sentences to illustrate the meaning and use of each preposition, like this:

There's a grocery store *next to* the drugstore. There are some hotels *on* Elm Street.

■ Ask questions around the class to elicit information about buildings on the school campus or in the neighborhood (e.g., "Is there a gym on campus?"/"Are there any restaurants on . . . Street?"). Write Ss' responses on the board, adding more examples of your own if necessary.

A

■ Go over the task. Ss work individually to write questions. Be sure Ss know they should include a preposition in each question. Write some examples on the board like these:

Is there a bank <u>opposite</u> the Jamison Hotel?
Are there any gas stations <u>on</u> Pine Street?

■ To check Ss' answers, elicit responses around the class.

Possible answers

See part B below.

B *Pair work*

This is a controlled fluency activity that provides extra oral practice.

■ Go over the example A/B dialog with the class. Then Ss form pairs and take turns asking each other their questions. Go around the class and give help as needed.

Possible answers

A: Is there a bank near here/around here/on Pine Street/close to the hotel?
B: Yes, there is. There's one across from/opposite/in front of the hotel.
A: Are there any gas stations near here/around here/on Pine Street?
B: No, there aren't, but there's one on the corner of First and Main.
A: Is there a department store around here/near here/close to the park/on Main Street?
B: Yes, there is. There's one next to the gym/across from the park.
A: Are there any grocery stores around here/near here/on Pine Street?
B: Yes, there are. There are some on Pine Street.
A: Is there a gym near here/around here/on Elm Street?
B: No, there isn't, but there's one on Main Street, between the post office and the department store.
A: Are there any hotels around here/near here?
B: No, there aren't. But there are some on Elm Street, close to the park.
A: Is there a laundromat around here/near here/close to the hotel/on First Avenue?
B: Yes, there is. There's one behind the post office.
A: Is there a pay phone near here/around here/close to the park/on Main Street?
B: Yes, there is. There's one across from the post office.
A: Is there a post office near here/around here/on Pine Street?
B: No, there isn't, but there's one on Main, in front of the park.
A: Are there any restaurants near here/around here/close to the hotel/on Maple Avenue?
B: Yes, there are. There's one on Maple Avenue and one on Elm Street.

Optional activity: *Game – Twenty questions*

■ See page T-28.

3 GRAMMAR FOCUS

There is, there are; one, any, some 🔊

Is there a laundromat near here?
    Yes, **there is.** There's **one** across from the shopping center.
    No, **there isn't**, but there's **one** next to the library.

Are there any grocery stores around here?
    Yes, **there are.** There are **some** on Pine Street.
    No, **there aren't**, but there are **some** on Third Avenue.

Prepositions
on
next to
across from/opposite
in front of
in back of/behind
near/close to
between
on the corner of

A Write questions about these places in the neighborhood map below.

a bank   a department store   a gym   a laundromat   a post office
gas stations   grocery stores   hotels   a pay phone   restaurants

Is there a pay phone around here?

Are there any restaurants on Maple Avenue?

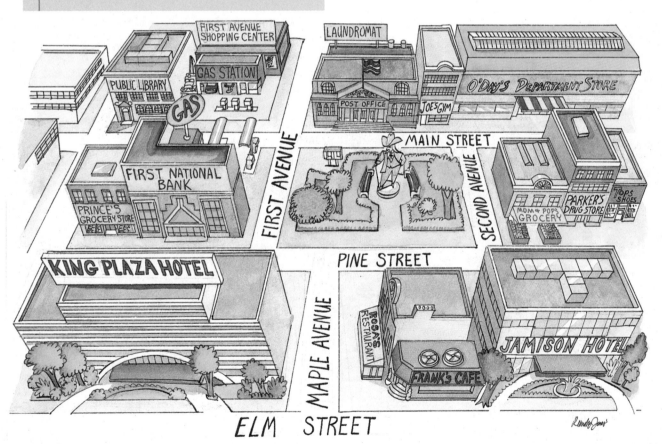

B *Pair work* Ask and answer the questions you wrote in part A.

A: Is there a pay phone around here?
B: Yes, there is. There's one across from the post office.

4 PRONUNCIATION *Reduced forms of* there is/there are

 Listen and practice. Notice how **there is** and **there are** are reduced in conversation.

There's a gym across from the shopping center.
There's a bookstore near the laundromat.

There are some restaurants on Elm Street.
There are some grocery stores across from the post office.

5 IN YOUR NEIGHBORHOOD

Group work Take turns asking and answering questions about places like these in your neighborhood.

a bookstore	dance clubs	a coffee shop	a music store	stationery stores
a gym	drugstores	movie theaters	a pay phone	a travel agency

A: Is there a good bookstore in your neighborhood?
B: . . .
A: And are there any drugstores?
B: . . .

useful expressions

Sorry, I don't know.
I'm not sure, but I think . . . .
Of course. There's one . . . .

6 LISTENING

CLASS
AUDIO
ONLY

 Some hotel guests are asking about places to visit in the neighborhood. Complete the chart.

Place	Location	Interesting?	
		Yes	No
Hard Rock Cafe	....	☐	☐
Science Museum	....	☐	☐
Aquarium	....	☐	☐

4 PRONUNCIATION *Reduced forms of* there is/there are

This exercise practices producing the reduced forms of *there is/there are*.

- Play the audio program once or twice. Ss listen and repeat. Point out that both *there is* and *there are* are often reduced in conversation. Explain also that although *there is* is often contracted in writing *(there's)*, *there are* is not.

5 IN YOUR NEIGHBORHOOD

This is a fluency activity and a follow-up to Exercises 3 and 4. Here, the purpose is to get Ss to respond quickly with correct pronunciation while giving facts about their own neighborhoods.

Group work

- Explain the activity by modeling how to use the example dialog and cues. Ask a volunteer to start with A's part while you take B's, like this:

  S: Is there a good bookstore in your neighborhood?
  T: Yes, there is. There's one on Fourth Street. It's called Just Books, and it's right next to a popular coffee shop called Perks. They have really great books there.
  S: And are there any drugstores?

  T: No, there aren't, but I think there are some downtown on Central Avenue. And how about your neighborhood? Is there a good bookstore . . . ?

- Go over the list of places. (*Note:* All of these words were presented in Exercises 1 and 3 except for *a music store.*) Then elicit additional places Ss may want to ask about in their classmates' neighborhoods. Write these on the board for Ss to use in their groups.
- Present the useful expressions. On the board, write other expressions of your own and those elicited from the class (e.g., Oh, I can't remember./Gee, I have no idea.).
- Ss practice the activity in small groups.

6 LISTENING

This exercise practices listening for locations of places and whether or not the places are interesting.

- Books closed. Ask the class "What places do you want to know about when visiting a city for the first time?" Write Ss' responses on the board.
- Set the scene: Two guests are asking the hotel clerk about some places to visit in the neighborhood. Play the audio program once. Ss listen.

Audio script

CLERK: Good morning. Can I help you?
GUEST 1: Yes. We need some directions.
CLERK: Sure. What are you looking for?
GUEST 1: Well, first of all, we're looking for the Hard Rock Cafe. How far is it from here?
CLERK: Oh, it's just a few minutes from here – right across from the National Bank.
GUEST 2: The National Bank on Park Avenue?
CLERK: Yes, that's the one.
GUEST 2: Is the Hard Rock Cafe a nice place?
CLERK: Well, I think so. The food is good, and there are some interesting things to look at in the restaurant – like one of Elvis's cars.
GUEST 2: Great! And where is the Science Museum?
CLERK: Well, that's near City Hall.
GUEST 1: Near City Hall. OK, I know where that is. And what's the museum like?
CLERK: Actually, it's not very good. It's small, and there isn't a lot to see there. It's really for young kids.
GUEST 1: Oh, then maybe we won't go there.
GUEST 2: Mmm, one last question – is there an aquarium in the city?

CLERK: Yes, there's a very good one. It's only about six blocks from here. It's in the park next to the train station.
GUEST 2: Oh, next to the train station.
CLERK: Yes. Definitely visit the aquarium.
GUEST 1: Great! Thanks a lot.
CLERK: You're welcome. Have a good day!

- Books open. Go over the task and play the audio program again. Ss complete the chart. Check answers around the class.

Answers

Place	Location	Interesting?
Hard Rock Cafe	across from the National Bank on Park Avenue	Yes
Science Museum	near City Hall	No
Aquarium	in the park next to the train station	Yes

 *Workbook*

Assign Exercises 1–4 on pages 43–45 in the Workbook as in-class work or for homework. Ss compare answers in groups when all exercises have been completed. Assign one exercise to each group, who is then in charge of checking Ss' responses around the class on that same task. (Answers can be found on page T-182 of the Workbook Answer Key in this Teacher's Edition.)

Cycle 2, Exercises 7–11

7 *SNAPSHOT* 10 important things to look for in a community

This graphic introduces the topic of features that are considered important in a community.

■ Books closed. Introduce the topic of various aspects within a community by asking the Ss these questions:

What features would you like in your town or city? What things do you not want?

Write the most suitable answers on the board.

■ Explain these words before Ss read the Snapshot:

community = the people living in a certain area
crime = an action that is against the law: robbery, murder, and so on
unemployment = the number of people who don't have jobs
relatives = family members
public transportation = buses, subways, trains, and so on

■ Books open. Model how the decimal numbers should be read (e.g., 9.1 = "nine point one"). Ss read the information.

■ Read aloud the tasks. For the first task, make sure Ss know how to rank the ten items by writing on the board:

1 = the most important
2 = important (but not as much as 1) . . .
10 = the least important

■ Ss do the tasks and then compare answers.

■ **Optional:** As a follow-up to the first task, take a class poll (through a show of hands) on which three items were generally considered to be the most important and which three were the least important. For the second task, allow Ss to compare answers in groups of four; then group secretaries write their three best or most interesting suggestions on the board. Encourage groups to act quickly by making a rule that no answer can be written more than once; this also promotes a healthy competitive spirit among groups.

8 *CONVERSATION* Describing neighborhoods

This exercise presents *how much* with uncountable nouns (e.g., *crime*) and *how many* with countable nouns (e.g., *restaurants*).

A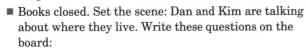

■ Books closed. Set the scene: Dan and Kim are talking about where they live. Write these questions on the board:

Where does Kim live? (In an apartment downtown)
What's it like? (There isn't much crime, but there is a lot of traffic.)
Where does Dan live? (In a house in the suburbs)
What's it like? (There isn't much to do there.)
What do Kim and Dan decide to do? (Trade places one weekend)

■ Play the first part of the audio program several times. Check Ss' answers to the questions on the board.

■ Books open. Refer to the pictures when presenting the conversation line by line. Explain any new words and expressions:

the suburbs = small towns outside a big city where people live but don't usually work
trouble = problem
trade places = here, to exchange homes

■ Model the pronunciation and stress in *down**town**, **sub**urbs,* and ***trou**ble.* Then Ss practice the conversation in pairs.

B

■ Read aloud the question that Ss need to focus their listening on. Then play the second part of the audio program once or twice. Ss take notes on additional information about Dan's and Kim's neighborhoods.

Audio script

DAN: How many restaurants are there in your neighborhood?
KIM: There are a lot, actually. There's a great pizza place on the corner. The pizzas are delicious and very cheap. And there's a good Chinese restaurant on the next block. Are there any good restaurants close to your place?
DAN: Unfortunately, there aren't any. But there is a big public park and a sports center just down the street.
KIM: Wow! You're really lucky!

■ If there's time, have pairs compare answers. Then check answers by eliciting Ss' responses around the class and writing them on the board.

Answers

Kim says there are a lot of restaurants in her neighborhood: There's a (great) pizza place on the corner; and there's a good Chinese restaurant on the next block.
Dan says there aren't any good restaurants close to his place.

7 SNAPSHOT

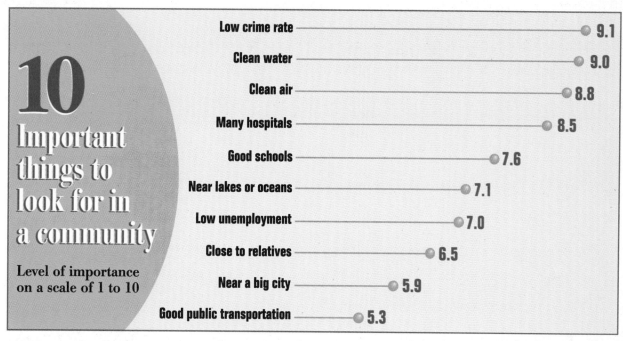

10
Important things to look for in a community

Level of importance on a scale of 1 to 10

Low crime rate ————————————————— 9.1
Clean water ————————————————— 9.0
Clean air ————————————————— 8.8
Many hospitals ————————————————— 8.5
Good schools ————————————— 7.6
Near lakes or oceans ————————— 7.1
Low unemployment ————————— 7.0
Close to relatives ——————— 6.5
Near a big city ————— 5.9
Good public transportation —— 5.3

Source: *Money* Magazine

Complete these tasks and talk about them.

What is important to you in a community? Rank the features above from the most important (1) to the least important (10).
List three other things you think are important in a community.

8 CONVERSATION *Describing neighborhoods*

A Listen and practice.

Dan: Where do you live, Kim?
Kim: I live in an apartment downtown.
Dan: Oh, that's convenient, but . . . how much crime is there?
Kim: Not much. But there is a *lot* of traffic. I can't stand the noise sometimes! Where do you live?
Dan: I have a house in the suburbs.
Kim: Oh, I bet it's really quiet. But is there much to do there?
Dan: No, not much. In fact, nothing ever really happens. That's the trouble.
Kim: Hey. Let's trade places one weekend!
Dan: OK. Great idea!

 B Listen to the rest of the conversation.

What do Dan and Kim say about restaurants in their neighborhoods?

9 GRAMMAR FOCUS

How much *and* how many

Uncountable nouns		Countable nouns	
How much crime is there?	There's **a lot**.	**How many** restaurants are there?	There are **a lot**.
	There's **a little**.		There are **a few**.
	There is**n't much**.		There are**n't many**.
	There is**n't any**.		There are**n't any**.
	There's **none**.		There are **none**.

A Write answers to these questions about your neighborhood.
Then practice with a partner.

1. How many apartment buildings are there? ....
2. How much traffic is there? ....
3. How many bookstores are there? ....
4. How much noise is there? ....
5. How many movie theaters are there? ....

B *Pair work* Write questions like those in part A about
these topics. Then ask and answer the questions.

crime   parks   pollution   restaurants   schools   stores

interchange 8

Neighborhood survey

Compare two
neighborhoods in
your city. Turn to
page IC-11.

10 WRITING

A *Group work* Talk about where you live.
Discuss these questions in groups.

Do you live in a house or an apartment?
Where is it?
How many rooms are there?
IIow much noise is there?
Are there any good restaurants nearby?
How many clubs/theaters/gyms are there
   in your neighborhood?
Is there any public transportation near
   your home?
How do you like it there?

B Write a paragraph about where you live.
Use the information you discussed in part A.

> *I live in a big apartment building in the city. There are two bedrooms,*
>
> *a living room, a dining room, and a kitchen. There's a lot of noise in*
>
> *my neighborhood because there's a dance club across from my building. . . .*

9 GRAMMAR FOCUS How much *and* how many

This exercise practices the structure *How much . . . is there?* with uncountable nouns (e.g., *crime*) and *How many . . . are there?* with countable nouns (e.g., *restaurants*). Certain quantity words, also known as quantity determiners (*a lot, a little/a few, much/many, any,* and *none*), are introduced here as well.

The distinction between countable and uncountable nouns is likely to be difficult for many Ss because:

1. Not all languages make this distinction.
2. For languages that make the distinction, words that are countable in English may be uncountable or vice versa.
3. Many nouns can be both countable and uncountable in English (e.g., *crimes/crime*).

■ Use the audio program to present the language in the boxes. Ss repeat. Then introduce the distinction between countable and uncountable nouns:

1. Explain that nouns taking a plural *-s* are thought of as discrete and countable units (e.g., *a restaurant/restaurants, a store/stores*). In fact, one can count them: one store, two stores, ten stores.
2. Contrast countable and uncountable nouns by explaining that uncountable nouns do not normally take a plural *-s* and are not thought of as discrete and countable units (e.g., *noise, traffic, pollution, crime*). We don't say "two traffics" or "many pollutions."
3. Point out that some nouns, however, can be both countable and uncountable. Write some examples like these on the board:

   Uncountable noun: There is a lot of _noise_ today.
   Countable noun: There are _two_ unusual _noises_ outside.

   Uncountable noun: _Crime_ is down this year.
   Countable noun: There are only _three_ _crimes_ this year so far in my neighborhood. Last year, there were _many_ crimes.

4. Clarify the fact that quantity words or determiners are used to describe differing amounts of countable and uncountable things. Put the following information on the board for Ss to copy into their notebooks; then elicit example sentences and write them on the board, too:

Quantity words used . . .
*with countable and uncountable nouns = _a lot, any, none_*
*only with uncountable nouns = _a little, much_*
*only with countable nouns = _a few, many_*

A

■ Explain the task by modeling how to answer the first question. Ss work individually and then compare answers in pairs. Elicit Ss' answers.

■ Before Ss work in pairs to take turns asking and answering the questions, check Ss' answers around the class.

Answers

> 1. There are a lot/a few/none./There aren't many/any.
> 2. There's a lot/a little/none./There isn't much/any.
> 3. There are a lot/a few/none./There aren't many/any.
> 4. There's a lot/a little/none./There isn't much/any.
> 5. There are a lot/a few/none./There aren't many/any.

B *Pair work*

■ Go over the instructions and the topics. To model the task, elicit "How many/much . . . ?" questions for the first two words in the list.

■ After Ss work individually to write questions, have them form pairs to take turns asking their questions. Then elicit Ss' responses around the class.

Answers

> How much crime is there?
> How many parks are there?
> How much pollution is there?
> How many restaurants are there?
> How many schools are there?
> How many stores are there?

Optional activity: *Game – What's the question?*
■ See page T-147.

 INTERCHANGE 8 Neighborhood survey
See page T-113 in this Teacher's Edition for notes.

10 WRITING

In this exercise, Ss practice talking and then writing about where they live.

A *Group work*

■ Go over the questions: Pronounce each one and have Ss repeat. To model the task, use the photo to ask the class some of the questions given here.

■ Divide the class into groups of four. Ss take turns asking and answering the questions. Encourage Ss to ask additional follow-up questions of their own.

B

■ Read aloud the example paragraph. Tell Ss to brainstorm their topics before beginning their compositions.

■ **Optional:** In pairs, Ss take turns reading their first drafts aloud. Then they make revisions to their drafts based on questions, comments, and ideas that they received as feedback.

11 *READING* City scenes

In this text, Ss explore characteristics of cities in Mexico, Japan, and Australia; they also practice scanning for positive and negative ideas, and making inferences.

■ Books closed. Use the pre-reading question given here – "What are cities like in your country?" – to stimulate a short class discussion or brainstorming activity on this topic. Write as many of the Ss' ideas on the board as possible.

■ Present the idea of a city's "positive" features by asking Ss which ideas on the board show good things about a city; circle those words. Do the same for any "negative" characteristics by asking which things are bad or unpleasant in a city; underline those words or use different-colored chalk.

A

■ Books open. Go over the task. Ss read the passage without using their dictionaries and try to complete the chart.

■ Ask if Ss have questions about any new vocabulary (e.g., *modern, traditional, influences, outings, rural, commute, churches, recreational facilities*). Rather than your explaining the words or expressions, see if other Ss in the class can define them by giving synonyms or examples or even drawing pictures to illustrate them on the board. If no one can provide a definition for a certain word, allow Ss to check their dictionaries.

■ **Optional:** Ss first compare answers in groups.

■ Elicit Ss' answers around the class.

Possible answers

1. Mexico
   Positive = modern cities; traditional Indian and Spanish influences; a central square; outdoor marketplaces; parks; a lot of excitement
   Negative = lots of traffic and air pollution
2. Japan
   Positive = cities a mix of traditional and modern characteristics; little crime; many parks and gardens
   Negative = houses are expensive; traffic, pollution, and crowds are problems
3. Australia
   Positive = cities not large; most people live in houses in suburbs – not apartments; suburbs usually have own churches, schools, shopping centers, and recreational facilities
   Negative = suburbs often far from center of town; traffic slow; many traffic jams

B *Pair work*

■ Go over the task with the class. Tell Ss to write down five characteristics mentioned in the article that are true about their own cities.

In a homogeneous class: Ss form pairs and scan the text together, looking for five characteristics that match their country's cities. If desired, let two pairs form a group of four to discuss their choices.

In a heterogeneous class: Give Ss several minutes to work individually while they skim the text for appropriate comparisons with cities in their own countries. Then Ss form pairs or groups to compare answers.

■ **Optional:** Ask Ss to look over their own lists from part B again. Tell them to circle the things that are positive characteristics and to underline those that are negative. Which characteristics do they have more of – positive ones or negative ones? Does this say anything about Ss' general feelings regarding the cities in their countries?

 Workbook

Tell Ss to do Exercises 5–9 on pages 46–48 in the Workbook or assign the exercises as homework. At the start of the next class, have Ss compare answers in pairs. Then elicit answers around the class to check Ss' work. (Answers can be found on page T-182 of the Workbook Answer Key in this Teacher's Edition.)

Optional activities

1 *How good is your memory?*

Time: 10–15 minutes. This activity is a fun "test your memory" map-drawing task.

■ Explain the activity: Ss draw maps of their school's campus (or of the immediate neighborhood that surrounds the school).

■ Model the task by drawing a simple diagram that shows the location of your school building and its immediate vicinity (e.g., nearby streets, the campus area, large trees, benches).

■ Ask Ss to think about the building their classroom is in and what other things are nearby (e.g., a pay phone, lawns, a bus stop, street lights, a parking lot, a cafeteria, small stores).

■ Ss work in pairs and try to draw a map of the school building with as much information as possible about things on the street and in the immediate surrounding area. Set a time limit of about five minutes.

■ When time is up, find out how many and what types of things Ss were able to add to their maps. Which pair added the most items?

■ **Optional:** If it's possible, Ss might enjoy taking a break and going outside the school building to check their maps for accuracy and for things they might have missed. Set a time limit of about fifteen minutes for this.

2 *Word associations*

■ See page T-149.

11 *READING*

City Scenes

What are cities like in your country?

In many countries around the world, more and more people live in cities. Cities share many characteristics, but are also different from country to country.

Mexico Mexico's cities are modern but have traditional Indian and Spanish influences. The most important buildings are around a central square, which also serves as a place to meet with friends. There are outdoor marketplaces, where people can find almost anything they need. On Sundays, parks are a popular place for family outings. Many people move to Mexico City from rural areas. It has a lot of excitement, but also lots of traffic and air pollution.

Japan Japan's cities also have a mix of traditional and modern characteristics. There are tall office and apartment buildings as well as traditional wooden houses. Many people prefer to live near the center of cities, but because houses there are expensive, they often commute from suburbs. Traffic, pollution, and crowds are problems.

However, there is little crime, and even very crowded cities have many parks and gardens.

Australia Although 80% of Australians live near cities, the cities are not as large as those in some other countries. Most people live in houses in suburbs – not in apartments. The suburbs usually have their own churches, schools, and shopping centers. They also have recreational facilities. In large cities, like Sydney, the suburbs are often far from the center of town. Because many people commute to work, traffic is slow and there are many traffic jams.

A Read the article and complete the chart. Write one positive feature and one negative feature of cities in the countries described.

	Positive	Negative
1. Mexico	....	....
2. Japan	....	....
3. Australia	....	....

B *Pair work* Find five characteristics of the cities above that are also true of cities in your country.

Review of Units 5-8

1 DO YOU DANCE?

A *Class activity* Does anyone in your class do these things? How often and how well do they do them? Go around the class and find one person for each activity.

	Name	How often?	How well?
dance	....	....	....
play basketball	....	....	....
do karate	....	....	....
play computer games	....	....	....
swim	....	....	....
play the piano	....	....	....

A: Do you dance?
B: Yes, I do.
A: How often do you go dancing?
B: Every weekend.
A: And how well do you dance?
B: Actually, not very well. But I enjoy it!

B *Group work* Tell your group what you found out.

2 LISTENING

CLASS AUDIO ONLY

A A thief robbed a house on Saturday. Detective Dobbs is questioning Frankie. The pictures show what Frankie did on Saturday. Listen to their conversation. Are Frankie's answers true (**T**) or false (**F**)?

B *Pair work* Answer these questions.

1. What did Frankie do after he cleaned the house?
2. Where did he go? What did he do? When did he come home?

1:00 P.M.   **T F**   3:00 P.M.   **T F**   5:00 P.M.   **T F**

6:00 P.M.   **T F**   8:00 P.M.   **T F**   10:30 P.M.   **T F**

Review of Units 5–8

This unit reviews the past tense and the present continuous along with asking questions with be, do, how often, how well, how much, and how many. It also reviews talking about cities, daily routines, and free-time activities.

1 DO YOU DANCE?

In this exercise, Ss review asking and answering questions with *do, how often,* and *how well* while interviewing one another on sports and other leisure activities.

A Class activity

- Read aloud the instructions and the six activities in the chart. Ss repeat.
- Model the A/B dialog with several volunteers; try to get detailed responses from them.

- Set a time limit of about ten minutes. Ss go around the class and take turns interviewing one another.

- Walk around the class and observe any difficulties Ss may be having. At the end of the activity, make some general observations to the whole class on any common problems Ss had with grammar or vocabulary usage.

B Group work

- Ss form small groups. Using their charts, Ss take turns sharing what they found out about one another.

2 LISTENING

This fun "whodunit" activity reviews listening for specific times and events; it also practices making inferences.

A 🔊

- Books closed. Set the scene: Detective Dobbs is interrogating Frankie, a suspect in a robbery, about what he did last Saturday. Play the audio program. Ss only listen.

Audio script

> DET. DOBBS: *(a knock on the door)* Well, Frankie. How was your weekend?
> FRANKIE: Oh, it's you, Detective. My weekend? What do you want to know about it?
> DET. DOBBS: Now just tell the truth. What did you do at one P.M. on Saturday?
> FRANKIE: Ah . . . one P.M. . . . on Saturday? Well, oh, I remember! I watched a baseball game on TV. Yeah. The Expos won, four to nothing. It was a great game!
> DET. DOBBS: OK . . . OK. What did you do at three P.M.?
> FRANKIE: Ah . . . at three? Ah, yeah, I went to my karate class like I always do, every Saturday at three.
> DET. DOBBS: Karate, huh? Well, well . . . OK. And what did you do on Saturday at five P.M.?
> FRANKIE: Ah, oh, yeah, ah, after karate, I visited some old friends of mine, Tom and Mary Kent, on Front Street.
> DET. DOBBS: Yeah? Tom and Mary Kent. We'll talk to them. Now, Frankie, six o'clock. Where were you at six?
> FRANKIE: Oooh! Gee . . . at six? Well, I went home at six . . . . yeah . . . to clean the house.
> DET. DOBBS: Yeah, yeah, so you cleaned the house. Now listen carefully, Frankie. What did you do at eight on Saturday night?
> FRANKIE: Gee . . . at eight? Uh . . . oh, yeah . . . I remember now. I watched a terrific movie on TV! Yeah . . . it was great!
> DET. DOBBS: Oh, you watched a movie on TV, did you? And what movie did you watch? What was the name of the movie, Frankie? Huh?
> FRANKIE: The movie? The name of the movie? Uh, let me think a minute. . . it was a fantastic movie.

> DET. DOBBS: Really?
> FRANKIE: No, wait! I remember, it was a . . . a . . . well, it was exciting . . .
> DET. DOBBS: OK, OK, Frankie . . .
> FRANKIE: . . . and I clearly remember that I went to bed at ten-thirty, uh, exactly . . . . Yeah, I watched the movie, and I went to bed right after . . . ahem . . . the movie. Yeah, boy, I was tired . . . a long day, like I said.
> DET. DOBBS: Interesting. Very interesting, Frankie. Come on, Frankie, let's go down to the police station.
> FRANKIE: The police station? Me? Why me? I was at home on Saturday night!
> DET. DOBBS: Sure, Frankie, sure. *(police siren)*

- Books open. Explain the task: Ss look at the pictures and listen for Frankie's answers to Detective Dobbs's questions. Tell the Ss that if the picture and Frankie's answer are the same, they should circle **T** for true; if the picture and Frankie's answer are different, they should circle **F** for false.

- Play the audio program again. Ss do the task individually and then compare answers in pairs. Check Ss' answers around the class.

Answers

1:00 P.M. T	3:00 P.M. T	5:00 P.M. T
6:00 P.M. T	8:00 P.M. F	10:30 P.M. F

B Pair work

- Go over the questions; Ss repeat. Then Ss work in pairs to use the pictures to answer the questions.

Answers

> 1. He went out after he cleaned the house.
> 2. He went to the house that was robbed. He robbed the house. He came home at 10:30 P.M.

3 WHAT CAN YOU REMEMBER?

This communicative activity reviews the past tense as Ss talk about what they did the previous day.

A *Pair work*

■ Go over the instructions. Model the correct pronunciation and intonation of each question. Ss repeat. Show how to give extended answers like these:

S1: What time did you get up yesterday?
T: Well, my alarm rang at six o'clock and I turned it off. Then I listened to the morning news on the radio for thirty minutes. Then I . . . .
S2: What did you wear to school?
T: Let me think. Oh, yes, I wore . . . *(naming at least four items of clothing and accessories).*
S3: Were you late for class?
T: No, I wasn't. I arrived ten minutes early. I got a cup of coffee and chatted with . . . .

■ Set a time limit of five minutes. Now Ss form pairs and take turns asking the questions. Encourage Ss to ask appropriate follow-up questions and to give lots of details in their responses. Go around and give help as needed, noting any incorrect past tense forms.

■ When Ss finish, write some questions and answers on the board that the class generally had trouble with. Then ask Ss to help correct them.

B *Group work*

■ Pairs separate into new groups of four. Explain the task: Ss try to ask as many questions as possible about what others in their group did yesterday. Tell groups to keep score of how many questions each person asks.

■ Ss do the task with books closed for about five minutes. Then find out which S asked the most questions in each group. Who asked the most questions in the whole class?

4 ROLE PLAY What's it like?

This role play reviews asking and answering questions about a classmate's city while using *how much/how many* and *there is/there are*.

■ Explain the activity by going over the roles for Students A and B. Allow the Bs to describe their hometowns or the city they are currently living in.

■ Go over the questions in the box. Ss repeat. Then model the task with one or two Ss.

■ Ss form pairs and try the role play. After about five minutes, have Ss change roles and try the activity again with the same partner or with a different one.

5 WHAT'S GOING ON?

This fun exercise involves listening to sound effects; its main purpose is to elicit the present continuous.

A

■ Explain the task: Ss will hear the sounds of people doing things (i.e., they won't hear people talking). Ask Ss to guess what each person is doing and to come up with interesting suggestions. They should answer the question in the chart with notes written in the present continuous. Write this structure on the board:

someone is + verb + *-ing*

■ Play the audio program several times. Ss complete the chart using the present continuous.

Audio script/Answers

Ss will hear four different sound effects, in this order:
1. someone mixing a drink with ice cubes in a blender
2. someone taking a shower and singing
3. someone vacuuming – a ring gets sucked into the vacuum
4. someone snoring, waking up, rolling over, and going back to sleep

B *Pair work*

■ Model how to use the example A/B dialog. Ss form pairs and use the dialog to talk about their answers. Then check Ss' suggestions around the class.

Test 2

See page T-152 in this Teacher's Edition for general instructions on using the tests. Test 2 covers Units 5–8. Photocopy the test (pages T-157–T-160) and distribute a copy to each S. Allow 45–60 minutes for the test. Listening material for the tests is at the end of the Class Audio Program. The Test Audio Scripts and Answer Key start on page T-169 of this book.

Optional activity: *True or false?*

Time: 10–15 minutes. This activity practices making descriptions.

■ Explain the activity: Ss write six statements about themselves – four should be true and two false.

■ Ss form groups and take turns reading their statements aloud while others try to guess which are true and which are false.

3 WHAT CAN YOU REMEMBER?

A *Pair work* Talk about what you did yesterday. Take turns asking these questions. Give as much information as possible.

What time did you get up yesterday?
What did you wear?
Were you late for class?
Did you meet anyone interesting?
How many phone calls did you make?
Did you drive or take the bus anywhere?
Did you buy anything?
How much money did you spend yesterday?
Did you watch TV? What programs did you watch?
Did you do any exercise?
Were you in bed before midnight?
What time did you go to sleep?

B *Group work* Close your books. Take turns.
How many questions can you ask?

4 ROLE PLAY *What's it like?*

Student A: Imagine you are a visitor in your city.
You want to find out more about it.
Ask the questions in the box.

Student B: You are a resident of your city.
A visitor wants to find out more about it.
Answer the visitor's questions.

Change roles and try the role play again.

> **Questions to ask**
>
> What's it like to live here?
> How much unemployment is there?
> How much crime is there?
> How many good schools are there?
> Is traffic a problem?
> What's public transportation like?
> Are there many places to shop? Where?

5 WHAT'S GOING ON?

A Listen to the sounds of four people doing different things.
What do you think each person is doing?

What's going on?	
1.	3. ....
2.	4. ....

B *Pair work* Compare your answers with a partner.

A: In number 1, someone is shaving.
B: I don't think so. I think someone is . . . .

9 What does he look like?

1 WORD POWER Appearance

A Look at these expressions. Can you add three more words or expressions to describe people? Write them in the box below.

Height

short   fairly short   medium height   pretty tall   tall

Age

young   middle aged   elderly

Looks

handsome   good-looking   pretty

Hair

straight black hair   curly red hair   short blond hair

long brown hair   bald   a mustache and beard

Other words or expressions
....
....
....

B *Pair work* Choose at least four expressions to describe yourself and your partner. Then compare. Do you agree?

A: You have curly blond hair and a beard.
    You're young and good-looking.
B: I agree! / I don't agree. My hair isn't very curly.

Me	My partner
....	....
....	....
....	....
....	....

54

9 What does he look like?

This unit introduces ways to describe people's physical appearance and to identify what they are doing and wearing. It practices questions and statements for describing people and presents modifiers with participles and prepositions.

Cycle 1, Exercises 1–5

1 WORD POWER Appearance

This exercise presents words and expressions used to describe people's physical attributes.

- Books closed. As a quick warm-up to this vocabulary-building exercise, ask a few volunteers to stand up. Then use the vocabulary from part A (and additional words and expressions of your own) to describe each volunteer's height, age, general appearance/looks, and hair, like this:

T: *(standing next to Sean)* Sean, you're medium height – about five feet seven, right? You're young and good-looking. You have short black hair and brown eyes.

Alternative presentation

Preparation: Find some color pictures of famous people in magazines or newspapers. Bring them to class to use during the warm-up activity.

A

- Books open. Tell Ss to look at the pictures and to study the vocabulary for a few minutes.
- Present the vocabulary by pronouncing each word or phrase. Ss repeat. Then start at the top left again and model how to use each word or expression in a sentence. Ss look at the picture and repeat the sentence for each one – for example:

T: *Height:* E.T. is short.
　　　Dustin Hoffman is fairly short.
　　　Marilyn Monroe was medium height.
　　　John Wayne was pretty tall.
　　　Frankenstein is tall.
　　Age: He's young.
　　　She's middle aged.
　　　He's elderly.
　　Looks: He's handsome.
　　　They're good-looking.
　　　She's pretty.
　　Hair: She has straight black hair.
　　　He has curly red hair.
　　　She has short blond hair.
　　　She has long brown hair.
　　　He's bald.
　　　He has a mustache and beard.

- Explain that *handsome* usually refers to men and *pretty* to women; however, *good-looking* can be used to describe both sexes. Also point out that the adverbs *fairly* and *pretty* are used to give the modified word a less strong meaning (e.g., He's *fairly* short. = He's short, but not very short./He's *pretty* tall. = He's tall, but not very tall.).

- Now Ss work alone to do the task: They need to add three more words or expressions. Walk around the class and give help as needed.
- Ss compare their responses in pairs or small groups.
- To check Ss' answers, write these six categories on the board:

Height　　*Hair type/style*
Age　　　*Hair color*
Looks　　*Other*

Elicit Ss' answers one at a time. Encourage the class to suggest which category is best for each one, and write it next to the appropriate heading on the board. Tell Ss to write the words and phrases in their notebooks for use in this unit and for future reference.

Possible answers

> *Height:* rather short, very tall, 5'2" (or five feet two), around six feet
> *Age:* in her/his teens/twenties/thirties, old
> *Looks:* cute, beautiful, ugly
> *Hair type/style:* permed, medium length, a ponytail, frizzy, wavy
> *Hair color:* blond, brunette, auburn, gray, white
> *Other:* Body type = athletic, muscular, heavy, thin, slender; Eye color = black, brown, blue, green, gray, hazel

- Ask each S to make a sentence using one word or phrase from part A or from the ones written on the board. Check that Ss use the correct grammar structures. (*Note:* If Ss have difficulty remembering which pattern to use, refer them to the Unit Summary on page S-10 for examples of structures with *be* + adjective and *have* + noun.)

B Pair work

- Go over the task by reading the instructions aloud.
- Ss first work individually to fill in the chart. Walk around the class and spot-check Ss' responses; give help as needed.
- Tell Ss to form pairs. Then model the A/B dialog with several volunteers.
- Pairs take turns describing each other as in the A/B dialog. Encourage them to give lively responses when agreeing or disagreeing.
- **Optional:** Volunteers form new pairs and sit back to back in front of the class. Find out how well they can describe each other without turning around.

T-54

2 CONVERSATION Describing someone

📻 This exercise introduces questions and statements for describing people.

- Books open. Use the picture to set the scene: The woman is looking for someone and is describing that person to the hotel clerk.

- Books closed. Play the audio program. Ss listen and take notes. Then ask the class some comprehension questions like these:

  Who is the woman looking for? (Martin Bock)
  What does he look like? (He's about 35, pretty tall, with red hair.)
  What's the woman's name? (Jean Taylor)
  Where is the man? (He's in the restaurant.)
  What's the woman going to do? (Go and look for him)

- **Optional:** If Ss had difficulty answering some of the questions, write those questions on the board and play the audio program again. Then let pairs compare answers before checking answers around the class.

- Books open. Present the conversation line by line. Explain any new expressions, such as:

  I'm afraid I missed him. = I'm worried that he (the person I came to meet) already left.
  Let's see. = I need to think for a moment.
  a few minutes ago = from one to ten minutes before now

- Ss form pairs and practice the conversation using the "Look Up and Say" technique.

- **Optional:** Tell pairs to cover the conversation and look only at the picture. Then have them try the practice again, this time using their own words.

3 GRAMMAR FOCUS Questions for describing people

📻 This exercise practices using Wh- and yes/no questions and statements to describe people's general appearance, age, hair color/length, and height.

(*Note:* Most of the vocabulary presented here has already been practiced in Exercises 1 and 2 in this cycle.)

- Play the audio program to present the questions and responses in the boxes. Ss repeat.

- If necessary, explain these expressions:

  in his twenties = between the age of 20 and 29
  medium length = between short and long

- Point out that there are several ways to give a person's exact height in English. Write these examples on the board:

  She's 152 centimeters. = She's five feet (tall).
  He's six two. = He's six feet two inches.
  I'm five foot six. = I'm five feet six inches (tall).

- Use the questions in the boxes to elicit responses about some Ss in the class, like this:

  T: What does . . . look like?
  S1: He's very tall.
  S2: He has short black hair.
  T: How old is he?
  S3: I think he's about 23.
  S4: Yes, he's in his twenties.
  T: Does he have a beard?
  S5: No, he doesn't.
  T: Does he wear contact lenses?
  S6: Gee, I don't know.
  T: OK, how about . . . ? What does she look like?

- **Optional:** Ss take turns asking the same questions around the class.

A

- Read aloud each of the six statements. Then go back to number 1 and elicit at least one appropriate question for it.

- Ss do the task individually and then compare answers with a partner. Check answers around the class.

Answers

1. How old is your brother?
2. How tall are you?
3. What color is Julia's hair?/What color hair does Julia have?
4. Does she wear glasses?
5. What does he look like?
6. What color are your eyes?/What color eyes do you have?

B *Pair work*

- Read the instructions aloud to the class. Make sure Ss understand that they can write five questions about any S in the class or five questions about you. Elicit a few questions that Ss might ask and write them on the board.

- Before Ss form pairs, have them write down their five questions individually. Then partners get together and take turns asking and answering each other's questions.

- Check Ss' answers around the class by calling on various pairs to ask you or one of their classmates their questions.

  (*Note:* If a S doesn't want to answer a question, tell him/her to smile and say "I'd rather not say.")

- **Optional:** While checking answers, write on the board any interesting or unusual questions that were given as responses. Have Ss copy the questions into their notebooks.

2 *CONVERSATION* Describing someone

Listen and practice.

Clerk: Good afternoon. Can I help you?
Jean: Yes, I'm looking for someone.
His name is Martin Bock.
I'm afraid I missed him.
Clerk: Well, what does he look like?
Jean: Let's see. He's about 35, I guess.
He's pretty tall, with red hair.
Clerk: Oh, are you Jean Taylor?
Jean: Yes, that's right!
Clerk: He asked for you a few minutes ago.
I think he's in the restaurant.
Jean: Thanks. I'll go and look for him.

3 *GRAMMAR FOCUS*

Questions for describing people

General appearance		Hair	
What does he **look like**?	He's pretty tall, with red hair.	**What color** is her hair?	Light brown.
Does he wear glasses?	Yes, he does.		She has dark brown hair.
Does he have a mustache?	No, he doesn't.	**How long** is her hair?	It's medium length.
Age		Height	
How old is he?	He's about 25.	**How tall** is she?	She's fairly short.
	He's in his twenties.		She's 152 cm (five feet).

A Write questions to match these statements. Then compare with a partner.

1. .... ? My brother is 26.
2. .... ? I'm 173 cm (five feet eight).
3. .... ? Julia has brown hair.
4. .... ? No, she wears contact lenses.
5. .... ? He's tall and very handsome.
6. .... ? I have brown eyes.

B *Pair work* Write five questions about your teacher's or a classmate's
appearance. Then take turns asking and answering your questions.

What color is Aki's hair?

4 WHO IS IT?

A Listen to the speakers describe these people.
Number the people from 1 to 5.

B *Pair work* Choose a person in your class.
Don't tell your partner who it is. Take turns.
Ask questions to guess the person your partner chose.

A: Is it a man or a woman?
B: A man.
A: How tall is he?
B: He's fairly short.
A: What color is his hair?
B: . . .

interchange 9

Find the differences

Compare two pictures of a party. Student A turns to page IC-12. Student B turns to page IC-14.

5 WRITING

A Write a description of a person in your class.
Don't put the person's name on it.

> *He's in his twenties. He's quite good-looking. He's tall, and he has short blond hair. He's wearing a red shirt, a black jacket, and khaki pants. He's sitting next to the window.*

B *Group work* Read your description to the group.
Can they guess who you are describing?

4 WHO IS IT?

This exercise practices listening for and giving descriptions of people.

A

- Books open. Read the instructions to the class. Explain that Ss need to listen to each description and write the number *1, 2, 3, 4,* or *5* in each box. Tell the Ss these numbers are based on the order in which the descriptions are heard on the audio program.

- Play the audio program once. Ss listen while they look at the picture and write a number in each box.

Alternative presentation

- Books closed. Set the scene: Five people are being described. Tell Ss to write down the numbers *1* through *5* on a separate piece of paper. Then Ss listen and take notes on each person in the order they hear each one being described. Play the audio program once, without stopping. Ss take notes. Then Ss compare notes in pairs or small groups before opening their books to look at the picture. How many of the people can Ss identify correctly with their notes?

Audio script

1. WOMAN: I think Brian's good-looking. He's pretty tall, with dark brown hair and a mustache. He's about thirty.
2. MAN: Tina's eighteen. She's got pretty red hair – shoulder length and very curly – and she always wears interesting glasses, just for fun.

3. WOMAN: Rosie is pretty tall for her age. She has long blond hair and wears contact lenses. She just turned ten.
4. MAN: Tim's about twenty-three. He's fairly short and a bit heavy. He needs to lose some weight.
5. WOMAN: Alice is very tall, and she's got long black hair. She's around twenty-five. Oh, and she's very slim. She looks like a fashion model.

- Elicit Ss' answers around the class.

Answers *(as pictured from left to right)*

2, 4, 1, 5, 3

B Pair work

- Read the instructions aloud. Then use the example A/B dialog to model the activity with one or two Ss.

- Ss form pairs. Each S secretly chooses one person to describe from the class. Then Ss take turns describing the person they chose while their partner tries to guess who it is. Walk around the class and give help as needed.

Optional activity: *Game – What's the question?*

- See page T-147.

 INTERCHANGE 9 Find the differences

See pages T-116 and T-117 in this Teacher's Edition for notes.

5 WRITING

In this exercise, Ss practice writing a description of a classmate.

A

- Go over the instructions and read the example description to the class.

- Ss work individually to write their descriptions. Remind Ss not to name the person they are describing. Go around and give help as needed.

B Group work

- Go over the activity. Model how to do the task with one or two groups.

- Ss form small groups and take turns reading their descriptions aloud. After each description is read, other Ss in the group try to guess who is being described.

- **Optional:** Have each group vote on which description was the best or the most interesting. Then that description is read by the writer to the whole class. How many Ss can guess who is being described?

Workbook

For homework or as in-class work, Ss complete Exercises 1–5 on pages 49–51. Use the Workbook Answer Key on page T-183 in this Teacher's Edition to check Ss' answers whenever convenient during the next class.

Optional activity: *Is this me?*

Time: 10 minutes. This provides additional practice in describing people.

- Ss write six statements about themselves – four that are true and two that are false.

- Ss work in groups and take turns reading their statements. If a S hears a false statement, he or she says "False!" and then gives the correct information, like this:

S1: *(reading statements)* I'm pretty tall. I have straight black hair.
S2: False! You don't have straight black hair. You have curly black hair.
S1: You're right! OK, my eyes are green. I have a mustache. I'm wearing jeans. I'm in my twenties.
S3: False! You're not in your twenties. You're 18!

6 *SNAPSHOT* *Thirty years of fashion*

This graphic introduces the topic of clothing and changing fashion styles.

■ As a quick warm-up, find out how much Ss know about the entertainers in the photos on the left and on the right:

Left: Marlon Brando (1924–) = U.S. movie actor (seen here in the 1954 film *The Wild One*)

Right: John Travolta (1954–) = U.S. movie actor (seen here in the 1977 film *Saturday Night Fever*)

■ Read aloud the Snapshot title. Explain that *the 1950s*

is the decade that includes the years 1951 through 1959. Ask "What does *the 1970s* mean? Which decade is it now?"

■ Pronounce the new words and have Ss repeat.

■ Go over the four questions. Decide how you want the class to work – individually, in pairs or groups, or as a whole-class activity; then instruct the class accordingly.

■ If Ss worked individually, let them form pairs or groups to compare answers. Then elicit responses around the class.

7 *CONVERSATION* *Identifying people*

This conversation introduces modifiers with participles and prepositions.

■ To introduce the topic of this conversation – asking about and identifying people at a party – ask the class:

Do you often go to parties? What kinds of people are usually there? Do you always know everyone? What do you do first after you arrive?
Have you ever gone to a party alone? How was it? How did you meet people there?

A 📼

■ Books closed. Set the scene: A man (Raoul) comes to a party alone, so a friend (Sarah) is telling him about people he doesn't know. Write these questions on the board:

Where's Margaret? (She couldn't make it. She went to a concert with Alex.)
Does Judy know anyone at the party? (No, she doesn't.)
Which one is she? (She's the tall one in jeans.)
Where is she? (She's standing near the window.)

■ Play the audio program once. Check Ss' answers to the questions on the board.

■ Books open. Play the audio program again while Ss look at the picture or read along silently. Present the conversation line by line. Explain new expressions:

Good to see you! = I'm happy to see you.
Oh = an exclamation used to express various emotions, such as the three different ones here: disappointment ("Oh, she couldn't . . . ."); surprise ("Oh! Well, why don't you . . . ?"), or pleasure ("Oh, I'd like to . . . .")
couldn't = here, the past of *can't;* wasn't able to
make it = come or go somewhere; do something

■ Ss practice the conversation in pairs.

B 📼

■ Ask some questions like these about the people in the picture:

Which one is Sarah? Raoul?
What's this man/woman wearing?

■ Go over the instructions. Pronounce the names of the four people. Explain that *label* means "write the names of the people in order to identify them."

■ Play part B of the audio program. Ss do the task.

Audio script

SARAH: Let's see. Who else is here? Do you know Kevin Phillips? He's really nice.
RAOUL: No, I don't. Which one is he?
SARAH: He's over there. He's the one wearing white slacks and . . .
RAOUL: . . . and a yellow polo shirt?
SARAH: That's right. And then there's Michiko Sasaki. She works with me at the office.
RAOUL: Oh? Which one is Michiko?
SARAH: Oh, Michiko's the very pretty woman in black pants and a green pullover sweater. She's wearing glasses.
RAOUL: Oh, I see her. She's the one talking to Kevin, right?
SARAH: Uh-huh.
RAOUL: And who are those two people dancing?
SARAH: Oh, that's my best friend. Her name is Rosa, Rosa Ramirez. She's really nice.
RAOUL: Yeah, and she's very attractive in that . . . purple dress.
SARAH: Uh-huh. And she's dancing with John DuPont, her new boyfriend.
RAOUL: John is Rosa's boyfriend?
SARAH: Yeah. Sorry, Raoul.
RAOUL: Oh! Gee, they're really good dancers, aren't they?
SARAH: Yeah, they are. Say, didn't you want to meet Judy?
RAOUL: Uh, Sarah? I'm sorry, but which one is Judy again? *(laughs)*

■ After Ss compare answers in pairs, check answers around the class.

Answers *(as pictured from left to right)*

Rosa, John, Michiko, Kevin

6 SNAPSHOT

THIRTY YEARS OF FASHION

1950s — cap, T-shirt, black leather jacket, gloves, jeans, heavy boots

1960s — teased hair, hat, sunglasses, wide belt, mini dress, miniskirt, knee socks, tights

1970s — polyester shirt, three-piece suit: jacket, vest, flared pants

Talk about these questions.

Which of these items are in style now? out of style?

What are three more things that are in style today?

What are two things you wear now that you didn't wear five years ago?

---

7 CONVERSATION *Identifying people*

A 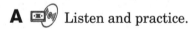 Listen and practice.

Sarah: Hi, Raoul! Good to see you! Where's Margaret?

Raoul: Oh, she couldn't make it. She went to a concert with Alex.

Sarah: Oh! Well, why don't you go and talk to Judy? She doesn't know anyone here.

Raoul: Judy? Which one is she? Is she the woman wearing glasses over there?

Sarah: No, she's the tall one in jeans. She's standing near the window.

Raoul: Oh, I'd like to meet her.

B 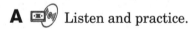 Listen to the rest of the conversation.

Can you label Kevin, Michiko, Rosa, and John in the picture?

8 GRAMMAR FOCUS

Modifiers with participles and prepositions 📟

		Participles
Who's Raoul?	He's **the man**	**wearing** glasses.
Which one is Raoul?	He's **the one**	**talking** to Sarah.
		Prepositions
Who's Sarah?	She's **the woman**	**with** the short black hair.
Which one is Judy?	She's **the tall one**	**in** jeans.
Who are the Smiths?	They're **the people**	**next to** the window.
Which ones are the Smiths?	They're **the ones**	**on** the couch.

A Rewrite these statements using modifiers with participles or prepositions. Then compare with a partner.

1. Jim is the tall guy. He's wearing glasses.
   Jim is the tall guy wearing glasses.
2. Bob and Louise are the good-looking couple. They're talking to Jim.
   ....
3. Lynne is the young woman. She's in a T-shirt and jeans.
   ....
4. Maria is the attractive woman. She's sitting to the left of Carlos.
   ....
5. Tom is the serious-looking person. He's listening to Maria.
   ....

B *Pair work* Complete these questions and add two questions of your own. Use the names of people in your class. Then take turns asking and answering the questions.

1. Who is .... ?
2. Which one is .... ?
3. Who's the man sitting next to............... ?
4. Who's the woman wearing .... ?
5. .... ?
6. .... ?

---

9 PRONUNCIATION Contrastive stress

A 📟 Listen and practice. Notice how the stress changes to emphasize a contrast.

A: Is Raoul the one wearing the red **shírt**?
B: No, he's the one wearing the **bláck** shirt.

A: Is Judy the short one in **jéans**?
B: No, she's the **táll** one in jeans.

B 📟 Mark the stress changes in these conversations. Listen and check. Then practice the conversations.

1. A: Is Rose the one sitting next to Kate?

   B: No, she's the one standing next to Kate.

2. A: Is Brian the man on the couch?

   B: No, Brian's the man behind the couch.

8 *GRAMMAR FOCUS* *Modifiers with participles and prepositions*

This exercise reviews Wh-questions and presents modifiers with present participles and prepositional phrases for descriptions; it also introduces the definite article *the* + noun and reviews the pronouns *one/ones*.

A participle ending in *-ing* is known as a present participle. A participial phrase functions as an adjective phrase, which is a reduction of an adjective clause. This type of phrase modifies a noun, does not contain a subject and a verb, and shows no tense:

He's the man *who is wearing glasses.* (adjective clause)
He's the man *wearing glasses.* (adjective phrase)

Ss need to know how to form a present participle (i.e., verb + *-ing*) and where to place the participial phrase in a sentence (i.e., after the noun or pronoun it modifies).

A prepositional phrase is made up of a preposition (e.g., *with, in, next to, on*) and its object, which is a noun or pronoun.

- Use the audio program to present the questions and responses in the box. Ss repeat. Then have a quick practice by asking questions about the Ss – for example:

  Who's Sal? Which one is Pedro?
  Which ones are Lee and Ben?

- Explain how to form a participle by writing this structure with some examples on the board:

  Participle =   verb + -ing
  wear + -ing = wearing
  dance + -ing = dancing
  sit + -ing = sitting

  You may also want to refer Ss to the Unit 5 Summary Grammar Extension on page S-6 of their textbook.

- Read aloud the first two questions and statements in the box again. Point out that the participles *wearing* and *talking* come after the words they describe (i.e., the noun *man;* the pronoun *one*).

- Now point out that the pronoun *one* replaces the singular noun *man* (or *person*) in "Which one is Raoul?" The pronoun *one* functions in the same way in "He's the *one* (or *man* or *person*) talking to Sarah." Also, *ones*

replaces the plural noun *people* in "Which ones are the Smiths?" "They're the ones on the couch."

- The definite article *the* is used when a speaker knows or assumes that the listener is familiar with and thinking about the same specific thing or person the speaker is talking about. Present these contrasts to help explain this difference between *a/an* and *the:*

  Indefinite article *a:* He's a man. (not a specific person; he is one man out of a whole group called *men*)
  Definite article *the:* He's the man + . . . (a specific person, e.g., the man/one/person who is wearing certain clothes or doing something in particular)

- If necessary, explain what a prepositional phrase is by writing this sentence on the board:

  She's the one with the short black hair.

  Elicit some other examples and write them on the board.

A

- Go over the first statement and the example answer to explain the task. After Ss work individually to rewrite the statements using modifiers with participles or prepositions, have them compare answers in pairs. Then elicit answers around the class.

Answers

1. Jim is the tall guy wearing glasses.
2. Bob and Louise are the good-looking couple talking to Jim.
3. Lynne is the young woman in the T-shirt and jeans.
4. Maria is the attractive woman sitting to the left of Carlos.
5. Tom is the serious-looking person listening to Maria.

B *Pair work*

- Model the task by completing one or two questions with several volunteers. Then Ss work alone to write their questions. Walk around the class, giving help as needed.

- Check Ss' questions before pairs work together.

- Ss work in pairs to take turns asking and answering their questions.

9 *PRONUNCIATION* *Contrastive stress*

This exercise practices the use of stress to focus on contrasting information in statements.

A

- Play the audio program once or twice; Ss repeat. Point out the stress in the contrasting words, i.e., the words in **bold type**.

B

- Go over the instructions: Ss circle or write a stress mark (´) over each word they think should be stressed.

- Play the second part of the audio program. Ss check and correct their guesses. Check Ss' answers before they practice the conversations in pairs.

Answers

1. A: Is Rose the one sitting next to **Kate**?
   B: No, she's the one **standing** next to Kate.
2. A: Is Brian the man on the **couch**?
   B: No, Brian's the man **behind** the couch.

10 **READING** *Hip-hop fashions*

This text explores a clothing trend popular among teenagers around the world; in the exercise, Ss scan for key words in order to match pictures to specific vocabulary in the text.

■ Books closed. To introduce the topic of current or "hot" new fashions, read aloud the two pre-reading questions at the top about clothing styles and "dressing up" or "dressing down." Explain that *dress up* means "to wear nice, expensive, new, or formal clothes," and *dress down* means "to wear old, worn, comfortable, or casual clothes." Elicit Ss' responses to these questions around the class.

Alternative presentation

■ Write the two questions on the board. Then give Ss about five minutes to work in groups to talk about them. When time is up, ask the groups to summarize their main ideas and to present them to the rest of the class.

A

■ Books open. Ss read the passage and try to guess the meanings of any unknown words. Tell Ss to circle or underline any words whose meanings they can't guess.

■ Go over the article and explain any words Ss don't know or can't find in the dictionary – for example:

Paragraph 1
hot style = something that is popular right now
urban = from big cities
heavy beat = strong bass rhythm
lyrics = the words in a song
loose-fitting = baggy, not tight
flannel = a kind of soft cotton fabric
Paragraph 2
African Americans = black Americans whose families originally came from Africa
Detroit and Chicago = two large cities in the midwestern region of the U.S.
influenced = had an effect on
mixture = a combination of things
sensation = excited interest
Paragraph 3
pride and joy = something or someone very special to a person
cartoon characters = e.g., Mickey Mouse, Snoopy

Alternative presentation

■ Assign this article as a homework assignment: Tell Ss to read it and to look up any difficult words and expressions in their dictionaries.

■ Go over the labeling task. Model how to do the first two items, like this: Tell Ss to look at the first two pictures. Then ask some questions – for example:

T: What type of clothing is this in the first picture?
CLASS: *(answer given in text)* Baggy jeans.
T: Right. Now how about the next one? What are these called?
S1: Black pants?

T: OK. What else are they called?
S2: Jeans? I think they're tight black jeans.
S3: They're called Levi's, right?

If Ss aren't sure what certain things are called in the pictures, tell them to scan the article for the names of various types of clothing that seem to be appropriate and may match the pictures.

■ As Ss work individually to write down the words for the various pieces of clothing and accessories, go around the class and give help as needed.

■ Explain the second part of the task: Ss look at all ten pictures again to decide if a clothing item is a hip-hop fashion or not. If yes, they check the box next to the picture; if no, they leave the box blank. Remind Ss to scan through the article again, this time checking to see if certain items pictured here were also mentioned as being hip-hop fashions.

■ **Optional:** Ss form pairs or groups to compare answers.

■ Elicit Ss' responses around the class.

Possible answers *(from left to right)*

> baggy jeans ✓
> tight black jeans
> brown cowboy boots
> black hiking boots ✓
> a red baseball cap ✓
> a hat
> a yellow jacket with sports logo ✓
> a brown jacket/blazer
> a blouse with cartoon character
> a flannel shirt ✓

B *Pair work*

■ Go over the three questions with the class. Then Ss form pairs and discuss their answers to each question. Walk around the class and give help as needed.

■ **Optional:** To check Ss' free responses, call on pairs to share their answers with the class.

Optional activities

1 *Game – Colorful things around us*

■ See page T-15.

2 *Sentence-making contest*

■ See page T-149.

 Workbook

Assign Exercises 6–11 on pages 52–54 for homework. At the beginning of the next class, have Ss compare answers in pairs. Then elicit answers around the class for a final check. (Answers can be found on page T-183 of the Workbook Answer Key in this Teacher's Edition.)

10 READING

Hip-Hop Fashions

**What kinds of clothing styles do you like to wear?
Do you like to "dress up" or "dress down"?**

Teenagers who listen to the same music often have a common "look." One hot style in music and fashion is hip-hop. Hip-hop is a type of urban music with a heavy beat. The lyrics are very important in this music. Hip-hop fashions are large or loose-fitting street clothes. The style includes baggy jeans, sweatshirts, hiking boots, and baseball caps (usually worn backward). However, teens add other clothing items like flannel shirts, jackets with sports logos, and athletic shoes. In the hip-hop style, boys and girls dress the same.

African American kids in Detroit and Chicago first made hip-hop fashions popular – they wore baggy street clothes to dance clubs. Then North American and European bands also began wearing this style. These bands influenced one another's music and clothing. This mixture made hip-hop into an international fashion sensation.

Hip-hop is now a teen fashion from Britain to Japan. Melanie Borrow, 17, of Manchester, England, says, "My pride and joy in life are my Levi's jeans." In Japan, hip-hop is replacing the usual outfit for teenage girls: blouses and skirts with cartoon characters on them. And in the United States, teens spend a lot of money on hip-hop fashions. David Bowen, 17, of Evanston, Illinois, has five pairs of hiking boots at $100 each. Bowen says, "They're popular because a lot of hip-hop performers wear them. They even rap about them."

A Read the article. Then look at these pictures and label them. According to the article, which of the clothing items are hip-hop fashions? Check (✓) the correct items.

baggy jeans ☐ .... ☐ .... ☐ .... ☐ .... ☐

.... ☐ .... ☐ .... ☐ .... ☐ .... ☐

B *Pair work* Talk about these questions.

1. Do you ever listen to urban or hip-hop music?
2. Do you ever wear hip-hop fashions? Describe what you wear.
3. What do you wear when you dress up or dress down?

10 Have you ever ridden a camel?

1 SNAPSHOT

Unusual Ways to Spend Time

Singapore:
Eat at a bird-singing cafe

New York City:
Go to a TV talk show

New Zealand:
Try bungee jumping

Réunion:
See people fire walking

Talk about these questions.

Which of these activities would you like to try? Why?
What are three unusual things you can do in your city or country?

2 CONVERSATION Going out

A 🔊 Listen and practice.

Ted: Are you enjoying your trip to New Orleans?
Brenda: Oh, yes. I really like it here.
Ted: Would you like to do something tonight?
Brenda: Sure. I'd love to.
Ted: Let's see. Have you been to a jazz club yet?
Brenda: Yes. I've already been to several clubs here.
Ted: OK. What about an evening riverboat tour?
Brenda: Uh, actually, I've gone twice this week.
Ted: So, what *do* you want to do?
Brenda: Well, I haven't been to the theater in a long time.
Ted: Oh, OK. I hear there's a terrific show at the Saenger Theater.
Brenda: Great! Let's make a reservation.

B 🔊 Listen to Ted call the Saenger Theater.

1. What's playing tonight?
2. Where is the theater?

10 **Have you ever ridden a camel?**

> This unit helps Ss expand their ability to talk about past events and experiences. It introduces the present perfect with already and yet, along with regular and irregular past participle forms.

1 SNAPSHOT Unusual ways to spend time

This graphic presents some interesting facts about unusual ways to spend time in various places around the world.

(*Note:* It would be helpful to have a world map for this activity.)

■ Books closed. As a warm-up, have a brainstorming activity with the class by doing one of the following:

(a) *In a heterogeneous class:* Introduce the topic by brainstorming like this: Ask the Ss to think of one interesting or unusual thing that can be done in their hometowns or cities. Have Ss write their activities on the board, but tell them not to include the location:

Brainstorming on interesting or unusual activities
– go to Stanley Market and look for some bargains
– visit the Butterfly Farm
– see a Bunraku puppet play

Then read aloud each activity and ask the class questions like these: "Where can you do this?" or "Where is this possible?" Elicit suggestions; then ask the S who wrote it to give the correct answer.

(b) *In a homogeneous class:* Broaden this brainstorming activity by allowing Ss to choose an activity from their hometowns, cities, country, or somewhere else they have visited or read about. Then continue the activity as described in (a) above.

■ Books open. Ss read the information in the Snapshot without using their dictionaries. Check if there are any words that Ss can't guess even after looking at the photos provided on the page. Point out or ask for volunteers to indicate on a map the four places listed:

> **Singapore** = the capital of the tiny island-nation of the same name, located in Southeast Asia
> **New York City** = an important city in the northeastern region of the U.S.
> **New Zealand** = a neighbor of Australia, located in the southwestern Pacific Ocean
> **Réunion** = an island in the Indian Ocean

■ Read each question aloud. Then Ss work individually to answer the questions. When they finish, have them form pairs or small groups to compare information.

2 CONVERSATION Going out

This exercise introduces the present perfect for referring to indefinite events in the past.

A 🎧

■ Books closed. Set the scene: Two friends are talking about possible things to do that night. Write some pre-listening questions like these on the board:

Is the woman enjoying her trip? (Yes, she is.)
What city is she visiting? (New Orleans)
Does she want to do something tonight? (Yes, she does.)
Where has she been already? (To several jazz clubs and twice on evening riverboat tours)
Where do they decide to go? (To the theater)

■ Play the first part of the audio program. Ss take notes. Then check Ss' answers to the questions on the board.

■ Books open. Play the audio program again, pausing it to present the conversation line by line. Allow Ss to repeat if they wish. Explain any new vocabulary:

> **New Orleans** = a city and port on the Mississippi River in the southern U.S. state of Louisiana
> **riverboat tour** = a short cruise on a boat with a flat bottom, which often has a paddle wheel moving it through the water

■ Ss practice the conversation in pairs.

B 🎧

■ Go over the instructions and the two questions. Then play part B of the audio program.

Audio script

> BOX OFFICE: *(phone rings; picks up)* Thank you for calling the Saenger Theater. How can I help you?
> TED: Um, what's playing tonight?
> BOX OFFICE: Tonight is the final performance of *The Mousetrap.*
> TED: *The Mousetrap.* That's a mystery, isn't it?
> BOX OFFICE: Yes, it is.
> TED: Great! I love mysteries. And where are you located?
> BOX OFFICE: We're at 143 North Rampart Street.
> TED: How do you spell the street name?
> BOX OFFICE: It's R-A-M-P-A-R-T.
> TED: So that's 143 North Rampart Street. Oh! Do you still have tickets?
> BOX OFFICE: Yes, we do.
> TED: I'd like to reserve two tickets for tonight.

■ Elicit Ss' answers around the class.

Answers

> 1. *The Mousetrap* is playing.
> 2. It's at 143 North Rampart Street.

3 GRAMMAR FOCUS *Present perfect; already, yet*

 This exercise practices the present perfect in questions and responses with *already* and *yet*; it also introduces regular and irregular past participles.

The present perfect expresses the idea that something happened (or never happened) before now; the time in the past is unspecified and unimportant. The present perfect can also show the repetition of an activity before now – again, the specific time is not important.

■ Put Figure 10.1 on the board to visually show Ss the two situations in which the present perfect is used:

The present perfect

A. *(one event – the specific   Present
    time is not important)*
    —————————×—————————|———————

Have you *cleaned* your room (yet)?
Yes, I*'ve* (already) *cleaned* it.

B. *(repeating events – the specific   Present
    time is not important)*
    ———×—————————×————————|————————

I've cleaned my room twice this week.

Figure 10.1

■ Play the audio program to present the questions and statements in the box. Ss repeat.

■ Explain how to form the present perfect: Use the verb *have* + the past participle form of a verb. Play the audio program to present the regular and irregular past participles in the box along with the contracted forms. Tell Ss to refer to the appendix at the back of the Student's Book for a list of additional irregular past participles whenever needed.

(*Note:* Ss will practice using the present perfect + *ever* along with a review of the past tense in Exercise 5 on page 62.)

■ Do a quick drill around the class by asking questions like these to elicit Ss' responses in the present perfect:

Have you been to . . . (e.g., a concert) lately/recently/this past month?
Have you seen . . . (e.g., *Star Wars, Baywatch*)?
Has Carlos been to . . . (e.g., Disneyland, the Grand Canyon, Paris, Hawaii)?
Have you done . . . (e.g., your homework, any exercise) this week?

■ **Optional:** Go back to the two diagrams that you put on the board earlier. Ask Ss to suggest additional examples. If a S's suggestion is grammatical, ask that S to write it under the appropriate diagram on the board.

A

■ Read the question and the instructions aloud. Present the useful expressions. Model how to use these expressions by reading aloud the examples for number 1.

■ Ss work alone to complete the task and then compare answers with a partner. Check Ss' answers around the class.

Possible answers

> 1. I've cleaned the house once/twice this week./I haven't cleaned the house this week.
> 2. I've made my bed seven times/every day this week./ I haven't made my bed this week.
> 3. I've cooked dinner every day/four times this week./ I haven't cooked dinner this week.
> 4. I've done laundry once/twice this week./I haven't done laundry this week.
> 5. I've washed the dishes every day/five times this week./I haven't washed the dishes this week.
> 6. I've gone grocery shopping once/twice this week./ I haven't gone grocery shopping this week.

B

■ Go over the instructions. Model the task by doing the first item with a volunteer, with you asking the question. Then Ss work individually. Encourage Ss to use contractions in their answers. Go around and give help as needed.

■ Elicit Ss' responses to check answers around the class.

Answers

> 1. Yes, I**'ve** already **been** to aerobics class four times.
> 2. No, I **haven't had** the time.
> 3. Actually, I **haven't seen** any yet.
> 4. No, I **haven't gone** to any parties for a while.
> 5. Yes, I**'ve** already **made** three calls.
> 6. I**'ve eaten** at fast-food restaurants a couple of times.

■ Ss form pairs and practice the dialogs.

C *Pair work*

■ Show Ss how to give their own information in this task by having the class ask you some of the questions in part B. Then have pairs do the activity together. Walk around the class and note any problems that Ss seem to be having. When pairs finish, go over the problems and their solutions with the whole class.

■ **Optional:** As a follow-up, ask pairs to share with the rest of the class the most interesting or unusual information they got from each other.

Optional activity: *Chain story – A terrible day!*
■ See page T-149.

 Workbook

For homework or as in-class work, Ss complete Exercises 1–4 on pages 55–57. Use the Workbook Answer Key on page T-184 in this Teacher's Edition to check Ss' answers whenever convenient during the next class.

3 GRAMMAR FOCUS

Present perfect; already, yet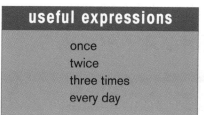

The present perfect is formed with the verb **have** + *the past participle form of a verb.*		Contractions
Have you **been** to a jazz club?	Yes, I**'ve already been** to several.	I have = I**'ve**
Have they **seen** the play?	No, they **haven't seen** it **yet**.	have not = **haven't**
Has she **gone** on a riverboat tour?	Yes, she**'s gone** twice this week.	she has = she**'s**
Has he **called** his parents lately?	No, he **hasn't called** them.	has not = **hasn't**

Regular past participles

call → call**ed**
hike → hik**ed**
jog → jog**ged**
try → tri**ed**

Irregular past participles

be → **been**   have → **had**
do → **done**   make → **made**
eat → **eaten**   see → **seen**
go → **gone**

For a list of irregular past participles, see the appendix at the back of the book.

A How many times have you done these things in the past week?
Write your answers. Then compare with a partner.

1. clean the house
2. make your bed
3. cook dinner
4. do laundry
5. wash the dishes
6. go grocery shopping

useful expressions
once
twice
three times
every day

> *I've cleaned the house once this week.*
>
> **OR**
>
> *I haven't cleaned the house this week.*

B Complete these conversations using the present perfect.
Then practice with a partner.

1. A: Have you done much exercise this week?
   B: Yes, I .... already .... to aerobics class four times. (be)

2. A: Have you played any sports this month?
   B: No, I .... the time. (have)

3. A: How many movies have you been to this month?
   B: Actually, I .... any yet. (see)

4. A: Have you been to any interesting parties lately?
   B: No, I .... to any parties for a while. (go)

5. A: Have you called any friends today?
   B: Yes, I .... already .... three calls. (make)

6. A: How many times have you gone out to eat this week?
   B: I .... at fast-food restaurants a couple of times. (eat)

C *Pair work* Take turns asking the questions in part B.
Give your own information when answering.

4 CONVERSATION *Describing events*

A 🔊 Listen and practice.

Dave: So, how was your weekend?
  Sue: Oh, really good. I went to see
        David Copperfield.
Dave: The magician?
  Sue: That's right. Have you ever seen him?
Dave: Yes, I have. I saw his show in Las Vegas
        last year. He's terrific.
  Sue: Yeah. He does some incredible things.
Dave: Have you ever been to Las Vegas?
  Sue: No, I've never been there.
Dave: You should go sometime. It's an interesting
        city, and the hotels are wonderful.

B Have you ever seen a magician? When? Where?
What did you think of the magician?

David Copperfield

5 GRAMMAR FOCUS

Present perfect and past tense 🔊

Use the present perfect for an indefinite time in the past. Use the past tense for a specific event in the past.

Have you ever **seen** a magic show?	Yes, I **have**.	I **saw** a magic show last year.
	No, I **haven't**.	But my sister **saw** David Copperfield.
Have you ever **been** to Las Vegas?	Yes, I **have**.	I **went** there in September.
	No, I **haven't**.	I've never **been** there.

A Complete these conversations. Use the present perfect and the
past tense of the verbs given and short answers. Then practice with
a partner.

1. A: .... you ever .... skiing? (go)
   B: Yes, I .... I .... skiing once in Colorado.

2. A: .... you ever .... something valuable? (lose)
   B: No, I .... But my brother .... his camera on a trip once.

3. A: .... you ever .... a traffic ticket? (get)
   B: Yes, I .... Once I .... a ticket and had to pay $50.

4. A: .... you ever .... a body-building competition? (see)
   B: Yes, I .... I .... the National Championships this year.

5. A: .... you ever .... late for an important appointment? (be)
   B: No, I .... But my sister .... 30 minutes late for her wedding!

B *Pair work* Take turns asking the questions in part A.
Give your own information when answering.

4 CONVERSATION *Describing events*

This exercise introduces the differences between the present perfect and the past tense; it also presents the adverb *ever* when used in *Have you ever . . . ?*

A 🔲🔊

- **Optional:** Books closed. Ask the class "How was your weekend?" or "Have you ever been to Las Vegas or Atlantic City?" (*Note:* Both American cities are popular gambling centers where the large luxury hotels also have clubs where famous entertainers often give live performances.) If a S answers "It was great!" or "Yes, I've been there," encourage the rest of the class to ask questions to get more information.

- Books closed. Set the scene: Two friends are talking about past experiences. Play the audio program; Ss only listen.

- Books open. Draw Ss' attention to the picture and present the conversation line by line. Explain any difficult vocabulary.

- Ss practice the conversation in pairs.

B

- Use the questions to stimulate a class discussion on magicians that Ss have seen. Have Ss take turns telling the class when and where they saw a certain magician.

---

5 GRAMMAR FOCUS *Present perfect and past tense*

🔲🔊 This exercise practices the use of the present perfect for an indefinite time in the past and the past tense for a specific event in the past.

The present perfect is used here to refer to events that occurred within a time period beginning in the past and continuing up to the present; thus, the present perfect is used for the "indefinite past." For example, "Have you ever seen a magic show?" also implies "at any time in your lifetime." In contrast, the simple past describes a specific event completed in the past as in "Yes, I saw a magic show *last year.*"

- Put Figure 10.2 on the board to visually show Ss the difference between the past and the present perfect.

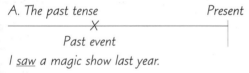

A. The past tense   *Present*
————————×————————————————|
          Past event

I *saw* a magic show last year.

B. The present perfect with ever

From . . . *Your birth to the . . .*   *Present*
—←————————←—————————————|
—→————————→—————————————|

Present perfect = sometime in your life

Have you ever *seen* a magic show?
Yes, I *have.*/No, I *haven't.*

Figure 10.2

- Point out that the present perfect can introduce a topic (e.g., Have you ever seen a magic show?). However, if we continue to talk about the topic (i.e., the magic show), we use the past tense (e.g., I saw it last year.) because the topic now refers to a definite event and time in the past.

- Use the audio program to present the questions and responses in the box; Ss repeat. Model the correct stress with *ever* in "Have you **ever seen** a **ma**gic show?"

- Ask Ss some additional questions beginning with "Have you ever . . . ?" Then let Ss take turns asking one another similar questions around the class.

A

- Go over the instructions. Model how to do number 1 with the class. Then Ss complete the task individually, or the whole class can do it orally as a chorus.

- If Ss do the task alone, let them compare answers in pairs; or they can check their own answers by using the irregular verb list in the appendix at the back of the Student's Book.

- Check Ss' answers around the class.

Answers

> 1. A: **Have** you ever **gone** skiing?
>   B: Yes, I **have**. I **went** skiing once in Colorado.
> 2. A: **Have** you ever **lost** something valuable?
>   B: No, I **haven't**. But my brother **lost** his camera on a trip once.
> 3. A: **Have** you ever **gotten** a traffic ticket?
>   B: Yes, I **have**. Once I **got** a ticket and had to pay $50.
> 4. A: **Have** you ever **seen** a body-building competition?
>   B: Yes, I **have**. I **saw** the National Championships this year.
> 5. A: **Have** you ever **been** late for an important appointment?
>   B: No, I **haven't**. But my sister **was** 30 minutes late for her wedding!

- Ss practice the dialogs in pairs.

B *Pair work*

- Model the task: Ask several Ss the first question in part A. Then pairs do the task together, asking the questions from part A and giving their own responses this time.

6 PRONUNCIATION Have

This exercise practices when and when not to reduce *have*.

A 🔊

- Play the audio program once. Ss only listen. Point out the reduced form of *have* /həv/ in the questions and its full forms /hæv/ and /'hævənt/ in the short answers.
- Play the audio program again. Ss listen and repeat.

B *Pair work*

- Go over the task: Ss work individually to write four questions of their own like those in part A above. Walk around the class, giving help as needed.
- Ss form pairs and take turns asking and answering their questions. Remind Ss to pay attention to the pronunciation of *have*.

7 LISTENING

🔊 This exercise practices listening for key information.

- Books closed. Explain the situation: Two friends are talking about some things they have done recently. Play the audio program once or twice; Ss only listen.

Audio script

> KARL: So, Clarice, what have you been up to lately?
> CLARICE: Oh, well . . . I tried a new restaurant last week. The Classical Cafe. Have you ever been there?
> KARL: No, I haven't. What's it like?
> CLARICE: It's wonderful! The food is great, and the prices are reasonable. But the most interesting thing is the waiters. They sing!
> KARL: The waiters sing? You're kidding!
> CLARICE: No, they're really terrific!
> KARL: I've got to go there.
> CLARICE: Yeah, you should, Karl. And what about you? Have you done anything interesting lately?
> KARL: Oh, well, I went mountain climbing last month.
> CLARICE: Really? I've never done that!

> KARL: Well, I was in Switzerland, . . .
> CLARICE: You went mountain climbing in Switzerland?
> KARL: Yeah. It was really exciting! Of course it was dangerous, but I enjoyed it a lot.
> CLARICE: Wow! I'm impressed!

- Books open. Play the audio program again. Ss listen and complete the chart. Point out that Ss need to write only key words and phrases – not full sentences.
- Check Ss' answers by asking for volunteers to write their responses on the board in chart and note form.

Answers

	Where he/she went	*Why he/she liked it*
Clarice	The Classical Cafe	wonderful; food great; prices reasonable; waiters sing
Karl	mountain climbing in Switzerland	really exciting

8 WORD POWER Collocation

This exercise practices collocation with verbs and nouns; these collocations will be used in Exercise 9.

A

- Explain the task. Read aloud the words in the list and the verbs in the box. Ss repeat.
- Explain any new vocabulary. Alternatively, if you prefer, have Ss use their dictionaries.

> **kiwi fruit** = an oval fruit with brown hairy skin and bright green flesh; Chinese gooseberry
> **rice wine** = an alcoholic drink made from the seeds of rice plants; often called *sake*

- Model how to do the first item in the chart. Then Ss complete the task individually. Give help as needed. If time permits, have pairs or groups compare answers. Then check Ss' answers around the class.

Answers

climb	a hill	a mountain
drink	goat's milk	rice wine
drive	a sports car	a truck
eat	kiwi fruit	raw fish
lose	your keys	your wallet
ride	a camel	a motorcycle

B

- Model the task by writing on the board the past participle form for the first verb listed in part A: *climb/climbed*. Again, Ss work alone to complete the task before comparing answers with a partner.
- Check Ss' answers, or tell the class to look at the list of irregular past participles in the appendix at the back of the Student's Book.

Answers

> climb/climbed; drink/drunk; drive/driven; eat/eaten; lose/lost; ride/ridden

6 *PRONUNCIATION* Have

A Listen and practice. In questions, **have** is usually
reduced to /həv/. In short answers, **have** is not reduced.

A: **Have** you ever been in a traffic accident?
B: Yes, I have.

A: **Have** you ever eaten Greek food?
B: No, I haven't.

B *Pair work* Write four questions like those in part A.
Take turns asking and answering the questions.
Pay attention to the pronunciation of **have**.

7 *LISTENING*

 Listen to Clarice and Karl talk about interesting things they've
done recently. Complete the chart.

	Where he/she went	Why he/she liked it
Clarice	....	....
Karl	....	....

8 *WORD POWER* Collocation

A Find two words or phrases in the list that are usually paired with each verb.

a camel	a hill	kiwi fruit	a mountain	rice wine	a truck
goat's milk	your keys	a motorcycle	raw fish	a sports car	your wallet

climb	....	....
drink	....	....
drive	....	....
eat	....	....
lose	....	....
ride	....	....

B Write the past participle forms of the verbs above. Then compare with a partner.

9 HAVE YOU EVER . . . ?

A *Group work* Ask your classmates questions
about each of the things in Exercise 8. Take notes
on the answers.

A: Have you ever ridden a camel?
B: Yes, I have.
A: Really? Where were you?
B: . . .

B *Class activity* Tell the class one
interesting thing you learned
about a classmate.

10 WRITING *I've never . . . .*

A Write a paragraph describing something that you've never
done but would like to do. Explain why you want to do it.

> I've never gone white-water rafting. I'd
> like to because it sounds exciting. My
> brother was on vacation in Canada
> two years ago and decided to try it. . . .

interchange 10

Lifestyles survey
Is your lifestyle easygoing
and relaxed or busy and
fast-paced? Turn to
page IC-13.

B *Pair work* Exchange your compositions.
Take turns asking and answering questions
with a partner.

9 *HAVE YOU EVER...?*

This is a fun information-exchange activity that gives Ss an additional opportunity to practice using the present perfect and the past tense.

A *Group work*

■ Read aloud the instructions. Then model the A/B dialog with several volunteers, using the words and phrases in Exercise 8, part A.

■ In groups, Ss take turns asking one another their questions. Remind everyone to take notes on their classmates' answers during this activity; these notes will be used in part B.

B *Class activity*

■ With the whole class, each S uses his or her notes to find and then share one interesting thing he or she discovered about a classmate during the part A activity.

10 *WRITING* *I've never ....*

This exercise gives Ss the chance to describe in writing a personal challenge and why they would like to try it.

A

■ Books closed. Ask the class this question: "What would you like to do that you've never done before?" Elicit some responses and write them on the board as examples. Then ask Ss to give reasons why they are interested in that particular activity.

■ Books open. Go over the instructions and read the example paragraph aloud. Use the picture to define the term *white-water rafting*.

■ Ss write a draft of their paragraphs. Walk around the class and give help as needed.

(*Note:* If classroom time is tight, writing the first draft could be given as a homework assignment.)

B *Pair work*

■ Go over the instructions. Read one or two Ss' compositions aloud and then show how to ask for more information, clarification, or details. Explain to the class that the S writer should be taking notes and making revisions during this peer-feedback session.

■ Encourage Ss to revise their drafts to improve them (e.g., clarify ideas, add more information and details, double-check grammar and spelling).

■ **Optional:** Ask for volunteers to read their paragraphs aloud to the class.

 INTERCHANGE 10 Lifestyles survey

See page T-118 in this Teacher's Edition for notes.

Optional activities

1 *Getting to know you – better!*

Time: 10–15 minutes. This fun activity allows Ss to get to know their classmates better by asking questions about their past experiences, which may include some regular types of experiences along with some rather unusual ones!

■ With the whole class, brainstorm some fun and unusual topics. Write as many phrases as possible on the board using past participles, such as:

won a prize　　　　driven in a snowstorm
seen a ghost　　　　met someone from Russia
gone on a safari　　missed the last train home
ridden a donkey　　gone to a party alone
climbed Mt. Fuji　　eaten spicy Indian food

■ **Class activity:** Ss take turns asking classmates questions starting with "Have you ever ...?"

S1: Carlos, have you ever won a prize?
S2: Yes, I have. I won a speech contest once. Jill, have you ever seen a ghost?
S3: Well, I'm not really sure, but one night I saw ....

2 *Game – Hangman*

Time: 20 minutes. This popular activity can review vocabulary in any unit; it also allows Ss to practice spelling words. (*Note:* In Unit 10, the focus could be on past participle verb forms.)

■ Ss form large groups of five or six. Each group chooses a word from the unit. Point out that this game is somewhat similar to the popular TV game show in North America called *Wheel of Fortune.*

■ Groups take turns going to the board. There, one group draws a hangman diagram and blanks – one blank for each letter of the word they have chosen.

Figure 10.3

■ Other groups take turns guessing which letters are in the word. If a group guesses a correct letter, it is written in the appropriate blank on the board; if it is incorrect, one part of the body is drawn on the hangman's gallows. There are nine body parts, which are drawn in this order: head, neck, left arm, right arm, body, left leg, right leg, left foot, and right foot.

■ The object of the game is for a group to guess the correct word before the picture of the hangman's body is completed. The group who guesses the word is the winner and gets to be "it," i.e., has a chance to be at the board. If there is enough classtime, play until every group has won and gotten a chance to be "it."

READING *Taking the risk*

In the text, Ss read about risky sports; they also practice scanning for main ideas.

- Books closed. Use the pre-reading questions to stimulate a short class discussion on the topic of participating in risky, or dangerous, sports.

Alternative presentation

- Do some brainstorming with the Ss: Write *RISKY (DANGEROUS) SPORTS* on the board. Then elicit examples from around the class and write each suggestion on the board. Can Ss explain why each of these sports might be considered risky?

A

- Books open. Go over the instructions, questions, and chart. Then Ss read the three interviews without using their dictionaries. As usual, ask them to circle, underline, or highlight any words whose meanings they can't guess from context.

- **Optional:** Allow Ss to work in pairs or small groups to discuss the article and to help one another define any new vocabulary they weren't able to guess.

- Before Ss complete the chart, use the pictures to help describe the three sports; also, go over any words or expressions that Ss still don't understand:

Jenny's interview
accident = something bad that happens unexpectedly or by chance
seriously injured = badly hurt
upside down = in a position with the top turned to the bottom
crashed = fell
landing = coming down from the air to the ground

Tom's interview
high altitudes = in the sky far above sea level
lack of oxygen = not enough air
tiredness = needing rest or sleep
dehydration = when the body badly needs water
avalanches = large amounts of snow and ice crashing down the side of a mountain
overcoming = fighting successfully against

Ray's interview
bubbles = hollow balls of air
rare = unusual
explore = look around a place; discover

- Ss look back through the interviews and complete the chart. Tell them to write their answers in note form. Go around the class and give help as needed.

- **Optional:** Encourage Ss to compare answers in pairs or small groups.

- Check Ss' answers around the class.

Possible answers

	Sport	*What they enjoy*	*The danger(s)*
1. Jenny	hang gliding	flying like a bird	can lose control; landing difficult
2. Tom	mountain climbing	overcoming danger	lack of oxygen; tiredness; dehydration; storms, avalanches, strong winds
3. Ray	scuba diving	exploring another world	the bends (death)

B *Pair work*

- Go over the questions. Then have Ss form pairs to take turns asking and answering the questions. Walk around the class and give help – but only if there is a communication breakdown.

- **Optional:** Find out which Ss have tried one of these sports. Ask them to come up to the front of the class to be on the "hot seat" (if there is only one S) or on a discussion panel (if there are two or more Ss). Then let the rest of the class ask as many questions as possible about their experiences with these risky sports.

Optional activity: *Picture story*

Time: 15–20 minutes. This creative storytelling activity practices the past tense.

Preparation: Ask each S to bring two or three pictures from magazines or newspapers showing interesting people, actions, scenes, and events. The pictures do not need to be related.

- Ss form small groups. Tell them to pool their pictures and to lay them out on a desk. They have to link the pictures to tell a story. Encourage Ss to be creative in making up interesting or unusual stories. If necessary, model how a story might begin by showing how some of the pictures from one group could be linked together.

- Set a time limit of about ten minutes. Move around the class and give help as needed.

- As a class activity, groups take turns telling their stories and the rest of the Ss ask them questions. After all the groups have finished, take a class vote: Which group told the most interesting story?

 Workbook

Assign Exercises 5–9 on pages 58–60 for homework. At the beginning of the next class, have Ss compare answers in pairs. Then elicit answers around the class for a final check. (Answers can be found on page T-184 of the Workbook Answer Key in this Teacher's Edition.)

11 *READING*

Taking the Risk

Sports World magazine spoke with Jenny Adams, Tom Barker, and Ray Lee about risky sports.

SW: Hang gliding is a dangerous sport. Jenny, what do you enjoy about the sport, and have you ever had an accident?

Jenny: No, I've never been seriously injured. Maybe I've just been lucky. Once, my glider turned upside down, and I lost control. I almost crashed, but I parachuted away just in time. And I've always felt hang gliding is quite safe – though landing is sometimes difficult. But it's fantastic to be able to fly like a bird!

SW: Tom, you've been mountain climbing for years now. What are some of the dangers that you've experienced?

Tom: High altitudes are hard on the human body. I've experienced lack of oxygen, tiredness, and dehydration. I've lived through storms, avalanches, and strong winds. But that's what I like about mountain climbing – overcoming danger.

SW: What exactly are the bends, Ray? And have you ever experienced them while scuba diving?

Ray: You get the bends when you've been deep under water. If you come up out of the water too quickly, bubbles form in your blood. The bends can be serious, and they can even cause death. But the bends are rare. Scuba diving isn't really dangerous. And it lets you explore another world.

A Read the article. What do Jenny, Tom, and Ray enjoy about the sports they describe? What is dangerous about each sport? Complete the chart.

	Sport	What they enjoy	The danger(s)
1. Jenny	....	....	....
2. Tom	....	....	....
3. Ray	....	....	....

B *Pair work* Talk about these questions.

1. Have you ever tried any of the sports described? What was it like?
2. Which of the sports would you like to try? Why?

11 It's a very exciting city!

1 WORD POWER Adjectives

A *Pair work* Match each word in column A with its opposite in column B. Then add two more pairs of adjectives to the list.

A	B
1. beautiful	a. boring
2. big	b. dangerous
3. cheap	c. dirty
4. clean	d. expensive
5. hot	e. stressful
6. interesting	f. small
7. safe	g. ugly
8. relaxing	h. cold
9.	i. ....
10.	j. ....

B Choose four adjectives from part A that describe your city. Then compare with a partner.

2 CONVERSATION Describing cities

Toronto

A 🔊 Listen and practice.

Linda: Where in Canada are you from, Ken?
Ken: I'm from Toronto.
Linda: Oh, I've never been there. What's it like?
Ken: It's a fairly big city, but it's not *too* big. The nightlife is good, too.
Linda: Is it expensive there?
Ken: No, it's not too bad.
Linda: And what's the weather like in Toronto?
Ken: Well, it's pretty cold in the winter, and very hot and humid in the summer. It's nice in the spring and fall, though.

CLASS AUDIO ONLY ▶ **B** 🔊 Listen to the rest of the conversation.

What does Ken say about entertainment in Toronto?

66

It's a very exciting city!

This unit practices describing hometowns, cities, and countries. It presents adverbs, adjectives, and conjunctions; it also introduces the modal verbs can and should to ask for and give suggestions.

Cycle 1, Exercises 1–6

1 WORD POWER Adjectives

This exercise presents adjectives used to describe cities; Ss will use these words often throughout the unit.

■ Books closed. As a warm-up to this topic and task, have a short brainstorming session with the class. Ask questions like these to get started:

What kind of place is . . . (the town or city the school is in; a famous city in your or the Ss' country)?
What does it look like? Can you describe it?

Write Ss' ideas on the board, like this:

(Name of town or city)

| a nice downtown | heavy traffic | terrible parking |
| a pretty park | a good museum | lots of graffiti |

(*Note:* Try not to classify the words on the board into positive/negative opposites.)

A Pair work

■ Books open. Model the pronunciation of the words in lists *A* and *B*; Ss repeat. Make sure Ss know that the word *interesting* has only three syllables /ˈɪntrɪstɪŋ/.

■ Go over the task and divide the class into pairs. Write this A/B dialog on the board and model how Ss can use it during the task:

A: What's the opposite of . . . ?
B: I think it's . . . .
A: Yes, that's right. (or) No, it's . . . .

■ Pairs work together – without using their dictionaries – to match each adjective with its opposite. Walk around and give help as needed. Then check Ss' answers.

Answers

| 1. g | 2. f | 3. d | 4. c | 5. h | 6. a | 7. b | 8. e |

■ Now pairs add two more sets of opposites. Ss may use their dictionaries for this if they wish.

■ To check pairs' answers, have them write their two sets of adjectives on the board; or have them reveal only one adjective while challenging the rest of the class to guess its opposite.

Possible answers

| new/old | good/bad | near/far |
| quiet/noisy | fantastic/horrible | warm/cool |

■ Remind Ss to write down the additional sets of opposite adjectives in their vocabulary notebooks.

B

■ Go over the instructions. Ss work individually to choose four adjectives to describe their own cities. Then they compare answers with a partner.

■ Elicit Ss' answers around the class. Find out if others agree with their classmates' choices.

2 CONVERSATION Describing cities

This exercise presents various adverbs and adjectives along with conjunctions (e.g., *but, and, though*).

A 🔊

■ Books closed. Set the scene: Two people are talking about a city. Write these questions on the board:

Where's Ken from? (He's from Toronto, Canada.)
What's Toronto like? (It's a fairly big city, but not too big. The nightlife is good, too.)
What's the weather like? (It's pretty cold in the winter, and very hot and humid in the summer. It's nice in the spring and fall.)

■ Play part A of the audio program. Ss listen for answers to the questions on the board. Then check Ss' responses.

■ Books open. Use the picture while presenting the conversation line by line; Ss repeat.

■ Ss practice the conversation in pairs.

B 🔊

■ Go over the question. Tell Ss to listen and take notes. Play the second part of the audio program.

Audio script

LINDA: So, what kind of entertainment is there in Toronto? Is there a lot to do?
KEN: Oh, sure! It's a very exciting city. There's wonderful theater and music.
LINDA: Wow! Anything else?
KEN: Well, there are some pretty fun dance clubs and really terrific jazz clubs, too.
LINDA: Toronto sounds like a great place to visit!

■ Ss compare notes. Then check Ss' answers.

Answer

He says there's wonderful theater and music. There are some pretty fun dance clubs and really terrific jazz clubs, too.

3 GRAMMAR FOCUS Adverbs and adjectives; conjunctions

🔊 This exercise practices describing cities with adverbs, adjectives, and conjunctions.

Adverbs can modify adjectives, which, in turn, describe nouns. Adverbs often answer the question "How?" The meaning and placement of adverbs *not* and *too* in negative sentences can be confusing for some Ss.

- Present and compare these sentences:

  It's ***not*** **a very exciting city. (or) It's *not* exciting.** = It's a boring place. (*negative*)

  It's ***too*** **expensive.** = It costs more than what the speaker wants to pay. (*negative*)

  It's ***not too*** **big.** = It isn't small, and it isn't big. (*neutral; neither positive nor negative*)

- Use the audio program to present the sentences in the box; Ss practice them once or twice.

- To help prevent Ss from using incorrect structures (e.g., It's interesting city./It's a too hot day.), write these patterns on the board and go over them:

  a. *be* + *adjective*
     It's   exciting.

  b. *be* + *adverb* + *adjective*
     It's   very   exciting.

  c. *be* + *article* + *adjective* + *noun*
     It's   an   exciting city.

  d. *be* + *article* + *adverb* + *adjective* + *noun*
     It's   a   very   exciting   city.

- Now explain that the conjunction *and* is used to connect two adjectives or ideas that are both considered positive or negative. Point out that the words *however, though,* and *but* are used to connect two opposite adjectives, descriptions, or ideas. Have Ss look at the Unit Summary for Unit 11 on page S-12 of their textbook.

- To practice these structures, elicit additional examples from the class. Then ask questions about some cities that Ss know: "What's . . . (e.g., London, Rio, Kyoto) like?"

A

- Explain the task. Have Ss work individually. Then check Ss' answers before pairs practice the conversations.

Answers

1. c	2. d	3. a	4. b

B *Pair work*

- Go over the task and briefly discuss the photos. Encourage Ss to include in their descriptions adverbs, adjectives, and conjunctions from the grammar focus box as well as other adjectives from Exercise 1 on page 66.

4 LISTENING

🔊 This exercise practices listening for key words and for general information about two people's hometowns.

- Books closed. Set the scene; play the audio program once without stopping. Ss only listen.

Audio script

1. WOMAN: So tell me about your hometown, Joyce.
   JOYCE: Well, it's a really small town . . . .
   WOMAN: What's it like there?
   JOYCE: Oh, I think it's a very boring place.
   WOMAN: Really? Why?
   JOYCE: Well, there's nothing to do. No good restaurants. No nightlife of any kind.
   WOMAN: Oh, that's too bad. But small towns are pretty inexpensive to live in.
   JOYCE: Well, yeah, it is fairly cheap. And lots of people love it there because it's very pretty.
   WOMAN: Yeah?
   JOYCE: Uh-huh. It has great scenery – lots of mountains and rivers, lakes, trees . . . .
   WOMAN: Well, I don't know, Joyce. It sounds like a lovely place!
   JOYCE: Well, yeah, if you like to go hiking in the summer and skiing in the winter. But, you know, I'm not the outdoors type! I'm a real city person.

2. WOMAN: Do you come from a big city, Nick?
   NICK: Yeah, I do. It's pretty big.
   WOMAN: So there's a lot to do there?
   NICK: Oh, sure. It's a really fun place! It has some fantastic art museums and wonderful theaters and terrific restaurants of all kinds.
   WOMAN: Uh . . . really? How are the prices? Is it expensive?
   NICK: I guess so. Food costs a lot . . . both in the supermarket and in restaurants. And apartments! The rents are pretty high.
   WOMAN: And what's it like there? What does it look like?
   NICK: Well, it's very clean, and it's really pretty, too. There are lots of parks and trees right in the center of the city.

- Books open. Go over the task and the chart. Play the audio program again. Ss complete the chart and compare answers. Check Ss' responses.

Answers

	Big? Yes/No	Interesting? Yes/No	Expensive? Yes/No	Beautiful? Yes/No
1. Joyce		✓	✓	✓
2. Nick	✓	✓	✓	✓

3 GRAMMAR FOCUS

Adverbs and adjectives; conjunctions 🔊

It's a **very** exciting city. It's **too** expensive, **however**.
It's **not very** exciting. It's **really** beautiful, **though**.
It's a **fairly** big city, **but** it's **not too** big.
It's **pretty** safe, **and** it's **very** friendly.

A Match the questions with the answers. Then practice
the conversations.

1. What's Hong Kong like?
   Is it an interesting place? ....

2. Do you like your hometown? ....

3. What's Sydney like?
   I've never been there. ....

4. Have you ever been to
   São Paulo? ....

a. Oh, really? It's beautiful, and it's very clean.
   It has a great harbor and beautiful beaches.

b. Yes, many times. It's a very modern city.
   It's too hot in the summer, though.

c. Yes, it is. It's very exciting.
   It's really crowded, however.

d. No, I hate it. It's not too small, but it's
   pretty boring. That's why I moved away.

B *Pair work* What do you think of these cities? Take turns describing them.

"San Francisco is a really exciting city, and it's very clean."

4 LISTENING

🔊 Listen to Joyce and Nick talk about their hometowns. What do they say?
Check (✓) the correct boxes.

	Big?		Interesting?		Expensive?		Beautiful?	
	Yes	No	Yes	No	Yes	No	Yes	No
1. Joyce	☐	☐	☐	☐	☐	☐	☐	☐
2. Nick	☐	☐	☐	☐	☐	☐	☐	☐

5 HOME SWEET HOME

Group work Take turns. Ask one student about his or her hometown.
Then ask follow-up questions to get more information.

What's your city like?

Is it an interesting place?   Is it very expensive?
Is it very big?   What's the nightlife like?
Is it safe?   What's the weather like?
Is it clean?   Do you like it there?

6 WRITING

Pair work Think of an interesting city in
your country. Write a short composition
about it. Then exchange compositions.
Can your partner suggest any information
to add?

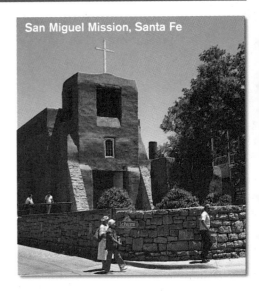
San Miguel Mission, Santa Fe

> My favorite city in the United States is Santa Fe.
> It's in New Mexico. It's an old city with lots
> of interesting Native American and Spanish
> buildings. It's fairly small, and it's really beautiful. . . .

7 SNAPSHOT

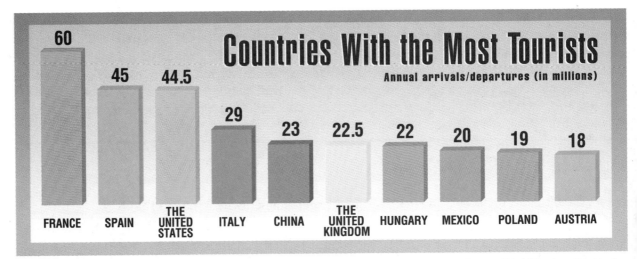

Countries With the Most Tourists
Annual arrivals/departures (in millions)

FRANCE	SPAIN	THE UNITED STATES	ITALY	CHINA	THE UNITED KINGDOM	HUNGARY	MEXICO	POLAND	AUSTRIA
60	45	44.5	29	23	22.5	22	20	19	18

Source: World Tourism Organization

Talk about these questions.

Why do you think France has the most tourists?
Which countries on this list would you most like to visit? Rank the countries from 1 to 10.
Which country did you rank number 1? Why?

5 HOME SWEET HOME

This is a fluency activity during which Ss describe their hometowns or cities.

Group work

■ Present the task and the questions.

■ Model the activity: Have Ss use the questions listed to ask about your hometown or city. Demonstrate how to give descriptive answers by using adjectives, adverbs, and conjunctions in your responses. Then elicit other questions that Ss can ask and write them on the board. Add these structures to the list:

> Is there a/an . . . (e.g., park, theater, historical site) in your hometown?
> Are there any interesting . . . (e.g., shops) there?
> How's the . . . (e.g., transportation, traffic, crime)?
> Where's a good place to . . . (e.g., hear music)?

■ Set a time limit of about ten minutes. Ss work in pairs, taking turns talking about their cities. Walk around the class and give help as needed.

6 WRITING

In this exercise, Ss practice writing a short description of a city in their country.

Pair work

■ Go over the task and read the example paragraph aloud. Can the class suggest any sentences to add to it?

■ Encourage Ss to brainstorm on their chosen cities in order to generate a lot of interesting information and details to include in their descriptive compositions. This can be done individually; or it can be done competitively in pairs, with each partner trying to write down the most words within a certain time (e.g., two minutes).

■ Ss write a first draft either in class or for homework. Remind them to use plenty of adverbs, adjectives, and conjunctions in their writing.

■ Before pairs exchange compositions, write these Wh-question words on the board for Ss to use while giving feedback: *Who? What? When? Where? Why?* and *How?*

■ Model how to use the Wh-words to have a helpful feedback exchange, like this: With a volunteer, demonstrate how to sit side by side so that both partners can read the same draft together. Explain that the writer lets his or her partner read the writer's composition aloud. The reader also asks for more information or clarification by using the Wh-words, like this (*T = Reader; S = Writer*):

T: *(reading aloud)* "My favorite city is . . . . It's very big and old. I often like to go there . . . ." *(stopping reading to ask)* **Why** do you often like to go there? **What** do you do? Give me an example.

S: Well, I love the downtown area. There's one coffee shop I always go to. It has delicious coffee and wonderful music.

T: That's very interesting! Add that information here. It improves your description.

S: Oh, really? OK. Good idea! *(adds new sentences or writes notes on the draft)*

T: *(waits for the writer to finish, and then continues)*

■ Ss work on writing and revising their final drafts, incorporating ideas from their feedback session.

 **Workbook**

Assign Exercises 1–6 on pages 61–64 in the Workbook as in-class work or for homework. Ss compare answers in groups when all exercises have been completed. Assign one exercise to each group, who is then in charge of checking Ss' responses around the class on that same task. (Answers can be found on page T-185 of the Workbook Answer Key in this Teacher's Edition.)

Cycle 2, Exercises 7–13

7 SNAPSHOT *Countries with the most tourists*

This graphic introduces the topic of countries that receive a lot of tourists.

■ Books closed. Ask the class this question: "Which three countries do you think get the most tourists every year?" Let Ss guess, and write their suggestions on the board.

■ Books open. Tell Ss to look over the Snapshot for the answer to the question above. Check answers (France, Spain, and the United States.)

■ Go over the information. Explain any new words or expressions, such as:

> **arrivals/departures** = number of visitors entering/ leaving a country
> **in millions** = add six zeros to each number given (e.g., 59 here = 59,000,000 = fifty-nine million)

■ Present the questions. For the second question, tell Ss that *1* = the country they would like to visit the most, *2* = the one they would like to visit next, and so forth. Ss answer the questions individually and then compare information and opinions around the class.

8 CONVERSATION Giving suggestions

This exercise introduces the topics of travel and taking vacations; it also presents the modal verbs *can* and *should* for asking for and giving suggestions.

A 🔊

■ Books closed. Set the scene: Two friends are talking about a certain city. Write these focus questions on the board:

Which city is the man asking about? (Mexico City)
What's a good time to visit? (Anytime)
What's the weather like? (It's always nice.)
How many places should he see there? (Three)

■ Play the audio program once or twice. Tell Ss to take notes as they listen. After Ss compare answers in pairs or groups, elicit Ss' responses.

■ Books open. Play the audio program again while Ss listen and look at the photos.

■ Present the conversation line by line. Explain these expressions, if necessary:

> **Can you tell me a little about . . . ?** = What do you know about . . . ?
> **What else?** = Is there anything more?
> **you shouldn't miss** = it's a good idea to see

(*Note:* The National Museum of Anthropology is one of the great museums of the world; its treasures include Mayan and Aztec artifacts. The Palace of Fine Arts is Mexico's most important theater; it also houses a permanent show of modern Mexican paintings. The Pyramid of the Sun is located about 30 miles from Mexico City in Teotihuacán, one of the best preserved and most beautiful archeological centers in Mexico.)

■ Ss practice the conversation in pairs.

B 🔊

■ Go over the two questions and play part B of the audio program. Ss listen for the answers.

Audio script

> MARIA: Where are you from again, David?
> DAVID: I'm from Miami, Florida.
> MARIA: Oh! I've always wanted to visit Miami. What's it like? What can you do there?
> DAVID: Well, there's a lot to do. But a visitor should definitely spend some time on the beach. The beaches there are beautiful.

■ Check Ss' responses around the class.

Answers

> 1. He's from Miami, Florida.
> 2. You should spend some time on the beach.

■ **Optional:** Has anyone ever been to Mexico City or Miami? Put him or her on the "hot seat," having the class ask for more information about the city.

---

9 GRAMMAR FOCUS Modal verbs can and should

🔊 This grammar focus practices the modal verbs *can* and *should* in questions and statements to ask for or make suggestions.

■ Explain that modal verbs or auxiliaries are usually added to a main verb and express a speaker's attitude or "mood"; here the modals *can* and *should* help the speaker give advice or make suggestions. Point out that modals do not take a final *-s* even when there is a third person singular subject: *he, she,* or *it.* Also, modals in sentences are followed immediately by a verb's simple, or base, form.

■ Clarify this pronunciation point: In affirmative (positive) statements and questions, the main verb – rather than the modal verb – is usually pronounced or stressed more strongly (e.g., "What can you **do** there? You can **see** . . . ."). However, in negative statements, both the modal verb *and* the main verb are usually stressed (e.g., "You **should**n't **miss** the Pyramid of the Sun."). (*Note:* Ss will also practice saying negative statements like these in Exercise 10 on page 70.)

■ Use the audio program to present the questions and responses in the box; Ss practice several times. Remind them to stress the correct words. Then elicit additional Wh-questions and statements with *can* and *should*.

A

■ Explain the task and go over the verb phrases in the small box on the right. Model how to do the first item with the class. Then Ss work individually to complete the sentences.

Answers

> 1. You **should visit** Paris.
> 2. You **can see** the Eiffel Tower.
> 3. You **should try** French food.
> 4. You **can go** shopping at the flea markets.
> 5. You **shouldn't miss** a boat ride on the Seine River.
> 6. You **should spend** a morning at the Louvre Museum.

■ After Ss compare answers in pairs, check answers around the class.

B *Pair work*

■ Go over the task and the example answer for number 1. Model the task by having Ss ask you some questions about your country. After answering a question, write that same response on the board. Then Ss work individually to do the task. Elicit Ss' responses around the class.

8 CONVERSATION *Giving suggestions*

A Listen and practice.

the Palace of Fine Arts

David: Can you tell me a little about Mexico City?
Maria: Sure I can. What would you like to know?
David: Well, what's a good time to visit?
Maria: I think you can go anytime. The weather is always nice.
David: Oh, good! And what should I see there?
Maria: Well, you should visit the National Museum and go to the Palace of Fine Arts.
David: What else?
Maria: Oh, you shouldn't miss the Pyramid of the Sun. It's very interesting.
David: It all sounds really exciting!

CLASS AUDIO ONLY ▶ **B** 📼 Listen to the rest of the conversation.

1. Where is David from?
2. What should you do there?

the Pyramid of the Sun

9 GRAMMAR FOCUS

Modal verbs can *and* should 📼

Can you tell me about Mexico? What **can** you do there?	Yes, I **can**./No, I **can't**. You **can** see the Palace of Fine Arts.
Should I go to the Palace of Fine Arts? What **should** I see there?	Yes, you **should**./No, you **shouldn't**. You **should** visit the National Museum. You **shouldn't** miss the Pyramid of the Sun.

A Complete these sentences about things to do in France. Use the verbs from the list.

1. You .... Paris.
2. You .... the Eiffel Tower.
3. You .... French food.
4. You .... shopping at the flea markets.
5. You .... a boat ride on the Seine River.
6. You .... a morning at the Louvre Museum.

should spend
can see
can go
should visit
should try
shouldn't miss

B *Pair work* Write answers to these questions about your country. Then compare with a partner.

1. What time of year should you go there?
2. What are three things you can do there?
3. Can you buy anything special?
4. What shouldn't a visitor miss?
5. What shouldn't people do?

1. You should go in the spring.

10 *PRONUNCIATION* Can't *and* shouldn't

A Listen and practice these sentences. Notice how the *t* in **can't** and **shouldn't** is pronounced.

You can't walk home on the streets late at night.
You shouldn't miss the night markets.
You can't go shopping on Sundays.
You shouldn't swim at the beaches.

B *Class activity* Are any of these statements true about your city?

interchange 11

City guide
Make a guide to fun and interesting places in your city. Turn to page IC-15.

11 *LISTENING*

CLASS AUDIO ONLY ▶ **A** Listen to three speakers talk about Japan, Argentina, and Italy. Complete the chart.

	Capital city	What visitors should see or do
1. Japan	....	....
2. Argentina	....	....
3. Italy	....	....

CLASS AUDIO ONLY ▶ **B** Listen again. One thing about each country is incorrect. What is it?

12 *ON VACATION*

Group work Has anyone in your group visited an interesting country or place in your country? Find out more about it. Start like this and ask questions like the ones below.

A: I visited Malaysia last summer.
B: Did you enjoy it?
A: Yes, I did.
C: . . .

What's the best time of year to visit?
What's the weather like then?
What should tourists see and do there?
What special foods can you eat?
What's the shopping like?
What things should people buy?
What else can visitors do there?

Kuala Lumpur, Malaysia

a market in Kuala Lumpur

10 PRONUNCIATION Can't *and* shouldn't

This exercise practices how to reduce the /t/ ending in *can't* and *shouldn't* when they are followed by a verb in a sentence.

A

- Read aloud the instructions. Explain that it is easier to reduce the *t* in *can't* and *shouldn't* than it is to pronounce it distinctly.
- Play each sentence on the audio program once or twice. Then play it again, pausing to allow Ss to practice each sentence several times.

B *Class activity*

- Have Ss take turns asking and answering the questions given in part A, like this:

  S1: Kevin, is it true that you can't walk home on the streets late at night in your city?

  S2: No, it's not true in . . . (city). In your city, Ty, you shouldn't miss the night markets, right?

INTERCHANGE 11 City guide

See page T-119 in this Teacher's Edition for notes.

11 LISTENING

This exercise practices listening for specific information.

A

- Books closed. Tell Ss they will hear people talking about three different countries. (*Note:* Don't tell them yet that some information here may be false, as that is the task in part B.) Play the audio program. Ss only listen.

Audio script

1. MAN 1: Today, I'm going to speak about Japan. Japan has several major islands and a lot of smaller islands. The capital city is Tokyo. The highest mountain in Japan is called Mount Everest. There are many beautiful Buddhist temples and Shinto shrines there. Visitors should try Japanese food, especially sashimi, which is raw fish.
2. WOMAN: Let me tell you about Argentina. Argentina is a country located in southeastern South America. It's a very large country. The capital city is Buenos Aires. The people all speak French. People visiting Buenos Aires shouldn't miss the downtown area, called the Plaza de Mayo. Many interesting people gather in this area.
3. MAN 2: Italy is a country in southern Europe, on the Atlantic Ocean. The country is shaped like a boot. And it's famous for its excellent food, especially pasta. Italy is also famous for its art, old buildings, and several beautiful cities – for example, the capital city of Rome.

- Ask the class some questions that won't give away answers needed for the chart – for example:

  Which three countries did they talk about? (Japan, Argentina, and Italy)

Which country is "very large"? (Argentina)

- Books open. Now go over the instructions and the chart. Play the audio program again. This time, Ss complete the chart. Elicit Ss' responses around the class.

Answers

	Capital city	*What visitors . . .*
1. Japan	Tokyo	see beautiful Buddhist temples and Shinto shrines; eat Japanese food
2. Argentina	Buenos Aires	go to downtown area
3. Italy	Rome	eat Italian food; see art, old buildings, several beautiful cities

B

- Read the instructions aloud. Explain that one statement about each place is incorrect. Play the audio program again; Ss take notes. Then check Ss' answers.

Answers

1. *Incorrect:* The highest mountain in Japan is called Mount Everest.
   Correct: The highest mountain in Japan is called Mount Fuji.
2. *Incorrect:* The people all speak French.
   Correct: The people all speak Spanish.
3. *Incorrect:* Italy is . . . on the Atlantic Ocean.
   Correct: Italy is . . . on the Mediterranean Sea.

12 ON VACATION

This fluency activity practices describing interesting vacation places; it also gives Ss additional practice with *can* and *should*.

Group work

- Read aloud the instructions. Then go over the questions and model the example dialog with several Ss.
- Ss form groups and take turns answering questions about an interesting place they have visited.

13 READING *Famous cities*

In this text, Ss read about three interesting world cities; the exercises practice reading for main ideas as well as scanning and making inferences.

- Books closed. Read the two pre-reading questions aloud. Ask for volunteers to respond; encourage other Ss to ask for more information.

A

(*Note:* This task can be done individually, in pairs or groups, or as a whole class activity.)

- Books open. Remind Ss that they do not need to know every word in the text. Tell them to try to guess the meaning of a new word from the context or through ideas surrounding it in the sentence or paragraph. For example, point out that Ss should be able to guess the meaning of the Italian word *gondolas* (see paragraph 1) because the text defines it for them: "Flat-bottomed boats called gondolas . . . ."

- Go over the instructions. Ss read the three descriptions. Remind them to identify the city being described in each paragraph by checking the correct name from the three choices given.

- **Optional:** Ss compare answers in pairs.

- Check Ss' answers around the class.

Answers

1. Venice	2. Chicago	3. Rio de Janeiro

- Tell Ss to look at each paragraph again. Ask how they chose the correct city. (*Note:* Doing this may help Ss become more aware of some other strategies they can use to make inferences.)

- If a S wasn't able to understand a particular word (e.g., *Renaissance*), ask the rest of the class to make a guess by giving a definition, an example or a synonym, or an antonym. Also, model how Ss should try to guess a word or expression from context – for example:

    T: If we try to make an educated guess here about the word *Renaissance,* we see that it refers to buildings. (*reading from paragraph 1*): "It has wonderful Renaissance buildings." So, we can guess that it probably describes some type of architecture, a style of building, or even a historical time in Venice.

(*Note:* It's not necessary for Ss to get the precise meaning of terms like *Renaissance* while reading a text. After Ss finish reading a passage, though, they can always check their dictionaries for the precise definition of a word or words they weren't sure about.)

- Go over any new words and expressions Ss may still have trouble understanding, such as:

Paragraph 1
islands = pieces of land surrounded by water
canals = waterways dug into the ground that allow boats to travel along them

the main means of transportation = the most important or popular way to travel in a place

Paragraph 2
opera = a musical play in which most of the words are sung

Paragraph 3
glamorous = charming and beautiful
Carnival = public fun and entertainment with eating, dancing, drinking, parades, and shows; a festival period before Lent in some Catholic countries, like Brazil
samba = a Brazilian dance of African origin
fabulous = fantastic

B

- Go over the task and the chart. Ss scan the three descriptions again and complete the chart individually. Then Ss compare answers with a partner. Elicit answers around the class.

Answers

Where is . . . ?	*What is . . . ?*	*What should . . . ?*
1. in northeastern Italy	no roads; canals, gondolas	see St. Mark's Square
2. in the Midwest U.S.	music, opera, theater, museums	visit Magnificent Mile, John Hancock Center
3. South America	Carnival; beaches and mountains	don't miss National Park of Tijuca

C *Class activity*

- Ss take turns telling the class which of the three cities featured in the reading they would most like to visit – and why.

Optional activities

1 *Let's go!*

- See page T-148.

2 *Game – Word Bingo*

- See page T-33.

3 *Crossword puzzle*

- See page T-146.

4 *Chain story – Visiting a foreign country*

- See page T-150.

 **Workbook**

Assign Exercises 7–10 on pages 65–66 for homework. At the beginning of the next class, have Ss compare answers in pairs. Then elicit answers around the class for a final check. (Answers can be found on page T-185 of the Workbook Answer Key in this Teacher's Edition.)

13 *READING*

FAMOUS CITIES

What cities are famous in your country? Why are they famous?

1.

This beautiful city in northeastern Italy is built on about 120 small islands. The city has no roads. Instead, people use boats to travel along the canals. Flat-bottomed boats called gondolas were once the main means of transportation, but today motorboats are more popular. You should see St. Mark's Square – the center of activity in this city. It has wonderful Renaissance buildings.

Which city:
- ☐ Paris
- ☐ Venice
- ☐ Rome

2.

This American city is the main business and cultural center of the Midwest. It is famous for its music, opera, and theater. It also has excellent museums. When shopping in this city, you can visit a long row of fashionable stores on North Michigan Avenue. This area is called the Magnificent Mile. One of the world's tallest buildings, the John Hancock Center, is also on this avenue.

Which city:
- ☐ New York
- ☐ San Francisco
- ☐ Chicago

3.

Travelers use many words to describe this South American city: beautiful, glamorous, sunny, friendly, and exciting. It is the city of the Carnival, when everyone dances the samba in the streets. Tourists also love to visit its fabulous beaches and mountains. You shouldn't miss the National Park of Tijuca – one of the largest city parks in the world.

Which city:
- ☐ Mexico City
- ☐ Rio de Janeiro
- ☐ Havana

A Read descriptions of the three cities. Check (✓) the correct city to match each description.

B Complete the chart with information about each city.
Then compare with a partner.

Where is this city?	What is special about this city?	What should visitors do there?
1.		
2.		
3.		

C *Class activity* Which city would you like to visit? Why?

12 It really works!

1 SNAPSHOT

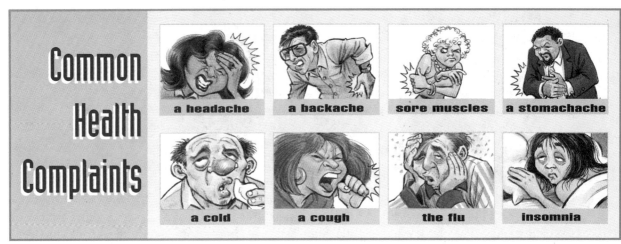

Common Health Complaints

a headache   a backache   sore muscles   a stomachache

a cold   a cough   the flu   insomnia

Source: National Center for Health Statistics

Talk about these questions.

Have you had any of these health problems recently? Which ones?
How many times have you been sick in the past year?
What do you do when you have a headache? a cold? insomnia?

2 CONVERSATION Health problems

A Listen and practice.

Joan: Hi, Craig! How are you?
Craig: Not so good. I have a terrible cold.
Joan: Really? That's too bad! You should be at home in bed. It's really important to get a lot of rest.
Craig: Yeah, you're right.
Joan: And have you taken anything for it?
Craig: No, I haven't.
Joan: Well, it's helpful to chop up some garlic and cook it in chicken stock. Then drink a cup every half hour. It really works!
Craig: Ugh!

CLASS AUDIO ONLY

B Listen to advice from two more of Craig's co-workers.

What do they suggest?

12 It really works!

This unit practices talking about health problems and buying over-the-counter medicines in a drugstore. It introduces infinitive complements for giving advice. It also presents making requests with the modal verbs can, could, and may, and provides additional language for giving suggestions.

Cycle 1, Exercises 1–5

1 SNAPSHOT Common health complaints

This graphic introduces the theme of common health complaints; it also practices some new vocabulary that Ss will use throughout the unit.

■ Books closed. Introduce the Snapshot topic by asking the class some general questions about common health complaints, such as:

T: Does anyone have a cold today?
S1: I have a little cold.
T: Oh, that's too bad, Sue. Do you often get colds?
S1: Well, I usually get one or two colds a year.
T: And how many colds do you get a year, Ed?
S2: Oh, I guess I get . . .

■ Books open. Tell Ss to look over the Snapshot

information. They shouldn't use their dictionaries; instead, they should try to guess the meanings of the new words by looking at the illustrations. Explain or mime any words that Ss still don't understand.

■ Model the pronunciation of -ache /eyk/ in headache, backache, and stomachache, and the word insomnia /ɪnˈsɑmniyə/. Have Ss repeat.

■ Go over the questions. Ss can first answer the questions individually, taking notes. Then have Ss talk about the questions in pairs or small groups.

■ Elicit Ss' answers around the class. Write any new vocabulary concerning health and medicine on the board for Ss to add to their notebooks.

2 CONVERSATION Health problems

This exercise continues the topic of the common cold; it also presents infinitive complements (e.g., It's important to + verb . . . .) for giving advice.

A 🔊

■ Books closed. Set the scene: A woman is asking a co-worker about his health. Write some questions on the board like these for Ss to focus their listening on:

What's the matter with Craig? (He has a terrible cold.)
What advice does the woman give him? (He should be at home in bed. It's really important to get a lot of rest.)
Has the man taken anything? (No, he hasn't.)
What does the woman tell him to do? (Chop up some garlic and cook it in chicken stock, then drink a cup every half hour.)
How does Craig reply? (Ugh!)

■ Play the audio program for part A. Ss listen and take notes. Check Ss' answers to the questions on the board.

■ Books open. Play the audio program again. Tell Ss to look at the picture as they listen.

■ Present the conversation line by line. Explain these words and expressions if necessary:

get a lot of rest = take time to relax or sleep
And have you taken anything for it? = Have you . . . (e.g., drunk, swallowed, eaten) any food or medicine to help you feel better?
chop up = cut in small pieces
chicken stock = the liquid made by boiling chicken in water
Ugh! = an exclamation used to express dislike or disgust

■ Ss practice the conversation with a partner.

B 🔊

■ Read the instructions and the question aloud. Play the audio program for part B. Tell Ss to listen and take notes.

Audio script

1. CRAIG: *(coughs and sneezes)*
   WOMAN: That cold sounds pretty bad, Craig!
   CRAIG: Yeah, it is. Don't get too close.
   WOMAN: Well, you know, it's important to drink a lot of liquids. I've got some herbal tea. Let me make you a cup.
   CRAIG: Gee, that's nice of you! What kind of herbal tea is it?
   WOMAN: I think it's ginseng.
   CRAIG: Oh, OK. That sounds good.
2. MAN: How's that cold, Craig?
   CRAIG: Not so good. I've still got it.
   MAN: Oh, too bad. Well, listen, it's a good idea to take some cold medicine. And you should go home and take a long, hot bath.
   CRAIG: You're right. Maybe I should. Thanks for the advice.

■ After Ss compare answers in pairs, check responses around the class.

Answer

The woman says it's important to drink a lot of liquids. The man says it's a good idea to take some cold medicine and Craig should go home and take a long, hot bath.

T-72

3 GRAMMAR FOCUS Infinitive complements

This grammar focus practices infinitive complements for giving advice.

The infinitive (*to* + simple form of the verb) and a phrase, known as an infinitive complement, is used after certain adjectives and nouns or noun phrases to "complete" the predicate.

An infinitive is commonly used in a sentence starting with *it* + *be,* where the pronoun *it* is often thought of as an "empty" subject while the verb *be* acts like an equal sign (=). Therefore, the *it* refers to and has the same meaning as the infinitive complement at the end of the sentence. For example:

Subject		Predicate	
It	is (=)	important	to get some rest.
		a good idea	to take vitamin C.
(subject pronoun)	*(linking verb)*	*(adjective or noun phrase)*	*(infinitive complement)*

- Use the audio program to present the question and pieces of advice in the box; Ss repeat.

- Do a quick question-and-response drill with the whole class, like this:

   T: What should you do for a cold? Please look at the grammar box and answer with "It's important to . . . ."
   Ss: It's important to get a lot of rest.
   T: Good. Now use "It's useful to . . . ."
   Ss: It's useful to get some cold medicine.
   T: *(switching focus)* Now ask me about the flu.
   Ss: What should you do for the flu?
   T: It's a good idea to see the doctor. Repeat.
   Ss: It's a good idea to see the doctor.
   T: Now ask me about a backache.
   Ss: What should you do for a backache?

- **Optional:** Explain that another way to answer the question "What should you do . . . ?" is to make a suggestion starting with "You should get/take/try . . ." (modal verb *should* + base verb + object). (*Note:* See also Exercise 8 on page 75 of the Student's Book.)

A

- Go over the instructions and present each item in the two lists called *Problems* and *Advice.* Model the correct pronunciation; Ss repeat. Use the pictures to explain any new words.

- Tell Ss that they should choose at least three pieces of advice that are appropriate for each problem. Then have Ss do the matching task individually.

- **Optional:** Ss form pairs to compare answers. Model how Ss can take turns checking their answers while using the structures in the box:

   T: What should you do for a sore throat?
   S1: Well, I think it's a good idea to (j) see the doctor.
   T: Yes, I agree. It's also important to (h) get some medicine from the drugstore.
   S2: Right. And it's useful to . . . .

- Elicit Ss' ideas around the class.

Possible answers

```
1. a, c, d, h, j
2. a, d, h, j
3. b, d, e, g, j
4. c, d, g, h, j
5. g, i
6. d, g, h, j
7. b, f, h, j
8. c, d, g, h, j
```

B Group work

- Go over the instructions. Then model the dialog with a volunteer.

- **Optional:** Brainstorm on other expressions for giving advice with infinitive complements. Write them on the board; Ss copy them into their vocabulary notebooks. Tell Ss to use them in this exercise and in other activities in the unit. Here are some examples:

   It's essential . . .
   It's best . . .
   It's common . . .
   It's smart . . .

- Ss form groups to practice giving advice about the problems in part A. Walk around the class and discreetly listen in. Offer help, particularly if there is a communication breakdown of any kind.

- Because Ss' answers will vary, ask groups to share some of the more interesting or unusual advice they heard during this activity.

C

- Go over the instructions, the list of problems, and the example. Find out if anyone can guess the problems of the people in the picture. (Answer: The man has stress. The woman has sore eyes.) Clarify any new words, if necessary (e.g., *stress* = a condition causing worry, depression, and other health problems).

- Ss do the task individually. Tell them to write their sentences on a separate piece of paper. Go around the class and give help as needed. (*Note:* Don't check Ss' answers or have Ss compare sentences at this time. Ss will be asked to do this in Exercise 4 on page 74.)

Optional activities

1 *Getting to know you – better!*
- See page T-64.

2 *Game – Simon Says*
- See page T-150.

3 *Absent again!*
- See page T-150.

3 *GRAMMAR FOCUS*

Infinitive complements 🔊

What should you do for a cold?	**It's important** to get a lot of rest.
	It's a good idea to take some vitamin C.
	It's useful to get some cold medicine.
	It's helpful to chop up some garlic and cook it.

A Look at these health problems. Choose several pieces of good advice for each problem.

a sore throat

a fever

a toothache

Problems

1. a sore throat ....
2. a cough ....
3. a backache ....
4. a fever ....
5. a toothache ....
6. a bad headache ....
7. a burn ....
8. the flu ....

Advice

a. take some vitamin C
b. put some ointment on it
c. drink lots of liquids
d. go to bed and rest
e. put a heating pad on it
f. put it under cold water
g. take some aspirin
h. get some medicine
   from the drugstore
i. see the dentist
j. see the doctor

a burn

B *Group work* Talk about the problems in part A and give advice. What other advice do you have for each problem?

A: What should you do for a sore throat?
B: It's a good idea to get some medicine from the drugstore.
C: Yes. And it's important to drink lots of liquids.
D: Well, I think it's useful to . . . .

C Write advice for these problems. (You will use this advice in Exercise 4.)

a cold
insomnia
sore eyes
sore muscles
stress

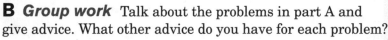

For a cold, it's a good idea to . . . .

stress

sore eyes

4 PRONUNCIATION *Reduced form of* to

A 🔊 Listen and practice. In conversation, **to** is usually reduced to /tə/.

A: What should you do for a fever?
B: It's important **to** take some aspirin.
   And it's a good idea **to** see the doctor.

B *Pair work* Now look back at part C of Exercise 3. Ask for and give advice about the health problems you wrote about. Pay attention to the pronunciation of **to**.

interchange 12

Talk radio
Imagine you are a talk show host. Give advice to some callers. Turn to page IC-16.

5 WHAT DID YOU DO?

A *Pair work* Take turns talking about these problems.

a stomachache   an insect bite   a sore throat   the hiccups

A: Have you ever had a stomachache?
B: Sure I have. Just last night, actually.
A: What did you do?
B: I took some antacid.

B *Group work* Compare with other pairs. Tell what you did for each problem.

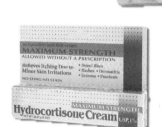

6 WORD POWER *Containers and medicines*

A Use the words in the list to complete these expressions. Then compare with a partner.

bottle   box   can   package   tube

1. a .... of ointment
2. a .... of aspirin
3. a .... of bandages
4. a .... of foot spray
5. a .... of tissues

B What is one more thing you can buy in each of the containers above?

C What common items do you have in your medicine cabinet?

4 PRONUNCIATION Reduced form of to

This exercise focuses on the reduction of *to* in conversation.

A

- Present the instructions and explanation. Then play the audio program; Ss only listen. Play the audio program again, this time pausing it after each line for a class chorus. Also, spot-check individual Ss' pronunciation.

B Pair work

- Go over the instructions: Pairs compare their sentences from part C of Exercise 3 on page 73. Remind Ss to use the reduced form of *to*.
- When pairs finish, elicit their most interesting piece of advice. Write it on the board.

INTERCHANGE 12 Talk radio

See page T-120 in this Teacher's Edition for notes.

5 WHAT DID YOU DO?

This exercise is an open-ended communication activity that practices giving advice with infinitive complements, at the same time recycling the present perfect and past tense.

A Pair work

- Go over the activity. Explain or mime any new vocabulary. Also, model the pronunciation of *hiccups* /'hɪkʌps/, *hydrocortisone* /ˌhaɪdrə'kɔrtəzown/, and *antacid* /æn'tæsɪd/.
- Model the example A/B dialog with one S. Then continue demonstrating the activity with the whole class by asking for advice about other problems, like this:

T: Have you ever had the hiccups?
S1: Sure I have! I always get them after I drink something very cold.
T: How do people usually get rid of the hiccups?
S2: Some people think it's useful to hold your breath.

- Ss practice the activity in pairs. One S acts as the secretary and writes down any advice given. Encourage Ss to suggest interesting or unusual home or folk remedies rather than standard drugstore medication. Walk around the class and give help as needed.

B Group work

- Two pairs form a group. The pairs use the two secretaries' notes to share remedies.

Workbook

Assign Exercises 1–4 on pages 67–69 in the Workbook for end-of-class work or for homework. Ss compare answers in pairs or groups when all the exercises have been completed. (Answers can be found on page T-186 of the Workbook Answer Key in this Teacher's Edition.)

Cycle 2, Exercises 6–12

6 WORD POWER Containers and medicines

This exercise presents partitive phrases – also known as unit expressions – used with countable and uncountable nouns (e.g., *a box of* tissues).

A

- Go over the task. Use the picture to present the container words (e.g., *bottle*). When doing this, be careful not to use a word with a phrase (e.g., a bottle of pills) as this is the Ss' task.
- Ss work alone to fill in the blanks and then compare answers in pairs. Check answers around the class.

Answers

1. a **tube** of ointment
2. a **bottle** of aspirin
3. a **package** of bandages
4. a **can** of foot spray
5. a **box** of tissues

- Use the answers to model how the preposition *of* in partitive phrases is unstressed; Ss practice.

B

- Go over the task. Allow Ss to work individually, in pairs or groups, or as a whole class. Then check Ss' ideas and write them on the board.

Possible answers

a bottle of vitamins/soda/ketchup/wine
a box of herbal tea/cereal/candy/cookies
a can of hair spray/soda/beer/paint/coffee/peas
a package of throat lozenges/gum/mints
a tube of toothpaste/lipstick/mascara/hand cream

C

- This could also be a pair, group, or whole class activity.

7 CONVERSATION *Giving suggestions*

This exercise introduces requests with *can, could,* and *may;* it also presents suggestions with the imperative "Try . . . ." along with the structures *I suggest* . . . . and *You should* . . . .

A 🔊

■ Books closed. Set the scene: A customer is in a drugstore talking to the pharmacist. Write some focus questions like these on the board:

What does the customer want? (She wants something for a cough.)
Why does she want it? (She thinks she's getting a cold.)
What does the pharmacist suggest? (A box of cough drops and a bottle of vitamin C)
What else does the customer want? (Something for dry skin)

■ Play the first part of the audio program. Ss listen for answers to the questions on the board. Then elicit Ss' answers.

■ Books open. Play the audio program again, this time with the Ss looking at the picture as they listen.

■ Present the conversation line by line. Explain any new vocabulary, if necessary. Point out that the word *some* is unstressed in the suggestion "Try some of this new lotion."

■ Ss practice the conversation in pairs. Remind them to use the "Look Up and Say" technique.

■ **Optional:** Books closed. Ss practice the conversation using their own words.

B 🔊

■ Go over the instructions and the question. Play the second part of the audio program. Ss listen for answers.

Audio script

> MAN: Excuse me.
> PHARMACIST: Yes? How can I help you?
> MAN: Um, what do you suggest for a backache?
> PHARMACIST: Well, you should take some aspirin. And it's also a good idea to use a heating pad.
> MAN: Thanks. Oh, and where are the aspirin?
> PHARMACIST: They're in aisle five. Right over there.
> MAN: OK. Thanks again.
> PHARMACIST: You're welcome.

■ After Ss compare answers in pairs, elicit responses around the class.

Answer

> He wants something for a backache.

■ **Optional:** Ask the class what the pharmacist suggests for this customer. (Answer: He should take some aspirin; it's also a good idea to use a heating pad.)

8 GRAMMAR FOCUS *Modal verbs* can, could, may *for requests; suggestions*

🔊 This exercise practices the modal verbs *can, could,* and *may* for polite requests; it also practices making suggestions using the imperative form with *Try* and the two other structures *I suggest* . . . . and *You should* . . . .

■ Explain that the modal expressions presented here are considered a more polite way of stating a request than direct requests such as "Give me . . . ." or "I want . . . ." Indirectness is a politeness strategy in English, as it is in many other languages. It distances the speaker from the request, which makes it less face-threatening.

■ Use the audio program to present the questions and statements in the boxes; Ss repeat.

■ Point out that the expression *something for* in the question "Could I have something for . . . ?" must be followed by the name of an illness or a health problem (e.g., a sore throat, a backache, the flu).

■ Give additional practice with modal verbs by saying phrases and then having Ss form requests. Conduct a quick class drill using *can, could,* and *may,* like this:

T: A box of cough drops.
S1: Can I have a box of cough drops?
T: *(continuing the drill with substitutions like these)* Something for a burn; A package of cold pills;

Something for a headache; A can of shaving cream; Something for mosquito bites.

■ After Ss look at the pictures, tell them to work alone to complete the conversations using the verbs given.

■ Ss compare answers with a partner. Then elicit and check responses around the class.

Answers

> 1. A: **Can/May** I help you?
>   B: Yes. **Can/Could/May** I have something for tired eyes?
>   A: Sure. I **suggest** a bottle of eye drops.
> 2. A: What do you **have/suggest** for sore muscles?
>   B: You **should** try a tube of this ointment. It's excellent.
>   A: OK. I'll take it.
> 3. A: **Can/Could/May** I have a box of cold tablets, please?
>   B: Here you are.
>   A: And what do you **have/suggest** for insomnia?
>   B: **Try** some of these sleeping pills.
>   A: OK. Thanks.

■ Ss practice the conversations in pairs. Walk around the class and give help as needed.

7 CONVERSATION *Giving suggestions*

A 🔊 Listen and practice.

Pharmacist: Hi. Can I help you?
Mrs. Webb: Yes, please. Could I have something for a cough? I think I'm getting a cold.
Pharmacist: Well, I suggest a box of these cough drops. And you should get a bottle of vitamin C, too.
Mrs. Webb: Thank you. And what do you have for dry skin?
Pharmacist: Try some of this new lotion. It's very good.
Mrs. Webb: OK. Thanks a lot.

CLASS
AUDIO
ONLY ▶

B 🔊 Listen to the pharmacist talk to the next customer.

What does the customer want?

8 GRAMMAR FOCUS

> ### *Modal verbs* can, could, may *for requests; suggestions* 🔊
>
> | | |
> |---|---|
> | **Can/May** I help you? | What do you have/suggest for dry skin? |
> | **Can** I have a box of cough drops? | Try some of this lotion. |
> | **Could** I have something for a sore throat? | I suggest some ointment. |
> | **May** I have a bottle of aspirin? | You should get some skin cream. |

Complete these conversations with the verbs *can, could, may, have, suggest, try,* or *should.* Then compare and practice with a partner.

1. A: .... I help you?
   B: Yes. .... I have something for tired eyes?
   A: Sure. I .... a bottle of eye drops.

2. A: What do you .... for sore muscles?
   B: You .... try a tube of this ointment. It's excellent.
   A: OK. I'll take it.

3. A: .... I have a box of cold tablets, please?
   B: Here you are.
   A: And what do you .... for insomnia?
   B: .... some of these sleeping pills.
   A: OK. Thanks.

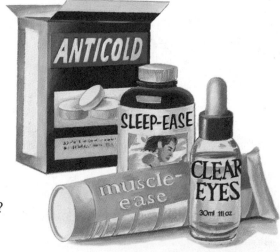

75

9 LISTENING

Listen to people talking about things in a drugstore.
Check (✓) the items they buy.

1.

☐   ☐

2.

☐   ☐

3.
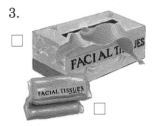

☐   ☐

4.
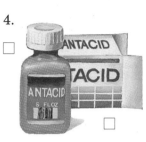

☐   ☐

10 ROLE PLAY *Can I help you?*

Student A: You are a customer in a drugstore. You need:

something for a sunburn
something for sore muscles
something for a sore throat

Ask for some suggestions.

Student B: You are a pharmacist in a drugstore. A customer needs some things.
Make some suggestions.

a can of sunburn spray   a tube of muscle ointment   a bottle of throat spray

Change roles and try the role play again. Make up your own information.

11 WRITING

A Write about an interesting home or folk remedy.

> *I have a good home remedy for a sore throat. I learned about it from*
> *my grandmother. Cut slices of meat, put pepper on them, and then tie*
> *them around your throat with a cloth. It's also a good idea to go to*
> *bed and rest. This always works (my grandmother says!).*

B *Pair work* Take turns reading your compositions. Which
home remedy is the most interesting?

9 LISTENING

This exercise develops Ss' ability to remember information in English while scanning pictures that relate to a specific topic.

- Books closed. Set the scene: Four different customers are talking to a pharmacist. Play the audio program once. Ss only listen.

Audio script

1. MAN: I think I've got a cold. My nose is stuffed up, and I have a sore throat.
   PHARMACIST: You should take some vitamin C.
   MAN: OK. May I have a large bottle, please?
2. WOMAN: What do you suggest for insect bites?
   PHARMACIST: Oh, this product is very good. And it comes in a can, so you just spray it on. I've tried it. It really works!
3. MAN: Excuse me, where are the tissues?
   PHARMACIST: They're right here on the counter.
   MAN: Thanks. I just need a couple of packages.

4. WOMAN: I've got a terrible stomachache! I think I ate too much last night.
   PHARMACIST: Here. Try these tablets. They work really fast. Just take two with a large glass of water.

- Books open. Explain the task: Ss listen and check the item that best matches the information discussed in each conversation.

- Play the audio program again. Ss do the task. Check Ss' answers around the class.

Answers

1. ✓ a large bottle of vitamins
2. ✓ a can of spray for insect bites
3. ✓ two small packages of tissues
4. ✓ a box of antacid tablets

10 ROLE PLAY Can I help you?

This fluency activity gives Ss the chance to use everything they have learned so far in the unit.

- Ss form pairs and choose A/B roles. Present the situation: Student A is a customer in a drugstore, and Student B is the pharmacist.

- Explain the activity: Student A has three things on a shopping list and should ask for each item, one at a time (i.e., Ss shouldn't ask for all three items in one question). Student B should suggest that the customer buy certain products, using the items pictured.

- Model how to start the role play, like this *(S = Student A, customer; T = Student B, pharmacist)*:

S: Good morning. I have a problem.
T: Oh? Can I help you?

S: Well, I went windsurfing yesterday and got too much sun. Could I have something for a sunburn?
T: Sure. I suggest a can of sunburn spray.

- Before Ss start the role play, ask them to cover their partner's information. Then set a time limit of about five minutes for pairs to do the activity. Move around the class, giving help as needed.

- **Optional:** Several pairs act out their role plays in front of the class. Follow up by giving or eliciting suggestions on what was good and how the role plays might be improved.

- Encourage Ss to use their own creativity and suggestions when they change roles (and partners, if desired) to do the activity again.

11 WRITING

This exercise practices writing a description of a home or folk remedy for a health problem.

A

- Go over the task and read the example paragraph aloud to the class. Explain any new words (e.g., *pepper, tie*).

- Allow Ss time to think of (or brainstorm on) an interesting home or folk remedy for a common illness or health problem (e.g., a sore throat, a headache). Then Ss work individually to quickly write down their ideas on a brainstorming map or in note form.

- Ss use their notes to compose one or two paragraphs. Go around the class and give advice. (*Note:* Writing the composition could be assigned as homework.)

- When Ss complete the first draft, remind them to check their spelling and grammar, especially the use of infinitive complements, modal verbs, and the structures used for giving advice and suggestions that they practiced in this unit.

B *Pair work*

- Decide if Ss should read their compositions in pairs, groups, or in front of the whole class. When all Ss have finished reading, find out (with a show of hands) which home remedy was the most interesting.

12 *READING* *Grandma knows best!*

In this text, Ss read about some simple home remedies for common health problems; the exercise practices reading for general ideas while challenging Ss to use their short-term memories to recall specific key words.

- Books closed. Present the pre-reading question to the whole class; or have Ss discuss the question in groups and then report their responses back to the rest of the class.

A *Pair work*

- Books open. Go over the instructions. While Ss read the article, encourage them to guess the meanings of any unfamiliar words while quickly reading the text for main ideas. Tell them to mark any words they don't understand.
- After reading the text, Ss work in pairs or small groups to discuss any new words. Tell them to ask each other the meaning of any that they still don't understand. Then Ss may use their dictionaries as a final check.
- Ss cover the article and complete the chart.
- **Optional:** Ss compare answers in pairs or small groups.
- While checking Ss' answers around the class, ask them which key words in each paragraph helped them choose the correct answer.

Answers

```
1. colds
2. insomnia
3. bee stings and insect bites
4. headaches
5. burns
6. coughs
```

B *Group work*

- Present the two questions. Then have Ss form large groups. Remind them to take turns asking and answering the questions. Encourage them to ask other questions of their own.
- **Optional:** For an extra writing assignment, ask Ss to use one or both of these questions as a topic for a short composition.

 Workbook

Tell Ss to do Exercises 5–8 on pages 70–72 in the Workbook or assign them as homework. Have Ss work in small groups to compare answers. Then elicit responses around the class. (Answers can be found on page T-186 of the Workbook Answer Key in this Teacher's Edition.)

Optional activities

1 *Wonder drug*

Time: 20–25 minutes. This fun and creative activity has Ss prepare a commercial for a new "miracle" drug.

- Explain the task: Ss work in small groups and think up a new wonder drug that can be used to solve an interesting "problem" (e.g., improve one's memory; make a person younger or taller; save someone from having to do any exercise). Ss prepare a 30-second commercial for radio or TV.
- Write these questions on the board to help Ss plan their commercials:

What is the drug for?
What does it look like?
What's it called?
Is this for a TV or for a radio commercial? Why?
How much does it cost?
Where do you buy it?
How often is it used?

- Set a time limit of about 15 minutes. Groups use their answers to the questions on the board to create their 30-second commercials. One S is the group secretary and records the final script. Go around the class, giving help and encouragement.
- As a class activity, groups read (for radio) or perform (for TV) their commercials in front of the room. Then let the class decide (1) which group has the most interesting wonder drug, and (2) which group has the best commercial.

2 *Game – Word Bingo*

- See page T-33.

3 *Crossword puzzle*

- See page T-146.

12 READING

Grandma knows best!

When you have a minor health problem, do you usually go to the doctor, get something from the drugstore, or use a home remedy?

When people have a cold, a fever, or the flu, they usually go to the doctor for help, or they get some medicine from the drugstore. But many people also use home remedies for common illnesses. Here are some simple home remedies.

Bee stings and insect bites

Wash the sting or bite. Put some meat tenderizer on a handkerchief and then put the handkerchief on the bite for half an hour. To avoid insect bites, it's helpful to eat garlic or take garlic pills.

Burns

Put the burn under cold water or put a cold handkerchief on it. It's important not to put ice on the burn.

Colds

Lots of people eat hot chicken soup when they have a cold. They find it clears the head and the nose. Some people rub oil on their chest for a cold. Other people drink a mixture of red pepper, hot water, sugar, lemon juice, and milk or vinegar.

Cough

Drink warm liquids or take some honey.

Headaches

Apply an ice pack or cold cloth to your head, or splash your face with cold water. It's also a good idea to put your hands into hot water and leave them there for several minutes. Also, you shouldn't read or watch TV.

Insomnia

Drink a large glass of warm milk. It's also a good idea to soak in a warm bath.

A *Pair work* Read the article. Then cover the article and complete the chart. What problems are these things good for?

Advice	Problem
1. hot chicken soup / rubbing oil on your chest	....
2. a warm bath / warm milk	....
3. garlic / meat tenderizer	....
4. an ice pack / putting your hands in hot water	....
5. cold water / cold handkerchief	....
6. honey / warm liquids	....

B *Group work* Do you use any of these remedies? What other home remedies do you use?

Review of Units 9–12

1 WHAT WAS IT LIKE?

Group work Ask these questions around the group.

Have you ever . . . ?

been on a camping trip
gotten a famous person's
   autograph
given first aid to someone
been on a blind date
lost your credit cards

gone windsurfing
been in an accident
had food poisoning
kept a diary
fainted

When someone answers "Yes," he or she
explains what happened, and the other
students ask for more information.

A: **Have you ever** gone windsurfing?
B: Yeah, I have. I tried it last year in Hawaii.
   It was really fun!
C: **What was it like?** Was it difficult?
B: Yes, it was at first. Has anyone else ever
   gone windsurfing?
D: . . .

2 ROLE PLAY Missing person

Student A: You are visiting an amusement
park with your English class.
One of your classmates is lost.
You are talking to a security
officer. Answer the officer's
questions and describe one of
your classmates. (Don't
give the student's name.)

Student B: You are a security officer at
an amusement park. Someone
is talking to you about a lost
classmate. Ask questions to
complete the form. Then look
around the class. Can you find
the lost student?

Change roles and try the role play again.

MISSING PERSONS REPORT

Name	
Age	
Height	
Hair	
Eyes	
Clothing	

Review of Units 9-12

This unit reviews the present perfect and the past tense; it also reviews how to describe a person's physical appearance. It practices using modifiers with participles and prepositions for identifying, and it gives Ss a chance to use infinitive complements for giving advice and making suggestions.

1 WHAT WAS IT LIKE?

This exercise reviews the present perfect and past tense while giving Ss practice in describing interesting experiences.

Group work

■ In a quick class drill, present each item on the list by modeling it with the given question, like this:

T: *(pointing to the picture)* Have you ever gone windsurfing? Repeat the question, please.

Ss: *(repeat question in unison)*

T: Have you ever been on a blind date? Repeat.

Continue until all the items are presented. Then explain any new words or expressions, such as:

autograph = signature
first aid = medical treatment quickly given to a sick or injured person before a doctor or an ambulance comes

blind date = a social meeting arranged at a certain time and place between two people who have never met before
food poisoning = sickness that comes from eating something bad
diary = a kind of book for a daily record of events, thoughts, etc.
fainted = lost consciousness (because of loss of blood, the heat, shock, alcohol, etc.); passed out

■ Read the instructions aloud and model the example dialog with several Ss. Remind the class to use the present perfect when asking about an indefinite event and the past tense when describing a particular event. Encourage Ss to give detailed answers.

■ Ss form groups and do the activity. Go around the class and discreetly listen in, giving help as needed.

2 ROLE PLAY Missing person

This exercise reviews describing a person's appearance.

■ Divide the class into A/B pairs. Use the picture to help explain the situation: On a trip to an amusement park, one of the Ss in the class gets lost. Student A gives a description of the missing classmate to Student B, who is a security officer at the amusement park.

■ Read aloud the role instructions for Student A and for Student B; go over the "Missing Persons Report." If the Ss have any questions about how to do the activity, model the task with a volunteer: S is Student A and looks around the class to secretly choose another S to describe as the "missing person." T is Student B, and shows the class how to use the "Missing Persons Report" in order to ask the necessary questions. Model how to write down the information received from Student A while having the conversation – for example:

S: Excuse me, Officer. My classmate is lost. Can you help me?
T: Sure. Um, is the person a man or a woman?
S: A woman.
T: OK. I need her age. How old is she?
S: Gee, I guess she's about nineteen.
T: All right. *(writing down* 19 *next to "Age" on the form)* And how tall is she?

■ Now the Student As look around the classroom and choose one of their classmates to be the "missing person" that they will describe. Tell them not to reveal that person's name to their partner. Also, remind the Student Bs to fill out the "Missing Persons Report" during their conversation. When the report is complete,

tell them to look around the room and find the "missing" student.

■ Set a time limit of about three minutes. Ss do the role play. Walk around and give help as needed.

■ As a follow-up, find out how many Student Bs were able to identify the missing students.

■ Ss change roles and partners, and try the role play again. Set another time limit of about three minutes.

Optional activity: *Cheap fun*

Time: 10–15 minutes. This activity practices describing events and activities in a city.

■ Explain the task: This is a brainstorming activity. Ss have to think of interesting and fun things they can do in their city for a fixed amount of money (e.g., for less than $5 each or for the equivalent amount in your currency). The group with the longest list is the winner.

■ Model the kinds of suggestions Ss can make, like this:

T: I think we should take the train to . . . Temple. We can look at the carvings on the temple walls. Then we can have lunch at the cafe outside. It costs two dollars for the train fare, one dollar for the temple entrance fee, and two dollars for a big bowl of noodles for lunch. That's only five dollars!

■ Ss form groups and choose a group secretary to take notes. Then they do the task. Set a time limit of about six minutes. Listen in and give help as needed.

■ Group secretaries read their suggestions to the class. Which group was the winner?

3 WHICH ONE IS BILL?

This exercise reviews modifiers with participles and prepositions.

Pair work

- Go over the instructions and the example answer. Then Ss work in pairs and do the activity. Walk around the class and give help as needed.
- Check Ss' responses around the class.

Possible answers

> Bill is the man in the black shirt./Bill is the one sitting next to Louisa.
> Kate is the woman in the jeans./Kate is the one standing next to the window.
> Louisa is the woman with the blond hair./Louisa is the one sitting next to Bill.
> Robert is the man with the black hair./Robert is the one wearing glasses.
> Maggie is the woman in the white blouse./Maggie is the one talking to Robert.

4 LISTENING

 This exercise practices listening for key points.

- Go over the task. Tell Ss to write only key words. Play the audio program. Ss listen and complete the chart.

Audio script

> MAN: So, you're from Hawaii, Jenny.
> JENNY: That's right.
> MAN: Where in Hawaii?
> JENNY: I'm from Honolulu – on the island of Oahu.
> MAN: Wow! Honolulu! That's a fairly big city, isn't it?
> JENNY: No, not really. It's not too big.
> MAN: The weather is great, though. Right?
> JENNY: Oh, yes. It is. It's very comfortable the whole year. Warm, but not too hot.
> MAN: I've heard that Honolulu is an expensive city. Is that true?
> JENNY: Well, yes, it *is* fairly expensive. Rents are high, and food is expensive, too. That's because everything

> comes in by plane from the mainland.
> MAN: And what are some places to see there?
> JENNY: Well, Waikiki Beach is probably the most famous place. That's where all the tourists go.
> MAN: Oh, yes. I've heard of Waikiki Beach.

- Elicit and check answers around the class.

Answers

> *What she says about . . .*
> 1. size   not too big
> 2. weather   very comfortable the whole year; warm, but not too hot
> 3. prices   fairly expensive; rents high, food expensive
> 4. a famous place   Waikiki Beach, where all the tourists go

5 DIFFICULT SITUATIONS

This exercise reviews infinitive complements for giving advice; it also practices making suggestions with modals *can* and *should*.

A Group work

- Read the instructions aloud. Present the five situations by modeling how to ask the given question with each one (e.g., What do you do when you have an argument with a friend?). Ss repeat. Then go over the example suggestion along with each useful expression.
- Explain any words that Ss don't know or can't remember (e.g., *argument, stressed, concentrate, apologize*).
- Model the task with several Ss. Show how to incorporate the useful expressions while giving elaborate answers during a discussion. Also, demonstrate how to take notes by writing the Ss' suggestions on the board – for example:

> S1: What do you do when you have an argument with a friend?

> T: Well, I think it's a good idea to apologize right away. (*writing on the board:* apologize right away)
> S1: Yes, I agree. Having a good friend is more important than winning an argument. (*writing on board:* friend more important than winning argument)
> S2: You're both right. And I think you should . . . .

- Ss do the task in small groups. Remind them to take notes on their group's answers to each question. Go around the class and give help as needed.

B Class activity

- Groups use their notes to share their ideas.

Test 3

See page T-152 in this Teacher's Edition for general instructions on using the tests. Test 3 covers Units 9–12. Photocopy the test (pages T-161–T-164) and distribute a copy to each S. Allow 45–60 minutes for the test. Listening material for the tests is at the end of the Class Audio Program. The Test Audio Scripts and Answer Key start on page T-169 of this book.

3 *WHICH ONE IS BILL?*

Pair work Look at this picture of a party. Write sentences identifying each person.

Bill is the man in the black shirt./Bill is the one sitting next to Louisa.

4 *LISTENING*

 Listen to Jenny talking about Honolulu. What does she say about these things? Complete the chart.

What she says about	
1. size	....
2. weather	....
3. prices	....
4. a famous place	....

5 *DIFFICULT SITUATIONS*

A ***Group work*** What do you do in these situations? Discuss each situation using expressions from the box. Write down your ideas.

What do you do when . . . ?

1. you have an argument with a friend
2. it's 2:00 A.M. and you can't sleep
3. you feel very stressed
4. you can't remember someone's name
5. you need to study, but you can't concentrate

useful expressions

It's useful to . . . .
It's helpful to . . . .
It's a good idea to . . . .
You can . . . .
You should . . . .

1. It's a good idea to apologize right away.

B ***Class activity*** Read your group's ideas to the class.

13 May I take your order, please?

1 SNAPSHOT

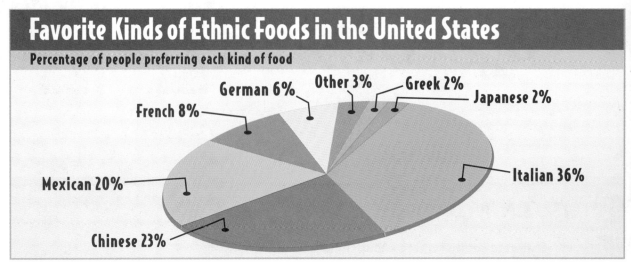

Favorite Kinds of Ethnic Foods in the United States

Percentage of people preferring each kind of food

German 6%
Other 3%
Greek 2%
Japanese 2%
French 8%
Italian 36%
Mexican 20%
Chinese 23%

Source: National Restaurant Association

Talk about these questions.

Are there restaurants in your city that serve these kinds of foods?
Which of the foods have you tried? Which would you like to try?
What other kinds of foods do you like?

2 CONVERSATION *Going out for dinner*

A Listen and practice.

Sandy: Say, do you want to go out to dinner tonight?
Bob: Sure. Where would you like to go?
Sandy: Well, what do you think of Indian food?
Bob: I love it, but I'm not really in the mood for it today.
Sandy: Yeah. I'm not either, I guess. It's a bit spicy.
Bob: Hmm. How do you like Japanese food?
Sandy: Oh, I like it a lot.
Bob: I do, too. And I know a nice Japanese restaurant near here – it's called Iroha.
Sandy: Oh, I've always wanted to go there.
Bob: Terrific! Let's go!

CLASS AUDIO ONLY ▶ **B** Listen to the rest of the conversation.

1. What time do they decide to have dinner? Why?
2. Where do they decide to meet?

80

13 May I take your order, please?

Cycle 1, Exercises 1–4

1 SNAPSHOT *Favorite kinds of ethnic foods in the United States*

This graphic introduces the theme of the unit – different types of foods and restaurants.

■ Books closed. Ask questions like these as a warm-up:

What kinds of (ethnic) foods do you like?
What's your favorite restaurant? What's good there?
What do you think are the three favorite types of ethnic foods in the U.S.?

■ Books open. Regarding the last question above, tell Ss to find the answer in the Snapshot now. (Answer: Italian, Chinese, and Mexican) Then Ss look over the other information.

■ Model the pronunciation of each type of ethnic food listed; Ss repeat. Then ask questions like these:

Do you like . . . (e.g., lasagna, baklava)?
What's your favorite . . . (e.g., Japanese) food?
How often do you eat . . . (e.g., sushi, pasta)?

■ Go over the four questions. Tell Ss to answer the first question about the town or city they are living or studying in now.

■ Ss first answer the questions individually and then compare answers in pairs or groups.

■ Compare Ss' information around the class. In general, does one type of ethnic food seem to be more popular with the class than others? If so, and particularly if the class is a heterogeneous one, try to find out why.

2 CONVERSATION *Going out for dinner*

This exercise introduces responses with *either* and *too* to show agreement.

A 🔊

■ Books closed. Set the scene: Two friends are talking about going out. Write some focus questions like these on the board:

What does Sandy invite Bob to do? (Go out to dinner)
What kinds of foods do they talk about? (Indian and Japanese)
Where do they finally decide to go? (To a Japanese restaurant [called Iroha])
Have they both been there before? (No, only Bob has.)

■ Play part A of the audio program. Ss listen. Then elicit Ss' answers to the questions on the board.

■ Books open. Ss look at the picture while listening again to the audio program. Then present the conversation line by line. Explain any new words and expressions, such as:

I'm not really in the mood for . . . . = I don't feel like having . . . .
a bit = a little
How do you like . . . ? = Do you like . . . ?

■ Pairs practice the conversation. Encourage Ss to have fun acting out the positive emotions in the conversation. For example, when a word or sentence shows agreement (e.g., "Sure." "I love it." "I'm not either, I guess." "Oh, I like it a lot." "I do, too." "Terrific!"), model ways in which Ss can improve on their communication by nodding for "yes" or shaking their head for "no," raising their eyebrows, opening their eyes wider, smiling, or frowning.

B 🔊

■ Go over the questions and encourage Ss to focus on the information that will answer them. Then play part B of the audio program. Have Ss take notes.

Audio script

> SANDY: So, do you want to eat early or late?
> BOB: Let's eat early. Then maybe we can go to a movie after dinner.
> SANDY: Good idea! Why don't we have dinner around six o'clock?
> BOB: Six is good. And where do you want to meet?
> SANDY: Let's meet at the restaurant, OK?
> BOB: Yeah, that's fine with me.

■ Elicit Ss' responses around the class.

Answers

> 1. They decide to meet at 6:00 because then maybe they can go to a movie after dinner.
> 2. They decide to meet at the restaurant.

■ **Optional:** Pairs act out the conversation in front of the class, using gestures and their own words. Assure them that it isn't necessary to repeat the exact words or sentences from the book. Also, encourage pairs to be creative and to use information about real restaurants. Give pairs about five minutes to prepare. After each performance, ask the rest of the class what was good or interesting about the conversation and what could be improved.

3 *GRAMMAR FOCUS* So, too, neither, either

🔊 This grammar focus practices expressing positive and negative opinions about food. It also introduces ways to show agreement when using the adverbs *so* and *too* in positive responses and *neither* and *either* in negative responses; various other contrastive responses showing disagreement are also presented.

The usage of the adverbs *so, too, neither,* and *either* in English grammar can be tricky for some Ss whose native language may have a different system of showing agreement and disagreement with a speaker's initial statement. These four adverbs can be defined as follows:

> **so** = usually used before the verbs *do, be,* and *have,* the modal *can,* and other auxiliary verbs to express the meaning "in the same way" or "similarly"
> **too** = used especially at the end of a sentence to show "in addition" or "also"
> **either/neither** = used with or as negative expressions to show that the listener agrees with the speaker's former negative comment

■ Use the audio program to present the statements and responses in the boxes; Ss practice several times. Make sure Ss understand that the expression *be crazy about* means "like very much."

■ Return to the information presented in the boxes. Explain that after each initial statement here, whether it is positive (in the first box) or negative (in the second box), there are two responses that show agreement and one that shows disagreement. Go over all of the information carefully with the class, as in these two examples:

Initial positive statement: I like Japanese food a lot.
Two responses showing agreement: So do I./I do, too.
One response showing disagreement: Really? I don't like it very much.

Initial negative statement: I don't like greasy food.
Two responses showing agreement: Neither do I./I don't either.
One response showing disagreement: Oh, I like it a lot.

■ Point out how the adverbs *so* and *too* are used to show agreement in responses to initial positive statements, like this:

1. When a verb other than *be* is in the initial statement (e.g., "I *love/like/enjoy* . . . ."), use *do* or *don't* in the response (e.g., "So *do* I./I *do,* too." for agreement, or "I *don't.*" for disagreement).

2. When the verb *be* is in the initial statement (e.g., "I'm crazy about . . . ."), use *am* or *'m not* in the response (e.g., "So *am* I./I *am,* too." for agreement, or "I'm *not.*" for disagreement).

3. When the modal *can* is in the initial statement (e.g., "I *can* eat . . . ."), use *can* or *can't* in the response (e.g., "So *can* I./I *can,* too." for agreement, or "I *can't.*" for disagreement).

■ Follow this with a similar type of explanation for the initial negative sentences, which use *neither* or *either* in responses showing agreement.

■ Have a quick statement-and-response drill with the class, like this:

T: I like . . . (e.g., tacos/pizza). What about you, Sara?
S1: So do I.
T: Tom?
S2: I do, too.
T: I'm crazy about . . . (e.g., apple pie). What about you, Marie?
S3: Oh, I'm not at all.
T: Kenjo, now you make a statement about something and ask for someone's opinion.
S4: OK. I can eat really hot food. How about you, Pravit?
S5: Yeah, so can I.

A

■ Present the seven new adjectives (*healthy* through *bland*) by pointing to each word and modeling its pronunciation; Ss repeat.

■ Read the instructions aloud. Explain that Ss need to write positive or negative responses that show agreement – not disagreement – with each statement. If helpful, model how to do number 1 by eliciting Ss' suggestions and writing the correct ones on the board.

■ Ss work individually to complete the task and then compare answers in pairs. Elicit Ss' responses around the class.

Answers

> 1. Neither am I./I'm not either.
> 2. So can I./I can, too.
> 3. So do I./I do, too.
> 4. Neither can I./I can't either.
> 5. Neither do I./I don't either.
> 6. So am I./I am, too.
> 7. So am I./I am, too.
> 8. Neither do I./I don't either.
> 9. So do I./I do, too.
> 10. Neither can I./I can't either.

B *Pair work*

■ Ss form pairs and take turns reading the initial statements in part A, this time responding with their own real opinions to show agreement and/or disagreement. Go around the class and listen in to check that Ss are responding correctly.

C

■ Go over the task and the three food categories that Ss need to write statements about. Model how to do the first one. Then tell the Ss to complete the task individually. (*Note:* Don't let pairs compare statements at this time as they will do this in part B of Exercise 4 on page 82.)

3 *GRAMMAR FOCUS*

So, too, neither, either 🔊

I like Japanese food a lot. **So** do I./I do, **too**. Really? I don't like it very much.	I don't like greasy food. **Neither** do I./I don't **either**. Oh, I like it a lot.
I'm crazy about dessert. **So** am I./I am, **too**. Oh, I'm not at all.	I'm not in the mood for Indian food. **Neither** am I./I'm not **either**. Really? I am.
I can eat really spicy food. **So** can I./I can, **too**. Oh, I can't.	I can't stand fast food. **Neither** can I./I can't **either**. Oh, I love it!

healthy   greasy   salty   rich   spicy   delicious   bland

A Write responses to show agreement with these statements.
Then compare with a partner.

1. I'm not crazy about French food. ....
2. I can eat any kind of food. ....
3. I think Mexican food is delicious. ....
4. I can't stand greasy food. ....
5. I don't like salty food. ....
6. I'm in the mood for something spicy. ....
7. I'm crazy about Korean food. ....
8. I don't enjoy rich food very much. ....
9. I always eat healthy food. ....
10. I can't eat bland food. ....

B *Pair work* Take turns responding to the statements in part A again.
Give your own opinion when responding.

C Write statements about these things. (You will use the statements
in Exercise 4.)

1. two kinds of food you like
2. two kinds of food you can't stand
3. two kinds of food you are in the mood for

4 PRONUNCIATION *Stress in responses*

A 🎧 Listen and practice. The last word of each response is usually stressed.

So do **Í**.   I do, **tóo**.   Neither am **Í**.   I'm not **éither**.
Neither do **Í**.   I don't **éither**.   So can **Í**.   I can, **tóo**.
So am **Í**.   I am, **tóo**.   Neither can **Í**.   I can't **éither**.

B *Pair work* Take turns reading the statements you wrote in part C of
Exercise 3. Pay attention to the stress in your responses.

A: I don't really like greasy food.
B: I don't **éither**. (Neither do **Í**.) It's not very healthy.

5 WORD POWER *Restaurant orders*

A *Pair work* Complete the chart with words from the list. Then add two
more words to each category. What's your favorite food in each category?

apple pie   cold pasta salad   chicken broth   chocolate cake   coffee
cole slaw   onion soup   grilled salmon   hamburger & fries   ice cream
iced tea   milk   mixed greens   roast turkey   clam chowder

Soups	Salads	Main dishes	Desserts	Beverages
......	......	......	......	......
......	......	......	......	......
......	......	......	......	......
......	......	......	......	......
......	......	......	......	......

B What foods do you think these people like best? Use items from
the chart above or your own ideas.

Jenny

Brenda

Grant

Mr. and Mrs. Dobson

1. ....   2. ....   3. ....   4. ....
....

CLASS AUDIO ONLY

C 🎧 Listen to each of the people above talking about their favorite
foods and take notes. How similar were your guesses?

4 *PRONUNCIATION* Stress in responses

This exercise focuses on the stressed words in responses with *so, too, neither,* and *either.*

A

■ Use the audio program to present the responses; Ss listen and repeat. Then model the timing of each response by clapping your hands or tapping on the desk and emphasizing the stressed word; Ss repeat.

B *Pair work*

■ Go over the task and model the example A/B dialog.

■ Ss form pairs and take turns reading their statements

from part C of Exercise 3 on page 81. Walk around the class, checking on individual Ss' responses, pronunciation, stress, and timing.

■ Elicit Ss' responses around the class.

Workbook

Assign Exercises 1–3 on pages 73–75 in the Workbook for end-of-class work or for homework. Ss compare answers in pairs or groups when all the exercises have been completed. (Answers can be found on page T-187 of the Workbook Answer Key in this Teacher's Edition.)

Cycle 2, Exercises 5–11

5 *WORD POWER* Restaurant orders

This exercise introduces ordering in a restaurant; it also presents vocabulary commonly found on menus in English.

A *Pair work*

■ Model the pronunciation of the words in the list and the headings in the chart; Ss repeat. Don't explain any of the words here as this is one of the Ss' tasks. However, go over the following pronunciation points:

1. The letter *l* in *salmon* is silent, 2. *chocolate* has two syllables, 3. & is a symbol for the word *and*, 4. *beverages* has three syllables.

■ Go over the three-part task: (1) Ss work individually to complete the chart without using their dictionaries; (2) Ss then add two more words to each category in the chart (let them use their dictionaries for this); and (3) Ss indicate their favorite food or drink in each category.

■ Ss do the task. Walk around the class and give help as needed.

■ Check Ss' responses around the class.

Answers (*extra examples in boldface*)

Soups	*Main dishes*	*Beverages*
onion soup	grilled salmon	iced tea
chicken broth	hamburger & fries	milk
clam chowder	roast turkey	coffee
gazpacho	**steak**	**soda**
minestrone	**fried chicken**	**juice**
Salads	*Desserts*	
cole slaw	apple pie	
cold pasta salad	chocolate cake	
mixed greens	ice cream	
Caesar salad	**cheese cake**	
spinach salad	**cookies**	

B

■ Present the pictures and go over the activity. Explain that Ss will make guesses about each person's food

preferences and then write down two food items under his or her picture. Have Ss do the task individually. (*Note:* Check Ss' answers after the audio in part C.)

C

■ Go over the task. Then play the audio program. Tell Ss to take notes and then compare their notes with their original answers they wrote in part B.

Audio script

1. MAN: What's your favorite food, Jenny?
   JENNY: Oh, that's easy – hamburgers and french fries.
   MAN: Is that all?
   JENNY: Well, I also like chocolate ice cream.
   MAN: Chocolate ice cream. Really!
2. WOMAN: What kind of food do you like best, Brenda?
   BRENDA: Well, one of my favorites is a big mixed green salad. I also like vegetable soup. I eat lots of vegetables. They're very good for you, you know.
3. MAN: What's your favorite kind of food, Grant?
   GRANT: Oh, my favorite is pasta. I love Italian food. I also like seafood. My favorite fish is grilled salmon. Mmm.
4. WOMAN: What are your favorite foods, Mr. and Mrs. Dobson?
   MRS. DOBSON: Well, we like fairly simple things. My favorite is chicken. I like baked chicken with potatoes.
   MR. DOBSON: And my favorite is roast turkey.

■ Elicit and check answers around the class.

Answers

1. hamburgers and french fries, chocolate ice cream
2. mixed green salad, vegetable soup
3. pasta, seafood (grilled salmon)
4. Mrs. Dobson: baked chicken with potatoes,
   Mr. Dobson: roast turkey

6 CONVERSATION Ordering a meal

🔊 This exercise introduces requests with the modal verbs *would* and *will* in the context of ordering a meal in a restaurant.

- Books closed. Set the scene: A customer is ordering a meal in a restaurant. Write some focus questions like these on the board:

  What does the customer order to eat? (A hamburger, a large order of french fries, and a mixed green salad)
  What kind of dressing does the person want? (Italian)
  What does the person order to drink? (A large soda)

- Play the audio program once or twice. After pairs compare answers to the questions on the board, elicit responses around the class.

- Books open. Play the audio program again. As Ss listen, they look at the picture or read along.

- Use the audio program to present the conversation, pausing it after each line for Ss to repeat. Model the stress and timing in these questions:

  And would you **like** a **sal**ad?
  What kind of **dres**sing would you **like**?
  And would you **like** anything to **drink**?

- Ss practice the conversation in pairs.

- **Optional:** Books closed. Pairs try the conversation again, this time using their own words and substituting other food items if they wish.

7 GRAMMAR FOCUS Modal verbs would and will for requests

🔊 This exercise practices the use of modal verbs *would* and *will* for making polite requests.

- *Will* is often incorrectly referred to as a future tense; *will* is not a tense in English but is part of the modal system and behaves like other modal verbs. It can also be used to refer to future time (e.g., *We'll leave tomorrow night.*), as can the simple present (e.g., *We leave tomorrow night.*) or present continuous (e.g., *We're leaving tomorrow night.*). Both *would* and *will* refer to intention here.

- Use the audio program to present the questions and statements in the box; Ss repeat. Then present the contractions in the same way.

- Point out that requests with *would* and *will* are usually considered more polite than more direct questions (e.g., "What would you like to eat?" is considered more polite than "What do you want to eat?").

- Go over the task. Ss complete it individually and then compare answers in pairs.

- Elicit and check Ss' answers around the class.

Answers

WAITRESS: What **would** you like to order?
CUSTOMER: **I'll** have the fried chicken.
WAITRESS: **Would** you like rice or potatoes?
CUSTOMER: Potatoes, please.
WAITRESS: What kind of potatoes **would** you like? Mashed, baked, or french fries?
CUSTOMER: **I'd** like french fries.
WAITRESS: OK. And what will you **have** to drink?
CUSTOMER: I guess **I'll** have a cup of coffee.
WAITRESS: Would you **like** anything else?
CUSTOMER: No, that **will** be all for now, thanks.
Later
WAITRESS: Would you **like** dessert?
CUSTOMER: Yes, **I'd** like ice cream.
WAITRESS: What flavor **would** you like?
CUSTOMER: Hmm. **I'll** have chocolate, please.
WAITRESS: OK. I'll bring it right away.

- Pairs practice the conversation. Encourage them to use the "Look Up and Say" technique.

Optional activity: *Restaurant Chez Moi*

Time: 15–20 minutes. This activity can be fun and encourages Ss to be creative. In pairs or groups, Ss prepare menus in English for their own restaurants.

- Brainstorm with the class on which categories Ss might want to include in a restaurant menu that is written in English. Write Ss' suggestions on the board – for example:

Restaurant menu

Appetizers	Main dishes	Desserts
Soups	Side dishes	Beverages
Salads		

- Elicit some unusual dishes that Ss might want to add to their menus, depending on the "fantasy" restaurant they are creating it for. Then model how to provide short descriptions for several menu items – for example:

  nasi goreng = an Indonesian dish of fried rice topped with chicken and egg
  sushi = individual pieces of thinly sliced raw fish on top of slightly pickled white rice with spicy Japanese horseradish

- Ss form pairs or groups and write their menus. Encourage Ss to think up a clever name for their make-believe restaurant.

- Ss put their handmade menus on the bulletin board for the rest of the class to see and compare. Find out if the class wants to vote on the best or the most interesting menu.

- **Optional:** Ss use their own menu (or another pair's or group's menu) to have a quick role play activity – as in Exercise 8 on page 84 – that involves some Ss ordering a meal while another takes their orders. Alternatively, make photocopies of some real restaurant menus written in English that you and the Ss have collected; use them for an extra role play activity.

6 CONVERSATION *Ordering a meal*

 Listen and practice.

Waiter: May I take your order?
Customer: Yes. I'd like a hamburger and a large order of french fries, please.
Waiter: All right. And would you like a salad?
Customer: Yes, I'll have a mixed green salad.
Waiter: OK. What kind of dressing would you like? We have vinaigrette, Italian, and French.
Customer: Italian, please.
Waiter: And would you like anything to drink?
Customer: Yes, I'd like a large soda, please.

7 GRAMMAR FOCUS

Modal verbs would and will for requests		
What **would** you **like** to eat?	I**'d like** a hamburger. I**'ll have** a small salad.	*Contractions* I will = I'll I would = I'd
What kind of dressing **would** you **like**?	I**'d like** Italian, please. I**'ll have** French.	
What **would** you **like** to drink?	I**'d like** a large soda. I**'ll have** coffee.	
Would you **like** anything else?	Yes, please. I**'d like** some water. No, thank you. That **will be** all.	

Complete this conversation. Then practice with a partner.

Waitress: What .... you like to order?
Customer: I .... have the fried chicken.
Waitress: .... you like rice or potatoes?
Customer: Potatoes, please.
Waitress: What kind of potatoes would you .... ? Mashed, baked, or french fries?
Customer: I .... like french fries.
Waitress: OK. And what will you .... to drink?
Customer: I guess I .... have a cup of coffee.
Waitress: Would you .... anything else?
Customer: No, that .... be all for now, thanks.

Later

Waitress: Would you .... dessert?
Customer: Yes, I .... like ice cream.
Waitress: What flavor .... you like?
Customer: Hmm. I .... have chocolate, please.
Waitress: OK. I'll bring it right away.

8 ROLE PLAY In a coffee shop

Student A: You are a customer in a coffee shop.
This is what you want to order for lunch:

tomato and cucumber salad   garlic bread
spaghetti and meatballs   iced tea with lemon

Student B: You are the waiter or waitress.
Take your customer's order.

Change roles and try the role play again. Make up your own information.

9 LISTENING

CLASS AUDIO ONLY ▶ **A** Listen to Tom and Tina ordering in a restaurant. What did each of them order? Fill in their orders.

CLASS AUDIO ONLY ▶ **B** Listen to the rest of the conversation. What happened?

Phil's Diner   No. 399825

Date _____

Thank You!   Total _____

10 WRITING Restaurant reviews

A Have you eaten out at a restaurant recently? How was it? Write a review of the restaurant and the meal you had there.

> The Surf and Turf Restaurant
>
> I had lunch at the Surf and Turf Restaurant last week. It's a steak and seafood restaurant. I ordered a steak and a Caesar salad. For dessert, I had chocolate cake and coffee. My meal cost about $24 with the tip.
>
> The waiter was helpful. The coffee wasn't very good, but the salad and steak were delicious. I'd go back to the Surf and Turf.

interchange 13

Are you ready to order?
Have lunch at The Corner Cafe. Student A turns to page IC-17. Students B and C turn to page IC-18.

B *Group work* Take turns reading your reviews to the group. Is there a restaurant you would like to try?

8 ROLE PLAY *In a coffee shop*

This fun activity provides a communicative follow-up to the grammar introduced in this cycle.

■ Set the scene: This is a role play in a coffee shop where Student As are customers and Student Bs are the waiters/waitresses. Go over the instructions and the tasks for Student As and Student Bs; then model the pronunciation of the food and drink items.

■ Model the activity with one or two Ss, changing roles at least once.

■ Now pairs try the role play. Set a time limit of about two minutes. Walk around the room and listen in on Ss' exchanges; give help if requested or needed.

■ Pairs change roles and do the role play again, this time using their own information for what to order.

9 LISTENING

This exercise practices listening for restaurant orders; it also includes recognizing a waiter's mistakes.

A

■ Books open. Read the instructions aloud and go over the restaurant order form. Then play part A of the audio program once or twice; Ss fill in the order form.

Audio script

WAITER: Hi. May I take your order?
TOM: Yes. I'll have a cup of coffee.
WAITER: Cream and sugar?
TOM: Oh, yes, please.
WAITER: And you?
TINA: I'd like a chicken sandwich. And I'll have some chips . . . oh, you call them french fries here. *(laughs)* Right. I'll have some french fries, please.
WAITER: All right. One coffee with cream and sugar and a chicken sandwich with french fries. Uh, anything else?
TINA: Yes, I'd like an iced tea, please.
WAITER: One iced tea. Thank you.
TOM: Oh, wait a minute! What kind of desserts do you have?
WAITER: Well, we have pie, cake, ice cream, chocolate mousse . . .
TOM: Oooo! What kind of pie do you have?
WAITER: I think today we have apple, cherry, lemon . . .
TOM: Hmm . . . , I think I'll have a piece of apple pie with my coffee. How about you, Tina?
TINA: Oh, maybe I'll have a piece later . . . or . . . I'll have some of yours! *(laughs)*
WAITER: Then it's one coffee, one apple pie, one chicken sandwich, an order of french fries, and an iced tea. Right?
TOM: Yes, thank you.
TINA: Thanks.

■ After Ss compare answers in pairs, check answers around the class.

Answers

Tom's order: coffee with cream and sugar, a piece of apple pie
Tina's order: a chicken sandwich, french fries, iced tea

B

■ Go over the task and the question. Play part B of the audio program. Ss listen and take notes.

Audio script

TINA: Oh, here comes our waiter!
TOM: Yeah, I wondered what took so long.
WAITER: *(rushing to table)* Whew! Here you are!
TINA: Uh, I ordered french fries with my chicken sandwich, and you brought me . . . ugh! . . . mashed potatoes with gravy!
WAITER: Oh, you ordered french fries?
TINA: Yes!
WAITER: Well, then, OK.
TOM: Uh, and could I have the apple pie I ordered?
WAITER: What apple pie? Did you order apple pie?
TOM: Uh-huh. Yeah, I did . . . with my coffee. Remember?
WAITER: Really? Gee, how did I forget that?
TINA: Uh, can I ask you a question?
WAITER: Yes?
TINA: How long have you been a waiter?
WAITER: Who me? Oh, uh, today is my first day. *(all laugh)* Well, I'll . . . I'll get your apple pie and the french fries right away. Sorry about that.
TOM: Oh, that's OK.
TINA: Yeah, thanks. Good luck!
WAITER: Thanks!

■ Elicit and check answers around the class.

Possible answer

Tina ordered french fries, but the waiter brought mashed potatoes with gravy. Tom ordered apple pie, but the waiter forgot to bring it. Tina asked, "How long have you been a waiter?" because he made two mistakes with their orders. He said it was his first day. They all laughed about it.

The teacher notes for Exercise 10 appear on the next page.

10 *WRITING* Restaurant reviews

This writing task practices describing a real restaurant.

A

- Go over the task and the example paragraph. Ss brainstorm individually on the information they need in order to write a real restaurant review.
- Ss use their brainstorming maps to make an outline. Tell them to write a two-paragraph first draft – one for the description and one for the evaluation.

B *Group work*

- Ss take turns reading their reviews in groups.

 INTERCHANGE 13 Are you ready to order?

See pages T-122 and T-123 in this Teacher's Edition for notes.

11 *READING* To tip or not to tip?

In this text, Ss read about tipping guidelines in the United States and Canada; the exercise practices reading for main ideas and scanning for key words.

- Books closed. Present the pre-reading discussion questions and elicit answers from the class. If time permits, discuss the custom of tipping and why people do it in some countries but not in others.
- Before Ss read the passage, explain these words if you think Ss might have trouble with them: *porters, bellhops, parking valet, hotel room attendants, service charge,* and *cafeterias.*

A *Pair work*

- Books open. Go over the instructions: Ss first read the passage individually and then form pairs to answer the questions. Explain that Ss have to do some simple mathematical calculations to decide on the amount needed as a tip for each item in question 2. Remind Ss to highlight, circle, or underline any word or expression whose meaning they can't guess from context.
- Ss do the tasks. Walk around the class, giving help as needed. Then check answers around the class.

Answers

---

1. takes your bag at an airport? $1.00
   parks your car at a hotel or restaurant? $1.00
   serves you in a fast-food restaurant? nothing
2. a $27 haircut? $2.70–$5.40
   a $50 restaurant check? $5.00–$10.00
   a $14 taxi fare? $1.40–$2.80

B *Group work*

- Present the question. Then Ss form groups to discuss their opinions about tipping. After about five minutes, ask groups to summarize their discussion for the class.

 Workbook

Tell Ss to do Exercises 4–8 on pages 76–78 in the Workbook or assign them as homework. Have Ss work in small groups to compare answers. Then elicit responses around the class. (Answers can be found on page T-187 of the Workbook Answer Key in this Teacher's Edition.)

Optional activities

1 *Restaurant guide*

Time: 10–15 minutes in class; 1–2 hours outside class. This activity is a natural follow-up to the writing assignment in Exercise 10 on page 84. Here, however, Ss write a local restaurant guide.

- Explain the project: Ss work in groups of three to five. Each group chooses a different area of the town or city (e.g., near your school, downtown, in a nearby shopping mall) and writes a local restaurant guide for it.

  The task is to make a list of three to five interesting places to eat. Then the group visits each one and writes a brief description of it – for example:

  > Name: Coffee Cantina
  > Address: 3443 Western Ave.
  > Telephone: (310) 555-9880
  > Hours: 7 A.M. to 10 P.M., Monday to Saturday

  The Coffee Cantina is a specialty coffee house. It has excellent espresso, cappuccino, and many different types of tea. It's a small, inexpensive cafe where you can drink delicious coffee and have a light snack like a bagel or a muffin. Also, the classical music there is very pleasant. You can sit inside or outside.

- Each group chooses one area of the city and plans which restaurants to include in the guide. Have them also schedule when they can go out together (or separately) to investigate the places on their list. Then they write the guide together as a group project.
- After the guides are written, groups put them on the bulletin board for the rest of the class to see. Or all of the guides could be combined, photocopied, and stapled into a larger class-made "Local Restaurant Guide" with a copy for each S to keep.

2 *What's your opinion?*

- See page T-150.

11 *READING*

To Tip or Not to Tip?

Do you tip for services in your country? When?

Canadians and Americans usually tip in places like restaurants, airports, hotels, and hair salons because many people who work in these places get low salaries. A tip shows that the customer is pleased with the service.

At airports, porters usually get a dollar tip for each bag. Hotel bellhops usually get a dollar for carrying one or two suitcases. A hotel door attendant or parking valet also gets about a dollar for getting a taxi or for parking a car. Many people also tip hotel room attendants, especially when they stay in a hotel for several days. They usually leave a dollar for each day.

The usual tip for other kinds of services – for example, for taxi drivers, barbers, hairdressers, waiters, and waitresses – is between 10 and 20 percent of the bill. The size of the tip depends on how pleased the customer is. In most restaurants, the check does not include a service charge. If the group is large, however, there may be an added service charge. There is no tipping in cafeterias or fast-food restaurants.

A *Pair work* Read the article. Then talk about these questions.

1. How much should you tip someone in North America who:

   takes your bag at an airport?
   parks your car at a hotel or restaurant?
   serves you in a fast-food restaurant?

2. What tip should you leave for the following:

   a $27 haircut?
   a $50 restaurant check?
   a $14 taxi fare?

B *Group work* Do you think tipping is a good or bad custom? Why?

14 The biggest and the best!

1 WORD POWER *Geography*

A Circle the word that doesn't belong in each list. Then compare with a partner.

1. canyon	2. lake	3. hill	4. desert
cliff	plateau	mountain	forest
swamp	river	volcano	plains
valley	sea	ocean	waterfall

B Find examples of some of the words above in this picture.
What other geography words can you think of?

C Add two names to these lists. Then compare with a partner.

Mountains	Rivers	Continents	Oceans
Mount Everest	the Amazon River	Africa	the Pacific Ocean

The biggest and the best!

This unit presents language that enables Ss to share their knowledge of world geography. It also reviews comparative adjectives, introduces superlative adjectives, and practices questions with how.

Cycle 1, Exercises 1–7

1 WORD POWER Geography

This exercise introduces the topic of this cycle – world geography – and practices vocabulary that Ss will use throughout the unit.

(*Note:* A world map would be useful for this activity and for other exercises in the unit.)

A

(*Note:* This first activity is based on the "Odd Man Out" game, which some Ss may have played before.)

■ Model the pronunciation of the words in the four lists; Ss repeat. Also point out the correct stress in **can**yon, pla**teau**, vol**ca**no, and **des**ert.

■ Go over the instructions. If Ss aren't sure how to do the task, write a simple example on the board using words the class knows (e.g., here, words from Unit 13):

Which word doesn't belong in this list?
   tea, milk, salad, coffee

Elicit Ss' ideas and circle the correct answer: *salad.* Then ask why it doesn't belong. (Answer: The word *salad* doesn't belong because it is something to eat while the others are things to drink.)

■ Ss complete the task individually, using a dictionary if necessary. Walk around and give help, if requested.

■ Ss compare answers in pairs. Then check answers around the class.

Answers

1. swamp	2. plateau	3. ocean	4. waterfall

B

(*Note:* The two tasks in this part can be done in pairs, in groups, or as a whole class activity.)

■ Read the instructions aloud. Then do the following:

First question: Give Ss a few minutes to look at the picture. Then tell them to check (✓) any words in the lists in part A that they can also find illustrated in the picture. When time is up, elicit Ss' responses.

Answers

1. canyon, cliff, valley	3. hill, mountain, volcano
2. lake, plateau, river	4. desert, forest, waterfall

Second question: Have Ss brainstorm to see how many words they can think of that relate to geography. Let Ss write as many as they wish on the board for everyone else to copy into their vocabulary notebooks.

Possible answers

Water-related terms: stream, creek, inlet, bay, pond, tide, waves
Land-related terms: continent, island, peninsula, rain forest, savanna
Climate-related terms: weather, climate, rain, storm, wind, snow, dry, wet, humid
Other terms: flora, fauna, city, town, village

C

■ Go over the task. Then model the words in the headings and the examples in the chart; Ss repeat.

■ Ss work individually to add two names of real geographical features in their own countries or elsewhere in the world. Then Ss compare answers in pairs.

■ Check Ss' answers and write some of them on the board.

Possible answers

Mountains: Aconcagua, Fujiyama, Kilimanjaro
Rivers: the Danube, the Huang, the Mississippi River
Continents: Antarctica, Asia, Australia, Europe, North America, South America
Oceans: the Arctic Ocean, the Atlantic Ocean, the Indian Ocean

Optional activity: *Guess the word*

Time: 10–15 minutes. This activity practices giving definitions and descriptions.

Preparation: Use index cards or pieces of paper (approx. 3" × 5") to make a set of vocabulary cards (around 20), with one word on each card. The words should be any that were generated while studying a certain exercise or cycle (e.g., here, the Word Power on page 86).

■ Divide the class into groups of four or five and place the cards facedown on a desk at the front of the class.

■ Explain the activity: Groups take turns. One S from a group comes to the front of the class and picks up a card. That S gives clues (i.e., short definitions or descriptions, synonyms, antonyms) to his or her group who, in turn, tries to guess the word on the card.

■ Model the game with the word *cliff,* like this:

It's higher than the low land next to it.
It's often on a coast above a beach.
It's the opposite of *canyon.*

■ Now start the activity. If a group can't guess the word in 30 seconds, the S gives the answer. Then a S from another group takes a turn. The winner is the group that guesses the most correct words.

2 CONVERSATION Describing countries

🔊 This exercise introduces comparisons with superlative adjectives (e.g., *the most famous* beaches/*the longest* coral reef).

■ Books closed. Introduce the topic of comparing countries by asking the class to compare any two countries that most Ss know something about – even if they haven't actually visited them (e.g., the U.S. and the U.K.; Japan and China; Brazil and Mexico). Elicit information from the class by asking questions like these:

Which is larger, . . . or . . . ? Is . . . warmer than . . . ? Where would you prefer to take a vacation, in . . . or in . . . ?

■ Now set the scene for the conversation: Someone is asking about another person's country. Play the audio program. Ss listen. Then check Ss' general

comprehension by asking what kinds of things the two people discussed. Write Ss' ideas on the board.

■ Books open. Play the audio program again. Present the conversation line by line. Explain any new words:

> **"down under"** = a nickname for Australia and New Zealand, which are below the equator in the Southern Hemisphere
> **the Great Barrier Reef** = a 2,000-km (1,250-mile) reef off the northeastern coast of Queensland, Australia *(See the photo on page 87.)*
> **coral** = a white, pink, or reddish stonelike substance formed from the bones of very small sea animals
> **reef** = a line of rocks, sand, or coral just above or just below the surface of the sea

■ Ss practice the conversation in pairs.

3 GRAMMAR FOCUS Comparisons with adjectives

🔊 This grammar focus reviews the comparative forms of adjectives with *-er* and *more* (+ *than*); it also presents the superlative forms of adjectives with *the* + *-est* or *most*.

■ Review how comparative adjectives are used when comparing two things (e.g., Which country is larger, Canada or China?). If necessary, quickly review how to form comparative adjectives. (*Note:* See the notes in Unit 3, Exercise 9 on page T-18 in this Teacher's Edition. Also, refer Ss to the Unit Summary for Unit 3 on page S-4 of their textbook.)

■ Explain how superlatives are always used with the definite article *the* (e.g., *the* largest/*the* most beautiful): (1) to compare three or more things (e.g., "Which is *the* largest: Russia, Canada, or China?" [Answer: Russia]); or (2) to compare two or more things when using the phrase *in the world* (e.g., What is *the* largest continent *in the world*, Africa or Asia? [Answer: Asia]).

■ Refer Ss to the Unit Summary for Unit 14 on page S-15 of their textbook. Then share with the class these guidelines for forming the superlative with adjectives. Write them on the board and encourage Ss to copy them into their notebooks for future reference:

1. For adjectives ending in two consonants, add -est (or just -st if the adjective ends in e): long – longest, large – largest.
2. For adjectives ending in y, change y to i and add -est: pretty – prettiest.
3. For adjectives ending in a single vowel + consonant, double the final consonant and add -est: big – biggest.
4. For other adjectives of two or more syllables, add most: famous – most famous, beautiful – most beautiful.

■ Use the audio program to present the adjective forms, questions, and responses in the boxes. Play the audio program once more, pausing it to allow Ss to repeat.

■ **Optional:** Elicit some adjective pairs from the class and write them on the board (e.g., *cheap/expensive, dirty/clean, safe/dangerous, interesting/boring*). Then ask for volunteers to try spelling the comparative and superlative forms for each one.

A

■ Read the instructions aloud. Then have Ss complete the task individually. Either elicit Ss' answers or have Ss check them against the list of adjectives in the appendix at the back of their textbook.

■ Ss compare answers in pairs. Then check answers around the class by having volunteers give their answers and write them on the board.

Answers

> 1. Which country is **smaller**, Monaco or Vatican City?
> 2. Which waterfall is **higher**, Niagara Falls or Angel Falls?
> 3. Which city is **more crowded**, Hong Kong or Cairo?
> 4. Which lake is **larger**, the Caspian Sea or Lake Superior?
> 5. Which mountain is **the tallest**: Mount McKinley, Mount Everest, or Fujiyama?
> 6. What is **the longest** river in the world, the Nile or the Amazon?
> 7. Which country is **the most popular** with tourists: Spain, France, or Italy?
> 8. What is **the deepest** ocean in the world, the Pacific or the Atlantic?

B Class activity

■ Ss work individually (or in pairs if the two Ss are from the same country) to write four questions like those in part A. Then Ss take turns asking the rest of the class their questions.

2 CONVERSATION *Describing countries*

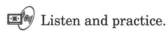 Listen and practice.

Paul: I'm going to Australia next year. Aren't
you from "down under," Kelly?

Kelly: That's right.

Paul: I hear there's not much pollution, and
the beaches are clean and beautiful.

Kelly: Oh, yes. Australia has some of the most famous
beaches in the world – like Bondi Beach.

Paul: What else should I see?

Kelly: Well, the Great Barrier Reef is there.
It's the longest coral reef in the world.

Paul: Wow! It sounds beautiful. You're lucky
to be an Australian.

Kelly: Thanks, but actually, I'm a New Zealander.

the Great Barrier Reef

3 GRAMMAR FOCUS

Comparisons with adjectives

Adjective	Comparative	Superlative
large	larger	the largest
long	longer	the longest
dry	drier	the driest
big	bigger	the biggest
beautiful	more beautiful	the most beautiful
famous	more famous	the most famous
good	better	the best
bad	worse	the worst

Which country is **larger**, Canada or China?
   Canada is **larger than** China.

Which country is **the largest**: Russia, Canada, or China?
   Russia is **the largest** country of the three.

What is **the most beautiful** mountain in the world?
   I think Fujiyama is **the most beautiful**.

For more information on comparatives and superlatives, see the appendix at the back of the book.

A Complete questions 1 to 4 with comparatives. Complete questions
5 to 8 with superlatives. Then ask and answer the questions.
Check your answers in the appendix.

1. Which country is .... , Monaco or Vatican City?   (small)
2. Which waterfall is .... , Niagara Falls or Angel Falls?   (high)
3. Which city is .... , Hong Kong or Cairo?   (crowded)
4. Which lake is .... , the Caspian Sea or Lake Superior?   (large)
5. Which mountain is .... : Mount McKinley, Mount Everest, or Fujiyama?   (tall)
6. What is .... river in the world, the Nile or the Amazon?   (long)
7. Which country is .... with tourists: Spain, France, or Italy?   (popular)
8. What is .... ocean in the world, the Pacific or the Atlantic?   (deep)

B *Class activity* Write four questions like those in part A about your
country or other countries. Then ask your questions around the class.

4 *PRONUNCIATION* *Questions of choice*

Listen to the intonation of questions where there is a choice.
Then practice the questions.

Which country is bigger, China or Russia?

Which is the largest desert in the world, the Australian or the Sahara?

Which country is the most interesting: Korea, Brazil, or France?

5 *IN YOUR OPINION*

Group work Answer these questions about your country.
Be ready to explain your answers. Then compare in a group.

What are the three most interesting places in your country?
What's the best time of year to visit?
What are the most famous tourist attractions?
What's the most beautiful place in your country?

interchange 14

How much do you know?

You probably know more than you think you do! Take a quiz. Turn to page IC-19.

6 *WRITING*

A Write about one of the places or things you discussed in Exercise 5.

> I think the most beautiful place in my country is a town called Ubud on Bali. It's located in the mountains, and there are lots of rice fields. Many artists live and work there. . . .

B *Pair work* Exchange papers and read each other's compositions.

Ubud, Bali, Indonesia

4 PRONUNCIATION Questions of choice

This exercise practices the intonation of questions where there is a choice.

- Play the audio program to present the questions. Model

the rising and falling intonation patterns. Then play the audio again; Ss repeat.

- **Optional:** For additional practice, elicit similar types of questions from the class.

5 IN YOUR OPINION

This is a communicative activity that practices using superlative forms of adjectives in questions and responses.

Group work

- Explain the task. Then read the four questions aloud; Ss repeat.

- Ss work individually to write down their answers.

  (*Note:* In a homogeneous class – and to add variety to the Ss' composition topics – Ss could choose to answer these questions about another country they have visited instead of their own.)

- Ss form groups to take turns asking and answering the questions. Encourage Ss to ask for and give additional information when possible; they should also give reasons for their answers if they can.

  (*Note:* In a heterogeneous class, it may be more interesting to form groups with Ss from different countries.)

 INTERCHANGE 14 How much do you know?

See page T-121 in this Teacher's Edition for notes.

6 WRITING

This exercise practices describing in writing one of the places that Ss discussed in Exercise 5 above.

A

- Go over the assignment and read the example aloud.

- Explain how to start a paragraph with a topic sentence. Write these examples on the board:

  I believe that . . . is the most interesting place in my country.
  The weather in my country is nice all year round, but the best time to visit is in . . . .
  There are many famous tourist attractions in my country, but I feel that . . . is the best.
  Many people agree that . . . is the most beautiful place in my country.

- Allow Ss to choose which place they want to write about. Encourage them to write a topic sentence. Tell them to use it to brainstorm on the kinds of information and details they need to include in their compositions in order to support the main idea.

- Ss use their topic sentences and brainstorming notes to compose the first draft. (*Note:* If you're short on classtime, this writing could be done for homework.)

- When Ss finish their drafts, remind them to check and correct grammar and spelling.

B Pair work

- Explain the activity: First, pairs exchange compositions and read them silently. Then they take turns reading each other's composition aloud. Encourage Ss to offer their input on their partner's composition.

- Remind the class how to participate in giving helpful peer feedback, like this:

  1. Your partner sits down next to you. Both of you look at the writer's composition while the partner (i.e., not the writer) reads it aloud straight through.

  2. Then the writer asks questions in order to get some helpful feedback from his or her partner. Write these peer feedback questions on the board and model how to use them with the whole class:

  Content: What did you like the most about my composition? What was the most interesting/boring part? Were there enough details? If not, where do I need to add more? Were there any sentences you couldn't understand?

  Organization: How was the organization? Did the topic sentence in each paragraph cover it like "an umbrella"? Were there any sentences that seemed out of place?

  Grammar/Spelling: Are there any grammar or spelling problems? Where? Can you help me edit them, please?

  3. While the partner is giving feedback, the writer makes notes on the draft on what is OK and revises anything that needs to be changed, added, or deleted.

  4. Now the other S reads his or her partner's draft aloud to give some feedback in the same manner.

- Allow pairs enough time to give feedback (e.g., about five to ten minutes for each composition). Then Ss make final revisions in class or for homework.

- Give your own feedback on content, organization, grammar, and spelling on Ss' second drafts.

7 *LISTENING* TV game show

This fun exercise involves listening for answers to common-knowledge questions.

- Read the instructions aloud to set the scene and then explain the task. Play the audio program once or twice. Ss check (✓) the correct answer to each question.

Audio script

> HOSTESS: *(music and applause)* Our contestants this evening are Jack, Susan, and Jonathan. And now, contestants, let's get right to our first question. Question number one: Which is the oldest: the Statue of Liberty, the Eiffel Tower, or the Empire State Building? *(buzzer)* Jack?
>
> JACK: The Statue of Liberty is the oldest. They built it in 1886. They didn't build the Eiffel Tower until 1889, and the Empire State Building until 1931.
>
> HOSTESS: That's correct! *(applause)* Question number two: Is a Concorde airplane bigger than a 747 or DC-10 airplane? *(buzzer)* Susan.
>
> SUSAN: No, a 747 is the biggest. It carries up to five hundred people; the Concorde only carries about a hundred passengers, and a DC-10 about 300 people.
>
> HOSTESS: That's right! *(applause)* Question number three: Which is the heaviest: a pound of gold, a pound of butter, or a pound of feathers? *(buzzer)* Jonathan.
>
> JONATHAN: They all weigh the same.
>
> HOSTESS: Yes! *(applause)* Question number four: Which country is the largest: the U.S., China, or Canada? *(pause)* Nobody knows? Does anybody want to guess? *(buzzer)* Jack.
>
> JACK: Uh . . . China is the largest. *(gong and audience sighs)*
>
> HOSTESS: No, sorry!
>
> JACK: Oh, shoot!
>
> HOSTESS: *(buzzer)* Jonathan.
>
> JONATHAN: Canada is the largest.
>
> HOSTESS: Correct! *(applause)* Question number five: Which is the biggest city: Moscow, New York, or Shanghai? *(buzzer)* Susan.
>
> SUSAN: New York is the biggest. It has over 14 million people. Shanghai has about 13 million, and Moscow has about 10.
>
> HOSTESS: Correct! *(applause)* Question number six: Which is the smallest: Australia, Argentina, or Brazil? *(buzzer)* Susan.

> SUSAN: Argentina is the smallest.
>
> HOSTESS: That's right! *(applause and music)* OK, contestants, the winner is . . . *(fade)*

- After Ss compare answers in pairs, elicit and check answers around the class.

Answers

1. the Statue of Liberty	4. Canada
2. 747	5. New York
3. gold, butter, and feathers	6. Argentina

Alternative presentation

- Before Ss listen to the audio program, read the following questions to the class and let Ss check their own answers (or guesses) for items 1–6.

  1. Which is the oldest: the Statue of Liberty, the Eiffel Tower, or the Empire State Building?
  2. Which airplane is the biggest: the Concorde, the 747, or the DC-10?
  3. Which is the heaviest: a pound of gold, a pound of butter, or a pound of feathers?
  4. Which country is the largest: the U.S., China, or Canada?
  5. Which is the biggest city: Moscow, New York, or Shanghai?
  6. Which is the smallest country: Australia, Argentina, or Brazil?

  Play the audio program. Ss compare their checked boxes with the correct answers they hear.

 Workbook

Assign Exercises 1–4 on pages 79–81 in the Workbook as in-class work or for homework. Ss compare answers in groups when all exercises have been completed. Assign one exercise to each group, who is then in charge of checking Ss' responses around the class on that same task. (Answers can be found on page T-188 of the Workbook Answer Key in the Teacher's Edition.)

Cycle 2, Exercises 8–11

8 *SNAPSHOT* The five tallest buildings in the world

This graphic focuses on the topic of comparing things – here, tall buildings around the world; it also continues the practice of superlative forms of adjectives.

- Books closed. Just for fun, ask some questions (or write them on the board) about items in the Snapshot, but without giving the correct answer. Let the class discuss answers to questions like these:

  What's the world's tallest building?
  Where's the famous Sears Tower located?
  What's the tallest building in China?

  Is the Empire State Building the tallest building in the United States?

- Books open. Ss read the information in the Snapshot to find the answers to the questions above.

- Ss do the two tasks individually and then compare their answers in groups. Elicit each group's most interesting information.

Optional activity: *That's not right!*

- See page T-151.

7 *LISTENING* TV game show

Three people are playing a TV game show. Listen to each question, and check (✓) the correct answer.

1. ☐ the Statue of Liberty
   ☐ the Eiffel Tower
   ☐ the Empire State Building

2. ☐ Concorde
   ☐ 747
   ☐ DC-10

3. ☐ gold
   ☐ butter
   ☐ feathers

4. ☐ the U.S.
   ☐ China
   ☐ Canada

5. ☐ Moscow
   ☐ New York
   ☐ Shanghai

6. ☐ Australia
   ☐ Argentina
   ☐ Brazil

8 *SNAPSHOT*

The five tallest buildings in the world
(Approximate height)

Petronas Towers Kuala Lumpur, Malaysia	Sears Tower Chicago, USA	Jin Mao Building Shanghai, China	World Trade Center New York City, USA	Empire State Building New York City, USA
452 meters (1,483 feet) Completed in 1996	442 meters (1,450 feet) Completed in 1974	421 meters (1,379 feet) Completed in 1998	417 meters (1,368 feet) Completed in 1973	381 meters (1,250 feet) Completed in 1931

Source: Council on Tall Buildings and Urban Habitats

Talk about these questions.

Would you like to visit any of these places? Which ones? Why?
Can you identify these buildings in your city?
  The tallest building: ....
  The oldest building: ....
  The most beautiful building: ....

9 **CONVERSATION** *Distance and measurements*

A Listen and practice.

Paul: So, what's New Zealand like?
Kelly: Oh, it's beautiful. It has lots of farms,
and it's very mountainous.
Paul: Mountainous? Really? I didn't know that.
How high are the mountains?
Kelly: Well, the highest one is Mount Cook.
It's about 3,800 meters high.
Paul: Hmm. How far is New Zealand from Australia?
Kelly: Well, I live in Auckland, and Auckland
is about 2,000 kilometers from Sydney.
Paul: Well, maybe I should visit you next year, too.
Kelly: That would be great!

Auckland, "the City of Sails"

CLASS AUDIO ONLY ▶ **B** Listen to the rest of the conversation.

What are some things New Zealand is famous for?

10 **GRAMMAR FOCUS**

Questions with **how** 🔊

How far is New Zealand from Australia?	It's about 2,000 kilometers.	(1,200 miles)
How big is Singapore?	It's 620 square kilometers.	(239 square miles)
How high is Mount Everest?	It's 8,848 meters **high.**	(29,028 feet)
How deep is the Grand Canyon?	It's about 1,900 meters **deep.**	(6,250 feet)
How long is the Mississippi River?	It's about 6,019 kilometers **long.**	(3,740 miles)
How hot is New Zealand in the summer?	It gets up to about 23° Celsius.	(74° Fahrenheit)
How cold is it in the winter?	It goes down to about 10° Celsius.	(50° Fahrenheit)

A Write the questions to these answers. Then practice with a partner.

1. A: ....?
   B: Angel Falls is 979 meters (3,212 feet) high.

2. A: ....?
   B: California is about 411,000 square kilometers (159,000 square miles).

3. A: ....?
   B: The Nile is 6,670 kilometers (4,145 miles) long.

4. A: ....?
   B: Washington, D.C., gets up to about 32° Celsius (90° Fahrenheit) in the summer.

B *Group work* Think of five questions with *how* about places in your country
or other countries you know. Ask and answer your questions in groups.

"How cold is Seoul in the winter?"

9 CONVERSATION Distance and measurements

This exercise practices describing a country and asking
questions about distance and measurements with *how.*

A 🔊

- Books closed. Ask Ss questions to find out what they
  know about New Zealand (e.g., Where is it? Do any un-
  usual animals live there? When is their summer/winter?).
- Write these pre-listening questions on the board. Find
  out if Ss already know some of the answers:
  What's New Zealand like? (It's beautiful, it has lots of
  farms, and it's very mountainous.)
  What's the highest mountain? (Mount Cook)
  How high is it? (It's about 3,800 meters high.)
  How far is New Zealand from Australia? (Auckland is
  about 2,000 kilometers from Sydney.)
- Play the first part of the audio program. Ss listen for the
  correct answers to the questions on the board. Check
  answers around the class.
- Books open. Point out that this conversation is a
  continuation of the one in Exercise 2 on page 87. Play
  the audio program again, pausing it to present the
  conversation line by line; Ss repeat. Explain any new
  words and expressions, such as:

Auckland = New Zealand's largest city and a seaport
Sydney = a seaport in southeastern Australia

- Pairs practice the conversation.

B 🔊

- Present the question. Play the second part of the audio
  program. Ss listen and take notes.

Audio script

PAUL: Tell me a little more about New Zealand, Kelly.
KELLY: Well, it has some great beaches. There are some
excellent beaches in the North Island for surfing.
PAUL: Well, I don't really like surfing, but I love boating.
KELLY: Really? Well, you can go boating in Auckland. It's
one of the most popular places for sailing. And you
should definitely try jet boating in the South Island.
PAUL: Oh, I'd love to do that! It sounds pretty exciting.
KELLY: It is. And there's good skiing in New Zealand in
the winter, too. Lots of people go there to ski.
PAUL: It sounds too good to pass up. Now I have to go!
KELLY: Yes, you do!

- Ss compare answers in pairs. Then elicit answers
  around the class.

Possible answers

New Zealand is famous for some great beaches; there
are excellent beaches in the North Island for surfing;
Auckland is very popular for boating and sailing; you
can try jet boating in the South Island; and there's good
skiing in the winter.

10 GRAMMAR FOCUS Questions with how

🔊 This exercise practices asking and answering
questions starting with *how + far, big, high,* and so on.

- Questions with *how* are used to ask about distance and
  other measurements. Quickly find out how much the
  class already knows about these two systems:

The Metric System = linear measurements using
centimeters, meters, kilometers, etc.
  1 centimeter = 0.01 m
  1 meter = 100 cm
  1 kilometer = 1,000 m
The Imperial System = linear measurements using
inches, feet, yards, miles, etc.
  1 inch = 2.54 cm
  1 foot = 12 in. = 0.3048 m
  1 yard = 3 ft. = 36 in. = 0.9144 m
  1 mile = 5,280 ft. = 1,760 yd. = 1.6093 km

- Present the questions and responses in the box by
  playing the audio program. Then play it again and
  pause it to allow Ss time to repeat.

A

- Read the instructions aloud. Then Ss do the task
  individually. Check Ss' answers before they form pairs
  to practice the dialogs.

Answers

1. How high is Angel Falls?
2. How big is California?
3. How long is the Nile?
4. How hot is Washington, D.C., in the summer?

B *Group work*

- Go over the task and the example question.
- Have Ss work individually to write down five questions
  with *how* (like the ones in the grammar focus box and in
  part A) about their own countries or other places that
  they know.
- Ss form groups and take turns asking their questions.
  Walk around and give help as needed.

Optional activities

1 *Game – What's the question?*
- See page T-147.

2 *Vacation snapshots and souvenirs*
- See page T-45.

3 *What an interesting place!*
- See page T-151.

READING *Things you can do to help the environment*

In this article, Ss explore various environmental issues; the exercise practices skimming and scanning.

- Books closed. Introduce the topics – the environment and pollution problems – by brainstorming with the class. Write these two topics on the board and then add Ss' suggestions under the appropriate headings:

The Environment	*Pollution Problems*
cities	*exhaust from cars and trucks*
rain forests	*chemicals in rivers*
oceans	*people not recycling enough*

- Books open. Read aloud the pre-reading question and the four choices. Ask Ss to check (✓) the answer that they think applies to their country. Then elicit Ss' responses around the class; you may wish to use Ss' answers as the basis for a short discussion on pollution in various countries.

A *Pair work*

- Ss read the article straight through to the end. Remind them to circle or highlight any words or expressions whose meanings they can't guess from context.

- When Ss finish reading the article, tell them to form pairs. Then have them compare any words they couldn't guess and help each other with the definitions. As a "last resort," encourage Ss to use their dictionaries. Go around and give help as needed.

- Explain any vocabulary that Ss couldn't guess from context or find in their dictionaries, such as:

Introduction
(to be) in trouble = to have difficulty with something
Cars
the atmosphere = a mixture of gases surrounding the earth
global warming = the heating up of the earth worldwide
ozone layer = a level of air high above the earth that contains a lot of ozone (a form of oxygen); it prevents harmful ultraviolet light from the sun from reaching the earth
Products
disposable products = things that can be (easily) thrown away after being used
recycled materials = collected and treated (trash) to produce useful materials that can be used again
Water
"low-flow" shower head = a device that controls or restricts the amount of water coming out of the shower faucet
leaky = that let water out even when they're not turned on

- Present each of the four questions. Then have Ss work in pairs to take turns asking and answering the questions. Go around the class and give help as necessary.

- Elicit Ss' responses around the class. Write the more interesting ones on the board.

Possible answers

> 1–3. Ss' answers will vary.
> 4. *Possible answers may include:* Don't buy products that aren't recyclable or made by companies that are known to pollute the environment. Plant trees instead of cutting them down. Continue to read and study about how people can recycle things and protect the environment. Turn off lights and appliances that are not being used to save electricity. Don't leave the water on when brushing your teeth. Wear heavy clothes inside when it's cold outside and light clothes when it's hot outside so you don't have to use heat and air conditioning.

B *Group work*

- Read aloud the description of the task. Model how to answer questions about the first photo, like this:

> T: Let's look at the first picture. Does it show an environmental problem or a solution?
> S1: I think it shows a problem.
> T: Yes, I agree. Can anyone describe what is wrong in this photo?
> S2: Well, there are lots of cars on the road.
> S3: Yeah, there's a lot of traffic.

- Ss form groups and discuss the eight photos in the same manner. Walk around the class and discreetly listen in on what each group is talking about. Interrupt and give help only if Ss request it.

- To check answers, let groups take turns and share their responses about one picture each.

Possible answers

> Photos that show environmental problems = 1, 3, 5, 7
> Photos that show solutions = 2, 4, 6, 8
> 1 Wrong: car exhaust polluting air; noisy cars causing noise pollution
> 2 Right: bicycling to work saves gas; prevents pollution
> 3 Wrong: throwing away too many recyclable items
> 4 Right: recycling aluminum cans, which can be made into new cans and used again
> 5 Wrong: wasting electricity, gas, or coal to heat or cool a house too much
> 6 Right: saving electricity with low-energy bulbs
> 7 Wrong: leaky faucets waste water
> 8 Right: using efficient shower head will save water

 Workbook

Assign Exercises 5–7 on pages 82–84 for homework. At the beginning of the next class, have Ss compare answers in pairs. Then elicit answers around the class for a final check. (Answers can be found on page T-188 of the Workbook Answer Key in this Teacher's Edition.)

11 *READING*

Things You Can Do to Help the Environment

Is pollution in your country: ■ serious? ■ under control? ■ increasing? ■ decreasing?

Our environment is in trouble. People and industries are polluting the air, rivers, lakes, and seas. You may think that there's nothing you can do to help. That's not true. In fact, there are many things you can do to help the environment. Here are a few.

Cars

The burning of gasoline is one of the biggest sources of carbon monoxide (CO) in the atmosphere. Some people believe that CO is causing global warming. They think CO thins the ozone layer, which protects us from the sun's rays. So try to walk, bicycle, or use public transportation. And if you drive a car, drive at a steady speed – this is more efficient than speeding up and slowing down.

Products

Don't use disposable products. In a single year, people in the United States use enough disposable diapers to reach to the moon and back seven times. If you use disposable products, use products made from recycled materials. Also, recycle whenever possible. Recycling one aluminum can saves enough energy to run a TV for three hours.

Energy

The biggest use of home energy is for heating and cooling homes. So turn the heat down, especially at night. Replace regular light bulbs with fluorescent or halogen bulbs, which use less energy.

Water

Showers use a lot of water. In one week a typical American family uses as much water as a person drinks in three years! Buying a special "low-flow" shower head or taking shorter showers can cut this use in half. Also, fix any leaky faucets.

A *Pair work* Read the article. Then talk about these questions.

1. Which of the advice above is new to you?
2. Do you follow any of the advice in the article?
3. Which are the three best pieces of advice?
4. What are two other things people can do to protect the environment?

B *Group work* Look at the photos in the article. Which ones show environmental problems? Which show solutions? Describe what is right or wrong in each photo.

15 I'm going to see a musical.

1 SNAPSHOT

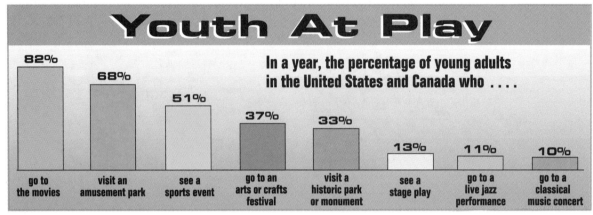

Youth At Play

In a year, the percentage of young adults in the United States and Canada who . . . .

- 82% go to the movies
- 68% visit an amusement park
- 51% see a sports event
- 37% go to an arts or crafts festival
- 33% visit a historic park or monument
- 13% see a stage play
- 11% go to a live jazz performance
- 10% go to a classical music concert

Source: National Endowment for the Arts

Talk about these questions.

Which of these activities have you done in the past year?
Which of these activities would you like to do?
What other activities do you like to do?

2 CONVERSATION *Talking about plans*

A Listen and practice.

Tony: Say, Anna, what are you doing tonight? Would you like to go out?

Anna: Oh, sorry, I can't. I'm going to work late tonight. I have to finish this report.

Tony: Well, how about tomorrow night? Are you doing anything then?

Anna: No, I'm not. What are you planning to do?

Tony: I'm going to see a musical. Would you like to come?

Anna: Sure, I'd love to! But let *me* pay for the tickets this time. It's my turn.

Tony: All right! Thanks!

CLASS AUDIO ONLY ▶ **B** Listen to the rest of the conversation.

1. What musical are they going to see?
2. What are they doing before the musical?
3. Where are they going to meet?
4. What time are they meeting?

This unit introduces the future with the present continuous and be going to; it also presents the use of tell and ask to leave messages with statements and requests.

1 SNAPSHOT Youth at play

This graphic presents the theme of the first cycle – how young people spend their free time.

- Books closed. To introduce the Snapshot activities informally, ask questions like these around the class:

  T: How often do you go to the movies, Rosa?
  S1: Oh, I usually go once a week.
  T: Oh, that's quite often. You must really like movies!
  S1: Yeah, I do!
  T: OK. And Kenji, how often do you see sports events?
  S2: Well, these days, I go to my sister's high school tennis match every Friday afternoon.

- **Optional:** Ss ask similar questions around the class starting with "How often do you . . . ?" about other free-time activities. (*Note:* This is also a good review of the adverbs of frequency and short answers with time phrases introduced in Unit 6.)

- Books open. Ss read the Snapshot information. Then answer Ss' questions about any words that may not have been introduced yet – for example:

arts/crafts festival = a fair where art and other handmade objects (e.g., household decorations, furniture, pottery) are sold
monument = a special place or object built to remember and show respect to a person or group of people
stage play = a piece of writing that is acted in a theater

- Read aloud the three questions. Have Ss complete the tasks individually. Walk around and give help as needed. Then Ss form pairs or small groups and compare answers.

- Check Ss' answers, like this:

First and second questions: Take a quick class survey (through a show of hands) to find out which activity was the most popular response to each question.

Third question: Tell Ss to write their "other activities" on the board. Then the class asks questions in order to get more information.

(*Note:* Additional vocabulary for leisure activities is presented in the Word Power on page 93.)

2 CONVERSATION Talking about plans

This exercise introduces the present continuous (What *are* you *doing* tonight?) and *be going to* + verb (I'm going to see a musical.) with future meaning.

A 🔊

- Books closed. To introduce the topic of dating and going out, ask the class some questions like these to stimulate a short discussion:

  Does anyone here like to date/go out?
  Where do you like to go on dates?
  Should one person pay for everything on the date?
  Where do young people go on special dates (e.g., high school proms; celebrating a special event or day like a graduation, a birthday, Valentine's Day)?
  Do you think it's OK for co-workers to date? Why?

- Books open. Use the picture to set the scene: Two co-workers are making plans to go out. Then play the audio program. Ss only listen.

- Use the audio program to present the conversation. Check that Ss understand that the expression *It's my turn.* means "You did something nice for me, and now I want to do something nice for you."

- Ss practice the conversation in pairs.

B 🔊

- Read the four questions aloud. Then play the second part of the conversation and tell Ss to listen and write down their answers.

Audio script

ANNA: So, what musical are we going to see?
TONY: It's called *Cats.*
ANNA: Oh, sure. *Cats.* I've heard a lot about it. When does it start?
TONY: It starts at eight. Maybe we can have a pizza before the show.
ANNA: OK. Great!
TONY: Should I pick you up at your house?
ANNA: Well, I'll be in the city tomorrow afternoon, so let's meet near the theater.
TONY: OK. Do you want to meet in front of the Pizza Palace on State Street? At a quarter to seven?
ANNA: A quarter to seven at the Pizza Palace? Great!

- Check Ss' answers around the class.

Answers

1. *Cats.*
2. Having a pizza.
3. In front of the Pizza Palace on State Street.
4. At a quarter to seven.

3 GRAMMAR FOCUS *Future with present continuous and* be going to

🔊 This grammar focus practices ways to express the future with the present continuous and *be going to;* it also presents future time expressions (e.g., *tonight, next week*).

(*Note:* Although the form of the present continuous was first introduced in Unit 5, its use to describe future events is new here.)

The present continuous is commonly used for describing future events. When contrasted with the simple present (e.g., I *watch* TV every night.), the simple present describes a regular, unchanging event. On the other hand, the present continuous describes an event that is neither regular nor typical (e.g., I'm *seeing* a movie tonight.). We can also use *be going to* + verb to show future intention (e.g., She's *going to work* late on Friday.).

■ Use the audio program to present the questions and responses in the box; Ss repeat.

■ Present each time expression and have Ss repeat. Use a calendar (or draw one on the board) and point to today's date. Give Ss a chance to use the new vocabulary by answering questions like these:

T: What day is tomorrow?
S1: It's . . . .
T: That's right. (*pointing to the coming Friday on the calendar*) Are you doing anything on Friday?
S2: Yes, I'm going to see a movie.
T: How about you, Pablo? What are you going to do on Friday?
S3: I'm studying.

■ Have Ss take turns asking and answering Wh- and yes/no questions around the class using the present continuous and *be going to* + verb for future meaning.

A

■ Read the instructions aloud. Show how to fill in the first blank in both columns with the appropriate structure. Ss work individually to do this part. Then elicit and check Ss' answers around the class.

Answers

1. What **are** you **doing** tomorrow? Would you like to go out?
2. **Are** you **doing** anything on Saturday night? Do you want to see a movie?
3. We**'re having** friends over for a barbecue on Sunday. Would you and your parents like to come?
a. Well, my father**'s going to visit** my brother at college. But my mother and I **are going to be** home. We'd love to come!
b. Sorry, I can't. I**'m going to work** overtime. How about Saturday?
c. Can we go to a late show? I**'m going to stay** at the office till 7:00. After that I**'m going to go** to the gym.

B

■ Explain the task: Ss match the invitations in column A to the responses in column B. Check answers before Ss practice the conversations in pairs.

Answers

1. b	2. c	3. a

Optional activity: *Are you doing anything on Saturday?*

■ See page T-151.

4 WORD POWER *Leisure activities*

This exercise continues the theme of leisure activities; it also presents additional language that Ss will find useful for other activities in the rest of the unit.

A

■ Read the instructions aloud. Then present the words and categories; Ss repeat. (*Note:* It's best not to give any definitions at this time as the Ss' initial task is to figure out the meanings and associations of these words.)

■ Model the task using several words from the list. Then Ss do the first part of the task either individually or in pairs. Go around the class, giving help as needed.

■ Now Ss work individually to add two more words to each category. To check answers, write the categories on the board; ask Ss to write their words under the correct headings, but without repeating any words.

Answers (*extra examples in boldface*)

Exhibitions	*Friendly gatherings*
art show	barbecue
car show	beach party
craft fair	picnic
dog show	**dinner party**
fashion show	**card game**

Spectator sports	*Live performances*
baseball game	comedy act
hockey game	play
tennis tournament	rock concert
football game	**ballet**
soccer match	**opera**

B *Pair work*

■ Present the two questions and model the A/B dialog with a S. Then pairs take turns making statements, or asking and answering questions, while using the words from the chart. Go around and give help as needed.

3 GRAMMAR FOCUS

Future with present continuous and be going to 🔊

With present continuous	**With be going to + verb**	**Time expressions**
What **are** you **doing** tonight?	What **is** she **going to do** tonight?	tonight
I**'m going** to a movie.	She**'s going to work** late.	tomorrow
		on Friday
Are you **doing** anything tomorrow night?	**Are** they **going to see** a musical tomorrow night?	this weekend
No, I'm not.	Yes, they are.	next week

A Complete the invitations in column A with the present continuous used as future. Complete the responses in column B with *be going to*.

A

1. What .... you .... (do) tomorrow? Would you like to go out?

2. .... you .... (do) anything on Saturday night? Do you want to see a movie?

3. We .... (have) friends over for a barbecue on Sunday. Would you and your parents like to come?

B

a. Well, my father .... (visit) my brother at college. But my mother and I .... (be) home. We'd love to come!

b. Sorry, I can't. I .... (work) overtime. How about Saturday?

c. Can we go to a late show? I .... (stay) at the office till 7:00. After that I .... (go) to the gym.

B Match the invitations in column A with the responses in column B. Then practice with a partner.

4 WORD POWER Leisure activities

A Complete the word map with activities from the list. Then add two more words to each category.

art show   craft fair
barbecue   hockey game
baseball game picnic
beach party   play
car show   rock concert
comedy act   tennis tournament

Leisure activities

Exhibitions

Friendly gatherings

Spectator sports

Live performances

B *Pair work* Are you going to do any of the activities on the chart? When are you doing them? Talk with a partner.

A: I'm going to see a rock concert.
B: Really? When?
A: On Friday.
B: . . .

5 ROLE PLAY An invitation

Student A: Choose an activity from Exercise 4 and invite a partner to go with you. Be ready to say where and when the activity is.

> A: Say, are you doing anything on . . . ?
> Would you like to . . . ?

Student B: Your partner invites you out. Either accept the invitation and ask for more information, or say you can't go and give an excuse.

Accept

> B: That sounds interesting. Where is it?

Refuse

> B: Oh, I'm sorry, but I can't go. I'm . . . .

Change roles and try the role play again.

interchange 15

What are you going to do?

Find out what your classmates are doing over the weekend. Turn to page IC-20.

6 CONVERSATION Telephone messages

 Listen and practice.

Secretary: Good morning, Parker Industries.
Mr. Kale: Hello. May I speak to Ms. Graham, please?
Secretary: I'm sorry. She's not in. Can I take a message?
Mr. Kale: Yes, please. This is Mr. Kale.
Secretary: Is that G-A-L-E?
Mr. Kale: No, it's K-A-L-E.
Secrctary: All right.
Mr. Kale: Please tell her our meeting is on Friday at 2:30.
Secretary: Friday at 2:30.
Mr. Kale: And would you ask her to call me this afternoon? My number is 356-4031.
Secretary: 356-4031. Yes, Mr. Kale. I'll give Ms. Graham the message.
Mr. Kale: Thank you. Good-bye.
Secretary: Good-bye.

To: _Ms. Graham_

Date: _August 10_   Time: _____

WHILE YOU WERE OUT

From: _Mr. Kale_

of: _____

Phone: _356-4031_   ext: ____

Message: _____
The meeting is on Friday at 2:30.
Please call him this afternoon.

Taken by: _____

5 ROLE PLAY An invitation

This role play is a fluency activity that is also an extension of Exercise 4. Ss improvise by thinking up information about a make-believe event and then practice making, accepting, and declining invitations.

- Divide the class equally into two groups: one half = Student As; the other half = Student Bs.

- Gather all Student As together and go over their instructions. Model the two example questions; Student As repeat. Elicit additional questions that Ss could use to invite someone out and write them on the board – for example:

  What are you doing on . . . ?
  Are you going to be busy . . . ?

  Also write the following cues on the board and have Student As use them to help plan their invitations:

  | *activity/event* | *transportation* | *day/date* |
  | *location/venue* | *place to meet* | *time* |

- While Student As are planning their invitations, gather all Student Bs together. Go over their instructions. Model the example statements to accept or refuse an invitation; Student Bs repeat. Then elicit Student Bs' additional suggestions on how to accept and politely decline invitations. Write the better (i.e., more polite and/or more appropriate) ones on the board for Ss to use during the role play. For example:

  Accepting an invitation
  Thank you! I've really wanted to . . . (e.g., see, do) that!
  Wow, that sounds really terrific! Thanks a lot!

Refusing an invitation
Mmm, I have to . . . (e.g., baby-sit, do homework).
Thanks for asking, but I already promised to . . . (e.g., see my brother, pick up a friend at the airport).

- Model the role play with several volunteers. Show Ss how to elaborate and use their own words, like this:

  T: Say, Andy, there's a great concert this weekend. Are you doing anything on Saturday night?
  S: Um, no. What kind of concert is it?
  T: It's a terrific rock group from Ireland.
  S: Yeah? Gee, that sounds interesting!
  T: Well, would you like to go?
  S: Sure! Where is it going to be?

- Ss form A/B pairs to practice the role play, using the cues in the book and on the board. Go around the class and give help as needed.

- Ss change roles and do the activity again.

 INTERCHANGE 15 What are you going to do?

See page T-124 in this Teacher's Edition for notes.

 Workbook

Assign Exercises 1–6 on pages 85–87 for homework or let Ss do them in class. Pairs or groups compare answers. Then elicit Ss' answers around the class. (Answers can be found on page T-189 of the Workbook Answer Key in this Teacher's Edition.)

Cycle 2, Exercises 6–12

6 CONVERSATION Telephone messages

This exercise introduces the use of *tell* and *ask* for relaying telephone messages.

- Books closed. Set the scene: A man is making a business phone call. Write these questions on the board:

  Who does the caller want to speak to? (Ms. Graham)
  Is she there? (No, she isn't.)
  What does the caller do? (He leaves a message.)
  What's the caller's name? (Mr. Kale)
  What's he calling about? (A meeting on Friday at 2:30)
  What's his phone number? (356-4031)

- Play the audio program. Tell Ss to listen and take notes. Then have Ss work in pairs to compare answers to the questions on the board. Check Ss' responses.

- Books open. Use the audio program and the picture to present the conversation.

- Pairs practice the telephone conversation – back-to-back, if possible, to make it more challenging.

Optional activity: *A fantastic weekend!*

Time: 15–20 minutes. This fun activity practices planning weekend activities for visiting guests.

- Explain the situation: Two wealthy friends are coming to visit you this weekend. They have *very* expensive tastes and like to enjoy the best of everything. Of course, they will pay all expenses, including yours.

- Ss work in groups of four. If Ss live in a big city, they should plan activities for that city. However, if they are in a small town, they should make plans to stay in the nearest big city. Write this information on the board:

  Things to think about for the weekend
  | *transportation* | *sightseeing* | *shopping* |
  | *hotel* | *entertainment* | *restaurants* |

  Weekend itinerary
  Friday evening (guests arrive at 6 P.M.)
  Saturday morning, afternoon, and evening
  Sunday morning and afternoon (guests leave at 3 P.M.)

- Groups plan their weekends. Go around the class and give help and encouragement as needed.

- Ask groups to report their weekend plans. Encourage others to ask questions in order to find out more details.

7 GRAMMAR FOCUS Tell *and* ask

 This exercise practices using *tell* and *ask* to relay messages; it also reviews object pronouns.

Using tell *in messages with a statement:* With a message based on a statement (e.g., The meeting is on Friday.), the statement remains intact when using the verb *tell* (e.g., Please *tell* Ann [that] <u>the meeting is on Friday.</u>/Would/Could you *tell* her [that] <u>the meeting is on Friday</u>?). Following *tell* + name/pronoun is the optional use of the relative pronoun *that*.

Using ask *in messages with a request:* In a message containing a request with an imperative (e.g., Call me this afternoon.), the imperative verb becomes an infinitive (i.e., *to* + base verb) when using the verb *ask* (e.g., Please *ask* him <u>to call me this afternoon.</u>/Would/Could you *ask* him <u>to call me this afternoon</u>?).

- Use the audio program to present the sentences in the box. Explain the differences (as described in the notes above) between messages made from statements using *tell* + name/pronoun + optional *that* and messages made from imperative requests using *ask* + infinitive. Also point out the punctuation needed with these two different types of messages: Messages beginning with *Please* are statements that end with a period; messages with *Would/Could you* are requests in the form of questions that end with a question mark.

- Give Ss additional examples of statements to change into messages with statements. Dictate them or write them on the board (e.g., The picnic on Sunday is at 2 P.M.); call on Ss to practice changing them into messages. Then conduct a similar drill with additional

examples of imperative requests (e.g., Call me this Friday.); Ss put them into messages with requests.

- Read the instructions aloud. Present messages 1–6. Explain any new words that Ss may ask about (e.g., *pick up, canceled*).

- Go over the first message again and point out the cue word, *could*. Then read aloud the example question and show how the statement was formed into a message with a statement beginning with *could*.

- Now Ss do the task. Walk around the class, giving help as needed and taking notes on how the Ss are doing.

- **Optional:** If many Ss seem to be having difficulty knowing which pattern to use with statements and which to use for requests, stop the activity. Go over each initial message again, this time asking "Is this a statement or a request?"

- Ss compare responses in pairs. Then elicit and check Ss' answers around the class.

Answers

1. Could you tell Kim the movie is at 7:00?
2. Would you ask Mike to pick me up at home around 4:00?
3. Please tell Maria (that) the concert on Saturday is canceled.
4. Could you ask Jim to bring the tickets for the hockey game tonight?
5. Would you tell Ann (that) the museum opens at 10:00 tomorrow morning?
6. Please ask Alex to meet us in front of the cafeteria at 12:15.

8 WRITING

This exercise gives Ss practice in writing real requests and then relaying them verbally as messages. This activity can be fun when Ss are willing to be enthusiastic and imaginative.

Pair work

- Go over the instructions and read aloud the example message. Using the example message, model with a volunteer how this activity works, like this (*S = Juan, the writer; T = Su Hee, the partner*):

The writer's tasks
1. The writer (Juan) writes a note to his partner (Su Hee). The note should include at least two messages to other people in the class.
2. Then he hands the written message to his partner.

The partner's tasks
1. The partner (Su Hee) reads the note and then gets up to relay the messages verbally to the people named in the note (here, Ms. King and Steve).

2. The partner goes up to the first person in the note, Ms. King, and relays the writer's message like this, "Excuse me, Ms. King. Juan isn't going to be in class tomorrow. Could you save any handouts for him?"
3. Then the partner goes up to the second person in the note, Steve, and says, "Oh, hi, Steve. Uh, Juan asked me to tell you that he isn't going to be in class tomorrow, so he can't meet you for dinner after class."

- Have Ss form pairs. Tell them to first work individually to write their notes – requests to their partners to give messages to at least two other people in the class. Encourage them to write interesting messages for their partners to relay. Walk around and give help as needed.

- Give Ss five to ten minutes to finish writing their requests. (*Note:* This writing task could be assigned for homework.) Then pairs exchange written notes. After partners read their requests, everyone gets up to deliver each request orally to the designated people in the class.

7 GRAMMAR FOCUS

Tell *and* ask 🔊

Statement	Messages with a statement
The meeting is on Friday.	**Please tell Ann (that)** the meeting is on Friday. **Would you tell her (that)** . . . ? **Could you tell her (that)** . . . ?
Request Call me this afternoon.	**Messages with a request** **Please ask him to** call me this afternoon. **Would you ask him to** . . . ? **Could you tell him to** . . . ?

Look at the message slips. Ask someone to pass on these messages.
Use the words in parentheses. Then compare with a partner.

1.
```
Kim -
The movie is at
7:00 tonight.
```
(could) *Could you tell Kim the movie is at 7:00?*

2.
```
Mike -
Pick me up at home
around 4:00.
```
(would)

3.
```
Maria -
The concert on Saturday
is canceled.
```
(please)

4.
```
Jim -
Bring the tickets for the
hockey game tonight.
```
(could)

5.
```
Ann -
The museum opens at
10:00 tomorrow morning.
```
(would)

6.
```
Alex -
Meet us in front of the
cafeteria at 12:15.
```
(please)

8 WRITING

Pair work You want to give messages to people in your class. Write a
request to your partner. Ask him or her to give the messages for you.

```
Dear Su Hee,
I'm not going to be in class tomorrow. Would you please ask Ms. King to save any
handouts for me? Also, could you tell Steve that I can't meet him for dinner after class?
                                    Thanks,
                                    Juan
```

9 PRONUNCIATION *Reduced forms of* could you *and* would you

A Listen and practice. Notice how **could you** and **would you** are reduced in conversation.

/cʊdʒə/
Could you tell Matt the meeting is at 5:00?

/wʊdʒə/
Would you ask him to pick me up at 4:30?

B Practice these questions with reduced forms.

Could you ask her to return my dictionary?
Would you tell him there's a picnic tomorrow?

10 LISTENING *Take a message*

CLASS
AUDIO
ONLY ▶ Listen to telephone calls to Mr. Kim and Ms. Carson, and write down the messages.

1.

To: _Mr._____
Date: _____ Time: _____

WHILE YOU WERE OUT

From: _____
of: _City_____
Phone: _____ ext:_____
Message: _____
_Call Mrs._____
_____
_____
Taken by: _____

2.

To: _Wendy_____
Date: _____ Time: _____

WHILE YOU WERE OUT

From: _____
of: _____National_____
Phone: _____ ext:_____
Message: _____
_____
_____
_____
Taken by: _____

11 ROLE PLAY *Who's calling?*

Student A: Call your friend David to tell him this:

There's a party at Bob's house on Saturday night.
Bob's address is 414 Maple St., Apt. 202.
Pick me up at 8:00 P.M.

Student B: Someone calls for your brother David. He isn't in.
Take a message for him.

Change roles and try another role play.

Student A: Someone calls for your sister Carol. She isn't in.
Take a message for her.

Student B: Call your friend Carol to tell her this:

There's no class next Friday afternoon.
The class is going to a movie at Westwood Theater.
Meet us in front of the theater at 4:30.

useful expressions
May I speak to . . . ?
Can I take a message?
I'll give . . . the message.

9 PRONUNCIATION Reduced forms of could you and would you

This exercise practices the reduced forms of *could you* and *would you* in questions.

A

■ Play the audio program. Model the consonant sounds *d + y* in *could you* and *would you*. Ss repeat.

B

■ Model the two questions for the class and have Ss repeat.

■ **Optional:** Have pairs go back to Exercise 7 on page 95 and practice the messages with "Could/Would you . . . ?"

10 LISTENING Take a message

This exercise practices listening to telephone messages and writing them down.

■ Go over the instructions and the message slips. Then play the audio program. Ss listen and write down the messages. Afterwards, Ss compare answers in pairs.

Audio script

1. RECEPTIONIST: *(phone rings)* Good afternoon, MBI. May I help you?
   MRS. PARIS: Hello. I want to speak to Mr. Kim, please.
   RECEPTIONIST: I'm sorry. Mr. Kim is in a meeting right now. Would you like to leave a message?
   MRS. PARIS: Yes, please. This is Mrs. Paris . . . of City Car Center.
   RECEPTIONIST: Mrs. Paris. Is that P-A-R-I-S?
   MRS. PARIS: Yes, that's right. Please ask him to call me at the City Car Center before three-thirty this afternoon. It's very important.
   RECEPTIONIST: All right. And your number, please?
   MRS. PARIS: Five-five-four, three-two-nine-zero.
   RECEPTIONIST: Five-five-four, three-two-nine-oh?
   MRS. PARIS: That's it.
   RECEPTIONIST: OK. I'll ask him to call you before three-thirty, Mrs. Paris.
   MRS. PARIS: Thank you. Good-bye.
   RECEPTIONIST: Good-bye. *(hangs up)*
2. RECEPTIONIST: *(phone rings)* This is Software Systems. Good morning.

SANDY: Good morning. May I speak to Ms. Carson, please?
RECEPTIONIST: Hmm . . . , do you mean Mrs. Carter?
SANDY: No, Carson, Ms. Wendy Carson. She's new there.
RECEPTIONIST: Let me check. Oh, yes, let me try to connect you. Hold on. *(phone rings)* I'm sorry. There's no answer. May I take a message?
SANDY: Yes. Would you please ask her to call Sandy at First National Bank?
RECEPTIONIST: Sandy . . . at First National Bank . . . .
SANDY: The number is four-six-two, one-one-eight-seven, extension three-one-three.
RECEPTIONIST: Four-six-two, eleven eighty-seven . . . extension three-one-three?
SANDY: That's right.
RECEPTIONIST: OK. I'll give her the message.
SANDY: Thanks so much. Bye.
RECEPTIONIST: Good-bye. *(hangs up)*

■ Check Ss' answers around the class.

Possible answers

1. To: Mr. **Kim** From: **Mrs. Paris** of: City **Car Center** Phone: **554-3290** ext. Message: Call Mrs. **Paris before 3:30 this** **afternoon. Very important!**	2. To: Wendy **Carson** From: **Sandy** of: **First** National **Bank** Phone: **462-1187** ext. **313** Message: **Call her.**

11 ROLE PLAY Who's calling?

This role play is an extension of Exercises 6–10. Here, Ss practice taking and leaving phone messages.

(*Note:* Before starting this activity, it might be helpful to review phone etiquette and language by having the class look back over the telephone conversation in Exercise 6 on page 94. Also, Ss might want to listen again to the audio program in Exercise 10 above.)

■ Divide the class into pairs and assign A/B roles. Present the first A/B role play: Explain the roles, go over the A/B cues, and model the useful expressions.

■ Model the role play with a volunteer. Sit back-to-back and pretend you are both holding phones. Play the role

of the caller (Student A) and use the cues to leave a message for your friend David; the S is David's brother (Student B), who should write down the message.

■ Ss do the first role play. Have Ss sit back-to-back if possible, while holding imaginary phones. Go around the class and give help as needed.

■ When pairs finish, ask for volunteers to do the role play in front of the class. Encourage the rest of the class to praise what was good in the role play; then elicit suggestions on what could be improved.

■ Go over the second role play and the A/B cues. Pairs try their new roles. Again, give help as needed.

12 *READING* *Ways to keep phone calls short*

This text presents useful and practical information about using the telephone; the exercise involves skimming, scanning, and making inferences.

■ Books closed. To stimulate a short class discussion on the main topic – ways to keep phone calls short – present the pre-reading questions.

A

■ Books open. Ss read the article once. Encourage Ss to try to guess the meanings of new words. Remind them to circle or underline any word or expression whose meaning they can't guess from its context within that particular sentence or other sentences surrounding it.

■ **Optional:** After Ss finish reading, tell them to scan the passage for any words or phrases that they marked. Then tell them to reread the whole sentence in which the new word occurs; have them reread the sentence that comes before and after it, too. Explain that this technique of looking carefully at the complete context in which an unknown word occurs can improve a reader's comprehension.

■ Either explain any new vocabulary, or have Ss form pairs or groups to help each other check words and definitions in their dictionaries. Here are some words and expressions that Ss may need help with:

Introduction
latest = most recent
rude = impolite
cut (someone) off = suddenly stop a person from talking or continuing on with a story
time management consultant = a person hired to study how quickly and accurately work is done in a particular location (e.g., in an office or on an assembly line in a factory) and then make suggestions for improvements
1. **impression** = idea
   chat = talk informally or casually
   get right to the heart of the matter = go directly to what is important
2. **time your calls** = plan when to phone
3. **time limit** = a fixed period of minutes/hours in which something has to be done
   run errands = go out on a short local trip to do something (e.g., mail letters at the post office, buy groceries at the supermarket, pick up dry cleaning)
4. **jump on (something)** = to act quickly
   pause = a short stop or break in time (e.g., taking a breath between sentences now and then when talking)
5. **forget niceties** = don't worry about being polite, pleasant, or agreeable
   take a hint = understand an indirect idea or suggestion
   pressed for time = in a hurry
   hang up = finish a telephone call by putting down the receiver

6. **"partner in crime"** = someone who helps another do something wrong or illegal; however, the quotation marks here show that this phrase is made in a lighthearted way and should not be taken seriously or literally
   signals = uses a nonverbal gesture (e.g., pointing with the hands, rolling the eyes, raising the eyebrows) to get someone's attention
7. **avoid** = don't use
   screen calls = listen in and pick up the phone only when it's someone you want to talk to
   chatterbox = a very talkative person

■ Now read aloud the instructions and go over the eight sentences in the list. Ss check (✓) the ones that are examples of things to say to keep phone calls short. If Ss aren't sure about some of the sentences, encourage them to reread or skim the passage. Walk around the class, giving help as needed.

■ **Optional:** Ss discuss their answers in pairs, in groups, or as a whole class activity.

Answers *(sentences that should be checked)*

2, 4, 7, 8

B *Pair work*

■ Go over the three questions. Then Ss work in pairs to discuss their answers to each question. After about five minutes, elicit Ss' answers around the class.

■ **Optional:** Since Ss' answers will vary for each question in part B, it might be fun to take a quick class poll on each question to find out which pieces of advice are the most popular or the most commonly used.

Optional activities

1 *Game – Word Bingo*
■ See page T-33.

2 *Crossword puzzle*
■ See page T-146.

3 *Sentence-making contest*
■ See page T-149.

 Workbook

Tell Ss to do Exercises 7–11 on pages 88–90 in the Workbook or assign them as homework. Have Ss work in small groups to compare answers. Elicit responses around the class. (Answers can be found on page T-189 of the Workbook Answer Key in this Teacher's Edition.)

12 READING

Ways to Keep Phone Calls Short

Do you like to talk on the phone?
Do you think that you spend too much time on the phone?

The phone rings. It's a friend who wants to tell you about his or her latest health problem. You hate to be rude and cut your friend off, but what can you do? Time management consultant Stephanie Winston, author of *Stephanie Winston's Best Organizing Tips,* offers this advice:

1. **Don't ask questions like "What's new?"** They give the impression that you have time to chat. After "hello," get right to the heart of the matter.

2. **Time *your* calls intelligently.** If you make a call right before lunch or dinner, or at the end of the workday, people chat less.

3. **Set a time limit.** Start with, "Hi, I've only got a few minutes, but I wanted to talk to you about …." Or, "Gee, I'd love to talk more, but I only have a couple of minutes before I have to run errands."

4. **Jump on a pause.** Even the most talkative caller has to pause now and then. Quickly say, "It has been great talking with you." Then end the conversation.

5. **Forget niceties.** Some people just don't take a hint. Interrupt your caller and say, "I'd like to talk to you longer, but I'm pressed for time. Good-bye." Then hang up. Don't ask for permission to end the conversation.

6. **Find a "partner in crime."** If nothing else works, ask someone in your home to help you. For example, one woman signals her husband, who yells, "Jane, I think the roast is burning!"

7. **Avoid the phone completely.** Use an answering machine to screen calls. If you have an important message for a chatterbox, leave the message when he or she isn't in.

A Read the article. Then look at these sentences. Check (✓) the things you can say to keep phone calls short.

☐ 1. I'm glad you feel better. What can I do for you?
☐ 2. I have to go now. Good-bye.
☐ 3. Hi. How are things?
☐ 4. I need to get off the phone now. There's someone at the door.
☐ 5. So, what else is new?
☐ 6. No, I'm not busy right now.
☐ 7. I'm sorry to call you at dinnertime, but I have just one question.
☐ 8. I only have three minutes before I have to leave.

B *Pair work* Talk about these questions.

1. Which advice have you used sometimes?
2. Which do you think are the three best pieces of advice?
3. What else can you do to keep phone calls short?

97

16 A change for the better!

1 SNAPSHOT

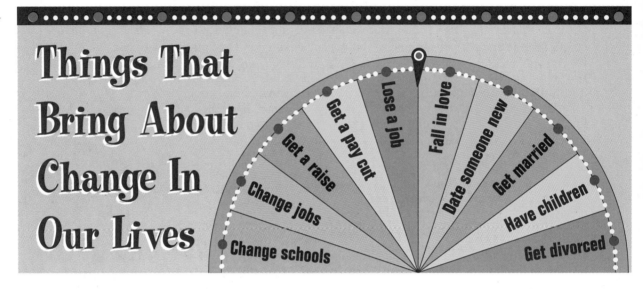

Things That Bring About Change In Our Lives

Lose a job
Get a pay cut
Fall in love
Get a raise
Date someone new
Change jobs
Get married
Have children
Change schools
Get divorced

Talk about these questions.

Have any of these things happened to you in the last few years?
How have they changed you?
What other things bring about change in our lives?

2 CONVERSATION Catching up

A Listen and practice.

Brian: Diane Grant? I haven't seen you for ages.
Diane: Brian! How have you been?
Brian: Pretty good. Say, you've really changed!
Diane: Oh, well, I've lost some weight. And my hair is longer than before.
Brian: Well, you look great! How are you?
Diane: I'm doing really well. I got married about three years ago. I have two kids now.
Brian: That's terrific!

B Listen to the rest of the conversation.

How has Brian changed?

98

16 A change for the better!

Cycle 1, Exercises 1–5

1 SNAPSHOT Things that bring about change in our lives

This graphic introduces the topic of this cycle – major changes or events in people's lives.

(*Note:* The Word Power on page 100 introduces additional phrases similar to those in the Snapshot. Ss will use them when discussing common, everyday things that change within people's lives.)

■ Books closed. Introduce the topic – important life-changing events – by asking some questions like these:

Getting married is an important change. Why?
How does moving to a new place change a person's life?
What other events are very important in our lives?

■ Books open. Ss read the Snapshot information. Answer any vocabulary questions Ss may have, or tell them to check their dictionaries.

■ Read the three questions aloud. Ss answer the questions individually; then pairs compare responses.

■ **Optional:** Elicit information that Ss feel comfortable sharing with the rest of the class; if Ss feel uncomfortable about sharing information that they think is too personal, tell them to simply respond by saying "I prefer not to talk about that."

(*Note:* If Ss keep an English journal or just want to write an extra composition for class, encourage them to use the questions here to brainstorm on this writing topic: "The Most Important Change in My Life.")

2 CONVERSATION Catching up

This exercise reviews various verb tenses and comparatives for talking about recent events and changes in people's lives.

■ Books closed. For a topic warm-up, present the information below and write it on the board. Tell Ss to brainstorm on the question in pairs or groups:

Situation: Two friends haven't seen each other for a few years. Then one day they run into each other.
Question: What things do they ask each other about?

■ Elicit Ss' suggestions and write them on the board.

A 🔊

■ Set the scene: Two old friends run into each other and talk about recent changes in their lives. Play the audio program. Tell Ss to listen and take notes.

■ Have Ss compare their earlier brainstorming suggestions with what Brian and Diane talked about.

■ Books open. Play the audio program again, pausing it line by line, and use the picture to present the conversation. Ss repeat.

■ Draw Ss' attention to the exclamation points in this dialog and explain that this punctuation mark shows the speakers' emotions and resulting changes in voice pitch and intensity. Model each of the four exclamatory sentences and encourage the class to repeat them with matching enthusiasm.

■ While Ss practice the conversation in pairs, encourage them to try to show real emotion when acting out their parts.

B 🔊

■ Read the question that Ss need to focus their listening on. Then play the second part of the audio program. Again, have Ss listen and take notes.

Audio script

> DIANE: And how about you, Brian? What have you been up to?
> BRIAN: Well, I moved away – to San Francisco. I'm just back here on some business today.
> DIANE: Oh, you have a new job?
> BRIAN: Yes, I work for a travel agency now.
> DIANE: Really? How do you like it?
> BRIAN: The work is wonderful! And my salary is much better than before.
> DIANE: That's great! You look different, too.
> BRIAN: Well, I've grown a mustache.
> DIANE: That's what it is! It looks good on you.
> BRIAN: *(laughs)* Thanks, Diane. You always were generous with the compliments.

■ Ss compare answers in pairs or groups.

Possible answer

> He moved away – to San Francisco; he has a new job in a travel agency; the work is wonderful, and his salary is much better than before; he's grown a mustache.

3 GRAMMAR FOCUS Describing changes

🔊 This grammar focus practices describing changes in a person's life, using the present tense, past tense, present perfect, and the comparative.

- Play the audio program to present the sentences in the boxes. Then use those sentence examples to briefly review the following grammar points:

Present tense = used for general statements of fact and to express habitual or everyday activity

Past tense = used to describe completed events at a particular time in the past

Present perfect = used to express that something happened (or never happened) before now and at an unspecified time in the past; it also expresses the repetition of an activity before now

Comparative = used to compare two things with adjectives

A

- Go over the instructions. Use the picture to model how to check (✓) any true statements and to correct any false statements in order to make them true. Put the following example on the board and go over it with the class:

☑ 1. *I've changed my hairstyle.*
☐ 2. *I dress differently now.* (T writes: *I dress the same.*)

- Ss work individually to complete the task. Remind them to pay attention to the various tenses and comparative forms that they use when correcting a false statement. Walk around and give help as needed. (*Note:* Ss' answers will be checked in part B below.)

B Pair work

- Go over the task. Then have Ss work in pairs to compare and discuss their part A responses.

- To check Ss' answers from part A, read aloud the items on the list; find out which statements Ss checked as true by asking for a show of hands. Then have Ss choose one of their false statements to share with the rest of the class and ask them to write the correct information for it – i.e., one sentence – on the board.

- **Optional:** Use the Ss' sentences on the board for a quick and fun editing activity, with the whole class participating. Encourage Ss to give suggestions on how to improve each sentence (when necessary) by correcting such things as verb tense, word choice, and spelling.

C Group work

- Explain the activity by reading the instructions aloud. If helpful, model or elicit some examples from the class and write them on the board – for example:

I'm now a college graduate.
I've cut my hair and changed the color of it.
I don't exercise very much anymore.
I have a full-time job now.
I became a vegetarian, so I eat different food now.

- Ss write five sentences. (*Note:* This writing task could also be assigned for homework.) Then Ss form groups to compare answers. After about five minutes, remind Ss to find out who in their group has changed the most.

4 LISTENING Memory lane

🔊 This exercise practices listening for main ideas, taking notes, and making inferences.

- Books closed. Set the scene: Two people are discussing how they have changed in recent years.

- Play the audio program once. Ss listen for general information and take notes.

Audio script

LINDA: What are you looking at, Scott?
SCOTT: Oh, just one of our photo albums.
LINDA: Oh, look – it's our wedding picture!
SCOTT: Yeah. Just think, we'll be celebrating our fifth wedding anniversary this month.
LINDA: Yeah, and I remember I couldn't stand you when we first met. But a year later, we fell in love and got married.
SCOTT: And here's a picture of our honeymoon. Wow! We sure look different now, don't we?
LINDA: Yes! My hair is much shorter now. And you've gained a little weight. You were always too thin! Oh,

and look, here's a picture of the day we brought Maggie home from the hospital.
SCOTT: She's adorable. And now we have two kids! Who would have guessed?
LINDA: Yeah. We're just lucky that they look like me!

- Books open. Present the task and go over the chart. Ss listen again, this time writing the information in the chart.

- Play the audio program again once or twice, if necessary, to help Ss complete the chart.

- Ss compare answers in pairs or groups. Then check responses around the class.

Answers

Changes
Her hair is (much) shorter.
He's gained (a little) weight.
They have two kids now.

3 GRAMMAR FOCUS

Describing changes

With the present tense	With the comparative	With the past tense	With the present perfect
I **have** two kids now.	My job is **more stressful** (now).	I **got** married.	I**'ve lost** weight.
I **don't smoke** anymore.	My hair is **longer** (**than** before).	I **moved** to a new city.	I**'ve grown** a mustache.

A How have you changed in the last five years?
Check (✓) the statements that are true
for you. If a statement isn't true, give the
correct information.

- ☐ 1. I've changed my hairstyle.
- ☐ 2. I dress differently now.
- ☐ 3. I've lost weight.
- ☐ 4. I moved into my own apartment.
- ☐ 5. I got married.
- ☐ 6. I'm more outgoing than before.
- ☐ 7. I don't go to many parties anymore.
- ☐ 8. My life is easier now.

B *Pair work* Compare your responses in
part A. Have you changed in similar ways?

C *Group work* Write five sentences
describing other changes in your life.
Then compare in groups. Who in the
group has changed the most?

4 LISTENING *Memory lane*

Linda and Scott are looking through a photo album.
Listen to their conversation. How have they changed?
Write down three changes.

Changes
....
....
....

5 WORD POWER Things that change

A Complete the word map with the phrases from the list. Then add two more examples to each category.

cut my hair short
do aerobics
eat more vegetables
get dressed up
get up early
grow a beard
learn to swim
learn to type
quit smoking
speak English
start cooking
wear contact lenses

Things that change

Appearance
....
....
....
....
....
....

Health
....
....
....
....
....

Skills/Abilities
....
....
....
....
....

B *Pair work* Have you changed in any of these areas?
Tell your partner about a change in each category.

"I get up earlier in the morning. I've started cooking. And I get dressed up for work now."

6 CONVERSATION Planning your future

A Listen and practice.

Alex: So what are you going to do after graduation, Susan?
Susan: Well, I've saved some money, and I think I'd really like to travel.
Alex: Lucky you. That sounds exciting!
Susan: Yeah. Then I plan to get a job and my own apartment.
Alex: Oh, you're not going to live at home?
Susan: No, I don't want to live with my parents – not after I start to work.
Alex: I know what you mean.
Susan: What about you, Alex? Do you have any plans yet?
Alex: I'm going to get a job *and* live at home. I'm broke, and I want to pay off my student loan!

CLASS AUDIO ONLY ▶ **B** Listen to the rest of the conversation.

1. What kind of job does Alex want?
2. Where would Susan like to travel?

5 WORD POWER Things that change

This exercise practices categorizing phrases; it also presents additional phrases for Ss to use when discussing changes in their lives in Exercises 7–10.

A

- Go over the task. Model each phrase and category in the word map; have Ss repeat for pronunciation practice.

- Explain any unfamiliar vocabulary; or you may prefer to have Ss look up any new words in their dictionaries.

- Ss complete the chart either individually or in pairs. Remind them to add two more examples to each category. Walk around and give help as needed.

- To check answers, write the category headings on the board. Ask each S or pair to add one or two words, but without repeating any words that have already been written on the board.

Answers (extra examples in boldface)

Health	Appearance	Skills/Abilities
do aerobics	cut my hair short	learn to swim
eat more vegetables	get dressed up	learn to type
get up early	grow a beard	speak English
quit smoking	wear contact lenses	start cooking
take vitamins	**let my hair grow long**	**take music/ art lessons**
eat less meat	**gain/lose weight**	**read more**

B Pair work

- Go over the task and the example. Elicit additional responses from a volunteer (see the example dialog below) and write them on the board:

 T: Is there something about your health that has changed in the past few years?
 S1: Yes, I get an annual checkup now. I have health insurance as a full-time student.
 T: (writing the S's first sentence on the board) And have you gotten any new skills or abilities in the past year?
 S1: Yes, I learned how to surf the Internet recently!

- Ss work together in pairs, taking turns asking each other similar questions. Tell them to respond orally first and then to write down their responses. Call on pairs to read aloud the most interesting changes they discussed.

Workbook

Assign Exercises 1–5 on pages 91–93 for Ss to do for homework or in class. Ss form small groups to compare answers. Elicit answers around the class. (Answers can be found on page T-190 of the Workbook Answer Key in this Teacher's Edition.)

Cycle 2, Exercises 6–12

6 CONVERSATION Planning your future

This exercise presents the use of verb + infinitive (e.g., *like to travel/plan to get*) to talk about future plans.

A

- Books open. Use the picture to set the scene. Play the first part of the audio program. Ss listen.

- Present the conversation line by line. Explain any new words and expressions like these:

 graduation = leaving school with a diploma
 I'm broke = I don't have any money
 pay off = make the final payment for something
 student loan = money given to a student, but which must be paid back (often with interest) when he/she finishes or leaves school

- Have Ss practice the conversation in pairs.

B

- Go over the two questions. Play the second part of the audio program. Tell Ss to listen closely for the answers.

Audio script

SUSAN: What kind of job are you looking for?
ALEX: Well, I've thought a lot about it, and I'd like to do computer programming. So I hope to get a job with a big computer company.
SUSAN: Hey, that sounds really interesting.
ALEX: Yeah. I've got an interview next week.
SUSAN: Well, good luck!
ALEX: And where do you plan to travel to, Susan?
SUSAN: Well, I'd like to travel around the United States a bit. There are so many beautiful places that I've never seen.
ALEX: Well, please send me lots of postcards while you're away.
SUSAN: All right, I will! And I hope you get the job!
ALEX: Me, too!

- After Ss compare answers in pairs, check answers around the class.

Answers

1. He wants to do computer programming (with a big computer company).
2. She'd like to travel around the United States.

7 GRAMMAR FOCUS *Verb + infinitive*

🔊 This grammar focus practices the structure verb + infinitive with various verbs (e.g., *I'm going to get* . . . , *I don't want/plan to* . . . , *I'd like/love to* . . . .) for talking about plans.

■ Play the audio program to present the statements in the box; Ss repeat. Point out the verb + infinitive structure in each sentence.

■ Point out that the modal *would* (or the contraction, *'d*) is used with the verbs *like* and *love* to talk about things people want to or hope to do in the future.

■ Give the class a quick drill, like this:

T: *(writing the question on the board)* What are you going to do this summer? Sam, use *going to* to answer the question.
S1: I'm going to take another English course.
T: Anita, please use *hope to.*
S2: I hope to take a little vacation.
T: Chan, use *don't plan to.*

A

■ Read over the instructions. Make sure Ss know that they should write about themselves. Encourage them to use all of the verbs from the box at least once.

■ **Optional:** Tell Ss to look at the photos. Lead a class discussion about the aspects of people's lives that the photos represent (e.g., families, working parents, getting married, becoming successful). Encourage thought and originality.

■ If necessary, show Ss how to complete number 1 before they work individually. Remind them to add three additional statements in the blanks for numbers 8–10. Walk around the class and give help as requested or needed. (*Note:* Don't check Ss' answers until the end of part B.)

B *Pair work*

■ Read aloud the instructions and questions. Ss form pairs to discuss their responses. Tell them to check (✓) the statements in their lists that are the same and to put an ✗ next to the ones that are different.

■ Elicit some "same" responses and some "different" responses from pairs in order to check Ss' answers.

Possible answers *(Accept as correct any answer that is logical and grammatically correct.)*

> 1. **I'm (not) going to** move to a new city.
> 2. I **(don't) plan to** get married.
> 3. I **(don't) want to** have a large family.
> 4. I **hope to** find a job where I can travel.
> 5. **I'd love to** make a lot of money!
> 6. **I'd like to** become very successful.
> 7. **I'd love to** retire at an early age.
> 8–10. Ss' answers will vary.

8 PLAN ON IT

This is an open-ended fluency activity in which Ss can talk about their real future plans or their dreams and hopes.

Group work

■ Introduce the task by modeling the correct pronunciation and intonation pattern of each question; Ss repeat. Remind Ss that Wh-questions usually have falling intonation and yes/no questions usually have rising intonation.

■ Before Ss form groups, have a quick question-and-answer practice with the whole class, like this:

T: What are you going to do after this English course is over, Yen?
S1: Gee, I guess I'm going to get a part-time job.
T: Oh? What kind of job do you want to get?
S1: Well, I don't want to work at . . . , but I hope to . . . .
T: That sounds good! All right, Yen, please ask someone else the next question.
S1: Ty, do you plan to study here again next year?

■ Groups take turns asking and answering the questions. Encourage Ss to ask follow-up questions to get more information and to show enthusiasm and interest in their classmates' future plans.

Optional activity: *End-of-the-class party*

Time: 15–20 minutes. This activity practices describing plans for a class party.

■ Explain the activity: Ss make plans for an end-of-the-class party. Write these topics on the board:

Date
Place
Time
Menu (food and drinks)
Activities
Entertainment
Responsibilities (who brings what/who does what)
Cost per student (if appropriate)

■ Ss form groups. Tell them to brainstorm on the topics to get ideas for their class party. Set a time limit of about ten minutes. Go around and give help as needed.

■ As a class activity, ask groups to take turns reporting their plans to the class. Take a vote (through a show of hands or with secret ballots): Who has the best plan? How many Ss really want to have a party? (*Note:* Consider the Ss' responses and then take it from there.)

7 GRAMMAR FOCUS

Verb + infinitive 🔲))

What **are** you **going to do** after graduation?
I'm (not) **going to get** a job right away.
I (don't) **plan to get** my own apartment.
I (don't) **want to live** with my parents.
I **hope to get** a new car.
I'd **like to travel** this summer.
I'd **love to move** to a new city.

A Complete these statements so that they are true for you. Use information from the grammar box. Then add three more statements of your own.

1. I .... move to a new city.
2. I .... get married.
3. I .... have a large family.
4. I .... find a job where I can travel.
5. I .... make a lot of money!
6. I .... become very successful.
7. I .... retire at an early age.
8. ....
9. ....
10. ....

B *Pair work* Compare your responses with a partner. How are you the same? How are you different?

8 PLAN ON IT

Group work What are your plans for the future? Ask and answer these questions.

What are you going to do after this English course is over?
Do you plan to study here again next year?
What other languages would you like to learn?
What countries would you like to live in? Why?
What countries wouldn't you like to live in? Why?
Do you want to get a (new) job in a few years?
What kind of job do you hope to get?

9 PRONUNCIATION *Reduced form of* to

A 🔊 Listen and practice. Notice that **to** is reduced to /tə/.

I hope **to** get married.   I'd love **to** move to a new city.
I plan **to** have a large family.   I'd like **to** live in a small town.

B *Pair work* Write four statements about yourself using the verbs above. Take turns reading your statements with a partner. Pay attention to the pronunciation of **to**.

10 WRITING

A Write about your plans for the future.

working in the Peace Corps

> I would like to join the Peace Corps for a couple
> of years. I have a degree in biology, so I hope
> to work in forestry or environmental education.
> I'd like to work with people in . . . .

B *Pair work* Compare your composition with a partner's. Ask and answer questions about each other's plans.

interchange 16

Unfold your future!
Imagine you could do anything, go anywhere, and meet anybody.
Turn to page IC-21.

11 LISTENING

CLASS AUDIO ONLY

A 🔊 Listen to three people discussing their plans for the future. What do they plan to do? What don't they want to do? Take notes.

	Plans to	Doesn't want to
1. Charlie	....	....
2. Leon	....	....
3. Marie	....	....

B *Group work* Which person do you think is most like you? Do your classmates agree?

9 PRONUNCIATION *Reduced form of* to

This exercise practices how to reduce *to* in statements formed with verb + infinitive.

A

- Play the audio program and point out the reduced form of *to* /tə/ (it sounds like "tuh"). Then play the audio again and have Ss repeat several times. If possible, check Ss' pronunciation individually around the class.

B *Pair work*

- Read over the task. Point out the four verbs in the examples in part A that Ss can use here.

- Ss first work individually. Then in pairs, they practice the reduced form of *to* while reading their statements aloud to each other. Walk around the class and monitor Ss' grammatical structures and pronunciation.

10 WRITING

This exercise gives Ss the opportunity to write a description of their future plans.

A

- Use the picture and the example paragraph to help explain the task: Ss write one or two paragraphs about what they would like to do someday. Tell them to include any changes in their lives that they would need to make in order to achieve a particular goal.

- Ss write a first draft – either in class or for homework.

B *Pair work*

- Ss form pairs. Remind them to sit next to each other so they can see their partner's composition. Encourage pairs to give helpful comments on content (e.g., Are there enough details? Should there be more examples?) and organization (e.g., Does each paragraph contain a main idea in a topic sentence?). Walk around the class and give help as needed.

 INTERCHANGE 16 Unfold your future!

See page T-125 in this Teacher's Edition for notes.

11 LISTENING

This exercise practices listening for main ideas about people's future plans; it also involves taking notes.

A

- Books closed. Read aloud the instructions to set the scene and explain the task. Then play the audio program once. Ss only listen.

Audio script

1. MAN: So, what are your plans, Charlie? Are you thinking much about the future?
   CHARLIE: Hmm, not really. I don't like to make plans. Oh, except for one thing.
   MAN: What's that?
   CHARLIE: I'm saving up for a new car. I really want to get a sports car.
   MAN: A sports car?
   CHARLIE: *(laughs)* Yeah, I'd love to get a Trans Am.
   MAN: Yeah, *(laughs)* who wouldn't?

2. WOMAN: Do you have plans for the future, Leon?
   LEON: Yeah, I do! I really want to open my own business. So right now I'm taking a course on running a small business.
   WOMAN: What kind of business?
   LEON: Oh, maybe a sports shop, or something like that. You know I love sports. But I want to do it on my own. I don't want to get a big loan from a bank. So I guess it's going to take me awhile.
   WOMAN: Yeah, but it's going to be worth it! Good luck!

3. WOMAN: Any big plans for the future, Marie? Would you like to get married soon?
   MARIE: *(laughs)* Oh, no, definitely not. That's one thing I don't plan to do for awhile. I want to save my money for the next few years and buy myself a little house. I'm really tired of living with my parents.
   WOMAN: Oh, yeah! I know what you mean. Well, let me know if you need a roommate once you get your own place!
   MARIE: *(laughs)* OK, I will.

- Books open. Play the audio program once more. This time, Ss listen and write notes in the chart.

- Ss compare notes in pairs. Then elicit Ss' responses.

Possible answers

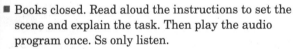

	Plans to	*Doesn't want to*
1. Charlie	get a sports car	–
2. Leon	open own business on his own	get a big loan from a bank
3. Marie	save her money for the next few years and buy a house	get married soon or live with parents

B *Group work*

- Read the questions aloud. Then Ss form groups to share their information. Find out if most group members agreed with each S's answer.

12 *READING* *The future looks bright*

This article is about three amazing young people; the exercise practices scanning for main ideas along with summarizing and making inferences.

- Books closed. Write the two pre-reading questions on the board to help prepare the class for the topic – how and why people set goals for themselves. Then stimulate a short, lively discussion on this topic by encouraging Ss (in groups or as a whole class) to give their own responses to the questions.

- Present any words that Ss might have difficulty understanding from the context. (*Note:* This could be done after Ss read the article instead.) For example:

Balamurati Krishna Ambati
advanced training = additional courses or experience in a certain field (e.g., learning to be a surgeon)
Catherine Charlton
composer = a person who writes music
Jasmin Sethi
a perfect score = 100% correct
blind = unable to see
editor = here, the person in charge of planning and directing other workers on a newspaper or magazine; also, someone who edits (changes/corrects) another person's writing
food collections = asking for cans and boxes of things to eat and then giving them to poor and hungry people

A

- Books open. Ss read the article straight through.

- Read aloud the two questions here and present the chart. Tell Ss to scan each paragraph again in order to look for each person's "interests" (i.e., what they enjoy doing) and their "goals" (i.e., what they hope to do in the future). Direct Ss to complete the chart in note form – only with single words and short phrases.

- Ss do the task individually. Walk around and give help as needed. Elicit Ss' answers around the class.

Answers

	Interests	Goals
1. Balamurati	medicine	wanted to be a doctor by 17; plans to get advanced training in Boston
2. Catherine	engineering, music	would like to design concert halls or manufacture pianos
3. Jasmin	the school paper, food collections	wants to go to a top university; would like to be a lawyer

B *Pair work*

- Present each question and have Ss repeat. (*Note:* If any Ss feel uncomfortable about giving personal answers, just tell them to make up imaginary goals to talk about,

or have them talk about someone that they know well, such as a relative or friend.)

- In pairs, Ss take turns asking and giving responses to each question. After about five minutes, you may want Ss to form groups to talk about the questions; alternatively, have all the Ss participate in a lively class discussion during which volunteers answer the questions.

- Check Ss' answers if only pairs and/or groups did the task.

Possible answers

1. Maybe designing and manufacturing sound systems or recording and acoustical equipment.
2. Yes, Balamurati needs more time to mature as an adult. (*or*) No, he must be a genius, which probably gives him the ability to be a good/competent doctor at such a young age.
3. With lots of determination, help from others, hard work, and never giving up.
4–6. Ss' answers will vary.

 Workbook

Tell Ss to do Exercises 6–10 on pages 94–96 in the Workbook or assign them as homework. Have Ss work in small groups to compare answers. Then elicit responses around the class. (Answers can be found on page T-190 of the Workbook Answer Key in this Teacher's Edition.)

Optional activity: *Good intentions*

Time: 15–20 minutes. This exercise give Ss' additional practice in talking about their future intentions.

- Explain the activity: Ss think of some real "good intentions" – things they would like to do but may not actually be able to. Encourage Ss to dream a bit. Write this information on the board:

Q: What are your good intentions?

1. I hope to be an interpreter at the Summer Olympics.
2. I'd like to go on a world cruise someday.
3. . . .

- Ss first work individually. They should think of three good intentions and write them down using the verb + infinitive structure presented in Exercise 7 on page 101. Then Ss work in pairs and take turns discussing their ideas.

- Set a time limit of five minutes. As a class activity, Ss get up and ask as many other classmates as possible the question on the board. When time is up, call on Ss to report to the rest of the class on some of the better intentions they heard.

(*Note:* If the end-of-the-class party was planned in Exercise 8 on page T-101 of this Teacher's Edition, give Ss some time to make final preparations, or hold the party now.)

12 READING

The Future Looks Bright

Do you like to set goals for yourself? What important goals have you reached recently?

Balamurati Krishna Ambati

At age three, Balamurati Krishna Ambati was badly burned and spent several months in the hospital. He decided then that he wanted to be a doctor. A few years later, he read in the *Guinness Book of Records* that the youngest doctor in the world was 18 years old. So he decided to become a doctor by the age of 17. Many people thought this was impossible, but at 11, Ambati was in college. He graduated from college at 14 and from medical school at 17. Now that he is a doctor, Ambati plans to go for advanced training in Boston.

Catherine Charlton

Catherine Charlton is studying engineering at Cornell University, but she has already achieved an important goal: She has worked for NASA (the National Aeronautics and Space Administration). Charlton's achievements aren't only in engineering, however. She is also a successful pianist and composer. Charlton hopes to combine her talents for engineering and music someday. For example, she would like to design concert halls or manufacture pianos.

Jasmin Sethi

The Scholastic Aptitude Test is the test American students take to enter college; each year, only a few students get a perfect score. One of those students was Jasmin Sethi. Her achievement was especially remarkable because she is blind. To take the test, someone read the test questions to her, and she gave the answers. She even solved difficult math problems in her head. Sethi has been the editor of her school newspaper and has organized food collections. She wants to go to a top university next year. Sethi would like to be a lawyer.

A Read the article. What are each student's interests? What goals has each student set?

	Interests	Goals
1. Balamurati	....	....
2. Catherine	....	....
3. Jasmin	....	....

B *Pair work* Talk about these questions.

1. Do you think Balamurati is too young to be a doctor?
2. What other careers would allow Catherine to combine her interests?
3. How do you think someone like Jasmin overcomes his or her disabilities?
4. How old were you when you started to think about your career goals?
5. Have you achieved a goal you set? What was it?
6. What other goals do you have?

Review of Units 13-16

1 FAVORITE RESTAURANT

A *Group work* Take turns talking about your favorite place to eat. One student makes a statement about a favorite restaurant. Other students ask questions.

My favorite place to eat is . . . .

Where is it?
What kind of food do they serve?
Does it have a nice atmosphere?
Is it expensive?

How much does dinner cost?
When is it open?
How often do you go there?
What do you usually order?

B *Class activity* Which place is the most interesting to you? Tell the class why.

2 LISTENING

CLASS AUDIO ONLY Listen and check (✓) the best response.

1. ☐ Yes, this way, please.
   ☐ Yes, please.

2. ☐ No, I don't.
   ☐ Yes, I'll have tea, please.

3. ☐ I'd like a steak, please.
   ☐ Yes, I would.

4. ☐ I'll have a cup of coffee.
   ☐ Italian, please.

5. ☐ Carrots, please.
   ☐ Yes, I will.

6. ☐ Yes, I'd like some water.
   ☐ No, I don't think so.

3 INTERESTING ADDRESSES

A *Pair work* Ask and answer questions about these places in your city.

Buildings

the biggest hotel
the most famous building
the oldest building

Streets

the busiest street
the best street for restaurants
the best street for shopping

Entertainment

the best place to go dancing
the best place to listen to music
the most interesting tourist spot

A: What's the biggest hotel?
B: I think it's the Hilton.
A: I do, too. / So do I. /
   Oh, I don't. I think it's the . . . .

B *Class activity* Compare your answers around the class.

This unit reviews describing a restaurant and the food, and using superlative adjectives to talk about places in a city. It also practices discussing weekend plans while using the present continuous and be going to. Finally, Ss use various structures to discuss changes in a person's life.

1 FAVORITE RESTAURANT

This exercise reviews describing a restaurant: the cuisine, prices, service, atmosphere, and so on.

A Group work

- Explain the task by reading the instructions aloud. Then present each question; Ss repeat.

- Elicit some words that are commonly used to describe a restaurant's atmosphere (e.g., *quiet, noisy, elegant, nice, relaxed*) and service (e.g., *excellent, very good, good, fair, poor, terrible*). Write them on the board.

- Model the activity by using the questions to talk about your favorite restaurant, like this:

  T: My favorite place to eat is the Hard Rock Cafe.
  S1: Oh? Where is that?
  T: It's downtown on the corner of First and Jones.
  S2: What kind of food do they serve?
  T: Well, they serve delicious hamburgers and french fries, and they have great chicken and rib dishes, too.

S3: Does it have a nice atmosphere?
T: Yes, it does. There are lots of interesting pictures and things on the walls, and the music is really good, too.
S4: Is it expensive?

- Divide the class into groups. Ss take turns talking about their favorite restaurants while others ask questions to get more information and details. Walk around the class and give help and suggestions as needed.

B Class activity

- Read the question aloud to the class. Have groups decide on the most interesting restaurant that they talked about. Remind them to give several reasons why.

- Groups take turns describing the restaurants they chose. Encourage others to ask more questions, especially to find out why the group preferred that particular restaurant.

2 LISTENING

This exercise practices listening to questions made in a restaurant setting, and choosing appropriate responses.

- Explain the task: Ss listen to each question and then check (✓) the correct response. Play the audio program once or twice. Ss do the task.

Audio script

1. MAN: Could I have a table for two, please?
2. WOMAN: Can I get you anything to drink?
3. WOMAN: What would you like for dinner?
4. MAN: What kind of dressing would you like?

5. WOMAN: What vegetable would you like?
6. MAN: Would you like dessert?

- Ss compare answers in pairs or groups. Then check Ss' answers around the class.

Answers

1. Yes, this way, please.	4. Italian, please.
2. Yes, I'll have tea, please.	5. Carrots, please.
3. I'd like a steak, please.	6. No, I don't think so.

3 INTERESTING ADDRESSES

This exercise reviews the superlative forms of adjectives used to describe places in a city.

A Pair work

- To help explain the task, go over the instructions and point out the picture. Then pronounce each item listed under the three categories; Ss repeat.

- Find out which city is the most interesting and appropriate for pairs to talk about – either the city your school is in or another city that all the Ss in the class know well. Write the name of that city on the board.

- Model how to get started by using the example A/B dialog with several volunteers. Encourage Ss to use

superlative adjectives during this activity (e.g., I think the Sheraton is *the biggest* hotel in the city.).

- Ss work in pairs and take turns asking questions about certain places in the city. Tell Ss to write down their answers for use in part B. Give help as needed.

B Class activity

- Compare Ss' answers around the class, like this: Write the three categories from part A on the board. Then tell pairs to choose their three most interesting sentences – one for each category – and to write them on the board under the appropriate headings. Tell Ss that duplicate statements are not allowed.

4 THE WEEKEND

This exercise reviews the future with the present continuous and *be going to*.

Pair work

- Read the instructions aloud. Present the phrases in the box and have Ss repeat.

- Ss do the activity in pairs. Walk around the class and note any difficulties Ss may be having.

- After about five minutes, go over any grammatical structures or word choices that Ss had trouble with.

Optional activity: *Charades*

- See page T-151.

5 ROLE PLAY Inviting a friend

This role play reviews calling a friend on the phone to invite him or her to go out. (*Note:* To make this role play more interesting and realistic, tell the Ss – the day before this activity is planned – to bring to class the entertainment section from a daily English-language newspaper or current city guide.)

A Pair work

- Use the picture to help explain the role play: One friend calls another friend and invites him or her to go out and do something fun. (*Note:* Assure the class that this activity is just a role play. Ss should have fun doing it and not worry about making a real "date" with a classmate.)

- Point out in the example dialog that A is the person being called ("the callee") and B is the person making the phone call ("the caller"). Then model how to use the A/B dialog with a S. Hold an imaginary phone in your hand while sitting back-to-back in front of the class (*S = A; T = B*):

A: *(phone rings and callee picks it up)* Hello?
B: Hi, . . . *(callee's name)*. This is . . . *(caller's name)*.
A: Oh, hi!
B: Say, are you doing anything **on Friday**?

A: Oh, yes. I'm sorry. I'm **going to be busy on Friday**.
B: Well, how about **Saturday**? **Are you doing anything then**?
A: No. What would you like to do?
B: **Let's see that new Harrison Ford movie. It's playing at the Varsity Theater downtown. Everybody says it's really great**!
A: I'd love to! What time **is the show**?
B: **Uh, it starts at 7:45**.
A: And where **do you want to meet**?
B: **How about in front of theater at 7:30**?
A: OK. See you on **Saturday then**. Bye!
B: Bye-bye.

- Ss form A/B pairs and sit back-to-back (if possible) while they do their role play phone conversation. (*Note:* If Ss brought newspapers or city guides to class, encourage them to use them here.) Go around the class and give help as needed.

B Pair work

- Have pairs change partners and roles and do the activity again.

- **Optional:** Volunteer pairs perform the role play in front of the class.

6 INTERVIEW

This exercise reviews ways to ask about and describe changes in a person's life while using a variety of verb tenses and structures.

A Pair work

- Explain the task by reading the instructions aloud. Then model each question; Ss repeat.

- **Optional:** Elicit additional questions Ss may want to ask each other. Write the more interesting or unusual ones on the board for everyone to use.

  (*Note:* This activity will work best if Ss are paired up with classmates that that they don't know very well.)

- Ss work in pairs and take turns. Each S uses the given questions – along with questions of their own – to interview the other. Walk around and give help as needed.

B Class activity

- Tell Ss to spend a minute thinking about three interesting things they learned about their partners. Then Ss share their information with the rest of the class.

Test 4

See page T-152 in this Teacher's Edition for general instructions on using the tests. Test 4 covers Units 13–16. Photocopy the test (pages T-165–T-168) and distribute a copy to each S. Allow 45–60 minutes for the test. Listening material for the tests is at the end of the Class Audio Program. The Test Audio Scripts and Answer Key start on page T-169 of this book.

4 THE WEEKEND

Pair work Which of the activities listed are you going to do this weekend? What else are you going to do? Talk with a partner.

Some activities
see a concert
meet someone special
go out to eat
work
play a sport or exercise
make a long-distance call

A: I'm seeing a concert this weekend.
B: What concert are you going to see?
A: A guitar concert at school.
B: Really? When is it?
A: It's on Saturday night. I'm going with my brother.

5 ROLE PLAY *Inviting a friend*

A *Pair work* Take turns inviting your partner to do something.

A: Hello?
B: Hi, ... This is . . . .
A: Oh, hi!
B: Say, are you doing anything (on) . . . ?
A: Oh, yes. I'm sorry. I'm . . . .
B: Well, how about (on) . . . ?
A: No. What would you like to do?
B: Let's . . . .
A: I'd love to! What time . . . ?
B: . . .
A: And where . . . ?
B: . . .
A: OK. See you on . . . . Bye!
B: Bye-bye.

B *Pair work* Change roles and try the conversation with a different partner.

6 INTERVIEW

A *Pair work* Find out more about a classmate. Ask your partner these questions or questions of your own.

Where have you lived?
What schools have you gone to?
What did you study? / What do you study now?
Are you married? / Do you hope to get married?
Do you have any children? / Do you want to have children?
What would you like to do in five years? ten years? when you retire?

B *Class activity* Tell the class about your partner.

Interchange Activities

Interchange Activities

interchange 1

This communicative activity draws upon the structures and much of the vocabulary presented in Unit 1. Ss will enjoy finding out more about their classmates while sharing some interesting information about themselves.

■ Books closed. As a warm-up to this activity, ask for a volunteer to come up to the front of the class and sit in the "hot seat." Ask the class questions like these:

What do you know about . . .
  (student's name)?
What's his/her nickname?
What's his/her family name?
What's his/her middle name?
Where is he/she from?
What foreign languages does he/she
  speak?

Then ask the S in the hot seat questions like these:

What is your father's first name?
What is your mother's name?
Are you named after a family
  member?
Are you good with names?

A *Class activity*

■ Books open. Use the pictures to help explain the activity. Go over the chart by reading aloud each "Find someone who . . . " statement, having the class repeat each accompanying question after you.

■ **Optional:** Find out how much Ss know about the famous people in the pictures: Tom Hanks in the first picture and Magic (Earvin) Johnson in the third. (*Note:* Tom Hanks [1956–] is a U.S. actor known for his roles in such films as *Apollo 13*, *Forrest Gump*, and *Philadelphia*, for which he won the Academy Award for best actor. Magic Johnson [1959–] is a popular U.S. athlete who played on the Los Angeles Lakers basketball team for twelve years before announcing his retirement from professional sports because he was infected with the virus that causes AIDS; Magic now devotes much of his

interchange 1 *GETTING TO KNOW YOU*

A *Class activity* Go around the class and find this information. Write a classmate's name only once.

Find someone who . . .	Name
1. . . . has the same first name as a famous person. "What's your first name?"	....
2. . . . has an unusual nickname. "What do people call you?"	....
3. . . . has an interesting middle name. "What's your middle name?"	....
4. . . . has the same last name as a famous person. "What's your last name?"	....
5. . . . is named after his or her father or mother. "Are you named after your father or mother?"	....
6. . . . always remembers people's names. "Are you good with names?"	....
7. . . . is from a beautiful city or town. "Where are you from?"	....
8. . . . speaks two foreign languages. "What languages do you speak?"	....

B *Pair work* Compare your information with a partner.

IC-2

time educating young people on the prevention of AIDS.)

■ If necessary, model how to go up to one S and ask some of the questions in the chart until his or her name can be written down. Then move on to another S and ask a few more questions.

■ Remind Ss not to write the same classmate's name more than once; in other words, once an interviewee's name has been written down in the chart, the interviewer should move on to another classmate.

■ Have Ss get up and move around the class. Set a time limit of about ten

minutes. Walk around the class and give assistance only if there is a communication breakdown. Note if there are any grammar or vocabulary problems that Ss continue to have. Go over these points after Ss have completed part B.

B *Pair work*

■ Ss form pairs and compare their information.

■ **Optional:** As a follow-up, elicit the most interesting piece of information that each S found out about a classmate.

interchange **2** *COMMON GROUND*

A Complete this chart with information about yourself.

	Time
I usually get up at	. . . .
I have breakfast at	. . . .
I leave for work or school at	. . . .
I have dinner at	. . . .
I go to bed during the week at	. . . .
I go to bed on weekends at	. . . .

B *Class activity* Take a survey. Ask five classmates for this information.

Names:	. . . . . .	. . . . . .	. . . . . .	. . . . . .	. . . . . .
What time do you . . . ?	**Times**				
get up	. . . . . .	. . . . . .	. . . . . .	. . . . . .	. . . . . .
have breakfast	. . . . . .	. . . . . .	. . . . . .	. . . . . .	. . . . . .
leave for work or school	. . . . . .	. . . . . .	. . . . . .	. . . . . .	. . . . . .
have dinner	. . . . . .	. . . . . .	. . . . . .	. . . . . .	. . . . . .
go to bed during the week	. . . . . .	. . . . . .	. . . . . .	. . . . . .	. . . . . .
go to bed on weekends	. . . . . .	. . . . . .	. . . . . .	. . . . . .	. . . . . .

C *Class activity* Compare the times you do things with the times your classmates do things. Whose schedule is the most like yours? Tell the class.

"Keiko and I have a similar schedule. We both get up at six and have breakfast at seven A.M. . . ."

useful expressions
We both . . . at . . . .
We . . . at different times.
My schedule isn't like anyone else's.

IC-3

---

interchange **2**

This is an information-sharing activity where Ss discover some facts about their classmates' routines by asking simple present Wh-questions.

A

■ Use the art at the bottom of the page to introduce the topic here – what time people do things each day – and to review the expressions that Ss will be using in this activity.

■ Point out that this communication activity gives Ss a chance to learn more about their classmates. Then read aloud the phrases in the chart; Ss repeat.

■ Tell Ss to work individually to write down true times from their daily routines in order to complete each statement in the chart. Set a time limit of about two minutes.

B *Class activity*

■ Model the correct pronunciation, stress, and rising intonation for the question "What **time** do you . . . ?" along with each of the six phrases in this chart. Ss listen and repeat.

■ Go over any new vocabulary in the chart, such as:

breakfast = a meal eaten in the morning as the first meal of the day

dinner = the main meal of the day, usually eaten in the evening between 6:00 and 8:00 P.M. in the U.S. and Canada

■ Explain the task: Ss go around the class to interview five students, one at a time. After they write down a S's name, they should ask all six questions starting with "What time do you . . . ?" Remind Ss to fill in the time in the chart for each response the interviewee gives.

■ Set a time limit of about ten minutes. Walk around the class and give support or advice as each pair's conversation warrants.

C *Class activity*

■ When time is up, Ss sit down and compare their own answers (in the part A chart) with the answers of the five Ss they interviewed (in the part B chart). Each S then decides which classmate's daily routine is most similar to his or her own.

■ Read aloud the example sentences and go over the useful expressions in the box. Then call on Ss around the class to share their findings.

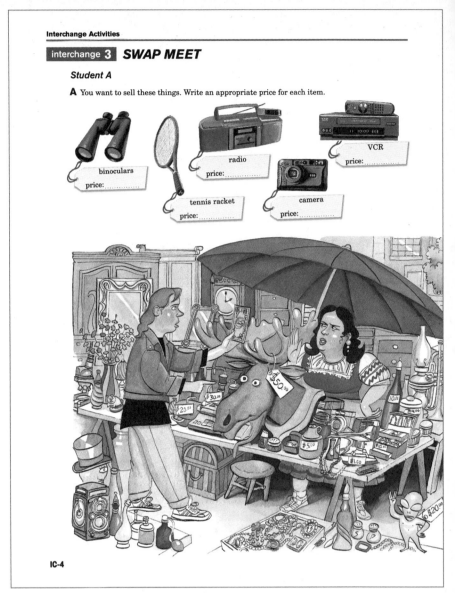

interchange **3** *SWAP MEET*

Student A

A You want to sell these things. Write an appropriate price for each item.

binoculars
price: ....

radio
price: ....

VCR
price: ....

tennis racket
price: ....

camera
price: ....

IC-4

interchange **3**

This role play practices asking about things for sale and responding with short and appropriate answers while trying to bargain.

A

■ Set the scene by explaining the term *swap meet*: In many cities in North America, people try to sell new and used things to the public by bringing the items to a designated place (e.g., a school or stadium parking lot).

■ **Optional:** In a heterogeneous class, find out which Ss come from countries where swap meets and bargaining are common events.

■ Go over the pronunciation of the

items pictured on the top half of Student As' and Student Bs' pages. Have Ss repeat.

■ Divide the class into pairs and assign A/B parts. Show how to write down a suitable price for the first object on each list, like this:

T: All Student As, what's a suitable (or fair) price for some used binoculars?
S1: Hmm. Maybe $20?
S2: I think $45.95 is better.
T: Both are OK. Please write down your own price for them here. And do the same for the other four items.
T: Now all Student Bs, what's a good price for an old bicycle like the one here?
S3: Maybe $15.99.
S4: Well, $5.00 is fair, I think.
T: All right. Write down your price on

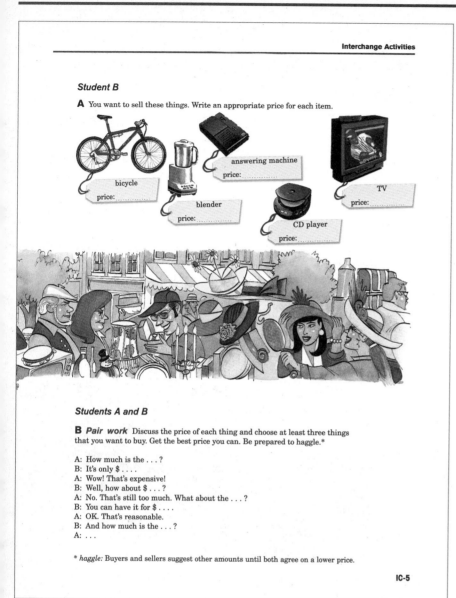

Student B

A You want to sell these things. Write an appropriate price for each item.

bicycle
price: ....

blender
price: ....

answering machine
price: ....

CD player
price: ....

TV
price: ....

Students A and B

B *Pair work* Discuss the price of each thing and choose at least three things that you want to buy. Get the best price you can. Be prepared to haggle.*

A: How much is the . . . ?
B: It's only $ . . . .
A: Wow! That's expensive!
B: Well, how about $ . . . ?
A: No. That's still too much. What about the . . . ?
B: You can have it for $ . . . .
A: OK. That's reasonable.
B: And how much is the . . . ?
A: . . .

* *haggle:* Buyers and sellers suggest other amounts until both agree on a lower price.

IC-5

the line. Also, write prices for the rest of your items.

■ As Ss are figuring out their prices, walk around the class and spot-check the amounts they are writing down. Do the prices seem reasonable, or are they fantastic? Encourage Ss to be inventive here.

B *Pair work*

■ Model the example A/B dialog with several Ss, showing that A is the buyer and B is the seller. Read the definition for *haggle* at the bottom of the page. Remind the class to use linked sounds with "How much is/are . . . ?"

■ Write a time limit of about ten minutes on the board. Explain that pairs need to take turns starting the dialog so that each person has the

chance to be the buyer and the seller until both partners are able to buy at least three things.

■ Walk around the class and give help, particularly if a communication breakdown seems to be happening.

■ **Optional:** Ask for volunteers to perform one of their swap meet transactions in front of the class. Alternatively, have Ss change partners and try the activity again.

interchange 4

This exercise practices writing creative invitations and responses and culminates in a fun communicative activity for the whole class to participate in.

Preparation: Each S will need six blank cards for this task. These can be index cards or simply pieces of paper all cut to the same size (about $3'' \times 5''$).

A

■ Go over the task and the three examples in the book.

■ Tell Ss to look at the picture of the young man at the bottom of the page. Ask "Which of the invitations matches his situation?" (Answer: The first one)

■ Elicit suggestions for similar kinds of invitations. Encourage Ss to think up invitations to interesting, funny, or unusual events or social activities.

■ Ss write out their three invitations – one invitation per card. (They don't need to put their names on the cards.) Walk around the class and give help as needed.

B

■ Before Ss prepare three response cards, go over the examples. Explain that they should write one acceptance and two refusals – one per card.

■ Elicit suggestions for other ways of accepting an invitation. Point out that there should be both an expression of interest or a direct acceptance along with a question about a time, day, or place to meet.

■ Go over the refusal cards in the same way. Encourage Ss to suggest silly or unusual reasons for refusing an invitation.

■ Tell Ss to look at the picture at the bottom of the page of the young girl holding the bird cage. Ask "Which of the refusals matches her situation?" (Answer: The first one)

■ Ss write their three response cards. (Again, there is no need for Ss' names on the cards.) Walk around the class again and give help as needed.

Interchange Activities

interchange 4 *WHAT AN INVITATION! WHAT AN EXCUSE!*

A Make up three invitations to interesting or unusual activities. Write them on cards.

Godzilla Meets Mightyman is at the Plaza Theater tonight at 8:00. Would you like to see it?

There's a dog and cat show at City Stadium on Saturday. It's at 3:00. Do you want to go?

I want to see the Turtle Races tomorrow. They're at 1:00 at the Civic Hall. Would you like to go?

B Write three response cards. One is an acceptance card.

That sounds great! What time do you want to meet?

The other two cards are refusals. Think of silly or unusual excuses.

I'd like to, but I want to take my bird to a singing contest.

I'm sorry. I'd like to, but I have to wash my hair.

C *Class activity* Put all the invitation cards in one pile and all the response cards in another pile facedown. Shuffle each pile. Each student takes three invitation cards and three response cards.

Go around the class. Invite people to do the things on your invitation cards. Use the response cards to accept or decline any invitation.

IC-6

C *Class activity*

■ Read the instructions aloud to explain the activity. Then collect the Ss' invitation cards and put them facedown in one pile. Do the same for their response cards and put them in another, separate pile.

■ Mix the cards in the invitation pile and put them facedown on a desk at the front of the classroom. Then mix the response pile in the same way, placing this deck on a separate desk.

■ Ask each S to come up and take three invitation cards and three response cards – for a total of six cards. Tell them to sit down for a few minutes to read the cards they took. (*Note:* If any Ss got three refusal cards, find out which S or Ss have more than one acceptance card. Then

help them switch cards so that each S ends up having one acceptance and two refusal cards to use as responses during the activity.)

■ Borrow a set of cards from one S and model the task with another S or two. Encourage Ss to get as many acceptances to their invitations as they can within a time limit of ten minutes.

■ Now tell the Ss to stand up and walk around the class. They should take turns extending invitations and responding to other people's invitations while using their six cards. Go around the class, giving help only if there seems to be a real breakdown in communication.

■ After the ten minutes are up, find out whose invitations received the most acceptances.

interchange 5 *FAMILY FACTS*

A *Class activity* Go around the class and find this information. Write a classmate's name only once. Ask follow-up questions of your own.

Find someone . . .	Name
1. . . . who is an only child. **"Do you have any brothers or sisters?"**	
2. . . . who has more than two brothers. **"How many brothers do you have?"**	
3. . . . who has more than two sisters. **"How many sisters do you have?"**	
4. . . . whose brother or sister is studying abroad. **"Are any of your brothers or sisters studying abroad? Where?"**	
5. . . . who lives with his or her grandparents. **"Do you live with your grandparents?"**	
6. . . . who has a great-grandparent still living. **"Is your great-grandmother or great-grandfather still living?"**	
7. . . . who has a family member with an unusual job. **"Does anyone in your family have an unusual job?"**	
8. . . . whose mother or father is working abroad. **"Is either of your parents working abroad? Where?"**	

B *Group work* Compare your information in groups.

IC-7

interchange 5

This enjoyable communicative activity reviews and practices the language and grammar studied in Unit 5. Ss are encouraged to ask follow-up questions of their own to find out more real information about their classmates.

(*Note:* Let Ss know that if they don't feel comfortable answering the questions with real information about their families, they can just make up other responses or answer with "I'd rather not say.")

■ As a warm-up to this activity, ask the class to look at the photos. Encourage Ss to ask one another questions around the class, like this:

T: Look at the middle photo. Please ask a question about it, Kendra.

S1: Where does this family live? Lee?
S2: They live in Africa.
T: Yes. Now ask another question.
S2: OK. How many are there in this family? Sita?
S3: There are four in the family. Greg, are these the grandparents?
S4: No, they're the parents.

A *Class activity*

■ Go over the task and the chart. Read aloud each of the eight statements beginning with "Find someone . . . " and the accompanying question. Have Ss repeat the questions in order to practice good pronunciation and intonation.

■ Model the task. Ask for one or two volunteers to come up to the front of the class to help you. Then show how to walk over to a S and ask questions

in the chart until that S's name can be written down. Demonstrate how to ask follow-up questions to get more information (while making a few notes):

T: (*asking question 1*) Do you have any brothers or sisters, Gabriel?
S1: Yes, I have some sisters.
T: Oh, really? (*now asking question 3*) How many sisters do you have?
S1: I have three sisters.
T: Wow! That's a lot! (*writing down Gabriel's name next to question 3 in the chart*) What are their names and ages?
S1: Well, Susita is twenty-two, Marta is . . . .
T: (*writing down additional notes in the chart: Susita 22, Marta . . .*)
S1: Now it's my turn to ask you about your family. Do you . . . ?

Encourage Ss to ask additional questions (e.g., about cousins, aunts/uncles, nephews/nieces), particularly when someone answers "No" to yes/no questions or says "I don't have any brothers/sisters" in response to questions beginning with "How many . . . ?" Explain that completing the chart is only one part of this activity; the other part is to have interesting conversations with their classmates so they can find out more about their families.

■ Set a time limit of about ten minutes. Remind Ss not to write down a S's name more than once in the chart. Ss do the activity by getting up and moving from classmate to classmate.

■ Walk around the class and observe how communication is going. Keep notes on any vocabulary or structural problems – especially question formation – that the Ss may be having. When time is up, go over any general problems and their solutions with the whole class.

B *Group work*

■ Ss form groups and compare information from their charts and from their follow-up questions.

■ **Optional:** Ask groups to share one or two interesting facts that they discovered about their classmates during their discussion.

interchange **6**

This activity involves a quiz on nutrition and fitness. Ss practice interviewing, listening for questions and choices, and talking about their levels of fitness and what to do to improve them.

A *Pair work*

■ As preparation, Ss quickly read each item on the quiz and circle any words they do not know. Then have them work in pairs and use their dictionaries to check definitions. Elicit any words that Ss still don't understand and explain them or give simple synonyms – for example:

> **fatty food** = food with a lot of fat (e.g., hamburgers, french fries, cheese, mayonnaise)
> **a complete physical** = a full examination by a doctor

Alternative presentation

■ If time is limited, have Ss read over the quiz for homework, looking up new vocabulary in their dictionaries. Then, in class, pairs can quickly begin their interviews.

■ Pairs take turns interviewing each other. Remind them to circle their partner's points for each item. Move around the class and give help as needed.

■ When Ss have finished, tell them to add up their partner's points in order to reach a total score for the fitness quiz. Then point out the numbers and information at the bottom of the quiz under "Rank your partner." Ask Ss to find where their partner ranks in the chart. Then they should read aloud his or her matching fitness profile.

B *Group work*

■ Go over the instructions. Model the questions and the example response; Ss repeat.

■ With several volunteers, show the class how to compare scores, like this:

T: What is your score, Sam?
S1: It's 49 points.
T: OK, and what does that say about you?
S1: It says: (*reading*) "Good job! Your health and fitness are above average."

T-112

Interchange Activities

interchange **6** *FITNESS QUIZ*

A *Pair work* Interview a partner using this simple quiz. Then add up your partner's score, and find his or her rank below.

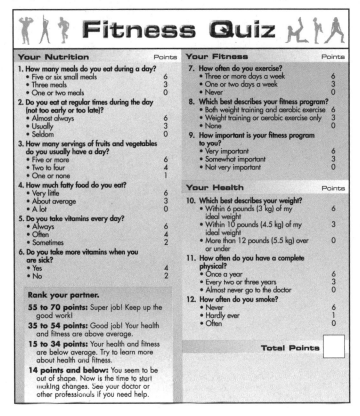

B *Group work* Compare your scores in groups. Who is the fittest? What can you do to improve your fitness?

"I need to . . . ."

IC-8

T: That's great! But what can you do to improve your fitness?
S1: I need to work out four times a week. Now I only go to the gym on Mondays and Thursdays.
T: Good. And how about you, Laura?
S2: Well, I only got 17 points. The quiz says that my health and fitness are . . . .

■ **Optional:** If you think Ss may have difficulty talking about how they *need to* or *can* improve their fitness, write some example sentences on the board like these:

I *need to exercise* every morning with a video.
I *need to work out* more and lose some weight.
I *can play* tennis on the weekend with friends.

I *can go* to the gym and take an aerobics class.

(*Note:* The modals *can* and *should* are introduced in Unit 11.)

Elicit additional sentences around the class and add them to the board.

■ Ss form groups of four. Groups take turns talking about their scores. Go around the class, giving help when requested.

■ **Optional:** As a class activity, discuss Ss' results: Do they feel the descriptions in the ranking are accurate? Why or why not?

interchange 8 **NEIGHBORHOOD SURVEY**

A *Group work* Imagine you are looking for a new home. You need to decide where you want to live. Compare two different neighborhoods in your city or town. Talk with your group and complete the survey.

What kinds of people live in each neighborhood – families, young people, working people, retired people?
Compare the neighborhoods' recreation facilities, stores, schools, and public transportation.
How much noise is there? pollution?
What's one advantage of living in each neighborhood?
 What's one disadvantage?

	Neighborhood 1:	Neighborhood 2: ....
people		
recreation facilities		
stores		
schools		
public transportation		
noise		
pollution		
an advantage of living in the neighborhood		
a disadvantage of living in the neighborhood		

A: What neighborhoods do you want to compare?
B: Let's look at Parkside and downtown.
C: OK. So what kinds of people live in Parkside?
D: There are lots of retired people. There aren't very many young people with families.
A: That's true. What about downtown?
C: . . .

B *Class activity* Study the results of the survey. Which neighborhood would you prefer to live in? Tell the class where and why.

IC-11

---

interchange **8**

This activity incorporates all of the vocabulary and grammar points presented in the unit. Ss should have fun comparing real neighborhoods in their city or town while trying to decide which one they'd like to live in.

A *Group work*

■ Read aloud the instructions and the questions; go over the survey form. Then use the example dialog to model the activity with the class.

■ **Optional:** Choose two different neighborhoods in your area and write their names or locations on the board. Then use the questions given above the survey form to do some quick brainstorming. Write Ss' ideas on the board. Use a chart similar to the one in the book:

	Neighborhood 1 2
kinds of people	
recreation facilities	
stores	
schools	
public transportation	
noise	
pollution	
an advantage	
a disadvantage	

■ Ss form groups of four or five. Remind Ss that they should use the questions and the example dialog to get started. Also, they need to fill in their survey form each time they finish discussing a particular item.

■ Set a time limit of about ten minutes. Walk around the class and stop by each group to listen in; offer help whenever needed.

B *Class activity*

■ Explain this follow-up task: Groups look over their survey forms and then take a vote on which neighborhood they would all prefer to live in.

■ Groups take turns sharing their findings with the class. Write these sentences on the board for the groups to use:

We would all prefer to live in . . . .
There are three main reasons why we decided on this neighborhood.
First, there is/are . . . .
Second, there is/are . . . .
Finally, ...

T-113

interchange **7** *VACATION PHOTOS*

Student A

A *Pair work* You went on a vacation to Mexico and took these photos. First, think about these questions. Then use the photos to tell your partner about your vacation. Give as much information as you can, and answer your partner's questions.

"I had a really interesting vacation. I went to Mexico . . . ."

Where did you go?
How long were you there?
Who did you go with?
What did you do there?
Did you enjoy it?
Where did you take this picture?
Who is this/that?
Is this a . . . ?

shopping

a bullfighter

Mexico City – a beautiful night

the Pyramid of the Moon

some Mariachis

B *Pair work* Listen to your partner talk about his or her vacation. Ask questions like the ones in part A about the vacation.

IC-9

---

interchange **7**

This role play incorporates much of the grammar and vocabulary presented in the unit. It also gives the Ss a chance to be creative as they make up descriptions of vacations in interesting places.

- Divide the class into pairs (preferably with Ss who haven't already worked together as pairs earlier in this unit). Then assign each pair their A and B roles.

- Model the pronunciation of the places: Mexico City /ˈmɛksɪkow ˈsɪtiy/ and Thailand /ˈtaylænd/. Then tell the Student As to look over their information on page IC-9 and Student Bs theirs on page IC-10. Give them a few minutes to do this.

A *Pair work*

- Show the class how to use the photos to help make notes next to the first five questions given here.

- Then model the activity with a volunteer (*T = Student A; S = Student B*). In particular, demonstrate how Ss can use this role play to make up wonderful and creative stories about a vacation in an exciting city or country.

- Encourage the class to ask additional questions of their own to get even more information from their partners.

- Pairs spend several minutes using their photos and questions to prepare their vacation stories.

Alternative presentation

- Gather all the Student As together in one area of the classroom and go

interchange 7 *VACATION PHOTOS*

Student B

A *Pair work* Listen to your partner talk about a recent vacation. Ask questions about the vacation and the photos.

Where did you go?
How long were you there?
Who did you go with?
What did you do there?
Did you enjoy it?
Where did you take this picture?
Who is this/that?
Is this a . . . ?

B *Pair work* Look at these photos of your vacation in Thailand. First, think about the questions in part A. Then use the photos to tell your partner about your vacation. Give as much information as you can, and answer your partner's questions.

"I had a really interesting vacation recently, too. I went to Thailand . . . ."

IC-10

over their photos of Mexico City along with the instructions and questions. When they understand what they are required to do, tell them to return to their desks and prepare their roles. Then do the same for the Student Bs and their information about Thailand.

■ Set a time limit of five minutes for this first part of the role play. The Student As start by showing the photos of Mexico City to their partners while giving information and answering questions. Walk around the class and take note of any common problems the Ss may be having.

■ When the time is up, go over any problems you observed with the whole class.

B *Pair work*

■ Now the Student Bs get to share their photos of Thailand and answer their partners' questions. Again, set a time limit of five minutes. Go around the class and give help, particularly to those Ss who may be having trouble thinking up things to say about their photos.

■ **Optional:** Ask one or two pairs (those who had entertaining or interesting role plays) to perform them in front of the class. When they finish, elicit what was good about their performance and what, if anything, could have been better.

interchange **9** *FIND THE DIFFERENCES*

Student A

A *Pair work* How many differences can you find between your picture here and your partner's picture? Ask questions like these to find the differences. (Look only at the people with names.)

How many people are there in your picture?
How many are standing? Who?
How many are sitting? Who?
What color is Dave's T-shirt? Kate's sweater?
Who is holding a drink?
What does . . . look like?
Does . . . wear glasses?
Does . . . have a beard?
What color is . . .'s hair?
How long is . . .'s hair?

Picture 1

B *Class activity* How many differences are there in the pictures? What are they?

"In picture 1, Dave's T-shirt is . . . . In picture 2, it's . . . ."

IC-12

---

interchange **9**

This enjoyable activity practices the present continuous; it also includes describing what people are doing or wearing.

■ Before starting the activity, divide the class into A/B pairs.

(*Note:* If possible, have partners sit across from – not next to – each other. This will make it harder for them to see each other's picture during the activity.)

■ Tell the Student As to look at page IC-12 and the Student Bs to look at page IC-14. Give the Ss a few minutes to look at their own page and picture; tell them not to look at their partner's picture.

A *Pair work*

■ Go over the instructions. Explain that the task here is for partners to get information from each other by asking questions – not by looking at each other's picture. Make sure all pairs understand that there are some differences between their two pictures and they must find those differences by asking and answering each other questions. Remind Ss to talk about only the people that have names.

■ Read aloud the questions given and the people's names in the pictures; Ss repeat to practice good pronunciation and intonation. (*Note:* All the instructions and questions on pages IC-12 and IC-14 are the same; only the pictures have slight variations.)

Encourage Ss to suggest other questions; write them on the board for the whole class to use during the activity.

■ Model the task with one or two volunteers to show how to ask questions about one picture in order to find a difference in the other one through a partner's response. For example (*T = A; S = B*):

T: How many people are there in your picture, Luis?
S: There are six.
T: Oh. That's the same number in my picture. OK, how many are standing in your picture?
S: There are three people standing in my picture. How about in yours?
T: Let me see. Oh, there are three in mine, too. Who is standing in yours?

Interchange Activities

interchange 9 *FIND THE DIFFERENCES*

Student B

A *Pair work* How many differences can you find between your picture here and your partner's picture? Ask questions like these to find the differences. (Look only at the people with names.)

How many people are there in your picture?
How many are standing? Who?
How many are sitting? Who?
What color is Dave's T-shirt? Kate's sweater?
Who is holding a drink?
What does . . . look like?
Does . . . wear glasses?
Does . . . have a beard?
What color is . . .'s hair?
How long is . . .'s hair?

Picture 2

B *Class activity* How many differences are there in the pictures? What are they?

"In picture 1, Dave's T-shirt is . . . . In picture 2, it's . . . ."

IC-14

S: Uh, Dave, Fay, and Kate are standing in picture 2.
T: Really? Gee, in picture 1, Dave, Ann, and Kate are standing. Great! Fay is sitting in my picture. Great! We found one difference already! Let's find some more. Now it's your turn to ask me some questions.
S: OK. . . .

■ Set a time limit of about five minutes. Pairs take turns asking questions to find the differences between their two pictures. Walk around the class, giving help only if there is a serious breakdown in communication.

B *Class activity*

■ Tell pairs to look over their answers (i.e., the differences they found between the two pictures) and to choose one to write on the board. Encourage them to come to the board quickly by making it a rule that no answer can be written twice.

■ To check the answers written on the board, ask the pair who wrote an answer to read it aloud for the class. Then find out if other Ss agree. If they do agree, go on to the next answer until all of them have been checked; if Ss don't agree, ask the class to look at both pictures again to check it.

Possible answers

In picture 1, Dave's T-shirt is white. In picture 2, it's black.
In picture 1, Ann has long hair and she's standing. In picture 2, she has short hair and she's sitting.
In picture 1, Nick isn't wearing glasses. In picture 2, he is.
In picture 1, Kevin has a beard and mustache. In picture 2, he doesn't.
In picture 1, Fay is sitting and has straight brown hair. In picture 2, she's standing and holding a drink, and she has curly red hair.
In picture 1, Kate's sweater is purple. In picture 2, it's orange.

interchange 10

This semi-controlled communicative activity gives Ss another chance to learn more about their classmates; it also practices the present perfect.

■ Books closed. Introduce these two types of lifestyles – easygoing and relaxed versus busy and fast-paced – by writing them on the board. Then do some brainstorming with the class: Ask Ss to suggest activities that people with each lifestyle might do; write the suggestions on the board – for example:

Easygoing and relaxed	Busy and fast-paced
read a lot of books	exercise every day
watch TV every day	go out every weekend
enjoy listening to music	use a cellular phone
take naps	eat out most of the time

A *Pair work*

■ Books open. Read the instructions aloud. Then have Ss look at the two pictures: Can they decide which lifestyle each person has? (Answer: The man seems to be easygoing and relaxed, the woman busy and fast-paced.)

■ Present all the questions in the survey: Read each question aloud in its full form (e.g., "How many times have you watched TV in the past week?"); have Ss repeat.

■ Model the activity by asking some of the questions from both sides of the chart while interviewing a volunteer. Also, demonstrate how to write down each of his or her responses under the column called "Number of times." Ss may also want to take notes on any additional information that their partners give them.

■ Now Ss form pairs. Tell them to take turns being the interviewer and the interviewee. Each interviewer should ask all ten questions and take notes on each answer that his or her partner gives. Set a time limit of about five minutes. Walk around the class, giving help only if there is a breakdown in communication.

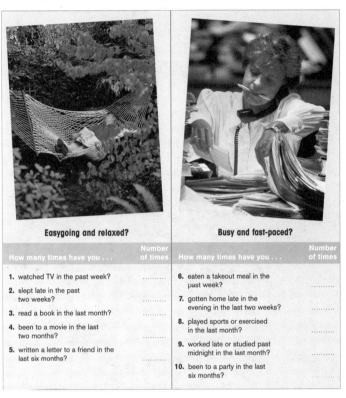

interchange 10 *LIFESTYLES SURVEY*

A *Pair work* What kind of lifestyle does your partner have: easygoing and relaxed or busy and fast-paced? Interview your partner using this survey.

Easygoing and relaxed?

Busy and fast-paced?

How many times have you . . .	Number of times
1. watched TV in the past week?	....
2. slept late in the past two weeks?	....
3. read a book in the last month?	....
4. been to a movie in the last two months?	....
5. written a letter to a friend in the last six months?	....

How many times have you . . .	Number of times
6. eaten a takeout meal in the past week?	....
7. gotten home late in the evening in the last two weeks?	....
8. played sports or exercised in the last month?	....
9. worked late or studied past midnight in the last month?	....
10. been to a party in the last six months?	....

B *Group work* Tell the group what you think your partner's lifestyle is like and why.

"Juan's lifestyle is busy and fast-paced. He hardly ever has time to watch TV, read a book, or go to the movies. He works late a lot, and he often eats takeout meals. . . . "

IC-13

B *Group work*

■ Go over the instructions. Model the example response and have Ss repeat.

■ **Optional:** Use the two pictures on the page to elicit additional example responses from the class. Write Ss' suggestions on the board, as in a short paragraph or a summary – for example:

This man's lifestyle is easygoing and relaxed. He really enjoys reading. In fact, he has read four novels in the past month! He likes to take a nap every afternoon, and he loves to watch TV. He has slept late six times in the past month. He has very little stress in his life.

This woman's lifestyle is busy and fast-paced. She has eaten takeout dinners five times in the past week. She has gotten home very late four times in the last two weeks. She hardly ever has any time for fun these days.

■ Now tell Ss to look over their survey forms and to prepare a summary of their partner's lifestyle. They can do this by writing down complete sentences or by simply making notes or a quick outline of what they want to say. Give them a few minutes to prepare.

■ Tell pairs from part A to separate and to form new small groups with other classmates. Ss take turns telling their group about their partner's lifestyle. Walk around the class listening in to groups' discussions; give help only if requested.

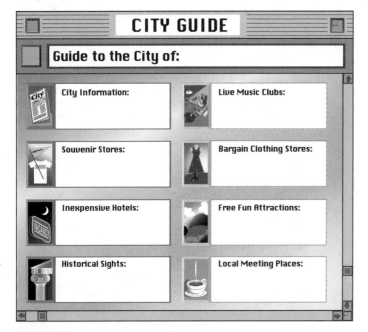

interchange 11 *CITY GUIDE*

A Where can you get information about your city? buy souvenirs? see historical sights? Complete the "City Guide" with information about your city.

CITY GUIDE

Guide to the City of:

City Information:	**Live Music Clubs:**
Souvenir Stores:	**Bargain Clothing Stores:**
Inexpensive Hotels:	**Free Fun Attractions:**
Historical Sights:	**Local Meeting Places:**

B *Group work* Compare your "City Guides" in groups. Ask these questions and your own questions. Add any additional or interesting information to your guide.

Where can you get information about your city?
Where can you buy souvenirs?
Are there any inexpensive hotels?
What historical sights should you see?
What's a good place to hear local music?
What's a cheap place to shop for clothes?
What fun things can you do for free?
Where do people often meet?

IC-15

historical sights = places of interest that were part of real events in a city's or country's past
bargain clothing stores = shops that sell clothes at cheaper prices than other stores
free fun attractions = places or things to do that don't cost any money (e.g., walking in a park, going window shopping, watching street performers)

■ Ss work individually to complete the guide with information about their cities. Walk around the room, giving help whenever needed.

(*Note:* The part A task can be assigned for homework, especially if classtime is tight or if Ss want to get more information about their cities before filling in the guide.)

Alternative presentation

■ Ss may wish to bring real information to class (e.g., brochures, maps, travel books or guides) about the city they have chosen to discuss in this activity. If that is the case, go over the questions, instructions, and new vocabulary in part A several days before this activity is scheduled to be done in class. Ss will then have enough time to gather materials that they might already have or to use the extra time to search the Internet or a local library in order to supplement their own knowledge about a particular city.

B *Group work*

■ Divide the class into small groups. (*Note:* Particularly in a homogeneous class, find out which cities Ss have chosen to talk about. Then try to place Ss in groups where each S has chosen a different city to talk about.)

■ Go over the instructions. Present each question; Ss repeat. Elicit additional questions that Ss can ask one another, and write them on the board for the groups to use.

■ Model the activity with one group by having them ask you questions about your city. Give elaborate answers and encourage the group to ask you lots of questions for more details and clarification.

---

interchange 11

This communicative activity gives Ss the chance to be "experts" about cities they choose to discuss.

■ Books closed. As a topic warm-up, write these questions on the board:

Do you come from a big or small city?
Is your city interesting or boring? Why?
Do many tourists go there? Why or why not?
Is there another city in your country that's more popular? If yes, do you know a lot about it?
Which city do you want to tell other people about?

■ Now model each of the questions on the board; Ss repeat.

■ Ss form pairs. Tell them to take turns asking and answering the questions on the board. Point out that Ss' goals in this warm-up task are: (a) to choose a city that they already know a lot about (e.g., their hometown, another city in their country, the city they are currently living in) and (b) to choose a city that they really want to tell other Ss about.

A

■ Books open. Go over the questions, instructions, and chart. Point out that the "City Guide" is set up as if it were being seen on the Internet. Explain any new vocabulary, such as:

souvenirs = things bought in a certain place to help remember that place or the trip taken there

interchange 12

This fluency activity challenges the Ss' ability to give thoughtful advice on some interesting questions; it also practices using infinitive complements.

■ As a topic warm-up, ask Ss if they ever listen to a talk radio program. If someone does, put him or her on the "hot seat"; if several Ss say "Yes," have them form a panel and sit at the front of the class. Then model how the other Ss can ask them questions, like this:

Which radio talk show do you listen to?

Is it in . . . (S's native language) or in English?

Who hosts that program?

What time/station is it on?

Do they discuss different topics every day?

What kinds of callers does it usually have?

Have you ever called a radio talk program? If yes, tell us about it.

Alternative presentation

■ Bring a portable radio to class (or a short-wave radio in order to get programs in English). Find a talk program and let the class listen to it for a few minutes. Alternatively, record an interesting segment from a popular local radio talk show (or the BBC, Voice of America, etc.) and play it for the class. How much can Ss understand?

A Group work

■ Go over the instructions and question. Make sure everyone understands that there are three parts to evaluating each of the four problems presented here:

1. The group reads the caller's question.
2. Ss take turns suggesting how to solve the caller's problem.
3. Then the group decides (or votes) on which suggestion is the best one to give that caller.

■ Ss form groups of four to six. Present the useful expressions.

■ Model how to get started by working with one group, like this:

Interchange Activities

interchange 12 TALK RADIO

A Group work Look at the four questions that people called a radio program about. What advice would you give each caller? Discuss suggestions to give each caller, and then choose the best one.

Caller 1: I'm visiting the United States. I'm staying with a couple of families while I'm here. What small gifts can I get for the families I stay with?

Caller 2: My dog barks loudly all night long. The neighbors are complaining about him. What can I do?

Caller 3: My doctor says that I'm not in good shape, and I need to lose about four and a half kilos (10 pounds). I don't like exercising though. Do you have any advice?

Caller 4: My school wants to buy some new gym equipment, so we want to have a fundraiser. What are some good ways to raise money?

HELP RAISE MONEY FOR NEW GYM EQUIPMENT

useful expressions
I think it would be useful to . . . .
One thing you could do is . . . .
It's a good idea to . . . .
It's important to . . . .
You should . . . .

B Class activity Share your group's advice for each problem with the class.

IC-16

T: OK. Let's read Caller 1's question (*reading the question aloud for the group*). Let's look at the picture here, too. The mother and father are in the kitchen fixing dinner, and their daughter and another girl are setting the table. The other girl is probably the one visiting the U.S.

S1: Yes. She looks Asian.

T: That's right. She's Asian, and she's visiting an American family. So let's talk about her "problem": What small gift can she get for this family she's staying with?

S2: Well, they're cooking. I think it would be useful to get something for the kitchen – something like a wok or a teapot.

S3: That's a good idea. But she could also get them a big box of chocolates.

S1: Well, I think it's a good idea to give them a nice plant. Then they can remember her each time they water it.

T: Well, these are all good ideas. Now let's vote on the best suggestion.

■ Set a time limit of about ten minutes for the groups to discuss all four callers' problems. Then groups start the activity. Go around the class and quietly sit near each group for a minute or two. It's probably best not to interrupt them during their discussion – unless they need some direction or they ask for help.

B Class activity

■ Groups take turns coming up to the front of the class to share their advice for each problem.

interchange **14** *HOW MUCH DO YOU KNOW?*

Pair work Take turns asking and answering these questions. Check (✓) the correct answer. If you and your partner don't agree, check (✓) the answer you think is correct.

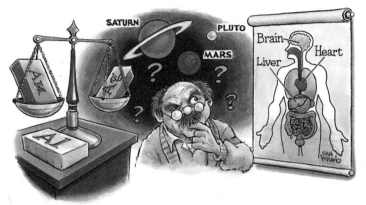

World Knowledge Quiz

1. Which metal is the heaviest?	☐ gold	☐ silver	☐ aluminum
2. Which planet is the coldest?	☐ Neptune	☐ Saturn	☐ Pluto
3. Which one is the biggest?	☐ Jupiter	☐ the Earth	☐ Mars
4. Which animal lives the longest?	☐ a whale	☐ an elephant	☐ a tortoise
5. Which one is the tallest?	☐ an elephant	☐ a giraffe	☐ a camel
6. Which of these is the heaviest?	☐ the brain	☐ the heart	☐ the liver
7. Which drink has the most calories?	☐ 1 liter of wine	☐ 1 liter of beer	☐ 1 liter of soda*
8. Which country is the driest?	☐ Egypt	☐ Peru	☐ Chile
9. Which one is closest to the equator?	☐ Malaysia	☐ Colombia	☐ India
10. Which shape has the most sides?	☐ a pentagon	☐ an octagon	☐ a hexagon
11. Which measurement is the longest?	☐ a yard	☐ a kilometer	☐ a mile
12. Which era is the oldest?	☐ the Renaissance	☐ the Dark Ages	☐ the Middle Ages

*1 liter = 35 ounces

Correct answers

How many did you get correct? (See the appendix at the back of the book for the answers.)

12 Perfect! Brilliant! You should be a teacher.
9–11 Very good! Do you watch lots of TV game shows?
5–8 Just OK. How often do you go to the library?
0–4 You should never be on a quiz show.

IC-19

---

interchange **14**

This is a lighthearted wind-up to the unit, in which Ss get to "test" their own world knowledge; it also practices the superlative forms of adjectives.

■ Books closed. As a quick warm-up, brainstorm with the class on various subjects that high school and college students study. Write them on the board, like this:

High School and College Classes
geography   history   foreign
algebra   biology   languages
chemistry   botany   English
astronomy   literature

Then find out how much Ss know about some of these subjects – for example:

T: How much do you know about geography – a lot, a little, or almost nothing?
S1: Um, I know a little about it. I took a geography class once.
S2: Well, I know almost nothing. I'm always forgetting where famous places are in the world.
S3: I know a lot about geography. It's my favorite subject!

Pair work

■ Books open. Read the instructions aloud. Then model the falling intonation for each question in the chart; have Ss practice. Also pronounce the three choices for each answer; Ss repeat. (*Note:* It's best not to explain any new words at this time as this might give away an answer.)

■ Divide the class into pairs. Before Ss begin the activity, model how to do the task by using the "Look Up and Say" technique, like this:

T: Which metal is the heaviest – gold, silver, or aluminum?
S: I think aluminum is the heaviest.
T: Oh? I'm not sure, but I think aluminum is much lighter than gold or silver.
S: You do? Well, maybe you're right.
T: Hmm, well, I think gold is the heaviest of the three metals.
S: And I think silver is.
T: OK, I guess we disagree here. So I'll check *gold*, and you can check *silver*. We'll find out later who got the correct answer for this one.
S: All right. Now it's my turn. Let's go on to question 2. (*looking at the question for a moment and then looking up at the T to ask the question*) Which planet is . . . ?

■ Set a time limit of about six minutes. Then pairs take turns asking and answering the questions. Remind them to check (✓) their answers in the chart after each discussion. If Ss have difficulty with any new words, allow them to use their dictionaries.

■ When time is up, present the final question below the chart. Then direct pairs to check their answers against those in the appendix at the back of their book.

■ **Optional:** If there is time and interest, go over each question and its correct answer with the class. Encourage Ss to find out more information about any topic that they find particularly interesting.

Answers

1. gold	7. a liter of wine
2. Pluto	8. Egypt
3. Jupiter	9. Colombia
4. a tortoise	10. an octagon
5. a giraffe	11. a mile
6. the liver	12. the Dark Ages

■ Go over the information in the score box at the bottom of the chart. Ss total their correct answers and then find that number in the score box and read the description provided.

interchange **13** *ARE YOU READY TO ORDER?*

Student A

You are the waiter or waitress at The Corner Cafe.
Take your customers' orders.

Taking the order
- Greet your customers.
- Ask what they would like. Write down each person's order on a separate piece of paper. (Use the menu to write down the orders and amounts.)
- Check the orders like this: "You ordered . . . ." and "You wanted . . . ."
- Ask if your customers want anything else (such as something to drink, a salad, or dessert).
- Go and get their orders.

Delivering the order
- Bring the orders to your customers. (You make a mistake. You give one customer the wrong thing.)
- Go and get the right order and bring it back.

Bringing the check
- Give each customer his or her check with a total at the bottom. (You make a mistake. You did not correctly add up one of the checks.)
- Walk away and wait for the customers to put the checks and money on the table.
- Pick up the checks and money. Bring back each customer's change.

The Corner Cafe

Soups	*Cup / Bowl*	*Salads*	
Chicken Noodle	$2.00/$3.00	Mixed Greens	$1.50
Clam Chowder	$2.00/$3.00	Pasta Salad	$2.75
French Onion	$3.00/$4.50	Chef Salad	$4.25

Sandwiches (served with Cole Slaw)		*Burgers (served with French Fries)*	
Tuna Salad	$4.25	Hamburger	$5.50
Roast Beef	$4.75	Cheeseburger	$6.00
Grilled Chicken Breast	$6.95	Turkey Burger	$5.75

Beverages	*Medium / Large*	*Desserts*	
Coffee or Tea	$.50/$1.00	Ice Cream	$1.50
Soda	$.75/$1.25	(Chocolate, Vanilla, or Strawberry)	
Iced Tea	$1.00/$1.50	Apple Pie	$2.25
Milk	$.75/$1.25	Chocolate Cake	$3.75

IC-17

---

interchange **13**

This creative role play practices both taking orders and ordering from a menu; it also involves using negotiation skills when mistakes are made in a restaurant situation.

- **Optional:** This activity might be fun to do in the school cafeteria or another large room that has tables and chairs rather than desks. If such a place is available, make arrangements to take the class there. You will need between fifteen and twenty minutes to complete the activity.

- With the whole class together, briefly explain the activity and the roles: Ss work in groups of three and imagine they are in a restaurant

called The Corner Cafe. The Student As are waiters/waitresses, and the Student Bs and Cs are customers.

- Divide the class into groups of three. Then assign the A/B/C roles to the three Ss in each group: The Student As look at page IC-17, and the Student Bs and Cs look at page IC-18. Tell Ss not to look at one another's pages either before or during the role play.

- Ask all Ss to silently read over their assigned roles and the menu for a few minutes. Tell them to mark (i.e., circle or underline) anything they don't understand and to ask about it when you go over their roles.

- Gather all the Student As (waiters/waitresses) together in one area of the room, if possible. Quietly go over their

instructions, using the pictures to help clarify their cues. (*Note:* Try not to let the Student Bs and Cs overhear what you are discussing.) Point out that there are three parts in their role play. Then answer any questions they may have about their roles or items on the menu.

- Do the same for the Student Bs and Cs (customers): Quietly go over their instructions, using the pictures to help clarify their cues. Point out that there are four parts in their role play – the extra part here involves the customers' tipping the waiter or waitress at the end. Then answer any questions they may have.

interchange 13 *ARE YOU READY TO ORDER?*

Students B and C

You are hungry customers in The Corner Cafe. You are having lunch.
The waiter or waitress comes to take your order.

Paying the check
- The waiter or waitress brings a check for each of you. Are they correct? If not, tell him or her like this: "Excuse me. This isn't right. It should be . . . ."
- Put the checks and money on the table for the waiter or waitress to pick up.

Ordering
- Look at the menu below. Order something to eat and drink.
- Ask the waiter or waitress to bring you something extra (such as a glass of water or another fork).

Being served
- The waiter or waitress brings your order. Is it correct? If not, tell him or her like this: "Sorry, I didn't order . . . . I ordered . . . ."

Tipping
- The waiter or waitress brings your change.
- Decide how much to leave for a tip.

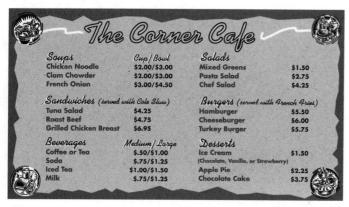

The Corner Cafe

Soups	Cup/Bowl	Salads	
Chicken Noodle	$2.00/$3.00	Mixed Greens	$1.50
Clam Chowder	$2.00/$3.00	Pasta Salad	$2.75
French Onion	$3.00/$4.50	Chef Salad	$4.25

Sandwiches (served with Cole Slaw)		Burgers (served with French Fries)	
Tuna Salad	$4.25	Hamburger	$5.50
Roast Beef	$4.75	Cheeseburger	$6.00
Grilled Chicken Breast	$6.95	Turkey Burger	$5.75

Beverages	Medium/Large	Desserts	
Coffee or Tea	$.50/$1.00	Ice Cream	$1.50
Soda	$.75/$1.25	(Chocolate, Vanilla, or Strawberry)	
Iced Tea	$1.00/$1.50	Apple Pie	$2.25
Milk	$.75/$1.25	Chocolate Cake	$3.75

IC-18

- Quickly model the pronunciation of the food and drink items on The Corner Cafe menu for the whole class; Ss repeat. Also, if time permits, go over the price for each item on the menu; Ss practice (e.g., $2.00 = "two dollars"; $3.50 = "three dollars and fifty cents" or "three fifty").

- Encourage Ss to be creative, to improvise, and most of all, to have fun.

- Now groups act out the role play. Set a time limit of ten to fifteen minutes. Walk around the room to observe how each group is doing. Try not to interfere with their role plays unless there is a serious breakdown in communication. If that occurs, quickly give whatever help is needed and then allow the group to continue with the activity.

Alternative presentation

- Let Ss listen again to some of the recording for Unit 13, Exercise 6 on page 83 and/or Exercise 9 on page 84. This may help the class be better prepared for this challenging role play. Then go over the roles and cues as outlined above before groups do the activity.

interchange 15

This activity provides an entertaining extension to the unit; it practices the future with the present continuous and *be going to* when asking and answering questions about weekend plans.

■ As a quick warm-up, ask questions like these around the class:

What are you doing this weekend?
Are you going to do anything special on . . . (e.g., Friday or Saturday night, Sunday afternoon)?
Are you going to a . . . (e.g., movie, party) this weekend?
What is . . . (S's name) going to do on . . . (day)?

■ **Optional:** Let the class put you on the "hot seat" to ask you questions about your weekend plans.

A *Class activity*

■ Read aloud the instructions and the headings in the chart. (*Note:* If all the Ss are married, tell them to cross out the first item in the chart.)

■ Present each of the eight phrases given here and have Ss repeat for good pronunciation, intonation, and stress. Then have volunteers form the questions from the phrases. The whole class practices each question. Here are examples of questions for the first two items in the chart:

go on a date
Are you going on a date next weekend?
Are you going to go on a date next weekend?

stay out all night
Are you staying out all night next weekend?
Are you going to stay out all night next weekend?

■ Point out that when Ss find someone who answers "Yes" to one of their questions about an activity in the chart, they need to write down that S's name next to the item. (*Note:* It makes for a livelier and perhaps more interesting activity with Ss talking to many more people if they write down a S's name only once.)

■ Use the picture and the A/B dialog to model the task with several volunteers. Show how Ss should react

Interchange Activities

interchange 15 *WHAT ARE YOU GOING TO DO?*

A *Class activity* What are your classmates' plans for the weekend? Go around the class and find people who are going to do these things. Ask for further information.

Find someone who is going to . . . next weekend.	Name
go on a date	....
stay out all night	....
go to an amusement park	....
go to a party	....
visit friends out of town	....
compete in a sports event	....
see a play	....
go to a garage sale	....

A: Are you going to an amusement park this weekend?
OR
A: Are you going to go to an amusement park this weekend?
B: Yes, I am, actually.
A: Oh, you are? Who are you going with?
B: . . .

B *Pair work* Compare your information with a partner.

IC-20

to hearing about someone's plans (e.g., "Oh, you are? Gee, that's great!" or "Wow! That sounds like fun!") and how to ask additional questions to get even more information from each person (e.g., "Who are you going with?" "Which . . . are you going to see?" "Did you already get the tickets?").

(*Note:* If any Ss feel uncomfortable talking about their real weekend plans, tell them to invent some interesting plans to talk about during the activity.)

■ Set a time limit of about ten minutes. Ss stand up and move around the class to do the task. Remind them to write down the name of anyone who answers "Yes" to a question about an activity on the list. Go around the class and listen in to see how Ss are doing.

(*Note:* It's best not to interrupt Ss during this exercise. This is a fluency activity where communication of real information is more important than grammatical or lexical accuracy.)

B *Pair work*

■ Ss form pairs and compare names in their charts. They should also share any other interesting pieces of information they heard during their conversations.

■ **Optional:** Ask pairs to share with the class the most interesting or unusual weekend plan that they heard about. Also, find out if any Ss are going to change their plans for next weekend as a result of doing this activity.

interchange 16 UNFOLD YOUR FUTURE!

A Complete this chart with information about yourself.

My Possible Future	
What are two things you plan to do next year?	....
What are two things you aren't going to do next year?	....
What is something you would like to change?	....
What is something you hope to buy in the next year?	....
What is a place you want to visit someday?	....
What is a place you would like to move to?	....
Who would you like to take a vacation with?	....
What famous person would you like to meet?	....

B *Group work* Compare your information in groups.
Be prepared to explain the future you have planned.

A: What are two things you plan to do next year?
B: Well, I'm going to travel to Italy and meet someone new.
C: Oh, really? Who are you going to meet?
B: I don't know, yet! What about you? What are two things you plan to do next year?
C: . . .

IC-21

interchange 16

This fluency activity is an appropriate wind-up to the unit. It is also a fun activity in which Ss, who have just successfully completed one goal – finishing the English course using *New Interchange Student's Book 1* – now have the chance to talk about other goals along with their real future plans and dreams.

A

■ For a quick warm-up to help the class start thinking about their possible futures – real and imaginary – tell Ss to cover the chart and look only at the picture. Then elicit some examples of questions that a person might ask a fortuneteller. Write them on the board:

Am I going to . . . (meet/marry someone; move/travel; change jobs/ friends; buy something expensive)? Where am I going to . . . (live/work/ travel to) next year?

■ Ss now look at the whole page. Explain the task: Ss answer each question in the chart called "My Possible Future" with real (or if some Ss prefer, made-up) information about themselves.

■ Model the pronunciation and intonation of each question in the chart; Ss practice.

■ Ss complete the chart individually. Walk around the class, giving advice as needed.

B *Group work*

■ Go over the task. Then have Ss form groups and take turns explaining their possible future plans.

■ **Optional:** Ask each group to choose the most interesting or unusual future plans that someone talked about. Then that S from each group tells the rest of the class about his or her plans. As usual, encourage other Ss to ask questions to show their interest and to get more information and details.

Unit Summaries

1 PLEASE CALL ME CHUCK.

KEY VOCABULARY

Nouns
back
bow
cheek
class
Dad
engineering
female
friend
greeting
handshake
hug
kiss
male
Mom
(first/last/full) name
nickname
parents
pat
student
(baseball/volleyball) team
women

Titles
Miss
Mr.
Mrs.
Ms.

Adjectives
married
same
single

Articles
a
the

Verbs
am
are
is

Adverbs
here
(over) there
too

Prepositions
from (Paris/France)
in (English 102/Canada)
on (the volleyball team/
   the back)

Conjunctions
and
but

Interjections
oh
well

EXPRESSIONS

Greeting someone
Hello.
Hi.

Exchanging personal information
What's your name?
  I'm . . . . /My name is . . . .
Where are you from?
  I'm from . . . .
How's everything?/
How are you?
  Not bad.
  Pretty good, thanks.

Introducing someone
This is . . . . /These are . . . .
  Nice to/Pleased to/
  Good to meet you.

Asking about someone
Who's that?
  That's . . . .
Who are they?
  Their names are . . . and . . . .

Checking information
How do you pronounce . . . ?
  It's Mandel, with the accent
  on "del."
How do you spell . . . ?
What do people call you?
  Please call me . . . .
  You can call me . . . .
  Everyone calls me . . . .
Excuse me, what's . . . again?
  It's . . . .
Are you studying . . . ?/
Are you on vacation?
  Yes, I am./No, I'm not.

Agreeing
That's right.
OK.

GRAMMAR EXTENSION Sentences with be

My name **is**   Amy.
    be + noun

I **am** from Korea.
    be + prepositional phrase

I **am** Korean.
    be + adjective

2 HOW DO YOU SPEND YOUR DAY?

KEY VOCABULARY

Nouns

Jobs/Professions
announcer
architect
carpenter
chef
company director
disc jockey
doctor
engineer
flight attendant
(tour) guide
nurse
police officer
professor
receptionist
sales manager
salesman
salesperson
secretary
security guard
supervisor
teacher
travel agent
word processor

Workplaces
airline
(construction/
  electronics)
  company
department store
hospital
office
radio station
(fast-food)
  restaurant
school

Classes
business
computer science
mathematics

Time
day
holiday
hour
week
year

Other
clothes
country
(computer)
  equipment

food
high school
house
instruction
lunch
music
(news)paper
passenger
patient
people
phone
snack
tour
TV
weather report
work

Adjectives
average
full-time
great
interesting
little
long
part-time

Article
an

Verbs
answer
arrive (at)
build
care for
cook
do
get (home)
get up
go (to bed/to
  school/to work)
have (a job/lunch)
leave
like
love
play (music)
read
sell
serve
sleep
sound (interesting)
spend (your day)
start
stay up
study
take
teach
wake up
watch
work

Adverbs
a lot
early
exactly
home
late
only
pretty (late)
then

Prepositions
about/around
  (10:00/noon)
after (midnight)
at (night/7:00/
  noon/midnight)
before (noon)
for (an hour)
in (the morning/
  the afternoon/
  the evening)
like (Peru)
on (weekends/
  weekdays/
  weeknights/
  Sundays)
until (midnight)

Interjection
so

EXPRESSIONS

Describing work/school
What do you do?
  I'm a/an . . . .
Where do you work?
  I work at/in/for . . . .
Where do you go to school?
  I go to . . . .

Asking for more information
What about . . . ?
Which . . . ?

Asking for and giving opinions
How do you like . . . ?
  I like . . . a lot./I love . . . .
  It's a great . . . .

Expressing interest
Really?
Oh, really?
That sounds interesting.

Talking about daily schedules
How do you spend your day?
  Well, I . . . . Then I . . . .
What time do you go to work/school?
  I leave at . . . .
And when do you get home?
  I get home around . . . .

Apologizing
Gee, I'm sorry.

GRAMMAR EXTENSION

1. Prepositions in sentences about work/school

I work	**for** Toyota.	*for* + name of company
	for Ms. Jones.	*for* + name of person
	for a lawyer.	*for* + person's job

I work	**in** a bank.	*in/at* + workplace
	at a restaurant.	

I work	**in** the sales department.	*in* + department/section
	in the front office.	

I go **to** Columbia University.	*to* + name of school

2. Articles

Indefinite articles
I'm **a** student.   *a* before consonants
He's **an** engineer.   *an* before vowel sounds

Definite article
I work for **the** *Daily News*.   *the* + specific place
  in **the** sales department.

3 HOW MUCH IS IT?

KEY VOCABULARY

Nouns
Clothes and jewelry
backpack
bag
boots
bracelet
cap
earrings
gloves
jacket
(pair of) jeans
necklace
pants
ring
Rollerblades
scarf
shirt
(athletic) shoes
sunglasses
sweater
tie
watch

*Materials**
cotton
gold
leather
plastic
polyester
rubber
silk
silver
wool

*Names of materials can be used as nouns or adjectives.

Other
adult
color
compact disc
cost
(room) decor
design
dollar
entertainment
(for) example
expenses
(gallon of) gas
haircut
health
money
(birthday) present
price
salary
savings
style
(price) tag
taxes
thing
transportation

Adjectives
attractive
bad
big
cheap
dark
different
each
expensive
good
large
light
medium
nice
OK
perfect
pretty
reasonable
small
warm
yearly

Verbs
buy
get
have on
let (me) + verb
look (= seem)
look at
pay (for)
prefer
spend (money)
try on

Adverbs
almost
better
more
right there

Preposition
for (you)

Conjunction
or

EXPRESSIONS

Talking about prices
How much is this sweater ?
  It's . . . .
That isn't bad.
How much are those shoes?
  They're . . . .
That's expensive.

Comparing
The black boots are more
attractive/prettier than the
brown ones.

Identifying things
Which one?
  The wool one.
Which ones?
  The blue ones.

Talking about preferences
Which one do you like better/more?
  I like the . . . one better/more.
Which ones do you prefer?
  I prefer the . . . ones.

Getting someone's attention
Excuse me.
Hey.
Look!

Making and declining an offer
Would you like to . . . ?
  Oh, no. That's OK.

Thanking someone
Thank you (anyway).
  You're welcome.

Asking for more information
Why?
Do you mean . . . ?
Oh, these?

Expressing doubt
Hmm.
I'm not sure.

Expressing surprise
Are you kidding?

GRAMMAR EXTENSION Comparative of adjectives

Adjectives with -er
Add *-er:*
Add *-r:*
Drop *y* and add *-ier:*
Double the final consonant and add *-er:*

cheap → cheap**er**
nice → nic**er**
pretty → prett**ier**
big → big**ger**

Adjectives with more
more + adjective: **more** perfect
               more expensive

For more information on comparatives, see the appendix at the back of the book.

4 DO YOU LIKE JAZZ?

KEY VOCABULARY

Nouns
Music*
classical
country
gospel
jazz
New Age
pop
rap/urban
rock
salsa

*Names of musical
styles can be used as
nouns or adjectives.

Movies
comedy
horror film
science fiction
thriller
western

TV programs
game show
news
soap opera
talk show

Entertainers
actor
actress
group
singer

Other
CD
date
dinner
fan
(baseball) game
gym
kind (of)
piano
play
theater
ticket
trumpet
video

Adjectives
best
favorite
new

Verbs
agree
ask
come over
go out
have to
know
listen to
meet
need
play (an instrument)
save
sing
think of
visit
want

Adverbs
just
really
tonight

Prepositions
for (dinner)
on (TV)
with (me)

EXPRESSIONS

Talking about likes and dislikes
Do you like . . . ?
   Yes, I do. I like . . . a lot.
   No, I don't. I can't stand . . . .
   No, I don't like . . . very much.
What kind of . . . do you like?
What do you think of . . . ?
What's/Who's your favorite . . . ?

Giving opinions
I like . . . . Do you?
I can't stand . . . . How about you?
I think . . . .
We don't agree on . . . .

Inviting and accepting/ refusing invitations
Would you like to . . . ?
   Yes, I would./I'd love to.
Do you want to . . . ?
   That sounds great.
   I'd like to, but I have to . . . .

Making suggestions
Why don't you . . . ?
Let's . . . .
   That sounds fine.

Asking about events
When is it?
Where is it?
What time does it start?
Where should we . . . ?

Asking for more information
How about . . . ?

GRAMMAR EXTENSION

1. Plural nouns

Add -*s:*	singer	→ singer**s**
Add -*es:*	actress	→ actress**es**
Drop *y* and add -*ies:*	comedy	→ comed**ies**

2. Prepositions

Do you want to go out **on** Saturday?   *on* + day
Let's meet **at** the theater.   *at* + place
       at 7:30.   *at* + time

5 TELL ME ABOUT YOUR FAMILY.

KEY VOCABULARY

Nouns

Family/Relatives
aunt
brother
children
cousin
daughter
father
grandfather
grandmother
grandparents
husband
mother
nephew
niece
sister
sister-in-law
son
uncle
wife

Other
acting
age
college
exhibition
fact
family tree
headline
home
(foreign) language
lawyer
painter
percent
semester
theater company
winter

Pronoun
anyone

Adjectives
divorced
elderly
famous
together
young

Verbs
break up
end
get (married/divorced)
live
look for
move
remarry
return
say
stay
take (a class)
take care of
talk
tell
travel
visit

Adverbs

Time expressions
again
ever
most of the time
never
(right) now
often
still
these days
usually
this month/semester/
    winter/year

Other
abroad
alone

Prepositions
at (a university/home)
by (the age of . . .)

EXPRESSIONS

Asking about someone
Tell me about . . . .
What is . . . doing these days?

Exchanging information about the present
Are you still looking for a job?
    Yes, I am./No, I'm not.
What are you studying this year?
    I'm studying a foreign language.
Is anyone in your family . . . right now?
    Yes, my . . . is.

Expressing interest
Is that right?
What an interesting . . . !
Wow!

Disagreeing
Do you think so? I think . . . .
I don't agree.
I don't think so.
It's different in my country.
Not really.

GRAMMAR EXTENSION Present participles

Add -*ing:*

go $\rightarrow$ go**ing**
work $\rightarrow$ work**ing**

Drop *e* and add -*ing:*
Double the final consonant and add -*ing:*

live $\rightarrow$ liv**ing**
get $\rightarrow$ get**ting**
shop $\rightarrow$ shop**ping**

KEY VOCABULARY

Nouns

Sports and fitness activities
aerobics
basketball
bicycling
football
jogging
racquetball
Rollerblading
soccer
swimming
tennis
weight training
yoga

Other
classmate
couch potato
fitness freak
free time
(fitness) program
sports fanatic
teen(ager)

Pronoun
nothing

Adjectives
good (at sports/for you)
fit
in (great) shape
middle-aged
old
popular
regular

Verbs
exercise
guess
keep
learn
lift (weights)
play (a sport)
stay
take (a walk)
work out

Adverb
hard
just (= only)
sometime
too

Prepositions
in (my free time)
for (a walk)
like (that)

Interjection
say

EXPRESSIONS

Talking about routines
How often do you . . . ?
  Three times a week/day/month.
  I don't . . . very often.
Do you ever . . . ?
How much time do you spend . . . ?
  Around two hours a day.

Talking about abilities
How well do you . . . ?
  Pretty well.
  Not very well.
How good are you at . . . ?
  I'm pretty good, I guess.
  Not too good.

Asking for more information
What else . . . ?

Expressing surprise
You're kidding!

Agreeing
All right.
No problem.

GRAMMAR EXTENSION Placement of adverbs of frequency

Questions
Is   he   usually at the gym after work?
be + subject + adverb

Statements
He   is   usually at the gym after work.
subject + *be* + adverb

He   isn't   usually there on weekends.
subject + negative *be* + adverb

Questions
Does he   usually go to the gym after work?
does + subject + adverb + verb

Statements
He   usually   goes to the gym after work.
subject + adverb + verb

He   usually doesn't   go on weekends.
subject + adverb + *doesn't* + verb

> *Always* usually goes between *don't / doesn't*
> and the main verb.

He   doesn't   always   go to the gym on weekends.
subject + *doesn't* + adverb + verb

7 WE HAD A GREAT TIME!

KEY VOCABULARY

Nouns
car
city
concert
(the) country
dancing
dishes
drive
housework
lake
neighbor
noise
party
picnic
trip
weather

Pronouns
anything
everyone
someone

Adjectives
all
boring
broke
cool
difficult
foggy
special
terrific

Verbs
baby-sit
complain
drive
enjoy
go shopping
have (someone) over
have (a[n] . . . time/
  [a lot of] fun)
invite (someone) out
see
snow
take (a day off)
work on

Adverbs
Time expressions
all day/month/year
all the time
as usual
last night/summer/weekend
the whole time
yesterday

Other
also
around
away
unfortunately

Prepositions
in (the country)
on (a trip/business/vacation)
over (the weekend)

EXPRESSIONS

Talking about past activities
Did you go out on Saturday?
What did you do . . . ?
How did you spend . . . ?
Where did you go . . . ?
What time did you go . . . ?
How long were you . . . ?

**Giving opinions about
past experiences**
How did you like . . . ?/
How was . . . ?
  It was . . . . /I really enjoyed it.
What was the best thing about . . . ?
  It's difficult to say.
Was the . . . OK?

**Making and responding
to suggestions**
Why don't you (just) . . . ?
  But then what would I do . . . ?

GRAMMAR EXTENSION Sentences about the weather

	it + be

How was the weather?	It was cool/cold/freezing.
	       warm/hot.
	       sunny/clear.
	       cloudy/rainy.
	       windy/foggy.

it + verb
It rained/snowed.

HOW DO YOU LIKE THE NEIGHBORHOOD?

KEY VOCABULARY

Nouns
Neighborhood/
Community places
apartment (building)
aquarium
bank
barber shop
bookstore
cafe
coffee shop
dance club
drugstore
gas station
grocery store
hotel
laundromat
library
(science) museum
park
pay phone
post office
shopping center

stationery store
street
travel agency

Other
air
bedroom
book
card
crime
dining room
idea
kitchen
living room
ocean
paper (= stationery)
pollution
public transportation
suburbs
traffic
unemployment
water

Adjectives
busy
clean
close
convenient
important
low
near
quiet
safe

Verbs
borrow
dry
happen
make (a reservation)
move in
trade (places)
wash

Adverbs
downtown
nearby

Prepositions
in (the shopping center/
   your neighborhood)
on (Pine Street/Third
   Avenue)

Interjections
by the way
in fact
of course

EXPRESSIONS

Asking for and giving locations
Is there a/an . . . around here?
   Yes, there is. There's one . . . .
   No, there isn't, but there's one . . . .
   Sorry, I don't know.
Are there any . . . near here?
   Yes, there are. There are some . . . .
   No, there aren't, but there are some . . . .
   I'm not sure, but I think . . . .

Complaining
That's the trouble.

Asking about quantities
How much . . . is there?
   There's a lot/a little/none.
   There isn't much/any.
How many . . . are there?
   There are a lot/a few/none.
   There aren't many/any.

Giving opinions
I bet . . . .

GRAMMAR EXTENSION

1. Countable and uncountable nouns

Countable

Singular	Plural
a bookstore	(**some**) bookstores
an apartment	(**some**) apartments

Uncountable

Singular	Plural
(**some**) traffic	–
(**some**) noise	–

2. *Some* and *any*

Questions
Is there **a** bookstore?
Are there **any** bookstores?

Statements
There are **some** bookstores.

Negatives
There aren't **any** bookstores.

Questions
Is there   traffic?
            any traffic?

Statements
There is **some** traffic.

Negatives
There isn't **any** traffic.

9 WHAT DOES HE LOOK LIKE?

KEY VOCABULARY

Nouns
beard
centimeter (cm)
contact lenses
couch
couple
eye
fashion
foot/feet
glasses
guy
hair
hand
height
length
man
mustache
person
T-shirt
window
woman

Adjectives
bald
blond
curly
good-looking
handsome
khaki
serious-looking
short
straight
tall

Verbs
ask for
change
miss
sit
stand
wear

Adverbs
ago
fairly
pretty
quite

Prepositions
in (a T-shirt and jeans/his thirties)
on (the couch)
to (the left [of])
with (red hair)

EXPRESSIONS

Greeting someone
Good afternoon.
Good to see you.

Offering help
Can I help you?
    Yes, I'm looking for . . . .

Asking about someone's appearance
What does she look like?
How old is she?
What color is her hair/are her eyes?
How tall is she?

Identifying people
Which one is Judy?
    She's the one talking to Tom.
Who's Brian?
    IIe's the man with curly blond hair/in jeans/
    behind the couch.

Expressing intention
I'll go and . . . .

Expressing regret
I'm afraid . . .

Hesitating
Let's see.

Confirming information
Are you . . . ?
    Yes, that's right.

GRAMMAR EXTENSION Be *and* have *to describe someone*

be + adjective
I'm 18.
He**'s** bald.
She**'s** tall.
They**'re** medium height.

have + noun
I **have** brown hair.
He **has** a mustache and a beard
She **has** blue eyes.
They **have** curly black hair.

KEY VOCABULARY

Nouns
accident
appointment
audience
bird
breakfast
bungee jumping
camel
camera
(body-building)
   competition
(a) couple (of)
fire
fish
grocery shopping
hill
kiwi (fruit)
laundry
magic
magician
(goat's) milk
motorcycle
mountain

pastime
pleasure
riverboat
skiing
sports car
truck
wallet
way
wedding
(a) while
white-water rafting
(rice) wine

Pronouns
several
something

Adjectives
every
exciting
incredible
raw
several
unusual
valuable
wonderful

Verbs
call
clean
climb
decide
drink
eat
hike
jog
lose
make (your bed)
ride
try

Adverbs
actually
already
lately
once
recently
today
twice
yet

Prepositions
for (a while)
in (a long time)

Conjunction
because

EXPRESSIONS

Exchanging information about past experiences
Have you ever . . . ?
   Yes, I have./No, I haven't.

Giving a suggestion
You should . . . .

Agreeing
Sure.

Checking and sharing information
The magician?
   That's right.
I hear . . . .

GRAMMAR EXTENSION *Time expressions*

With present perfect	*With past tense*
Time expressions refer to indefinite times in the past.	Time expressions refer to specific times in the past.

I've **already** seen that show.
I've seen it **twice**.
I haven't seen it **yet**.
I haven't been to the movies **in a long time**.

I saw it **last night**.
I saw it **yesterday**.
I saw it **last Friday**.
I went to the movies **about a month ago**.

11 IT'S A VERY EXCITING CITY!

KEY VOCABULARY

Nouns
Seasons
fall
spring
summer
winter

Other
arrival
beach
departure
harbor
hometown
(flea) market
million
nightlife
tourist
visitor

Pronoun
you (= anyone)

Adjectives
beautiful
cold
crowded
dangerous
dirty
friendly
hot
humid
modern
relaxing
stressful
ugly

Verbs
Modals
can
should

Other
hate

Adverb
anytime

Prepositions
at (the beach)
in (the fall)
on (the street)

Conjunctions
however
though

EXPRESSIONS

Describing something
What's . . . like?
  It's . . . , but it's not too . . . .
  It's . . . , and it's . . . .

Asking for a favor
Can you . . . ?
  Yes, I can./Sure I can.
  No, I can't.

Asking for and giving suggestions
What should I . . . ?
  You should . . . .
  You shouldn't . . . .
Should I . . . ?
  Yes, you should./
  No, you shouldn't.

Talking about advisability
What can you do?
  You can . . . .
  You can't . . . .

GRAMMAR EXTENSION Sentences with and, but, however, though

These sentences mean the same: They contrast something good (*a beautiful city*) and something bad (*very hot*).

This is a beautiful city, **but** it's very hot in the summer.
        It's very hot in the summer, **however**.
        It's very hot in the summer, **though**.

In this sentence, the conjunction *and* adds information.

This is a beautiful city, **and** there's always a lot to do.

12 IT REALLY WORKS!

KEY VOCABULARY

Nouns
Health problems
backache
burn
cold
cough
dry skin
fever
flu
headache
hiccups
insect bite
insomnia
muscle
pain
sore throat
stomachache
stress
sunburn
toothache

Containers and medicines
antacid
aspirin
bandage
bottle
box
can
cold tablets
cough drops
(anti-itch/skin) cream
(eye) drops
heating pad
lotion
ointment
package
sleeping pills
spray
tissue
tube
vitamin (C)

Other
chicken stock
dentist
garlic
liquid
meat
medicine cabinet
pepper
pharmacist
remedy
rest
slice

Adjectives
excellent
folk
half
helpful
lots of
sore
tired
useful

Verbs
Modals
could
may

Other
chop up
cut
get (a cold)
put
rest
take (medicine/ something for . . .)
tie
suggest
work (= succeed)

Prepositions
in (bed)
under (cold water)

EXPRESSIONS

Talking about health problems
How are you?
  Not so good. I have . . . .
That's too bad.

Offering and accepting assistance
Can/May I help you?
  Yes, please. Could/Can/May I have . . . ?
Here you are.
  Thanks a lot.

Asking for and giving advice
What should you do . . . ?
  It's helpful/a good idea to . . . .

Asking for and giving suggestions
What do you have/suggest for . . . ?
  Try/I suggest/You should get . . . .

Expressing dislike
Ugh!

GRAMMAR EXTENSION Sentences with have got to talk about health problems

What's the matter? **I've got** a bad cold.
  She's got the flu.

Contractions
I have = **I've**
She has = **She's**

KEY VOCABULARY

Nouns
Food and beverages
bread
broth
(chocolate) cake
(clam) chowder
(cup of) coffee
cole slaw
cucumber
dessert
dressing
flavor
(french) fries
(mixed) greens
hamburger
ice cream
lemon
main dish
meal
meatballs
milk
pasta

(apple) pie
potato
rice
salad
salmon
seafood
spaghetti
soda
(onion) soup
steak
(iced) tea
tomato
turkey
vegetable
vinaigrette

Other
customer
order
tip
waiter
waitress

Pronoun
all

Adjectives
baked
bland
delicious
ethnic
fried
greasy
grilled
healthy
mashed
rich
roast
salty
spicy

Verbs
Modals
will
would

Other
bring
go back
order

Adverbs
a bit
(not) at all
for now
right away

Preposition
with (lemon)

EXPRESSIONS

Expressing feelings
I'm crazy about . . . .
I'm (not) in the mood for . . . .

Agreeing and disagreeing
I like . . . .
  So do I./I do, too.
I don't like . . . .
  Neither do I./I don't either.
I'm crazy about . . . .
  So am I./I am, too.
I'm not in the mood for . . . .
  Neither am I./I'm not either.
I can . . . .
  So can I./I can, too.
I can't . . . .
  Neither can I./I can't either.

Ordering in a restaurant
May I take your order, please?/
What would you like?
  I'd like/I'll have a/an/the . . . .
What kind of . . . would you like?
  I'd like/I'll have . . . , please.
Would you like anything else?
  Yes, please. I'd like . . . .
  No, thank you. That will be all.

GRAMMAR EXTENSION Polite requests

Imperative
Please bring me a glass of water.

Questions with can/could/will/would
Can you please bring me a glass of water?
Could . . . .
Will . . . .
Would . . . .

14 THE BIGGEST AND THE BEST!

KEY VOCABULARY

Nouns

Geography
canyon
cliff
continent
desert
"down under" (= Australia
    and New Zealand)
farm
field
forest
plain
plateau
(coral) reef
river
sea
swamp
valley
volcano
waterfall

Measurements
degree
    (Fahrenheit/Celsius)
kilometer
meter
(square) mile
temperature

Other
artist
attraction
butter
feather
town

Adjectives
deep
far
heavy
high
located
lucky
mountainous

Verbs
get up (to)
go down (to)

Prepositions
in (the mountains/the world)
of (the three)
on (Bali)

EXPRESSIONS

Talking about distance and measurements
How far is . . . from . . . ?
    It's about . . . kilometers/miles.
How big is . . . ?
    It's . . . square kilometers.
How high is . . . ?
    It's . . . meters/feet high.
How deep is (the) . . . ?
    It's . . . meters deep.
How long is (the) . . . ?
    It's . . . kilometers long.
How hot is . . . in the summer?
    It gets up to . . . degrees.
How cold is . . . in the winter?
    It goes down to . . . degrees.

Making comparisons
Which country is larger, . . . or . . . ?
    . . . is larger than . . . .
Which country is the largest: . . . , . . . , or . . . ?
    . . . is the largest of the three.
What is the most beautiful . . . in the world?
    I think . . . is the most beautiful.

GRAMMAR EXTENSION Superlative of adjectives

Adjectives with -est
Add -*est:*
Add -*st:*
Drop *y* and add -*iest:*
Double the final consonant and add -*est:*

high → high**est**
large → large**st**
dry → dr**iest**
big → big**gest**

Adjectives with most
most + adjective: **most** famous
                              most mountainous

See the appendix at the back of the book for a list of adjectives.

15 I'M GOING TO SEE A MUSICAL.

KEY VOCABULARY

Nouns
(comedy) act
(leisure) activity
address
amusement park
barbecue
cafeteria
(telephone) call
dictionary
(craft) fair
(arts/crafts) festival
gathering
handout

hockey
meeting
message
monument
musical
plan
spectator
(tennis) tournament
turn

Adjectives
canceled
historic
live

Verbs
finish
give
open
pick (someone) up
plan
return
speak

Adverbs
in
overtime
tomorrow

Prepositions
at (college)
till (7:00)

Conjunction
that

EXPRESSIONS

Talking about plans
What are you doing tonight?
  I'm going . . . .
Are you doing anything tomorrow/
tonight?
  No, I'm not.
What is he going to do tonight?
  He's going to . . . .
Is he going to . . . tomorrow night?
  Yes, he is.

Apologizing and giving reasons
I'm sorry, but I can't go.
I'm working late.

**Accepting and refusing
invitations**
Would you like to . . . ?/
Do you want to . . . ?
  I'd love to.
  Oh, sorry, I can't.

Making a business call
Good morning, ...
  Hello. May I speak to . . . , please?
. . .'s not in. Can I take a message?
  Yes, please. This is . . . . Would
you ask . . . to call me? My number
is . . . .
I'll give . . . the message.
  Thank you. Good-bye.

Leaving and taking messages
Can/May I take a message?
  Please tell . . . (that) . . . .
  Please ask . . . to . . . .
  Would/Could you tell . . . (that) . . . ?
  Would/Could you ask . . . to . . . ?

GRAMMAR EXTENSION Future sentences

With be going to

The verb *be* is always used in the *be going to* form – never in the present continuous.

Where **are** you **going to be** tomorrow?
  I'm going to be at home.

With present continuous

Arrive, come, go, leave, and *stay* are usually used in the present continuous.

We're **arriving** tomorrow.
    coming
    going
    leaving
    staying

16 A CHANGE FOR THE BETTER!

KEY VOCABULARY

Nouns
biology
course
degree
(environmental) education
forestry
graduation
hairstyle
kid
life/lives
(student) loan
photo album
weight

Adjectives
dressed up
easy
outgoing
own
successful

Verbs
become
bring about
date
dress
fall (in love)
grow
hope
join
pay off
quit
retire
smoke
start
type

Adverbs
anymore
differently
for ages

Prepositions
at (an early age)
into (a new apartment)

EXPRESSIONS

Exchanging personal information
How have you been?
  Pretty good.
How are you?
  I'm doing really well.

Describing changes
You've really changed!
  I'm married now.
  I don't wear glasses anymore.
  My job is easier (now).
  I'm heavier (than before).
  I got divorced.
  I've grown a mustache.

Talking about plans for the future
I'm (not) going to . . . .
I (don't) plan to . . . .
I (don't) want to . . . .
I hope to . . . .
I'd like/love to . . . .

GRAMMAR EXTENSION Review: Wh-questions

What's your name?
What do you do?
What time do you get up?
What kind of music do you like?
What do you look like?
What color are your eyes?
What are you like?
What are you doing these days?
What did you do last night?
What do you think of Brad Pitt?

When do you get home?
When are you leaving?

Where are you from?
Where do you work?
Where did you go yesterday?
Where were you?
Which jeans do you like better,
  the light ones or the dark ones?
Which one is Tom?

Who is that?
Who's your favorite actress?
Who did you go out with last night?
Who's Sarah?

How do you like your job?
How do you spend your day?
How did you spend your last birthday?
How was your trip?

How much is that blouse?
How much crime is there in your city?
How many restaurants are there in your neighborhood?

How often do you exercise?
How well do you play?
How good are you at sports?
How long do you spend working out?
How long were you away?
How much time do you spend at the gym?
How old are you?
How long is your hair?
How tall are you?

Why don't you buy a new car?

Appendix

COUNTRIES AND NATIONALITIES

This is a partial list of countries, many
of which are presented in this book.

Argentina	Argentine	Germany	German	the Philippines	Filipino
Australia	Australian	Greece	Greek	Poland	Polish
Austria	Austrian	Hungary	Hungarian	Russia	Russian
Brazil	Brazilian	India	Indian	Singapore	Singaporean
Bolivia	Bolivian	Indonesia	Indonesian	Spain	Spanish
Canada	Canadian	Ireland	Irish	Switzerland	Swiss
Chile	Chilean	Italy	Italian	Thailand	Thai
China	Chinese	Japan	Japanese	Turkey	Turkish
Colombia	Colombian	Korea	Korean	Peru	Peruvian
Costa Rica	Costa Rican	Lebanon	Lebanese	the United Kingdom	British
Ecuador	Ecuadorian	Malaysia	Malaysian	the United States	American
Egypt	Egyptian	Mexico	Mexican	Uruguay	Uruguayan
England	English	Morocco	Moroccan		
France	French	New Zealand	New Zealander		

NUMBERS

0 zero	1 one	2 two	3 three	4 four	5 five	6 six	7 seven	8 eight
9 nine	10 ten	11 eleven	12 twelve	13 thirteen	14 fourteen	15 fifteen	16 sixteen	17 seventeen
18 eighteen	19 nineteen	20 twenty	21 twenty-one	22 twenty-two	30 thirty	40 forty	50 fifty	60 sixty
70 seventy	80 eighty	90 ninety	100 one hundred (a hundred)			1,000 one thousand (a thousand)		

COMPARATIVE AND SUPERLATIVE ADJECTIVES

1. Adjective with -er and -est

big	dirty	high	old	tall
busy	dry	hot	pretty	ugly
cheap	easy	large	quiet	warm
clean	fast	light	safe	wet
close	friendly	long	scary	young
cold	funny	mild	short	
cool	great	new	slow	
deep	heavy	nice	small	

2. Adjectives with *more* and *most*

attractive	exciting	outgoing
beautiful	expensive	popular
boring	famous	relaxing
crowded	important	stressful
dangerous	interesting	difficult
delicious		

3. Irregular adjectives

good → better → best
bad → worse → the worst

PRONUNCIATION OF REGULAR PAST FORMS

with /d/	*with* /t/	*with* /ɪd/
studied	worked	invited
stayed	watched	visited

IRREGULAR VERBS

Present	Past	Participle	Present	Past	Participle
(be) am/is, are	was, were	been	make	made	made
bring	brought	brought	meet	met	met
buy	bought	bought	put	put	put
come	came	come	quit	quit	quit
cut	cut	cut	read	read	read
do	did	done	ride	rode	ridden
drink	drank	drunk	run	ran	run
drive	drove	driven	see	saw	seen
eat	ate	eaten	sell	sold	sold
fly	flew	flown	set	set	set
fall	fell	fallen	sit	sat	sat
feel	felt	felt	sleep	slept	slept
get	got	gotten	speak	spoke	spoken
give	gave	given	spend	spent	spent
go	went	gone	take	took	taken
grow	grew	grown	teach	taught	taught
have	had	had	tell	told	told
hear	heard	heard	think	thought	thought
keep	kept	kept	wear	wore	worn
lose	lost	lost	write	wrote	written

ANSWER KEY   Unit 14, Exercise 3, page 87

1. Vatican City — (.44 square kilometers/.17 square miles)
2. Angel Falls — (979 meters/3,212 feet)
3. Hong Kong — (247,501 people per square mile)
4. the Caspian Sea — (378,400 square kilometers/146,101 square miles)
5. Mount Everest — (8,848 meters/29,028 feet)
6. the Nile — (6,670 kilometers/4,145 miles)
7. France — (60 million tourists)
8. the Pacific Ocean — (average depth of 4,028 meters/13,215 feet)

ANSWER KEY   Interchange 14, page IC-19

1. gold
2. Pluto (temperature = −230°C/−382°F)
3. Jupiter (diameter =142,984 km/88,846 miles)
4. a tortoise (maximum age = 150 years)
5. a giraffe (height = 5.5 meters/18 feet)
6. the liver (weight = 1,560 grams/55 ounces)
7. 1 liter of wine
8. Egypt (rainfall = 100–200 mm/4–8 inches)
9. Colombia (The equator runs through Colombia.)
10. an octagon (An octagon has 8 sides.)
11. a mile (1 mile = 1,760 yards = 1.6 kilometers)
12. the Dark Ages (from around 500–1,000 A.D.)

Acknowledgments

ILLUSTRATIONS

Barbara Griffel 15 *(top)*, 17 *(top)*, 18, 59
Randy Jones 5 *(top)*, 9, 23, 29, 37 *(top)*, 38, 46 *(top)*, 47, 52, 53, 54, 56, 63, 66, 75 *(top)*, 80, 85, 86, 94, 100, 104, IC-4 and IC-5 *(bottom)*, IC-16, IC-20
Mark Kaufman 74, 75 *(bottom)*, 76, 83 *(top)*, 84, IC-4 *(top five items)*, IC-5 *(top five items)*
Kevin Spaulding 3 *(bottom)*, 4, 5 *(bottom)*, 14, 15 *(bottom)*, 28, 37 *(bottom)*, 49, 55, 57, 60, 72 *(bottom)*, 78 *(bottom)*, 79, 92, 98, 105, IC-12, IC-14, IC-17, IC-18
Sam Viviano 2, 3 *(top)*, 11, 17 *(bottom)*, 26, 27, 31, 35, 40, 46 *(bottom)*, 61, 64, 72 *(top)*, 73, 78 *(top)*, 83 *(bottom)*, 89, 97, 99, IC-2, IC-3, IC-6, IC-19

PHOTOGRAPHIC CREDITS

9 *(left to right)* © Jon Riley/Tony Stone Images; © SuperStock; © Bruce Byers/FPG International; © Dennis Hallinan/FPG International; © Michael Krasowitz/FPG International; © Bruce Ayres/Tony Stone Images
10 © Flip Chalfant/The Image Bank
11 © James Levin/FPG International
12 © Jon Riley/Tony Stone Images
13 *(left to right)* © Mary Kate Denny/PhotoEdit; © Peter Correz/Tony Stone Images; © Jeffrey Sylvester/FPG International
16 *(top row, left to right)* Courtesy of IBM Corporation; courtesy of Kmart Corporation; courtesy of Kmart Corporation; courtesy of SWATCH; *(bottom row, left to right)* courtesy of IBM Corporation; Jeans by GUESS, photo © Richard Bachmann; courtesy of Reebok; courtesy of Kmart Corporation
19 *(left to right)* © Michael Keller/The Stock Market; © Ed Bock/The Stock Market; © Cybershop
21 *(top)* © Christian Ducasse/Gamma Liaison; *(bottom)* © Alpha/Globe Photos
22 *(clockwise from top)* © Fitzroy Barrett/Globe Photos; © Alpha/Globe Photos; © Paramount Pictures/Globe Photos
23 A scene from *The Phantom of the Opera*, photograph © Clive Barda
25 *(Bonnie Raitt)* © Alain Benainous/Gamma Liaison; *(Cui Jian)* © Forrest Anderson/Gamma Liaison; *(Caetano Veloso, performing at SummerStage in Central Park)* © Robert L. Smith
27 © Randy Masser/International Stock
29 *(left to right)* © Adam Scull/Globe Photos; © Bob V. Noble/Globe Photos; © Andrea Renault/Globe Photos; © R. Henry McGee/Globe Photos; © Imapress/Globe Photos; © Michael Ferguson/Globe Photos
30 © Chuck Kuhn Photography/The Image Bank
32 © Jim Cummins/FPG International
33 © Rob Gage/FPG International

35 © Donna Day/Tony Stone Images
38 © Paul Loven/The Image Bank
39 © Kevin Horan/Tony Stone Images
41 © Michael Keller/The Stock Market
42 © Peter Ginter/The Image Bank
43 *(ex.8, top)* © Gary Irving/Tony Stone Images; *(ex. 8, bottom)* © Hiroyuki Matsumoto/Tony Stone Images; *(ex. 9, clockwise from top)* © Zeynep Sumen/Tony Stone Images; © Ed Pritchard/Tony Stone Images; © Joe Cornish/Tony Stone Images
44 © Cliff Hollenbeck/Tony Stone Images
45 *(top to bottom)* © Matthew Weinreb/The Image Bank; © Wayne H. Chasan/The Image Bank; © Joseph Van Os/The Image Bank
48 © Schmid-Langsfeld/The Image Bank
50 © Ron Chapple/FPG International
51 © Jose Fuste Raga/The Stock Market
57 *(left to right)* © Springer/Corbis-Bettmann; © Helmut Gritscher/FPG International; © Paramount/The Kobal Collection
60 *(left to right)* © Alain Evrard/Gamma Liaison; © Globe Photos; © Paul McKelvey/Tony Stone Images; © Alexis Orand/Gamma Liaison
62 © Alpha/Globe Photos
64 © Dann Coffey/The Image Bank
65 *(top to bottom)* © Elan Sun Star/Tony Stone Images; © David Madison/Tony Stone Images; © Darryl Torckler/Tony Stone Images
66 © Richard Simpson/Tony Stone Images
67 *(left to right)* © Chip Vinai/Gamma Liaison; © Porter Gifford/Gamma Liaison; © Sylvain Grandadam/Tony Stone Images; © Tony Stone Images
68 © J. Blank/H. Armstrong Roberts
69 *(top)* © Don Klumpp/The Image Bank; *(bottom)* © Poulides/Thatcher/Tony Stone Images
70 *(left)* © Paul Chesley/Tony Stone Images; *(right)* © Glen Allison/Tony Stone Images
71 *(left to right)* © George Hunter/ H. Armstrong Roberts; © Travelpix/FPG International; © Will & Deni McIntyre/Tony Stone Images
74 © Richard Bachmann
81 *(left to right)* © Tony Stone Images; © Laurence Dutton/Tony Stone Images; © Luis Castaneda, Inc./The Image Bank; © James Jackson/Tony Stone Images; © Alberto Incrocci/The Image Bank; © Kenneth Mengay/Gamma Liaison; © Richard Bachmann
82 *(left to right)* © Paul Barton/The Stock Market; © Ron Chapple/FPG International; © Paul Barton/The Stock Market; © Ron Chapple/FPG International
87 © Stephen Frink/Tony Stone Images
88 © R. Kord/H. Armstrong Roberts
90 © Chad Ehlers/Tony Stone Images
91 *(top row, left to right)* © Ed Pritchard/Tony Stone Images ; © Ariel Skelley/The Stock Market; © Stephen Simpson/FPG

International; © Mug Shots/The Stock Market; *(bottom row, left to right)* © Richard Bachmann; courtesy of Philips Lighting Company; © Kevin Laubacher/FPG International; courtesy of Niagara Conservation Corporation
101 *(top to bottom)* © SuperStock; © Tom Wilson/FPG International; © Michael Keller/The Stock Market; © L.O.L. Inc./FPG International
102 © Eddie Adams/The Stock Market
103 *(left to right)* PEOPLE Weekly © 1995 Frank Veronsky; © Ted Rice; © Ed Hill/*The Bergen Record*, Hackensack, NJ
104 © Travelpix/FPG International
IC-7 *(left to right)* © Chuck Mason/International Stock; © Stephen Simpson/FPG International; © Michael Krasowitz/FPG International
IC-9 *(top row, left to right)* © Cliff Hollenbeck/International Stock; © Bruce Byers/FPG International; © Cliff Hollenbeck/International Stock; *(bottom row, left)* © Cliff Hollenbeck/International Stock; *(bottom row, right)* © Cathlyn Melloan/Tony Stone Images
IC-10 *(top row, left to right)* © Telegraph Colour Library/FPG International; © Darryl Torckler/Tony Stone Images; *(bottom row, left to right)* © Telegraph Colour Library/FPG International; © Josef Beck/FPG International; © Hugh Sitton/Tony Stone Images
IC-13 *(left)* © John Terence Turner/FPG International; *(right)* © Bruce Ayres/Tony Stone Images
IC-21 © Vera R. Storman/Tony Stone Images

TEXT CREDITS

The authors and publishers are grateful for permission to reprint the following items.

41 Adapted from "Smart Moves," by Susan Brink, *U.S. News and World Report,* May 16, 1996, page 76.
49 *(Snapshot)* Reprinted from the September 1994 issue of *MONEY* by special permission; copyright 1994, Time Inc.
97 Adapted from *Stephanie Winston's Best Organizing Tips,* by Stephanie Winston, Simon & Schuster, 1995.
103 *(Balamurati Krishna Ambati)* Adapted from "Prodigy, 12, Fights Skeptics, Hoping," by Alessandra Stanley, *New York Times,* May 7, 1990, pages A1, B9. Copyright © 1990 by The New York Times Co. Reprinted by permission. *(Catherine Charlton)* Adapted from "The Top Ten College Winners," *Glamour,* October 1994, Vol. 92, No. 10, page 118. *(Jasmin Sethi)* Adapted from "Blind Student Aces SAT," by Paul J. Toomey, *The Bergen Record* (Hackensack, NJ), November 20, 1995.
IC-7 Adapted from "Lifstyle Quiz," by Linda Henry, *Muscle & Fitness,* September 1994, pages 230–231. Reprinted with permission.

Optional Activities Index

Note: **(G)** = a "generic" activity, i.e., it can be used in any *New Interchange* unit by using it as is or by slightly adapting it to other topics, grammar points, or vocabulary.

Additional Optional Activities

Scrambled letters (G)

Time: 5–10 minutes. This activity can be used with any unit for a fun vocabulary review and spelling exercise.

Preparation: Near the end of a cycle, choose ten words and scramble the letters of each one. Use the Unit Summaries in the back of the Student's Book to help you. If possible, choose ten words that are related to one another in some way (e.g., words for jobs in Unit 2; words for clothing in Unit 3; all nouns).

■ In class, write the scrambled words on the board. To make the task easier, give Ss the first letter:

```
1. d e n f i r     (f_____)
2. t s a e p r n   (p_____)
3. e t t u s n d   (s_____)
4. e n m          (m_____)
5. r e t e h      (t_____)
6. l e a m        (m_____)
7. g e n i l s    (s_____)
8. s l a c s      (c_____)
9. e w n o m      (w_____)
10. k e n m i c a n (n_____)
```

■ Pairs rearrange the letters to find the words. Check Ss' answers.

Answers

1. friend	5. there	8. class
2. parents	6. male	9. women
3. student	7. single	10. nickname

Lots of languages

Time: 5 minutes. This activity introduces the names of languages that Ss speak.

In a heterogeneous class:

■ Find out how many different first languages there are in the class. Ask questions like these and write the information on the board for Ss to copy into their notebooks:

T: What's your first language, Celia?
S: Spanish.
T: How many of you speak Spanish as a first language?

In either a homogeneous or heterogeneous class:

■ Find out how many different foreign languages Ss are studying or know how to speak. Ask questions like these and write the information on the board:

T: Who is studying another foreign language?
S1: I'm studying Chinese.
S2: I'm studying French.
T: And who speaks another foreign language?
S3: I speak German.

Who am I? (G)

Time: 10–15 minutes. This activity practices yes/no questions.

Preparation: Cut out magazine pictures (one for each S) of well-known people that Ss are sure to know (e.g., famous entertainers, TV personalities, politicians, people currently in the news).

■ Introduce or review the names for different kinds of entertainers (e.g., *actor, actress, singer, musician*) and for other famous people (e.g., *politician, government leader, president, prime minister, king, TV personality, talk show host*).

■ Ask each S to come to the front of the class. Pin or tape a picture to the S's back without him or her seeing it. If possible, use pictures of women for female Ss and pictures of men for male Ss.

■ Explain the task: Each S tries to guess whose picture is on his or her back. Ss can use only yes/no questions to find out who it is.

■ Model the task by asking a S to pin a picture on your back (e.g., the picture here is of Boris Yeltsin):

T: Am I an entertainer?
S: No, you aren't.
T: Am I a politician?
S: Yes, you are.
T: Do I live in North America?
S: No, you don't.
T: Do I speak Russian?
S: Yes, you do.
T: Am I President Yeltsin?
S: Yes, you are!

■ Now Ss move around the class trying to identify their pictures. When a S correctly guesses the person's name, he or she sits down.

■ Stop the activity after about ten minutes. Find out how many Ss guessed their person's name correctly.

Crossword puzzle (G)

Time: 15 minutes. This activity is good for reviewing vocabulary in any unit and for practicing spelling.

■ Ss form pairs or groups and then make a crossword puzzle grid of 12 by 12 lines.

■ Ss use words from the unit and try to fit in as many as possible on their grids. (*Note:* The example grid below uses words connected to family and relatives from Unit 5.)

a	u	n	t					g		
	e		n					r		
	p		i			h		a		
	h		e			u		n		
	e			c		s		d		
	w	i	f	e		b		p		
		a				a		a		
		t				n		r		
		c	h	i	l	d	r	e	n	
	e							n		
	r				s	i	s	t	e	r
								s		

- After ten minutes, stop the activity and find out who has the most words on the grid. Ask that S to read each word aloud and to spell each one; the rest of the class listens and circles the same words on their grids.

What's his/her job?

Time: 10 minutes. In this activity, Ss guess people's jobs while using Wh- and yes/no questions and short responses.

Preparation: Ask Ss to look through magazines and newspapers for pictures of people who seem to have interesting or unusual jobs. Tell each S to bring about four pictures to class.

- Collect the pictures, mix them up, and divide them into sets – one set for each group.
- Form Ss into groups and give each a number (e.g., Group 1, Group 2). Explain the activity: Ss try to identify each person's job. When the group agrees on a job title for a person, the secretary writes the group number on the back of the picture, along with the name of the job. Let Ss use their dictionaries.
- Write these dialogs on the board and model them:

  A: *Is he/she a/an . . . ?*
  B: *Yes, he/she is.* **(or)** *No, he/she isn't.*

  A: *What's his/her job?*
  B: *I think he's/she's a/an . . . .*
  C: *Yes, I agree.* **(or)** *No, I think he's/she's a/an . . . .*

- Give one set of pictures to each group. Set a limit of five minutes. While groups work, walk around and give help as needed.
- When time is up, tell groups to choose the three most interesting pictures and to pass them on to another

group. Without looking at the back of the picture, the new group tries to identify each job. Do they agree with the previous group's suggestions?

Game – What's the question? (G)

Time: 10–15 minutes. This activity reviews Wh-questions.

Preparation: Each S will need three blank cards.

- Divide the class into two teams – Teams A and B. (*Note:* This activity can also be done in groups.) Give each S three blank cards.
- Ss think of three statements that could be answers to Wh-questions (e.g., She works in a zoo. He's a flight attendant for United. I study dance at UCLA.). Then Ss write one statement on each card. Walk around the class and give help when needed.
- Collect all of the Ss' cards and put them in a pile facedown.
- Team A starts: One S picks up a card and reads it aloud to a S from Team B. That S then tries to make a suitable Wh-question for it. Ss on both teams decide whether the question is correct or not. If it is, Team B wins a point; if it isn't, a S from Team A tries to correct it. If the correction is acceptable, Team A gets the point instead. Keep a tally of the scores on the board. The team with the most points wins.

Game – Tic-Tac-Toe (G)

Time: 5–10 minutes. This activity practices making past tense questions and statements with regular and irregular verbs. It can be adapted for use with any unit's verb forms or vocabulary.

- Draw a grid with nine squares on the board (i.e., 3 rows by 3 columns). Ask Ss to call out past tense verbs (e.g., *drove, enjoyed, saw*) and write them on the grid.
- Divide the class into two teams – Team X and Team O. Team X starts by choosing a verb and making either a question or a statement with it. If it is not correct, Team O gets a chance to use the same word in a question or statement. If Team O makes a correct sentence, write an O on the grid. Then it is Team O's turn. The game continues until one team gets tic-tac-toe (i.e., three Xs or Os together in a row, in a column, or diagonally through the grid).
- **Optional:** This game could also be played in pairs or groups, which would give each S more chances to make questions or sentences.

Likes and dislikes

Time: 15–20 minutes. This activity practices Wh- and yes/no questions.

Preparation: During an earlier class, ask Ss to write three statements on a piece of paper about their likes and dislikes on the topics of music and entertainment – for example:

I can't stand talk shows.
I like Mozart.
My favorite actor is Harrison Ford.

Collect the statements and use the information to make a class grid. In the first box on the grid, write the three sentences from one S (do not include the S's name). Continue by writing three more statements in the next box until all Ss' statements have been included. Make one photocopy for each S.

- Give each S a copy of the grid. Explain the task: Ss move around the class trying to find out who wrote the information in each box on the grid. They do this by asking one another questions. When Ss find the correct person, they write down that S's name in the box on the grid.

- Model the task. Tell Ss to look at the first box on the grid. Elicit example questions and write them on the board:

  Do you like talk shows?
  Do you like Mozart?
  What do you think of Harrison Ford?

- Set a time limit of about 15 minutes. Ss get up and go around the class asking questions. Remind Ss to write down the correct S's name in each box.

- When time is up, find out who has written down the most names. Then check that all the names are correct by asking each S to read his or her statements aloud to the class.

Let's go!

Time: 20 minutes. This is a two-part exercise that practices writing descriptions of events in a city – using real information – and then extending invitations.

Preparation: Ask Ss to bring English-language newspapers to class for this task. If there are none available, Ss could translate information from other sources into English. Alternatively, you could bring newspapers or other local printed sources with information about events in your town or city and make copies for all Ss to use in class.

- Explain the first task: Ss scan the newspaper for interesting local events. Then they choose three events and write short summaries about each one:

  There is a classic Japanese movie at the Star Theater. The movie is *The Seven Samurai*. It's on Thursday at 8 o'clock.

Ss should add other information as appropriate (e.g., type of movie, main actors, ticket price, location of the theater).

- Ss work individually, in pairs, or in groups to write descriptions of three events. Move around the class and give help as needed. (*Note:* This first part could also be done for homework.)

- Explain the second task: Ss work in pairs and take turns reading aloud their three descriptions to each other. Then they invite their partners to do something, using the information about their three events.

Guess who! (G)

Time: 5–10 minutes. This activity practices yes/no questions. It could be adapted for any unit.

- Have Ss form groups, or divide the class into two teams.

- Explain the activity: One S thinks of someone in the classroom. The other Ss try to guess who it is by asking yes/no questions. The S who guesses correctly has the next turn. Model the task, like this:

  T: I'm thinking of someone in the classroom.
  S1: Is it a man?
  T: Yes.
  S2: Is he sitting near the window?
  T: No.
  S3: Does he wear glasses?
  T: Yes.
  S4: Does he have curly black hair and a red shirt?
  T: Yes.
  S5: Is it Eduardo?
  T: Yes, it is! Now it's your turn.
  S5: OK. I'm thinking of someone . . . .

- Now Ss play the game in groups or teams.

Question and answer (G)

Time: 10 minutes. This activity practices asking questions about world geography or about your country; it also reviews comparative and superlative adjectives. This type of activity could be easily adapted for any unit's grammar and vocabulary.

Preparation: Make a set of Wh-questions and questions with *how* on cards; write one question on each card. Then make a corresponding set of answers on cards; write the answer to each question on a separate card – for example:

Question cards	Answer cards
What's the capital of France?	Paris
How cold is New Zealand in the winter?	It goes down to about 10° Celsius (50° Fahrenheit).

Question cards	Answer cards
What's the longest river in the world?	*The Nile*

Make enough question and answer cards so that half of the Ss have one question card each and the other half have one answer card each. (*Note:* In a small class, you may want to give more than one question or answer card to each S.) The questions should be about local geography, your country, or the world, and they should be relatively easy for Ss to answer.

■ In class, mix up both sets of cards and hand out one card (either a question or an answer card) to each S.

■ Explain the task: Ss move around the class and try to match their questions and answers. To do this, they can either read their questions and answers aloud or they can use these phrases, like this:

S1: What's your question?
S2: (*reads his or her question aloud*)
S1: No, my answer doesn't match. (*or*) Yes, that matches my answer (*reads answer aloud*)!

■ Set a time limit of about five minutes. When two Ss find a question and answer that match, they sit down.

■ Check answers by having Ss read their questions and answers aloud to the rest of the class.

Chain story – A terrible day! (G)

Time: 10 minutes. This activity practices telling stories in the past tense.

■ Ss work in groups. Explain the task: Each group makes up several interesting stories about a terrible day when everything went wrong. One S starts the first story, and then the other Ss in the group take turns adding sentences to it.

■ Model the task, like this:

T: Yesterday was a terrible day! We went to the beach.
S1: There was no sun.
S2: And it rained for two hours.
S3: Then we went to a restaurant for lunch.
S4: The food was horrible there.
S1: And then . . . .

■ Ss form groups and do the task. Set a time limit of about five minutes. Go around the class and give help as needed.

■ Each group chooses one of their stories. Then groups take turns telling their stories to the class. Which group told the best story?

Word associations

Time: 10 minutes. This activity reviews vocabulary used to describe places.

■ Write six words on the board from any one of the last four units in Student's Book 1 (e.g., from Unit 14, *Canada, Australia, city, beach, mountain, river*). Explain the task: Ss brainstorm and try to think of as many word associations as they can for each one.

■ Model the task by eliciting word associations for the word *Canada* and writing them on the board under it:

Canada

snow	Air Canada	mountains
skiing	Vancouver	French

■ Ss work in groups. Set a time limit of about ten minutes for groups to finish brainstorming on all six words. Walk around the class and give help as needed.

■ Find out which groups made the most word associations for each word. Those groups take turns reading their words aloud; other groups listen and check off those same words on their own lists.

Sentence-making contest (G)

Time: 10–15 minutes. This activity reviews describing people, their careers, and changes in their lives.

Preparation: In the class before the activity is done, each S brings one color magazine picture showing several people doing various activities. Collect the pictures and choose the best ones for this task. The number of pictures should equal the number of groups (e.g., class size 20 = 4 Ss in each group = 5 pictures needed). Then number each picture (e.g., *#1, #2*).

■ **Group work:** Give each group a picture and explain the game: Ss try to make as many different sentences as they can – in three minutes – about the people in the picture. On a separate piece of paper, the group secretary writes down the picture's number and every sentence the group can think up.

■ When the first three-minute time limit is up, groups exchange pictures (clockwise around the class) and do the task again with the next picture. On the same piece of paper, the group secretary again writes down the picture's number and all the sentences that the group forms. Continue the activity until every group has written sentences for each picture passed around.

■ **Class activity:** Now find out which group has written the most sentences for each picture. Then that group holds up the picture while the group secretary reads their sentences aloud to the class.

Chain story – Visiting a foreign country (G)

Time: 10 minutes. This activity practices narrating a story in the past tense while using adverbs, adjectives, and conjunctions.

■ Explain the task: Ss tell a story about visiting a foreign country. One S gives the first sentence of the story. The next S repeats that sentence and adds another sentence. Model the task with several Ss:

T: I went to France.
S1: I went to France, and I stayed in Paris.
S2: I went to France, and I stayed in Paris, but it was very expensive there.
S3: I went to France, and I stayed in Paris, but it was very expensive there. However, I bought a nice . . . .

■ Have Ss form groups. Ss take turns adding sentences around the group until the story comes to an interesting end.

Game – Simon Says (G)

Time: 5–10 minutes. Most Ss will enjoy this game, which reviews parts of the body and practices basic action verbs. This game could also be adapted to other units with different types of action verbs (e.g., Unit 4: *sing, play an instrument, go out, listen to*).

■ Explain the rules of the game: Ss stand up. You give a series of commands – one at a time, with most of them starting with the phrase "Simon says," like this:

T: Simon says touch your toes.

The class must obey these commands. Sometimes, however, you give a command without "Simon says":

T: Touch your toes.

When Ss hear a command without "Simon says," they shouldn't do anything. Tell Ss that if they do an action without hearing "Simon says" or if they do the wrong action, they're out and they have to sit down. The last S standing is the winner and gets to lead the next game.

Absent again!

Time: 10–15 minutes. This practical activity shows Ss how to make telephone calls and give medical excuses for when they must be absent from class.

■ Explain the activity: One S is calling the teacher or the school office to give a medical excuse for not being able to come to school. Encourage Ss to think of some interesting excuses for being absent. Model the task with a volunteer, like this:

T: Hello? This is . . . (*giving own name or school's name*). How can I help you?
S: Hello. This is Chuck Chen. I'm sorry I can't come to (*giving name of teacher or course number – e.g., Ms. Johnson's, English 100A*) class today.
T: Oh? I'm sorry to hear that, Chuck. What's wrong?
S: Well, I went skydiving with some friends on Saturday and I hurt my ankle.
T: Oh, that's too bad! Well, I hope you feel better soon. Take care now!
S: Thanks. Good-bye.
T: Bye.

■ Pairs choose roles and then sit back-to-back to practice making telephone calls. Go around the class and give help as needed.

■ Ss switch roles and try the activity again.

■ **Optional:** Ask pairs to volunteer to perform the activity in the front of the class.

What's your opinion?

Time: 10 minutes. This exercise practices giving opinions and making short responses.

■ Explain the activity: Each S writes down statements that express his or her strong opinions about five things. These statements should be about things that other Ss in the class may also know something about. In addition, the statements should be generally of a light and inconsequential nature. Give some examples like these:

I think the food in the school cafeteria is terrible!
I can't stand the color of the new building next door!
I hate heavy metal music!
I think *Star Wars* is a really terrific movie!

■ Ss work individually to write their five statements. Walk around the class and give help as needed.

■ With the whole class, Ss take turns reading one of their opinions aloud. Then they name a classmate, and he or she must make a suitable response with *so, too, neither,* or *either* when agreeing, or use other expressions for contrastive responses, like this:

S1: I think the food in the school cafeteria is terrible! What's your opinion, Terry?
S2: Yeah, I do, too. . . . Uh, I love to eat kiwi fruit! May?
S3: Ugh! Oh, I don't! I can't stand them. Jay, . . . ?

That's not right!

Time: 15 minutes. This is a world-knowledge quiz.

- Explain the task: In pairs, Ss think of a country and write down six statements about it – five true and one false. These should be factual statements, not opinions (e.g., I think X is more beautiful than Y.). Write these example sentences on the board:

  The Netherlands is a small country. It's in northern Europe. It's also known as Holland. The people speak French. The capital city is Amsterdam. There are a lot of windmills in the Netherlands.

  (Answer: The false statement here is "The people speak French." Correction: Dutch.)

- Ss work in pairs to do the activity.

- Now groups of four (two pairs each) get together. The members of one pair take turns reading their statements aloud. The other pair tries to identify the false statement and to correct the false information in it.

What an interesting place!

Time: About 3 minutes for each group's presentation. This activity requires Ss to do some outside research for a group presentation to the class.

- Describe the task: Ss work in groups and choose a country or city that none of them has ever visited but one they would all like to go to someday. Then they prepare a short, three-minute class presentation on it, using information from guidebooks, encyclopedias, and/or travel brochures. Write these topics on the board for the groups to focus their research on:

place	best time of the year
location	what to see and do
weather	why it's interesting
shopping	
people	
food	

- **Class activity:** Group members divide up the topics and take turns presenting different facts and information on the country or city they chose, like this:

  S1: Algeria is a beautiful country in North Africa. The weather is . . . .
  S2: There are many things to see in Algeria. For example, you can/should . . . .

- **Optional:** If time permits, allow the class to ask a few questions after each group's presentation in order to get additional information about the place.

Are you doing anything on Saturday?

Time: 10–15 minutes. This role play practices extending, accepting, and declining invitations.

Preparation: Ss bring in information from English language newspapers and magazines about local events (e.g., movies, concerts, sports events, fairs).

- Explain the activity: Ss work in pairs (or groups) and practice inviting each other to real events in the city or town by using local English newspapers and magazines. One S tells a partner about an event that he or she would like to see and then invites the partner to it. The partner either accepts or declines the invitation.

- If necessary, explain that this activity is just a role play – i.e., Ss should not feel obliged to actually go out with someone in the class as a result of this practice.

Game – Charades (G)

Time: 20 minutes. This activity reviews the vocabulary for any activity or situation that was presented in Units 13–16. This game can also be adapted to use with any other unit or units.

- Ss form groups. Each group thinks of several situations (e.g., ordering in a restaurant; eating an ice cream cone; talking about the size of a fish that got away; refusing an invitation) – one situation for each member of the group to mime.

- Groups take turns miming or acting out their situations in front of the class. Remind each group not to speak while performing their situation; they can only nod their heads when a group guesses the situation correctly. The other groups call out their guesses (e.g., "You're ordering a meal in a restaurant." "You're refusing an invitation to go somewhere.") Keep score on the board: Each group that guesses correctly gets one point.

Tests

The following set of four tests may be used to assess students' mastery of the material presented in *New Interchange* Student's Book 1. Each test covers four units. Not only will these criterion reference tests allow the teacher to determine how successfully students have mastered the material, but the tests will also give students a sense of accomplishment. For information about these tests — and about testing in general — see "Testing Students' Progress" on page x in the Introduction to this Teacher's Edition 1.

When to give a test

- Give the appropriate test after the class has completed each quarter of Student's Book 1, i.e., four units and the accompanying review unit.

Before giving a test

- Photocopy, collate, and staple the test — one for each student in the class.

- Schedule a class period of about 45–60 minutes for the test.

- Locate and set the recorded Part A for the test listening section on the Class Audio Cassette or Audio CD. The tests are at the end of the cassettes (cassette 2, side 4) or CDs (CD2, tracks 54–57).

- Tell the students that they are going to have a "pencil and paper" test (i.e., oral production will not be tested). Suggest that they prepare for the test by reviewing the appropriate units and unit summaries. In studying for the test, students should pay particular attention to the Conversations, Grammar Focus points, and Word Power exercises. Tell Ss that the test will also contain a listening section and a short reading section.

How to give a test

- Explain that the point of the test is not to have students compete with each other for the highest grade; rather, the test will inform each student (and the teacher) about how well the material was learned and what material, if any, may need extra review and practice.

- On the day of the test, hand out one photocopy of the test to each student.

- Encourage Ss to take about five minutes to look through the test, without answering any of the test items. Make sure students understand the instructions, e.g., "Check (✓) the correct answers." "Complete the conversations." "Circle **T** for true or **F** for false."

- Tell Ss that about five minutes of the test time will be used for the listening section, part A, which is the first item on the test. However, it is up to the teacher to decide whether to give the listening section near the beginning or the end of the test-taking time.

- Tell Ss that they are not allowed to use their Student's Books or dictionaries during the test.

- To help Ss use their time efficiently and to finish on time, write the total time for the test on the board before beginning the test:

Total time: 45 minutes

- After the test begins, revise the time shown on the board every ten minutes or so to tell the class how much time is left.

- When giving the listening section of the test, direct the class to part A, and go over the instructions. Advise Ss just to listen the first time they hear the audio recording, and then to listen and mark their answers during the second playing. Afterward, play the audio recording twice, straight through without stopping or pausing.

Alternative presentation

- If the teacher does not wish to use the class time for the test, tell Ss to complete the whole test at home except for part A, the listening test item. Advise the Ss to complete the test at home in 40 minutes and not to use their Student's Books or dictionaries. During the following class, take five minutes to play the audio recording and to complete part A of the test.

How to score a test

- Either collect the test and use the Test Answer Key to score it, or go over the test with the class while allowing each student to correct his or her own test. Alternatively, tell the students to exchange tests with a partner and correct each other's answers as the teacher elicits or reads the answers aloud.

- Each test has a total score of 100 points (50 correct answers are possible at 2 points each). If a letter grade is useful to the teacher and the Ss, this scoring system can be used:

90 – 100 points	=	A or Excellent
80 – 89 points	=	B or Very good
70 – 79 points	=	C or Fair
69 or below	=	Need to review the unit(s)

A 🔊 Listen to Rosemary, Ken, and Yoko talking.
Check (✓) the correct answers.

1. Her last name is ☐ Yoko.
☐ Miyake.
☐ Miyaki.

2. Ken is ☐ an engineer.
☐ a student.
☐ a chef.

3. They all ☐ can't stand Bonnie Raitt's music.
☐ don't like
☐ like

4. The concert tickets are ☐ $42 each.
☐ $7 each.
☐ $24 each.

B Complete each question with information about yourself.

1. What's your first and last name? _____

2. Where are you from? _____

3. What do people usually call you? _____

C Complete each conversation. Use the correct form of *be*.

1. A: Is Joseph Davis from the United States?

   B: Yes, _____ . He's from Chicago.

2. A: _____ ?

   B: No, Mr. and Mrs. Sanchez aren't Brazilian. They're American.

3. A: Are you in English 201?

   B: No, _____ . I'm in English 101.

4. A: _____ ?

   B: Yes, my first name is Amy.

D Read the passage. Then circle **T** (true) or **F** (false).

Names

In English-speaking countries, many people have three names – a first name, a middle name, and a last or family name (for example, John Fitzgerald Kennedy). Sometimes people use a short name or nickname (Bob for Robert, Liz for Elizabeth). People use a title (Ms., Mr.) with a first and last name (Ms. Mary Murphy) or with only a last name (Ms. Murphy). Many Americans and Canadians use first names at work or at school. In colleges and universities, teachers often call their students by their first names.

1. **T F** Many people have a middle name in English-speaking countries.

2. **T F** Bob is a nickname for Robert.

3. **T F** People use a title with a first name, such as Ms. Mary.

4. **T F** American and Canadian teachers don't call their students by their first names.

E Complete the question in each conversation.

1. A: Where _____ you work?

   B: I work in a department store.

2. A: What _____ she do?

   B: She's an architect.

3. A: Where does Jason _____ to school?

   B: He goes to U.C. Berkeley.

4. A: How _____ she like the class?

   B: Oh, she likes it a lot.

F Read each set of sentences and circle the word that doesn't fit. Write the correct word or words on the blank for the incorrect one.

Example: He's a chef. He works for a construction company. He builds houses.
    carpenter

1. I am a salesperson. I work for an airline. I serve meals to the passengers.
    _____

2. Ken works for King Travel. He's a receptionist. He takes people on tours.
    _____

3. Judy Johnson is a nurse. She works in a bank. She cares for patients.
    _____

G Write a short paragraph (about 3–5 sentences) describing your daily schedule or routine.

Example: I get up at 7:00 in the morning on weekdays. Then I . . . .

_____

_____

_____

_____

H Read each question. Circle the correct word in each answer.

1. A: How much is that ring?

    B: **(That / They're / It's)** only $29.

2. A: How much are those boots?

    B: Oh, **(these / they're / it's)** $65.

3. A: Which one do you prefer?

    B: I prefer the leather one. It is **(cheap / big / more attractive)** than the silk one.

4. A: Which one do you like better?

    B: I like the red one better. It's **(pretty / nicer / good)** than the blue one.

I Complete these sentences. Use the correct form of the adjective.

Example: That purple T-shirt is _____ *nicer than* _____ this pink one.   **(nice)**

1. Are these boots _____ the ones over there?   **(large)**

2. Usually leather jackets are _____ the wool ones.   **(good)**

3. Silk is _____ cotton.   **(expensive)**

4. Which shirt is _____ , the green one or the yellow one?   **(pretty)**

J Complete each conversation with the correct form of *do*.

1. A: _____ you like California, Kenji?

   B: Yes, I _____ . I really like it.

2. A: _____ John play the piano?

   B: Yes, he _____ .

3. A: What kind of music _____ they like?

   B: They really like rock a lot.

K Complete these sentences with object pronouns.

1. Julia Roberts is my favorite actress. I like _____ a lot.

2. Music videos aren't very interesting. Do you like _____ ?

3. Ellen can't stand the actor Sylvestor Stallone. What do you think about _____ ?

4. *Baywatch* is my favorite TV program. Do you like _____ ?

L Answer each question with a complete sentence about yourself.

1. What do you do? _____

   _____ .

2. Where do you go to school? _____

   _____ .

3. What do you usually do before 8 A.M.? _____

   _____ .

4. When do you usually get home on Mondays? _____

   _____ .

5. What is something you do on Saturdays? _____

   _____ .

6. What kind of TV program do you like? _____

   _____ .

7. What do you think of horror films? _____

   _____ .

8. Would you like to go out on Friday? _____ , but _____

   _____ .

Name: _____

Date: _____

Score: _____

A 🔊 Listen to people talking. Circle **T** (true) or **F** (false).

1. **T F** Peggy has four sisters and four brothers.

2. **T F** Janet usually goes to the gym to work out about three times a week.

3. **T F** John went to dinner in the mall on Sunday with his girlfriend.

4. **T F** There's not much traffic or crime in Peter's new neighborhood.

B Complete each conversation. Use the present continuous
(for example, *is going, are taking*).

1. A: Are _____ this Sunday afternoon?

   B: No, I'm not. I'm not doing anything on Sunday. Would you like to do something?

2. A: Is your sister coming to the picnic tomorrow?

   B: Yes, _____ .

3. A: Where _____ this summer vacation?

   B: My parents are going to France this summer. They really want to see Paris.

4. A: When are you playing tennis this week?

   B: _____ on Friday morning. Do you want to play, too?

C Rewrite these sentences using determiners.

Example: In China, 50% of women get married by the age of 22.

   In China, many women get married by the age of 22. .

1. About 5% of Americans use public transportation to get to work.

   _____ .

2. In the U.S., 80% of divorced people get married again.

   _____ .

3. Thirty percent of American mothers return to work one year after having a baby.

   _____ .

4. Ninety-eight percent of homes in the U.S. have at least one color TV set.

   _____ .

D Rewrite each question or sentence and put the adverb in the correct place.

1. I have eggs for breakfast. (**often**)

   _____ .

2. Do you eat lunch at the cafeteria? (**ever**)

   _____ ?

3. I watch TV in my free time. (**sometimes**)

   _____ .

4. What do you do on Saturday night? (**usually**)

   _____ ?

E Read each conversation and complete the question.

1. A: How _____ exercise?
   B: Not very often. I exercise only about an hour on Saturday morning.

2. A: Do _____ ?
   B: No, I never drive to school. I ride my bicycle most of the time.

3. A: What _____ usually _____ ?
   B: I usually stay home on the weekend. I often have lots to do around the house.

4. A: How _____ at tennis?
   B: Well, I guess I'm pretty good. I played on the tennis team in school.

5. A: How _____ spend working out?
   B: Oh, I spend about two hours every day at the gym. I'm a real fitness freak!

F Complete this story using the past tense (for example, *did, walked*).

I _____ (**have**) a great day last Saturday. In the morning, my best friend and I
_____ (**drive**) to the City Museum where we _____ (**see**) a wonderful art
exhibit. Then we _____ (**go**) bicycling in the park all afternoon. What fun! After
dinner, we _____ (**watch**) an old movie on TV. It was really a wonderful day!

G Answer these questions about yourself. Write complete sentences.

1. What did you do on Saturday? _____

   _____ .

2. Did you do anything special on Sunday? _____

   _____ .

3. Where did you go on your last vacation? _____

   _____ .

4. How long were you away on that vacation? _____

   _____ .

5. Were you out last night, or did you stay at home? _____

   _____ .

H Use the map to write a complete answer for each question.

Example: Is there a police station near here?

Yes, there is. There's one on Fox Street next to the post office.

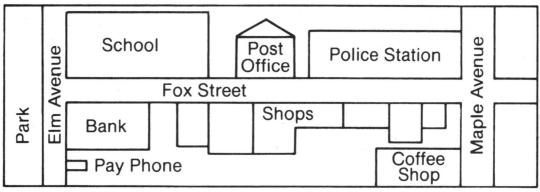

1. Is there a bank around here?

   _____ .

2. Are there any hotels near the school?

   _____ .

3. Are there any shops in this neighborhood?

   _____ .

4. Are there any coffee shops near here?

   _____ .

5. Is there a pay phone near the park?

   _____ .

I Read each sentence and circle the one word that doesn't fit. Then write the correct word on the blank.

1. On Saturday, I always take my clothes to the drugstore to   _____
   wash and dry them there. After that, I go to the library to
   make a book for the weekend. Then I go to the grocery store   _____
   and buy movies for my dinner.   _____

2. There's a barber shop in my neighborhood where I always
   get a good work. Also, near my house, there are several nice   _____
   banks where I like to eat dinner twice a week. On the corner   _____
   of First Avenue and Pine, there's a drugstore where I exercise   _____
   about an hour a day.

J Read the questions below. Answer them by writing a short paragraph (about 4–6 sentences) to describe your neighborhood.

Do you live in a house or an apartment? Where is it? Is there much noise? How much traffic is there in your neighborhood? How much crime is there? How many restaurants are there? Are there any stores or shops near your home? How do you like it there?

_____

_____

_____

_____

_____

K Read Rosa's letter to Gary. Circle **T** (true) or **F** (false).

> Dear Gary,
>
> Berkeley is an interesting city. I really like it here! There's always a lot to do. Every day after school, I usually go to Telegraph Avenue. I always like to go to my favorite coffee shop and meet my friends there for coffee. In the evening, there is always something interesting to do in the town or on the university campus, such as see a movie or hear some live music.
>
> On Saturday, my friends and I usually take the bus to San Francisco for the day. San Francisco is a beautiful place. I love the shops and restaurants, and it's a great city for just walking around or Rollerblading in Golden Gate Park. We always go to Chinatown to have lunch, and then we go shopping in the afternoon.
>
> On Sunday, I like to play tennis with friends, or we watch a sports event, like a football game or a baseball game, on TV at home. I think American football is very exciting!
>
> Well, that's all for now. Take care. Hope to hear from you soon.
>
> Love,
>
> Rosa

1. **T F** Rosa doesn't like Berkeley.

2. **T F** She always studies after school.

3. **T F** She spends the weekend in San Francisco.

4. **T F** She really likes to watch football.

Name: _____

Date: _____

Score: _____

A 🔊 Listen to people talking and check (✓) the correct information.

1. ☐ She is short and in her thirties.
   ☐ She is medium height and in her twenties.
   ☐ She is fairly short and about twenty-five.

2. ☐ He had a great vacation in Paris last year in July.
   ☐ He hasn't been to Paris, France, yet.
   ☐ He can't wait to go to Paris in August.

3. ☐ You shouldn't go to the Ramblas because that's a very long street.
   ☐ You shouldn't miss some of the wonderful museums in Barcelona.
   ☐ You should visit Spain in January.

4. ☐ It's important to get some rest for a backache.
   ☐ You shouldn't take aspirin.
   ☐ It's helpful to get a lot of exercise and to play lots of sports.

B Read these descriptions of people. Circle the correct word in each sentence.

1. My sister is (**in / on / at**) her thirties. She (**does / has / is**) long blond hair, and she (**have / is / does**) medium height. She (**is / wears / does**) contact lenses.

2. My brother (**has / is / are**) pretty tall, and he (**does / is / has**) a beard and a mustache. He (**is / has / are**) twenty years old.

C The police are looking for two people. Read each description and circle the correct picture of the person.

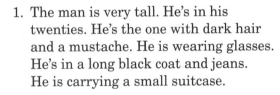

1. The man is very tall. He's in his twenties. He's the one with dark hair and a mustache. He is wearing glasses. He's in a long black coat and jeans. He is carrying a small suitcase.

2. The woman is short and in her forties. She has curly blond hair. She is in a cap, a white T-shirt, and dark pants. She isn't wearing glasses. She is the woman with a camera around her neck.

D Complete each conversation. Use the present perfect.

Example: A: _Have you been to San Diego?_
            B: No, I haven't been to San Diego yet, but I'm planning to go next year.

1. A: Have the children eaten anything this morning?

   B: No, _____ . So they should eat lunch soon.

2. A: _____ ?

   B: No, the movie hasn't started yet. I think it's going to begin in about 10 minutes.

3. A: Has your mother called you today about your sister's birthday party?

   B: No, _____ , but I talked to her yesterday about it.

4. A: Has Carol's brother ever seen the movie *Star Wars*?

   B: Yes, _____ already _____ twice.

5. A: _____ ever _____ ?

   B: No, I have never studied French. I speak Spanish and a little Italian though.

E Circle the correct adjective.

1. Bill's car is never clean. Why does he drive such a (**boring / dirty / noisy**) car?

2. It's not safe to walk there at night. It's really (**interesting / quiet / dangerous**).

3. It isn't cheap to stay at the Plaza Hotel. The rooms are very (**small / old / expensive**).

4. The movie wasn't interesting. It was so (**exciting / beautiful / boring**) that I left.

5. Hawaii is a very relaxing place. It's not (**hot / stressful / small**), like New York.

F Read Sam's composition. Then circle **T** (true) or **F** (false).

Mexico

One of my favorite places for a vacation is Mexico. I really like the weather because it never gets cold there. The people are very nice, too. They never laugh at my bad Spanish. And the food is wonderful!

Mexico City is a very interesting place to visit. It has some great museums and lots of fascinating old buildings. And the hotels are not too expensive. But you can stay in other places in Mexico. For example, you should go to one of the beach resorts — like Acapulco. And you shouldn't miss the Mayan temples near Merida.

1. **T F** Sam likes warm weather.

2. **T F** His Spanish is very good.

3. **T F** There's a lot to see and do on a vacation in Mexico.

4. **T F** The hotels in Mexico City are pretty expensive.

5. **T F** The Mayan temples are in Mexico City.

G Answer these questions about your hometown. Use complete sentences.

1. What's your hometown like? _____

_____

2. What's the weather like? _____

_____

3. When's a good time to visit? _____

_____

4. What can you do downtown? _____

_____

5. What should a visitor see there? _____

_____

6. What is one thing a visitor shouldn't miss? _____

_____

7. What can you buy there? _____

_____

H Read each set of sentences, and circle the one word that doesn't fit. Then write the correct word for it on the blank.

1. I feel terrible today. I have the flu and a headache. I know

   it's a good idea to get some bandages soon from the drugstore.   _____

2. You really have a bad cold! Everyone thinks that it's

   important for you to go to bed and get some stress.   _____

3. He picked up a very big suitcase yesterday, and now he has a

   bad backache. He should go to the dentist this morning.   _____

4. If you hurt your hand on something that's too hot, it's helpful to

   put the cough under cold water. Then put some ointment on it.   _____

I Look at each picture. Then circle the correct word for each description.

1. a (**bag** / **tube**) of cough drops
2. a (**can** / **bottle**) of aspirin
3. a (**tube** / **box**) of ointment
4. a (**bottle** / **box**) of bandages
5. a (**can** / **tube**) of sunburn spray

J Read each conversation. Check (✓) the correct response.

1. A: Well, what does your friend look like?
   B: ☐ No, he doesn't.   ☐ Yes, I do.   ☐ She's pretty short.

2. A: Would you like to do something tonight?
   B: ☐ No, I hate it!   ☐ Sure. I'd love to!   ☐ Yes, it's very expensive!

3. A: Does Paris have nice weather in the fall?
   B: ☐ Yes, it is.   ☐ It's not too bad.   ☐ Oh, really?

4. A: What can you do there?
   B: ☐ Sounds interesting. ☐ You should take a boat ride. ☐ No, you can't.

5. A: I have a terrible cold today.
   B: ☐ Oh, that's too bad!   ☐ Gee, that's great!   ☐ Here you are.

6. A: May I help you?
   B: ☐ It's excellent.   ☐ Could I have something for insomnia?   ☐ Try this lotion.

A 📀 Listening.

1. Listen to a waiter take an order in a restaurant. Fill in the restaurant check.

2. Listen to this telephone conversation. Complete the message form.

```
┌─────────────────────────────────────┐
│  🍔   RESTAURANT CHECK   🍔          │
│   🍾  1 ..............................│
│   🍾  1 large order of               │
│   🍦  .............................. │
│   ⚫  to drink:..................... │
│   ⚫  .............................. │
└─────────────────────────────────────┘
```

```
┌─────────────────────────────────────┐
│ Message  Donna called                │
│          The ........................│
│          is on ............... at ...│
│          It's in .....................│
│          Bring your .................│
│          .............................│
└─────────────────────────────────────┘
```

B Check (✓) the correct response.

1. I'm not in the mood for dessert.
   ☐ I can't either.
   ☐ So do I.
   ☐ Neither am I.

2. I'm crazy about spicy food!
   ☐ I am, too.
   ☐ Oh, I can't.
   ☐ Neither do I.

3. I like Mexican food a lot.
   ☐ So am I.
   ☐ I do, too.
   ☐ I'm not either.

4. I can't stand greasy food!
   ☐ Really? I am.
   ☐ I can, too.
   ☐ Oh, I love it!

C Circle the correct word.

1. What **(would / will)** you like to eat?

2. **(I'll / I'd)** have chocolate ice cream, please.

3. **(Would / Will)** you like anything else?

4. Yes, please. I'd **(like / have)** some water.

D Read Joanna's restaurant reviews. Then circle **T** (true) or **F** (false).

Two New Restaurants in Town

This week I tried two new restaurants – Michelle's and Anton's. They are both French restaurants downtown. Michelle's is a small place with about twenty tables. The waiters and waitresses are very friendly, and the service is excellent. I ordered chicken with orange sauce along with rice and a salad. Then I had chocolate cake and coffee. The chicken was delicious, but the cake was too dry. The meal cost about twenty dollars.

Anton's is a much bigger restaurant, and it was very crowded on that night. I waited twenty minutes for a table. Anton's is noisier than Michelle's, and the waiter was very slow with my meal. I ordered soup and a steak with fried potatoes and vegetables. The soup wasn't very hot. The steak was OK, but the vegetables weren't very good. For dessert, I had ice cream. The meal was really expensive – about forty-five dollars! Now you know why I would go to Michelle's again, but not to Anton's.

1. **T F** Joanna didn't have dessert at Michelle's.

2. **T F** Michelle's is smaller than Anton's.

3. **T F** The service was very good at Anton's.

4. **T F** She liked Michelle's restaurant better than Anton's.

E Circle the correct word.

1. There are lots of beautiful trees in the (**sea** / **forest** / **volcano**).

2. A (**desert** / **continent** / **hill**) is a very hot and dry place.

3. I love swimming in the (**waterfall** / **plateau** / **ocean**). I hate swimming in a pool.

4. A (**swamp** / **mountain** / **river**) is higher than a valley.

F Complete each sentence with the correct form of the adjective (for example, *smaller, more exciting, the biggest, the most beautiful*).

1. Is Rio _____ than Buenos Aires?   (**crowded**)

2. Which is _____ , the plains or the desert?   (**dry**)

3. Is Disneyland _____ amusement park in the world?   (**famous**)

4. California is _____ than France.   (**large**)

5. Which is _____ river in the world: the Nile, Amazon, or Danube?   (**long**)

G Read each conversation. Complete the question or response.

1. A: How _____ Australia from New Zealand?
   B: Oh, I think it's only about 1,200 miles away.

2. A: _____ is Angel Falls?
   B: It's 3,212 feet high.

3. A: How _____ Washington, D.C., in the summer?
   B: It gets up to about 32 degrees Celsius – that's around 90 degrees Fahrenheit.

4. A: _____ is the Mississippi River?
   B: It's about 3,740 miles long or 6,019 kilometers.

H Answer these questions about yourself. Write complete sentences.

1. Are you doing anything tomorrow night?

_____

2. What are you going to do tonight?

_____

3. Are you doing anything on Saturday? Would you like to see a movie?

_____

4. What are you going to do next week?

_____

I Circle the correct word or phrase.

1. Please (**tell** / **to tell**) Mary there's a school party on Saturday.

2. Would you ask Bill (**bring** / **to bring**) the concert tickets tonight?

3. Could you (**tell** / **ask**) her that the movie starts at 8:15 on Friday evening?

J Look at each message. Complete the request by using the name in parentheses.

1. The test on Thursday is at 1:00 P.M.

   Please tell _____ . (**Kim**)

2. Meet me after class today.

   Would you ask _____ ? (**Alex**)

3. There's a volleyball game tonight at six.

   Could you tell _____ ? (**Ann**)

4. Come to the picnic on Saturday.

   Please ask _____ . (**Mike**)

K How have you changed in the last five years? Write a short paragraph (about 3–5 sentences) describing some changes about yourself.

_____

_____

_____

_____

_____

_____

_____

L Answer these questions about your plans. Use complete sentences.

1. What are you going to do after this test today? _____

_____

2. Do you plan to take an English class again next term? _____

_____

3. Which other language would you like to learn? _____

_____

Test Audio Scripts

Test 1: Units 1–4

A Listen to Rosemary, Ken, and Yoko talking. Check the correct answers.

1.
ROSEMARY: Hi, Ken!
KEN: Hi, there, Rosemary! Good to see you again.
ROSEMARY: Yeah, I'm glad to see you, too. Uh, Ken, this is my new friend, Yoko Miyake. She's from Japan.
KEN: Hello, Yoko. Nice to meet you.
YOKO: Hi, Ken. It's good to meet you, too.
KEN: Um, I'm sorry, Yoko, but what was your last name, again?
YOKO: Oh, it's Miyake. M-I-Y-A-K-E.
KEN: Ah, Miya*ke* (pronounced "Mee-yah-KEH") . . . "keh" . . . *not* Miya*ki* (pronounced "Mee-yah-KEY") . . . . (*laughs*)
YOKO: (*laughs*) Yes, very good! That's right.

2.
KEN: Are you here on vacation, Yoko?
YOKO: No, I'm a student.
ROSEMARY: Yoko and I are in the same engineering class at the university.
KEN: Oh, really? That's great!
YOKO: Uh-huh. And what do you do, Ken? Are you a student, too?
KEN: No, I'm not. I work in a restaurant downtown.
YOKO: Oh? What do you do there?
KEN: I'm a chef.
YOKO: Wow, you're a chef! Gee, that sounds really interesting!

3.
ROSEMARY: By the way, there's a Bonnie Raitt concert this Friday night. Would both of you like to go with me?
KEN: Sure! I'd love to!
ROSEMARY: And Yoko, what about you? Do you like Bonnie Raitt? She sings country music along with the blues and rock.
YOKO: Yes, I do. I like her a lot, and I'd really like to see her in concert!
ROSEMARY: Good!
KEN: Yeah, that's great!

4.
YOKO: Uh, Rosemary, what time is the concert on Friday?
ROSEMARY: It's at eight o'clock.
YOKO: OK. That's fine. And how much are the tickets?
ROSEMARY: They're only twenty-four dollars each. What do you think?
KEN: Gee, twenty-four dollars each. I think that's very reasonable!
YOKO: Me, too. I don't think that's expensive at all.
ROSEMARY: All right. So let's meet at my house at seven o'clock on Friday, and we can go to the concert in my car. OK?
KEN: OK.
YOKO: Yes, that sounds great!

Test 2: Units 5–8

A Listen to people talking. Circle **T** for true or **F** for false.

1.
MAN: So tell me about your family, Peggy. How many brothers and sisters do you have?
PEGGY: Well, I have four sisters – Mary, Liz, Debbie, and Sue.
MAN: Oh, that's nice! And do you have any brothers?
PEGGY: Yes, I have four brothers – Dick, Ted, Sam, and Harry.

2.
WOMAN: How often do you exercise, Janet?
JANET: Well, I go jogging about three times a week.
WOMAN: Oh! Do you ever go to the gym to work out?
JANET: Yes. I usually go to the gym on Tuesdays, Thursdays, and Saturdays.
WOMAN: Wow! And how much time do you spend at the gym?
JANET: Oh, around three or four hours each time I go there.

3.
WOMAN: What did you do on the weekend, John?
JOHN: Well, I saw an action movie at the new movie theater in the mall. I went there with my girlfriend on Saturday.
WOMAN: And where did you go on Sunday?
JOHN: I went to the Laundromat, and then my parents invited me over for dinner at their house. We had a great barbecue.
WOMAN: Gee, you were pretty busy!
JOHN: Yeah. (*laughs*) I guess I was.

4.
WOMAN: Hi, good morning!
PETER: Hi. I'm your new neighbor, Peter Curtis. I just moved into the apartment building yesterday.
WOMAN: Oh, nice to meet you, Peter.
PETER: Uh, is there a post office near here? I have to mail some letters.
WOMAN: No, I'm sorry, there isn't one around here. But there's a mail box on the corner of First and Main Street. That's about five blocks from here.
PETER: OK. Thanks. Mmm. What's this neighborhood like, anyway? How much traffic and crime is there around here?
WOMAN: Oh, well, there isn't much. It's really pretty quiet in this neighborhood.

Test 3: Units 9–12

A Listen to people talking and check the correct information.

1.

MAN: Excuse me. I'm looking for someone. Her name is Sharon Beck.

WOMAN: Well, what does she look like?

MAN: Mmm, let's see. She's about twenty-five, I guess, and she's fairly short.

WOMAN: Look over there. Is she the one with the long black hair . . .

MAN: Huh? Where?

WOMAN: . . . who is sitting at the table next to the window?

MAN: Yes! There she is! Thanks a lot!

WOMAN: Oh, you're welcome.

MAN: *(walking away)* Hi, Sharon! Sorry I'm late. . . .

2.

WOMAN: Have you ever been to Paris, France?

MAN: Yes, I have. I went there last year in July.

WOMAN: How did you like it?

MAN: It's a wonderful city! I had really a great vacation there!

WOMAN: And what about this year? Have you taken a vacation yet?

MAN: No, I haven't, but I plan to go hiking in the mountains later this summer. Probably sometime in August.

WOMAN: Sounds good!

MAN: Yeah, I can't wait!

3.

FIRST MAN: Can you tell me a little about Spain?

SECOND MAN: Sure. What would you like to know?

FIRST MAN: Well, what's Barcelona like?

SECOND MAN: Oh, it's beautiful, and it's very exciting!

FIRST MAN: What should I see there?

SECOND MAN: You should visit some of the wonderful museums there, like Picasso's and Miro's. And you shouldn't miss the Ramblas; that's a very long street where you can walk and stop for a drink or a meal.

FIRST MAN: Sounds great! And when's a good time to visit?

SECOND MAN: Oh, I went there in June, and the weather was perfect then.

FIRST MAN: OK. Thanks a lot for the information.

SECOND MAN: Sure. My pleasure.

4.

DOCTOR: Have you ever had a backache like this before, Mr. Brown?

MR. BROWN: No, I haven't, doctor. I get a lot of exercise and I play lots of sports, but I've never had such a terrible backache. What should I do for it?

DOCTOR: Well, it's important to get a lot of rest.

MR. BROWN: Uh-huh. Um, I got a little extra sleep. And today I took some aspirin, but it really didn't help.

DOCTOR: Well, let's have a look at it.

MR. BROWN: OK. Thanks.

Test 4: Units 13–16

A Listening.

1. Listen to a waiter take an order in a restaurant. Fill in the restaurant check.

WAITER: May I take your order, please?

CUSTOMER: Yes, I'll have a hamburger.

WAITER: One hamburger. And would you like french fries with that?

CUSTOMER: Yes, please. Give me a large order of french fries.

WAITER: All right. One large order of fries. And how about a salad?

CUSTOMER: No, thanks, but I'd like a cup of coffee.

WAITER: OK. Would you like to have your coffee now or later?

CUSTOMER: I'd like it now, please.

WAITER: All right. Thank you very much.

CUSTOMER: OK. Thanks.

2. Listen to this telephone conversation. Complete the message form.

MAN: Hello?

DONNA: Hello. May I speak to David, please?

MAN: Sorry. He's out. Would you like to leave a message?

DONNA: Yes. This is Donna. I'm calling about the meeting. Would you tell him the meeting's on Friday evening at eight o'clock?

MAN: Sure. *(writing down the message)* Friday evening at eight P.M.

DONNA: And it's in Room 251 at the high school.

MAN: OK. Room two-five-one . . . at the high school. Uh-huh.

DONNA: And please ask him to bring his cassette recorder.

MAN: Bring your cassette recorder. OK, Donna, I'll give David your message.

DONNA: Thanks a lot.

MAN: You're welcome. Bye.

DONNA: Bye.

Test Answer Keys

Test 1: Units 1–4

A   [4 × 2 = 8]
1. Miyake   2. a chef   3. like   4. $24 each

B   [3 × 2 = 6]
Any logical and grammatically correct sentence is acceptable. For example:
1. My name is Charles Chang.
2. I'm from Hong Kong.
3. Well, everyone calls me Chuck.

C   [4 × 2 = 8]
1. B: Yes, <u>he is</u>. He's from Chicago.
2. A: <u>Are Mr. and Mrs. Sanchez Brazilian?</u>
3. B: No, <u>I'm not</u>. I'm in English 101.
4. A: <u>Is your first name Amy?</u>

D   [4 × 2 = 8]
1. T   2. T   3. F   4. F

E   [4 × 2 = 8]
1. do   2. does   3. go   4. does

F   [3 × 2 = 6]

Circled words	Written words
1. salesperson	flight attendant
2. receptionist	(tour) guide
3. bank	hospital

G   [3 × 2 = 6]
Any logical and grammatically correct paragraph with 3–5 sentences is acceptable. For example:
I get up at 7:00 in the morning on weekdays. Then I read the paper and have coffee. I go to work at 8:30. I have lunch around noon. After work, I go to school and study until 9:00 P.M.

H   [4 × 2 = 8]
1. It's   3. more attractive
2. they're   4. nicer

I   [4 × 2 = 8]
1. larger than   3. more expensive than
2. better than   4. prettier

J   [5 × 2 = 10]
1. A: <u>Do</u> you like California, Kenji?
   B: Yes, I <u>do</u>. I really like it.
2. A: <u>Does</u> John play the piano?
   B: Yes, he <u>does</u>.
3. A: What kind of music <u>do</u> they like?

K   [4 × 2 = 8]
1. her   2. them   3. him   4. it

L   [8 × 2 = 16]
Any logical and grammatically correct sentence is acceptable. For example:
1. I'm a student.
2. I go to UCLA Extension.
3. I drink coffee.
4. I usually get home at 5:00.
5. I clean the house.
6. I like game shows.
7. I like them a lot.
8. Yes, I'd like to, but I have to study.

Cross-reference Index: Units/Cycles and Areas Tested

Exercise	Items	Unit/Cycle	Areas tested
A	1	1	**Listening:** Spelling a person's last name
	2	2	**Listening:** A person's job
	3	4	**Listening:** People's likes and dislikes; making inferences
	4	3	**Listening:** Prices of tickets; numbers
B	1–3	1/1	**Grammar:** Wh-questions and statements with *be* **Function:** Introducing oneself **Topic:** Names
C	1–4	1/2	**Grammar:** Yes/No questions and short answers with *be*
D	1–4	1/1	**Reading:** Topic on names; true/false comprehension check
E	1–4	2/1	**Grammar:** Simple present Wh-questions and statements with *do*
F	1–3	2/1	**Vocabulary:** Jobs, workplaces, and job descriptions
G		2/2	**Grammar:** Time expressions **Writing:** Describing one's daily schedule or routine
H	1–2	3/1	**Grammar:** Demonstratives
	3–4	3/2	**Grammar:** Preferences; comparisons with adjectives
I	1–4	3/2	**Grammar:** Comparisons with adjectives
J	1–3	4/1	**Grammar:** Yes/No and Wh-questions with *do* and short responses
K	1–4	4/1	**Grammar:** Object pronouns
L	1–2	2/1	**Grammar:** Simple present Wh-question and statement **Function:** Talking about oneself
	3–5	2/2	**Grammar:** Time expressions **Function:** Describing one's schedule or routine
	6–7	4/1	**Grammar:** Wh-questions with *do* and short responses **Function:** Talking about likes and dislikes
	8	4/2	**Grammar:** *Would;* verb + *to* + verb **Function:** Responding to an invitation

Test 2: Units 5–8

A　　　　　　　　　　　　　　　[4 × 2 = 8]

1. T　　2. T　　3. F　　4. T

B　　　　　　　　　　　　　　　[4 × 2 = 8]

1. A: Are <u>you doing anything</u> this Sunday afternoon?
2. B: Yes, <u>she is.</u> She's coming to the picnic (tomorrow).
3. A: Where <u>are your parents going</u> this summer vacation?
4. B: <u>I'm playing tennis</u> on Friday morning. Do you want to play, too?

C　　　　　　　　　　　　　　　[4 × 2 = 8]

Any logical and grammatically correct sentence is acceptable. For example:

1. Not many/A few/Few Americans use public transportation to get to work.
2. In the U.S., most/many/a lot of divorced people get married again.
3. Some/Not many/A few/Few American mothers return to work one year after having a baby.
4. All/Nearly all/Most homes in the U.S. have at least one color TV set.

D　　　　　　　　　　　　　　　[5 × 2 = 10]

1. I <u>often</u> have eggs for breakfast.
2. Do you <u>ever</u> eat lunch at the cafeteria?
3. I <u>sometimes</u> watch TV in my free time. *(or)* <u>Sometimes</u> I watch TV in my free time.
4. What do you <u>usually</u> do on Saturday night?

E　　　　　　　　　　　　　　　[5 × 2 = 10]

1. How <u>often do you (usually)</u> exercise?
2. Do <u>you ever drive to school</u>?
3. What <u>do you usually do on the weekend</u>?
4. How <u>good are you</u> at tennis?
5. How <u>long do you</u> spend working out? *(or)* How <u>much time do you</u> spend working out?

F　　　　　　　　　　　　　　　[5 × 2 = 10]

I <u>had</u> a great day last Saturday. In the morning, my best friend and I <u>drove</u> to the City Museum where we <u>saw</u> a wonderful art exhibit. Then we <u>went</u> bicycling in the park all afternoon. What fun! After dinner, we <u>watched</u> an old movie on TV. It was really a wonderful day!

G　　　　　　　　　　　　　　　[5 × 2 = 10]

Any logical and grammatically correct sentence is acceptable. For example:

1. I stayed home and studied.
2. Yes, I did. I saw a good movie.
3. I went to Canada.
4. I was away for three weeks.
5. I was out last night with friends.

H　　　　　　　　　　　　　　　[5 × 2 = 10]

Any logical and grammatically correct sentence is acceptable. For example:

1. Yes, there is. There's one on the corner of Elm Avenue and Fox Street.
2. No, there aren't.
3. Yes, there are. There are some on Fox Street.
4. Yes, there is/are. There's one on Maple Avenue.
5. Yes, there is. There's one next to the bank on Elm Avenue.

I　　　　　　　　　　　　　　　[6 × 2 = 12]

Circled words	Written words
1. drugstore	laundromat
make	borrow *(or)* get
movies	food *(or)* groceries
2. work	haircut
banks	restaurants
drugstore	gym

J　　　　　　　　　　　　　　　[4 × 2 = 8]

Any logical and grammatically correct paragraph with 4–6 sentences is acceptable. For example:

I live in a big apartment building in the city. There's a lot of noise and traffic downtown. But there's isn't much crime. There are a lot of restaurants and shops. I really like the area a lot! It's a very exciting place.

K　　　　　　　　　　　　　　　[4 × 2 = 8]

1. F　　2. F　　3. F　　4. T

Cross-reference Index: Units/Cycles and Areas Tested

Exercise	Items	Unit/Cycle	Areas tested
A	1	5	**Listening:** Family members; numbers
	2	6	**Listening:** Leisure activities/routines; frequency
	3	7	**Listening:** Past weekend activities; places
	4	8	**Listening:** Neighborhoods
B	1–4	5/1	**Grammar:** Present continuous　**Topic:** Leisure time activities
C	1–4	5/2	**Grammar:** Determiners　**Function:** Describing statistics in general terms
D	1–4	6/1	**Grammar:** Adverbs of frequency　**Function:** Asking and talking about daily routines
E	1–3	6/1	**Grammar:** Adverbs of frequency　**Function:** Asking about routines and exercise
	4–5	6/2	**Grammar:** Questions with *how*　**Function:** Asking about exercise
F		7/1	**Grammar:** Past tense　**Function:** Describing a past event
G	1–3	7/1	**Grammar:** Past tense　**Function:** Describing weekend activities and a vacation
	4–5	7/2	**Grammar:** Past tense of *be*　**Function:** Describing a vacation and the night before
H	1–5	8/1	**Grammar:** *There is; there are; one, any, some*　**Function:** Describing locations of places
I	1–2	8/1	**Vocabulary:** Places and things to do there
J		8/2	**Grammar:** *How much* and *how many*　**Writing:** Describing one's neighborhood
K	1–4	8	**Reading:** Topic on cities; true/false comprehension check

Test 3: Units 9–12

A   [4 × 2 = 8]
1. She is fairly short and about twenty-five.
2. He had a great vacation in Paris last year in July.
3. You shouldn't miss some of the wonderful museums in Barcelona.
4. It's important to get some rest for a backache.

B   [7 × 2 = 14]
1. My sister is in her thirties. She has long blond hair, and she is medium height. She wears contact lenses.
2. My brother is pretty tall, and he has a beard and a mustache. He is twenty years old.

C   [2 × 2 = 4]
1. (circled) the man on the left
2. (circled) the woman on the left

D   [5 × 2 = 10]
1. B: No, they haven't. So they should eat lunch soon.
2. A: Has the movie started yet?
3. B: No, she hasn't, but I talked to her yesterday about it.
4. B: Yes, he has already seen it twice.
5. A: Have you ever studied French?

E   [5 × 2 = 10]
1. dirty   3. expensive   5. stressful
2. dangerous   4. boring

F   [5 × 2 = 10]
1. T   2. F   3. T   4. F   5. F

G   [7 × 2 = 14]
Any logical and grammatically correct sentence is acceptable. For example:
1. It's a fairly big city, but it's not too big.
2. It's pretty cold in the winter and hot in the summer.
3. Spring is a good time to visit my hometown.
4. You can visit the City Museum downtown.
5. A visitor should see the beautiful river near the park.
6. A visitor shouldn't miss the flea market on Saturday morning.
7. You can buy old clothes and interesting books.

H   [4 × 2 = 8]

Circled words	Written words
1. bandages	medicine (or) aspirin
2. stress	rest
3. dentist	doctor
4. cough	burn (or) hand

I   [5 × 2 = 10]
1. bag   3. tube   5. can
2. bottle   4. box

J   [6 × 2 = 12]
1. She's pretty short.
2. Sure. I'd love to!
3. It's not too bad.
4. You should take a boat ride.
5. Oh, that's too bad!
6. Could I have something for insomnia?

Cross-reference Index: Units/Cycles and Areas Tested

Exercise	Items	Unit/Cycle	Areas tested
A	1	9	**Listening:** A person's general appearance and age
	2	10	**Listening:** Vacations, cities, times during the year
	3	11	**Listening:** Description of a country and city
	4	12	**Listening:** Health remedies
B	1–2	9/1	**Grammar:** Statements for describing people
C	1–2	9/2	**Grammar:** Modifiers with participles and prepositions **Function:** Matching peoples' pictures with descriptions
D	1–3	10/1	**Grammar:** Present perfect; *already, yet*
	4–5	10/2	**Grammar:** Present perfect and past tense; *ever*
E	1–5	11/1	**Vocabulary:** Adjectives to describe places and things
F	1–5	11/1	**Reading:** Topic on a vacation in Mexico; true/false comprehension check
G	1–3	11/1	**Grammar:** Adverbs and adjectives; conjunctions **Writing:** Describing one's hometown
	4–7	11/2	**Grammar:** Modal verbs *can* and *should* **Writing:** Giving suggestions on what to do in one's hometown
H	1–4	12	**Vocabulary:** Health-related words
I	1–5	12/2	**Vocabulary:** Containers and medicines
J	1	9/1	**Grammar:** Questions for describing people and responses
	2	10/1	**Function:** Inviting someone out; responding to an invitation
	3	11/1	**Function:** Talking about the weather
	4	11/2	**Grammar:** Modal verb *can*
	5	12/1	**Function:** Talking about health problems and responding
	6	12/2	**Grammar:** Modal verb *may* for requests

Test 4: Units 13–16

A [8 × 2 = 16]

1. Restaurant Check:
   1 <u>hamburger</u>
   1 large order of <u>french fries</u>
   to drink: <u>(a cup of) coffee</u>

2. Message: Donna called. The <u>meeting</u> is on <u>Friday evening</u> at <u>8:00 (P.M.)</u>. It's in <u>Room 251 at the high school</u>. Bring your <u>cassette recorder</u>.

B [4 × 2 = 8]

1. Neither am I.
2. I am, too.
3. I do, too.
4. Oh, I love it!

C [4 × 2 = 8]

1. would
2. I'll
3. Would
4. like

D [4 × 2 = 8]

1. F   2. T   3. F   4. T

E [4 × 2 = 8]

1. forest   2. desert   3. ocean   4. mountain

F [5 × 2 = 10]

1. more crowded
2. drier
3. the most famous
4. larger
5. the longest

G [4 × 2 = 8]

1. How <u>far is</u> Australia from New Zealand?
2. <u>How high</u> is Angel Falls?
3. How <u>hot is</u> Washington, D.C., in the summer?
4. <u>How long</u> is the Mississippi River?

H [4 × 2 = 8]

Any logical and grammatically correct sentence is acceptable. For example:

1. Yes, I am. I'm going to a concert (tomorrow night).
2. I'm going to work late (tonight).
3. No, I'm not (doing anything on Saturday). Sure, I'd love to (see a movie)!
4. I'm going to visit my friend (next week).

I [3 × 2 = 6]

1. tell   2. to bring   3. tell

J [4 × 2 = 8]

1. Please tell <u>Kim (that) the test on Thursday is at 1:00 P.M.</u>
2. Would you ask <u>Alex to meet me after class today?</u>
3. Could you tell <u>Ann (that) there's a volleyball game tonight at six?</u>
4. Please ask <u>Mike to come to the picnic on Saturday.</u>

K [3 × 2 = 6]

Any logical and grammatically correct paragraph with 3–5 sentences is acceptable. For example:

I've changed a lot in the last five years. I got married, and I've lost weight. My husband and I moved to a new town. I got a new job there. I work as a secretary in an international trading company. So I think my English is better now.

L [3 × 2 = 6]

Any logical and grammatically correct sentence is acceptable. For example:

1. I'm going to go out to dinner with my friend.
2. Yes, I do. I'd like to take English 102 next term.
3. I'd love to learn Italian. I'd like to go to Italy someday.

Cross-reference Index: Units/Cycles and Areas Tested

Exercise	Items	Unit/Cycle	Areas tested
A	1	13/1	**Listening:** A meal in a restaurant; writing down an order
	2	15/2	**Listening:** A telephone message; writing down a message
B	1–4	13/1	**Grammar:** *So, too, neither, either* **Function:** Agreeing and disagreeing
C	1–4	13/2	**Grammar:** Modal verbs *would* and *will* for requests
D	1–4	13	**Reading:** Topic on restaurant reviews; true/false comprehension check
E	1–4	14/1	**Vocabulary:** Geography words
F	1–5	14/1	**Grammar:** Comparisons with adjectives **Function:** Making comparisons
G	1–4	14/2	**Grammar:** Questions with *how* **Function:** Talking about distance and measurement
H	1–4	15/1	**Grammar:** Future with present continuous and *be going to* **Function:** Talking about plans
I	1–3	15/2	**Grammar:** *Tell* and *ask*
J	1–4	15/2	**Grammar:** *Tell* and *ask* **Function:** Giving messages
K		16/1	**Grammar:** Describing changes (with the present tense, the comparative, the past tense, the present perfect) **Writing:** Describing changes about one's life
L	1–3	16/2	**Grammar:** Verb + infinitive **Function:** Describing future plans

Workbook Answer Key

1 Please call me Chuck.

Exercise 1
Answers will vary.

Exercise 2

A

2. M James	5. M Robert	8. F Jennifer
3. F Catherine	6. F Susan	
4. F Elizabeth	7. M William	

B

b. 3 Kate	d. 2 Jim	f. 1 Joe	h. 7 Bill
c. 8 Jenny	e. 4 Liz	g. 6 Sue	

C

2. Kate
3. Michael Charles Kennedy
4. Smith

Exercise 3
2. A: My name is Jim Holmes.
   B: <u>Nice to meet you, Mr. Holmes.</u>
3. A: This is Jenny Parker.
   B: <u>Nice to meet you, Ms. Parker.</u>
4. A: Hello, I'm William Dean. Please call me Bill.
   B: <u>Pleased to meet you, Bill.</u>
5. A: Excuse me, what's your name again?
   B: <u>Joe King.</u>
6. A: How do you spell your first name?
   B: <u>C-H-A-R-L-E-N-E.</u>

Exercise 4
2. JIM: <u>What's your last name?</u>
   BOB: My last name's Hayes.
3. JIM: Who<u>'s that?</u>
   BOB: That's my wife.
4. JIM: What<u>'s her name?</u>
   BOB: Her name is Rosa.
5. JIM: Where<u>'s she from?</u>
   BOB: She's from Mexico.
6. JIM: Who <u>are they?</u>
   BOB: They're my wife's parents.

Exercise 5
2. We're students. <u>Our</u> classroom number is 108-C.
3. Excuse me. What's <u>your</u> last name again?
4. That's Mr. Kim. <u>He</u> is in my class.
5. <u>My</u> name is Elizabeth. Please call me Liz.
6. This is Paul's wife. <u>Her</u> name is Jennifer.
7. My parents are on vacation. <u>They</u> are in South Korea.
8. I'm from Venice, Italy. <u>It</u> is a beautiful city.

Exercise 6
AMY: Oh, they <u>are</u> on the volleyball team. Let me introduce you. Hi, Surachai, this <u>is</u> Lisa Neil.
SURACHAI: Pleased to meet you, Lisa.
LISA: Nice to meet you, too, Surachai. Where <u>are</u> you from?
SURACHAI: I <u>am</u> from Thailand.
AMY: And this <u>is</u> Mario. He <u>is</u> from Brazil.

LISA: Hi, Mario.
Pablo: And my name <u>is</u> Pablo. I <u>am</u> from Colombia.

Exercise 7

A
Answers will vary.

B
(*Note: Words in italics were given as examples.*)

Name	Where from?	Languages	Sports?
1. *Mario*	Cali, Colombia	Spanish and French	volleyball
2. Eileen	*Mozambique, Africa*	Swahili and Portuguese	
3. Su Yin	Taiwan	*Mandarin Chinese and English*	volleyball
4. Ahmed	Luxor, Egypt	Arabic and English	*baseball*

Exercise 8
SARAH: Pretty good, thanks. Are you a student here?
RICH: <u>No, I'm not. I'm on vacation. Are you a student?</u>
SARAH: Yes, I am.
RICH: <u>And what are you studying?</u>
SARAH: I'm studying Spanish.
RICH: <u>Oh, really? Is Susan Miller in your class?</u>
SARAH: Yes, she is. Is she your friend?
RICH: <u>No, she's not. She's my sister!</u>

Exercise 9
TINA: Hi. <u>I'm</u> Tina Fernandez.
AMY: Are you from South America, Tina?
TINA: Yes, <u>I am.</u> I'm from Argentina.
   Where are you and your sister from, Alex?
ALEX: <u>We're</u> from Taiwan.
TINA: Are you from Taipei?
ALEX: No, <u>we're not. We're</u> from Tainan.
   Say, are you in English 101?
TINA: No, <u>I'm not.</u> I'm in English 102.

Exercise 10
2. A: <u>Are you from Spain?</u>
   B: No, we're not from Spain. We're from Mexico.
3. A: <u>Are they on the same baseball team?</u>
   B: No, they're not on the same baseball team. They're on the same volleyball team.
4. A: <u>Are Kim and Mika in your class?</u>
   B: Yes, Kim and Mika are in my class.
5. A: <u>Is it a nice class?</u>
   B: Yes, it's a nice class.
6. A: <u>Is your teacher Mr. Brown?</u>
   B: No, my teacher isn't Mr. Brown. I'm in Ms. West's class.

Exercise 11
1. How are you?	Saying "hello"
2. See you later.	Saying "goodbye"
3. Take care.	Saying "goodbye"
4. How's everything?	Saying "hello"
5. Good evening.	Saying "hello"
6. Good night.	Saying "goodbye"

Exercise 12
Answers will vary.

How do you spend your day?

Exercise 1
2. disc jockey
3. word processor
4. police officer
5. security guard
6. tour guide

Exercise 2
2. *She* works in a travel agency and takes people on tours. She's a tour guide.
3. *He* works in an office. He's a word processor. He likes computers a lot.
4. *She's* a disc jockey. She works in a night club. She plays music.

Exercise 3
2. She works for <u>a</u> travel company and arranges tours. She's <u>a</u> travel agent.
3. He has <u>an</u> interesting job. He's <u>a</u> teacher. He works in <u>a</u> high school.
4. She's <u>an</u> architect. She works for <u>a</u> large company. She builds houses. It's <u>a</u> great job.
5. She works with computers in <u>an</u> office. She's <u>a</u> word processor. She's also <u>a</u> part-time student. She takes <u>an</u> English class in the evening.

Exercise 4
TOM: What <u>*does*</u> your husband <u>do</u> exactly?
LIZ: He <u>works</u> for a department store. He's a store manager.
TOM: How <u>does</u> he <u>like</u> it?
LIZ: It's an interesting job. He <u>likes</u> it very much. But he <u>works</u> long hours. And what <u>do</u> you <u>do</u>?
TOM: I'm a student. I <u>study</u> architecture.
LIZ: Oh, really? Where <u>do</u> you <u>go</u> to school?
TOM: I <u>go</u> to Lincoln University. My wife, Jenny, <u>goes</u> there, too.
LIZ: Really? And what <u>does</u> she <u>study</u>?
TOM: She <u>studies</u> hotel management.
LIZ: That sounds interesting.

Exercise 5
VICTOR: I work for American Express.
MARK: And what <u>do you do</u> there?
VICTOR: I'm in management.
MARK: How <u>do you like it</u>?
VICTOR: It's a great job. And what <u>do you do</u>?
MARK: I'm a salesperson.
VICTOR: Really? What <u>do you sell</u>?
MARK: I sell computers. Do you want to buy one?

Exercise 6
1. *He*'s a chef.
2. He makes TV programs about Chinese cooking.
3. *She* finishes at eight or nine o'clock in the evening.
4. She's an electrician.

Exercise 7
Answers will vary. Possible answers:
2. Where does he work?
3. What does he do exactly?
4. How does he like his job?

Exercise 8
Everyone knows Pat at the hospital. Pat is a part-time night nurse. He cares for patients at night. <u>*On*</u> Saturdays and Sundays, Pat sleeps most of the day and wakes up a little <u>before</u> nine <u>in</u> the evening, usually at 8:45 or 8:50. He has breakfast very late, <u>around</u> 9:30 or 10:00 P.M.! He watches television <u>until</u> eleven o'clock, and then starts work <u>at</u> midnight. <u>Early</u> in the morning, usually around 5 P.M., he leaves work, has a little snack, goes home, goes to bed, and sleeps <u>late</u>. It's a hard schedule, but he loves his work.

Exercise 9

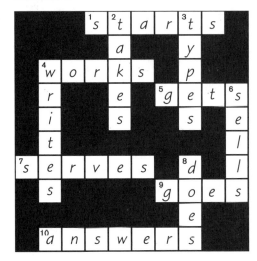

Exercise 10
2. What does he do?
3. She serves food in a restaurant.
4. He goes to the university.
5. She stays up late.
6. He works part time.

Exercise 11
1. New York Hospital needs *nurses*. Work during the day or <u>at night</u>, weekdays or <u>weekends</u>, full time or <u>part time</u>. Call 278-1191.
2. <u>Interesting</u> job for language student. Mornings only. Take people on <u>tours</u>. Need good English and Spanish. Call 989-3239.
3. No need to work <u>long hours</u>! Only work from 6:00 <u>until</u> 11:00 four evenings a week. Our <u>restaurant</u> serves great food! Work as our <u>manager</u>. Call 735-6845.

3 How much is it?

Exercise 1

SAM: The light blue ones over there. They're nice.
REBECCA: Yes. But I don't really like light blue!
SAM: Hmm. Well, what about that sweater? It's perfect for you.
REBECCA: Which one?
SAM: This red one.
REBECCA: Well, I like it, but it's expensive.
SAM: Hey, let me buy it for you. It's a present!
REBECCA: Oh, Sam. Thank you very much.

Exercise 2

2. A: How much are those bracelets?
   B: They're $29.
3. A: How much are these shoes?
   B: They're $64.
4. A: How much is that dog?
   B: That's my dog, and he's not for sale!

Exercise 3

1. *backpacks*
2. bookshelves
3. dresses
4. companies
5. gloves
6. hairbrushes
7. necklaces
8. rings
9. scarves
10. sweaters
11. ties
12. dishes

Exercise 4

Answers will vary. Possible answers:

2. That's cheap.
3. That's pretty expensive!
4. That's reasonable.
5. That's not bad.
6. That's cheap.

Exercise 5

1. CLERK: It's $195.
   LUIS: And how much is that one?
   CLERK: It's $255.
   LUIS: Oh, really? Well, thanks, anyway.

2. KIM: Excuse me. How much are those jeans?
   CLERK: They're only $59.
   KIM: And how much is this sweater?
   CLERK: Which one? They're all different.
   KIM: I like this green one.
   CLERK: It's $34.
   KIM: Well, that's not bad.

3. SONIA: I like those sunglasses over there.
   CLERK: Which ones?
   SONIA: The small brown ones.
   CLERK: They're $199.
   SONIA: Oh, they're expensive!

Exercise 6

Cotton	Gold	Leather	Silk	Plastic	Wool
pants	bracelet	boots	pants	boots	pants
gloves	ring	pants	gloves	bracelet	gloves
shirt	necklace	gloves	shirt	ring	shirt
jacket		jacket	jacket	necklace	jacket

Exercise 7

1. A: These cotton gloves are nice.
   B: Yes, but the leather ones are *nicer*.
   A: They're also more expensive.

2. A: Those silk jackets look more attractive than the wool ones.
   B: Yes, but the wool ones are warmer.

3. A: This purple shirt is an interesting color!
   B: Yes, but the color is prettier than the design.
   A: The design isn't bad.
   B: I think the design on that red shirt is better than the design on this purple one.

4. A: Hey, look at this gold ring! It's nice. And it's cheaper than that silver ring.
   B: But it's smaller than the silver one.
   A: Well, yeah. The silver one is bigger than the gold one. But look at the price tag. One thousand dollars is a lot of money for a ring!

Exercise 8

Clothing	Electronics	Jewelry
cap	computer	bracelet
dress	compact disc player	earrings
athletic shoes	television	necklace
sweater	laptop computer	ring

Exercise 9

Answers will vary. Possible answers:

2. Which cap do you like more, the wool one or the leather one?
   I like the wool one more. *or* I like the leather one more.

3. Which ones do you like more, the high-tops or the tennis shoes?
   I like the high-tops more. *or* I like the tennis shoes more.

4. Which one do you prefer, the laptop computer or the desktop computer?
   I prefer the laptop computer. *or* I prefer the desktop computer.

5. Which television do you like better, the 19-inch one or the 25-inch one?
   I like the 19-inch one better. *or* I like the 25-inch one better.

Exercise 10

A

1. d	3. a
2. c	4. b

B

1. False	3. True
2. True	4. True

C

Answers will vary.

Do you like jazz?

Exercise 1
Answers will vary.

Exercise 2
Answers will vary. Possible answers:
2. Do you like Tom Cruise? Yes, I do. I love <u>him</u>.
3. Do you like rap? No, I don't. I can't stand <u>it</u>.
4. Do you like Demi Moore? Yes, I do. I like <u>her</u> a lot.
5. Do you like TV game shows? No, I don't. I can't stand <u>them</u>.
6. Do you like soap operas? No, I don't. I don't like <u>them</u> very much.

Exercise 3
1. Mariah Carey is <u>a pop singer.</u>
2. The Rolling Stones are <u>a rock group.</u>
3. Oprah Winfrey is a <u>TV talk show host.</u>
4. Bruce Willis is <u>an actor.</u>

Exercise 4
1. SARAH: Yes, I <u>like</u> it a lot. I'm a real fan of Garth Brooks.
   ED: Oh, <u>does</u> he play the guitar?
   SARAH: Yes, he <u>does</u>. He's my favorite musician.
2. ANNE: <u>What</u> kind of music <u>do</u> your parents <u>like</u>, Jason?
   JASON: They <u>like</u> classical music.
   ANNE: Who <u>do</u> they <u>like</u>? Mozart?
   JASON: No, they <u>don't</u> like him very much. They prefer Beethoven.
3. SCOTT: Teresa, <u>do</u> you <u>like</u> Mariah Carey?
   TERESA: No, I <u>don't</u>. I can't stand her. I like Celine Dion.
   SCOTT: I don't know her. What kind of music <u>does</u> she sing?
   TERESA: She <u>sings</u> pop songs. She's really great!

Exercise 5
Answers will vary.   Possible answers:
1. <u>*What kinds*</u> of movies   I like comedies and
   do you like?   musicals.
2. <u>What</u> is your   My favorite movie is
   favorite movie?   *Star Wars*.
3. <u>What kind/kinds</u> of TV   I like game shows.
   shows do you like?
4. <u>Who</u> is your favorite   My favorite TV actor is
   TV actor or actress?   Michael J. Fox.
5. <u>What</u> is your favorite My favorite song is
   song?   "Let It Be."
6. <u>Who</u> is your favorite   My favorite rock group is
   rock group?   U2.

Exercise 6
Answers will vary. Possible answers:
2. Which movies are more interesting, thrillers or science fiction films?
   <u>Science fiction films are more interesting than thrillers.</u>
3. Which films are scarier, horror films or thrillers?
   <u>Horror films are scarier than thrillers.</u>
4. Which films are more exciting, comedies or thrillers?
   <u>Thrillers are more exciting than comedies.</u>

Exercise 7
A

play	listen to	watch
the piano	jazz	videos
the guitar	music	TV
the trumpet	CDs	a film

B
Answers will vary.

Exercise 8
A
1. Then and Now
2. A Question of $1 Million
3. The Best Man Wins

B
1. science fiction
2. comedy
3. western

Exercise 9
2. A: Do you like gospel music?
   B. <u>I can't stand it.</u>
3. A: There's a baseball game tonight.
   B. <u>Great. Let's go.</u>
4. A: What do you think of Tina Turner?
   B: <u>I'm not a real fan of hers.</u>

Exercise 10
A
1. No
2. Yes
3. Yes
4. No
5. Yes

B
Answers will vary.

Exercise 11
1. KATE: Yes, I do. <u>I like</u> it a lot.
   ROBIN: There's a concert on Friday. <u>Would you like</u> to go with me?
   KATE: Yes, <u>I'd love to</u>. Thanks.
2. CARLOS: <u>Would you like</u> to go to a French film at 11:00 tonight?
   PHIL: <u>I'd like to</u>, but I have to study tonight.
   CARLOS: Well, <u>do you like</u> Brazilian films?
   PHIL: Yes, I <u>do</u>. I love them!
   CARLOS: There's a great Brazilian movie on TV tomorrow. <u>Would you like</u> to watch it with me?
   PHIL: <u>I'd love to</u>. Thanks.

Exercise 12
2. Richard can't stand classical music.
3. I love horror films!
4. She's not a fan of country music.
5. Would you like to go to a baseball game?

5 Tell me about your family.

Exercise 1

Male	Female
brother	*aunt*
father	daughter
husband	mother
nephew	niece
son	sister
uncle	wife

Exercise 2

DON: No, I'm not. My brother and sister <u>are staying</u> with me right now.
We go to bed after midnight every night.

JOEL: Really? What <u>are they doing</u> this summer? <u>Are they taking</u> classes, too?

DON: No, they aren't. My brother is on vacation now, but he <u>is looking</u> for a part-time job here.

JOEL: What about your sister? <u>Is she working</u>?

DON: Yes, she is. She has a part-time job at the university. What about you, Joel?
Are you in school this summer?

JOEL: Yes, I am. <u>I'm studying</u> two languages.

DON: Oh, <u>are you taking</u> French and Spanish again?

JOEL: Well, I'm taking Spanish again, but <u>I'm starting</u> Japanese.

DON: Really? That's exciting!

Exercise 3

2. *Peter is* Liz's husband.
3. I'm not married.
4. We have a son and (a) daughter.
5. My father-in-law is a painter.
6. Michael is looking for a job right now.

Exercise 4

CHRIS: Wow! Do you like it?
PHILIP: <u>Yes, I do. I like it a lot.</u>
CHRIS: And is your brother still working in Hong Kong?
PHILIP: <u>Yes, he is. He loves it.</u>
CHRIS: And how about your parents? Are they still living in Florida?
PHILIP: <u>No, they aren't. They're living in New York these days.</u> How about you and your family, Chris? Are you still living here?
CHRIS: <u>Yes, we are. We really love San Francisco.</u>

Exercise 5

1. This is my aunt Barbara. *She lives* in Rome, but <u>she's visiting</u> Chile this summer. <u>She has</u> a summer house there.
2. And these are my parents. <u>They work</u> in London, but <u>they're visiting</u> my aunt in Chile this month.
3. And here you can see my grandparents. <u>They live</u> in New York, but <u>they're staying</u> at my parents' house in London now.
4. This is my brother-in-law, Edward. <u>He wants</u> to be a company director. <u>He's studying</u> business in Canada right now.

5. And this is my niece, Christina. <u>She goes</u> *or* <u>She's going</u> to high school. <u>She likes</u> mathematics, but she doesn't like English.
6. And you <u>know</u> this person, of course. It's me.

Exercise 6

A

Answers will vary.

B

1. False: Many college students live in university housing.
2. True
3. False: Few young people in the United States live with their parents.
4. False: Nearly all university students live with their parents.
5. True
6. False: (Rents in the city are very expensive.) Many young people continue to live with their parents after they marry.

Exercise 7

1. *all*
2. nearly all
3. most
4. many
5. a lot of
6. some
7. not many
8. a few
9. few
10. no

Exercise 8

1. *Many children start school before the age of 5.* All children go to school after the age of five.
2. Nearly all young people get a job after they finish high school.
Only a few go to college.
3. Not many people over 65 have part-time jobs.
Few people like to travel abroad.
Many people over 65 like to stay with their grandchildren.

Exercise 9

In my country, some <u>couples</u> get married fairly young. Not many marriages <u>break up</u>, and nearly all <u>divorced</u> people remarry.
Elderly couples often <u>live at home</u> and take care of their grandchildren.

Exercise 10

Answers will vary.

How often do you exercise?

Exercise 1

Team sports	Individual sports	Exercise
basketball	swimming	yoga
baseball	jogging	swimming
football	bicycling	jogging
	tennis	aerobics
		bicycling
		tennis

Exercise 2

2. They hardly ever play tennis.
3. How often do you go jogging?
4. We often do yoga on Sunday mornings.
5. Does Charlie ever do aerobics?
6. What do you usually do on Saturdays?

Exercise 3

2. A: <u>What do you usually do?</u>
   B: Well, I usually do karate on Saturdays and yoga on Sundays.
3. A: <u>Do you ever go to the gym after work?</u>
   B: No, I never go to the gym after work.
4. A: <u>How often do you exercise?</u>
   B: I don't exercise very often at all.
5. A: <u>Do you ever play sports (on weekends)?</u>
   B: Yes, I sometimes play sports on weekends – usually baseball.
6. A: <u>What do you usually do in your free time?</u>
   B: I usually play tennis in my free time.

Exercise 4

A

Answers will vary.

B

Answers will vary.

Exercise 5

JERRY: I always go jogging <u>at</u> seven o'clock. How about you, Susan?
SUSAN: I usually go jogging <u>around</u> noon. I jog <u>for</u> about an hour.
JERRY: And do you also play sports <u>in</u> your free time?
SUSAN: Not very often. I usually go out <u>with</u> my classmates in my free time. What about you?
JERRY: I go to the gym <u>on</u> Mondays and Wednesdays. And sometimes I go bicycling <u>on</u> weekends.
SUSAN: Wow! You really like to stay in shape.

Exercise 6

Crossword puzzle:
4 (across) exercise
6 (across) do
7 (across) shape
8 (across) training
10 (across) jogging
1 (down) fitness
2 (down) fitness
3 (down) aerobics
5 (down) football
9 (down) goes

Exercise 7

B

	Hiking Club	Adult Education Program	YWCA/ YMCA
1. play indoor sports			✓
2. do outdoor activities	✓		
3. take evening classes		✓	
4. go dancing			✓
5. learn to cook		✓	
6. meet new people	✓	✓	✓

Exercise 8

2. A: How long do you spend in the swimming pool?
   B: <u>About 45 minutes.</u>
3. A: And how well do you swim?
   B: <u>I'm about average.</u>
4. A: How good are you at other sports?
   B: <u>Not too good, actually.</u>
5. A: How much time do you spend working out?
   B: <u>Around an hour a day.</u>

Exercise 9

2. A: <u>How often do you go</u> for a walk?
   B: Almost every day. I really enjoy it.
3. A: <u>How much time do you spend jogging?</u> *or* <u>How long do you spend</u> jogging?
   B: I spend about an hour jogging.
4. A: <u>How good are you</u> at racquetball?
   B: I'm pretty good at it. I'm on the school team.
5. A: <u>How well do you play basketball?</u>
   B: Basketball? Pretty well, I guess. I like it a lot.

Exercise 10

2. Tom doesn't exercise very often.
3. Philip tries to stay in shape.
4. Jill often works out at the gym.
5. How much time do you spend at the gym?
6. How well do you play tennis?

Exercise 11

Answers will vary.

We had a great time!

Exercise 1

A

2. enjoyed   5. studied   8. washed
3. invited   6. tried   9. watched
4. loved   7. visited

B

2. give   6. spend
3. meet   7. take
4. see   8. go
5. sleep

C

Answers will vary.

Exercise 2

2. Who did you meet at the party?
   I met someone very interesting.

3. What time did you and Eva get home?
   We got home a little after 1:00.

4. How did you and Bob like the art exhibition?
   We liked the art exhibition a lot.

5. What did you buy?
   I *or* We bought the new Madonna CD.

6. Where did Jeff and Joyce go on vacation?
   They went to the country (on vacation).

Exercise 3

Answers will vary.

Exercise 4

A: What did you do?
B: Well, on Saturday, we went shopping.
A: And did you do anything special in the evening?
B: No, nothing special.
A: Where did you go on Sunday?
B: We went to the amusement park.
A: How did you like it ?
B: We had a great time. In fact, we stayed there all day.
A: Really? What time did you get home?
B: We got home very late, around midnight.

Exercise 5

2. A: I stayed home from work yesterday. Did you take the day off, too?
   B: No, I didn't take the day *or* yesterday off. I worked all day until six o'clock.

3. A: I slept in all weekend. Did you spend the weekend at home?
   B: No, I didn't spend the weekend at home. I went out with friends.

4. A: I studied all weekend. Did you and John have a lot of homework, too?
   B: No, we didn't have a lot of homework. We finished our homework on Saturday.

5. A: Carl drove me to work this morning. Did you drive to work?
   B: No, I didn't drive to work. I took the bus.

6. A: Kathy went to the baseball game last night. Did you and Bob go to the game?
   B: No, we didn't go to the game. We watched it on TV.

Exercise 6

2. d. He took a day off.
3. e. He did housework.
4. c. He didn't do laundry.
5. a. He had people over.
6. b. He had a good time.

Exercise 7

A

Answers will vary.

C

	William	Sue
1. visited Thailand for the first time.	✓	✓
2. stayed for two days in Bangkok		✓
3. visited the floating market	✓	✓
4. bought food in Bangkok		✓
5. saw some historic ruins		✓
6. took a trip on the river	✓	
7. loved the food the most	✓	
8. enjoyed everything		✓

Exercise 8

B: It was great. I really enjoyed it.
A: How long were you there?
B: We were there for two weeks.
A: Were you in Lima all the time?
B: No, we weren't. We were in the mountains for a few days.
A: And how was the weather? Was it good?
B: No, it wasn't good at all. The city was very hot, and the mountains were really cold!

Exercise 9

B: It was a great trip. I really enjoyed South Africa and Namibia.
A: How long were you in South Africa?
B: For ten days.
A: And how long were you in Namibia?
B: I was in Namibia for about five days.
A: Wow, that's a long time. How was the weather?
B: It was hot and sunny the whole time.
A: And how did you like it?
B: Oh, it was wonderful. And the wildlife was terrific – we saw some meerkats!

Exercise 10

1. The neighbors had a noisy party till 3:00 A.M. We complained about it.

2. We didn't see very much in the mountains. The weather was foggy.

3. We went on a tour of the ruins.

4. I worked very hard in Switzerland. I was there on business.

Exercise 11

A

Answers will vary.

B

Answers will vary.

What does he look like?

Exercise 1
2. light
3. young
4. short
5. tall

Exercise 2

A
2. fairly long
3. good-looking
4. medium height
5. middle aged

B
2. A: How long is his hair?
   B: It's fairly long.
3. A: What color is his hair?
   B: It's dark brown.
4. A: How old is he?
   B: He's middle aged.
5. A: How tall is he?
   B: He's medium height.

Exercise 3
JIM: And how long is her hair?
STEVE: It's medium length.
JIM: How tall is she?
STEVE: She's fairly tall.
JIM: And how old is she?
STEVE: She's in her early twenties.
JIM: Does she wear glasses?
STEVE: Sometimes. I think she's wearing them now.
JIM: OK. I think I see her over there.

Exercise 4
Answers will vary.

Exercise 5
1. This man is in his late forties. He's pretty tall. He has a black mustache, and he's bald. He's wearing a dark shirt and jeans.

   He isn't bald. He has short, curly hair.
2. This woman is about 25. She's very pretty. She's medium height. Her hair is long and blond. She's wearing a black sweater and tennis shoes. She's standing next to her motorcycle.

   She isn't wearing tennis shoes. She's wearing boots. She isn't standing next to her motorcycle. She's sitting on her motorcycle.
3. This woman is in her early twenties. She's pretty serious looking. She has glasses and straight blond hair. She's fairly tall, and she's wearing a good-looking skirt and blouse.

   She doesn't have glasses. She doesn't have straight blond hair. She has curly black hair.

Exercise 6

Formal	Casual
blouse	boots
dress	jeans
scarf	shorts
shirt	running shoes
suit	T-shirt
tie	cap

Exercise 7
2. Edward and Kate are the ones wearing sunglasses.
3. Mandy is the tall woman carrying a jacket.
4. Alice is the woman talking to the man.
5. Giorgio is the one standing next to Alice.

Exercise 8
Possible answers:
2. A: Which one is Carlos?
   B: He's the one behind the couch.
3. A: Which ones are Dan and Cindy?
   B: They're the ones next to Maria.
4. A: Which one is Angela?
   B: She's the one on the couch.
5. A: Who's Kim?
   B: He's the one with short black hair.

Exercise 9
2. A: Which ones are the teachers?
      Who are the teachers?
   B: They're the ones on the couch.
      They're the ones sitting on the couch.
3. A: Which one is Larry?
      Who is Larry?
   B: He's the guy wearing the coat.
      He's the guy in the coat.

Exercise 10
There's a good-looking middle-aged woman walking her dog, and a young guy talking on the phone. Two people are standing next to him. Hey! The one wearing a baseball hat is my classmate! Some people are waiting at the bus stop. A serious-looking woman is asking for directions. And hey, here comes a really cute woman carrying a backpack. Wait a minute! I know her. That's my old girlfriend. I have to go now! Bye.

Exercise 11
2. A: Who's Sam?
   B: The handsome guy near the door.
3. A: Is she the one on the couch?
   B: That's right.
4. A: How tall is she?
   B: Pretty short.

Have you ever ridden a camel?

Exercise 1
2. e. called
3. b. done
4. j. eaten
5. a. gone
6. h. had
7. f. jogged
8. g. made
9. c. seen
10. i. tried

Exercise 2
2. A: <u>Has she gone</u> running lately?
   B: Yes, she usually runs in the morning and evening.
3. A: <u>Have you eaten</u> at the new Brazilian restaurant?
   B: Yes, we've already eaten there. It's excellent, but very expensive.
4. A: How many times <u>have you gone</u> shopping at the mall this month?
   B: Actually, I haven't gone at all. Let's go today! I hear there's a new music store there.
5. A: How many international phone calls <u>have you made</u> this week?
   B: Only one – on my father's birthday.

Exercise 3
A
Answers will vary.
B
Answers will vary.

Exercise 4
Answers will vary.

Exercise 5
A
Answers will vary.
C

1	stayed in the mountains
2	lost a wallet
1	enjoyed the view
1 and 2	got no exercise
2	spent time on a boat
1	waited for help
2	went swimming
1 and 2	had a terrible day

Exercise 6
2. A: Have <u>you ever seen a sumo wrestling match?</u>
   B: Actually, I saw a sumo wrestling match last month on TV. It was terrific.
3. A: <u>Have you ever been camping?</u>
   B: No, I haven't. I've never been camping.
4. A: <u>Have you ever eaten oysters?</u>
   B: Yes, I have. I ate oysters last year in France.
5. A: <u>Have you ever gone wall climbing?</u>
   B: Yes, I went wall climbing on Friday night.
6. A: <u>Have you ever ridden a motorcycle?</u>
   B: Yes, I have. My brother once let me ride his motorcycle.
7. A: <u>Have you ever been to India?</u>
   B: No, I've never been to India.
8. A: <u>Have you ever had a bad dream?</u>
   B: Yes, I had a bad dream just last night.

Exercise 7
Answers will vary.

Exercise 8
B: Yes, I <u>lost</u> my watch last month.
A: <u>Have</u> you <u>found</u> it yet?
B: No. Actually, <u>I've</u> already <u>bought</u> a new one. Look!
A: Oh, that's nice. Where <u>did</u> you <u>buy</u> it?
B: I <u>got</u> it at the street market last weekend. What about you? <u>Have</u> you ever <u>lost</u> anything valuable?
A: Well, I <u>left</u> my address book in a pay phone a couple of months ago.
B: How annoying! Maybe that's why you <u>haven't called</u> me for a while.
A: That's right. I can't even remember my own phone number! But you <u>haven't called</u> me in a long time. What's your excuse?
B: I told you. I <u>lost</u> my watch, so I <u>haven't had</u> the time!
A: Very funny!

Exercise 9
2. A: Are you having a good time?
   B: <u>Really good.</u>
3. A: How many times has he seen the show?
   B: <u>Twice.</u>
4. A: What about a tour of the city?
   B: <u>Sure. I hear it's great.</u>

It's a very exciting city!

Exercise 1

2. My hometown is not an exciting place.
   The nightlife there is pretty <u>boring.</u>
3. Rome is a beautiful old city.
   There are not many <u>modern</u> buildings.
4. Some parts of this city are fairly dangerous.
   They're not very <u>safe</u> late at night.
5. Athens is a very quiet city in the winter.
   The streets are never <u>crowded</u> at that time of the year.

Exercise 2

A: <u>What's your hometown like?</u>
B: My hometown? Oh, it's a pretty nice place.
A: <u>Is it big?</u>
B: No, it's fairly small, and it has a lot of beautiful buildings.
A: <u>What's the weather like?</u>
B: The winter is wet and too cold. It's very nice in the summer, though.
A: <u>Is the nightlife exciting?</u>
B: No! It's really boring after six o'clock in the evening.

Exercise 3

2. Prague is a very nice place. The winters are terribly cold, <u>though.</u>
3. Sydney is a relaxing city, <u>and</u> it has a wonderful harbor.
4. My hometown is a great place for a vacation, <u>but</u> it's not too good for shopping.
5. Our hometown is fairly ugly and dirty. It has some beautiful old houses, <u>however.</u>

Exercise 4

2. _____ Restaurants are very cheap in Mexico.
3. ✓ Copenhagen is <u>a</u> clean city.
4. _____ The buildings in Paris are really beautiful.
5. _____ Apartments are very expensive in Hong Kong.
6. ✓ Amsterdam is <u>a</u> fairly crowded city in the summer.
7. _____ Toronto has good museums.
8. ✓ Rio is <u>an</u> exciting place to visit.

Exercise 5

Travel Britain

London <u>is</u> Britain's biggest city. It <u>has</u> a very old capital and dates back to the Romans. It <u>is</u> a city of interesting buildings and churches, and it <u>has</u> many beautiful parks. It also <u>has</u> some of the best museums in the world. London <u>is</u> very crowded in the summer, but it <u>is</u> not too busy in the winter. It <u>is</u> a popular city with foreign tourists and <u>has</u> more than eight million visitors a year. The city <u>is</u> famous for its shopping and <u>has</u> many excellent department stores. London <u>has</u> convenient trains and buses that cross the city, so it <u>is</u> easy for tourists to get around.

Exercise 6

B

City	Date founded	Population	Weather	Tourist attractions
Budapest	*1872*	*3 million*	very cold in the winter	the Danube nightlife
Los Angeles	1781	3.5 million	smoggy dry and warm	film studios Hollywood Boulevard beaches Disneyland
Taipei	18th century	2.3 million	humid not pleasant	museum shopping

C

2. <u>Los Angeles</u> has good beaches nearby.
3. <u>Budapest</u> was once two cities.
4. <u>Los Angeles and Taipei</u> were both founded in the eighteenth century.

Exercise 7

2. You <u>shouldn't stay</u> near the airport. It's too noisy.
3. You <u>shouldn't miss</u> the museum. It has some new exhibits.
4. You <u>can take</u> a bus tour of the city if you like.
5. You <u>shouldn't walk</u> alone at night. It's too dangerous.
6. You <u>should travel</u> by taxi if you're out late.

Exercise 8

B: <u>You shouldn't</u> miss Jogjakarta, the old capital city. There are a lot of beautiful old buildings. For example, <u>you should</u> see the temple of Borobudur.
A: Sounds great. Bali is very popular, too. <u>Should I</u> go there?
B: Yes, <u>you should.</u> It's very interesting.
A: <u>Should I</u> take a lot of money with me?
B: No, <u>you shouldn't.</u> Indonesia is not an expensive country.
A: So when <u>should I</u> go there?
B: Well, it's always hot and humid, so it really doesn't matter.

Exercise 9

Possible questions:

2. What can you see and do there?
3. What shouldn't you do there?
4. What special foods should you try?
5. What should you buy there?
6. What other interesting things can you do?

Exercise 10

2. The streets are always crowded.
3. It's a fairly ugly city.
4. What's a good time to visit the city?
5. You really shouldn't miss the flea markets.
6. What should we do there?

It really works!

Exercise 1

A

Suggested answers:

2. a headache: take some aspirin
3. a bad cold: go to bed and rest
4. an insect bite: put anti-itch cream on it
5. the hiccups: drink lots of hot water

B

Possible answers:

2. A: What should you do for a headache?
   B: It's useful to take some aspirin.
3. A: What should you do for a bad cold?
   B: It's important to go to bed and rest.
4. A: What should you do for an insect bite?
   B: It's a good idea to put anti-itch cream on it.
5. A: What should you do for the hiccups?
   B: It's helpful to drink lots of hot water.

Exercise 2

Possible answers:

2. For a sore throat, it's a good idea not to talk too much.
3. For a burn, it's important not to put ice on it.
4. For insomnia, it's helpful not to drink coffee at night.
5. For a fever, it's important not to get out of bed.

Exercise 3

Answers will vary.

Exercise 4

A

Answers will vary.

B

1. False
2. False
3. True
4. True
5. False
6. True
7. True
8. True

Exercise 5

A

Bottle	Box	Can	Tube
eye drops	cough drops	insect spray	ointment
pills	tissues	sunburn spray	cream

B

Possible answers:

2. Mary has a bad cold.
   She should buy a box of tissues.
3. Andrew and Carlos have a lot of insect bites.
   They should buy a can of insect spray.
4. David has dry skin.
   He should buy a tube of cream.

Exercise 6

1. CUSTOMER: Yes. Can I have a package of bandages?
   PHARMACIST: Here you are.
   CUSTOMER: And what do you have for a sunburn?
   PHARMACIST: I suggest this lotion.
   CUSTOMER: Thanks.
2. PHARMACIST: Hi. Can I help you?
   CUSTOMER: Yes. Could I have something for sore muscles?
   PHARMACIST: Sure. Try this ointment.
   CUSTOMER: Thanks. And what do you suggest for the flu?
   PHARMACIST: Try some of these tablets. They really work.
   CUSTOMER: OK, thanks. I'll take them. And could I have a box of tissues?
   PHARMACIST: Sure. Here you are.

Exercise 7

A: Wow, you don't look very good! Do you feel OK?
B: No, I think I'm getting a cold. What should I do _for_ it?
A: You should stay _at_ home and go _to_ bed.
B: You're probably right. I've got a really bad cough, too.
A: Try drinking some hot tea _with_ honey. It really helps.
B: Anything else?
A: Yeah, I suggest you get a big box _of_ tissues!

Exercise 8

Possible answers:

2. I think I'm getting a cold.
   You should get a bottle of vitamin C.
3. I have a backache. And don't tell me to go to bed!
   I suggest a heating pad.
4. I have a terrible stomachache.
   Try some antacid.

May I take your order, please?

Exercise 1
2. So do I.
3. I am, too.
4. Neither do I.
5. I don't either.
6. I do, too.

Exercise 2

A
Answers will vary.

B
Answers will vary.

Exercise 3

A
Answers will vary.

C

	Trattoria Romana	Dynasty	Beirut Cafe
Food	*Italian*	American	Lebanese
Atmosphere	*quiet and relaxing*	boring	lively
Specialties	desserts	steak and potatoes	meze
Service	very good	slow and unfriendly	very friendly
Price/person	about $25	$22	about $18
Reservation	yes	no	yes

Exercise 4

Kate's Diner

Main Dishes
(includes salad and choice of potatoes)
grilled *salmon*
roast beef
turkey sandwich

Soups
chicken noodle soup
French onion soup
clam chowder

Salads
chicken salad
pasta salad
mixed greens

Desserts
chocolate cake
apple pie
ice cream

Beverages
coffee   milk   tea

Exercise 5
WAITER: What kind of dressing would you like on your salad – French, Italian or vinaigrette?
CUSTOMER: French, please.
WAITER: And would you like anything to drink?
CUSTOMER: Yes. I'll have iced coffee.
WAITER: Anything else?
CUSTOMER: No, thanks.

Exercise 6
2. A: What kind of soda would you like?
   B: I'll have a cola.
3. A: Would you like anything to drink?
   B: No, thanks.
4. A: What flavor ice cream would you like?
   B: Vanilla, please.
5. A: Would you like anything else?
   B: That will be all, thanks.

Exercise 7
SHERRY: It's delicious. I like it a lot.
WHITNEY: I do, too. It's my favorite kind of food. Let's call Chiang Mai restaurant for home delivery.
SHERRY: Great idea! Their food is always good. I eat there a lot.
WHITNEY: So do I. Well, what would you like tonight?
SHERRY: I'm in the mood for some soup.
WHITNEY: So am I. And I think I will have spicy chicken and special Thai rice.
SHERRY: OK, let's order. Oh, wait a minute, I don't have any money.
WHITNEY: Neither do I. What should we do?
SHERRY: Well, let's look in the refrigerator. Hmm. Do you like boiled eggs?
WHITNEY: I can't stand them.
SHERRY: Actually, neither can I.

Exercise 8
2. Baked potatoes are less greasy than french fries.
3. Many people like dressing on their salad.
4. Some people rarely cook with spices. They prefer bland food.
5. Vanilla is a popular ice cream flavor.

The biggest and the best!

Exercise 1

A
2. b. forest
3. c. swamp
4. a. lake
5. c. volcano
6. a. desert

B
2. Amazon River
3. Lake Superior
4. Mount Fuji
5. Mediterranean Sea
6. Niagara Falls
7. Pacific Ocean
8. Sahara Desert

Exercise 2

2. cooler	the coolest		7. older	the oldest
3. friendlier	the friendliest		8. safer	the safest
4. heavier	the heaviest		9. smaller	the smallest
5. nicer	the nicest		10. wetter	the wettest
6. noisier	the noisiest			

Exercise 3

IAN: Well, it certainly has some of <u>the most famous</u> cities in the world – Rome, Milan, Venice.

VAL: Yeah. I had <u>the best</u> time in Venice.
It's <u>the most beautiful</u> city I've ever seen.
Of course, it's also one of <u>the most popular</u> tourist attractions.
It was <u>the most crowded</u> city I visited this summer, and there weren't even any cars!

IAN: I've always wanted to visit Venice. What's it like in the winter?

VAL: Actually, that's <u>the worst</u> time to visit.
Venice is one of <u>the coldest</u> and <u>foggiest</u> places in Italy in the winter.

Exercise 4

3. <u>The highest</u> waterfall in the world is in Venezuela.
4. The Suez Canal joins the Mediterranean and Red seas. It is 190 kilometers (118 miles) long. It is <u>longer than</u> the Panama Canal.
5. The Atacama Desert in Chile is <u>the driest</u> place in the world.
6. Mount Walialeale in Hawaii gets 1,170 centimeters (460 inches) of rain a year.
It is <u>the wettest</u> place on earth!
7. <u>The hottest</u> capital city in the world is Muscat, in Oman.
8. The continent of Antarctica is <u>colder than</u> any other place in the world.
9. The Himalayas are some of <u>the most dangerous</u> mountains to climb.

10. Badwater, in California's Death Valley, is <u>the lowest</u> point in North America.
11. Mont Blanc in the French Alps is <u>higher than</u> the Matterhorn in the Swiss Alps.
12. The Pacific Ocean is <u>deeper than</u> the Atlantic Ocean. In some places the Pacific Ocean is 11,033 meters (36,198 feet) deep.

Exercise 5

A
Answer will vary.

C
1. False
2. False
3. True
4. False
5. False
6. False

Exercise 6

2. How far is New Zealand from Australia?
a. It's about 2,000 kilometers (1,200 miles).
3. How long is the Amazon River?
a. It's 6,437 kilometers (4,000 miles) long.
4. How cold is Antarctica?
b. It gets down to minus 88.3 degrees Celsius.
5. How big is the Amazon Rain Forest?
a. It's 6 million square kilometers (2½ million miles).
6. How deep is the Grand Canyon?
b. It's about 1.6 kilometers deep.

Exercise 7

Crossword:
1 Down: colder
2 Across: smallest
3 Down: earliest
4 Down: most
5 Down: hotter
6 Across: good
7 Across: longer
8 Across: better
9 Across: best
10 Across: far
11 Across: highest
11 Down: hottest
12 Down: worst
13 Across: wettest
14 Across: cold
15 Across: tallest

I'm going to see a musical.

Exercise 1

have	see
a beach party	a play
a barbecue	a rock concert

visit	watch
an amusement park	a ballgame on TV
a museum	a video

Exercise 2
Possible answers:
2. On Monday, she's working overtime to finish the report.
3. On Tuesday evening at 7:00, she's seeing a play with Tony.
4. On Wednesday night, she's watching the hockey game with Kate and Sam.
5. On Thursday, she's having a barbecue at noon.
6. On Friday, she's staying home and watching the late show on TV.
7. On Saturday afternoon, she's going to an arts festival.

Exercise 3
MARK: I'm going to go to an art gallery on Saturday.
MARTA: That sounds interesting.
MARK: Yeah. There's a new exhibit at the Modern. And how about you, Marta?
MARTA: Well, Brain and I are going to see a ballgame in the afternoon.
MARK: And what are you going to do in the evening?
MARTA: Brian's going to visit his mother in the hospital. But I'm not going to do anything really.
MARK: Well, I'm going to have some friends over for a barbecue. Would you like to come?
MARTA: Thanks. I'd love to.

Exercise 4
2. A: Do you want to visit the street fair with us tomorrow?
   B: Sure, I'd love to.
3. A: We're having friends over for dinner tonight. Would you like to come?
   B: I'm working late tonight. I'm sorry.
4. A: How about dinner at the Mexican restaurant tonight?
   B: Great! But it's my turn to pay.

Exercise 5
Answers will vary.

Exercise 6
Answers will vary.

Exercise 7
A
Answers will vary.

B
Answers will vary.

C
1. True
2. False: It is possible to send letters and reports by faxing them over telephone lines.
3. True
4. False: You can carry a cellular phone in your pocket.
5. False: Now you can take your calls with you every where.

Exercise 8
Possible answers:
1. Please ask her to bring the last fax from New York.
2. Could you tell Mr. Alvarez that we need the report by noon? Please ask him to call Ms. James as soon as possible.
3. Would you tell Dr. James that the new fax machine is ready? Could you tell her to pick it up this afternoon?

Exercise 9
Possible answers:
1. Please ask Michael not to meet me at the airport until midnight. Would you tell him that the plane is going to be late?
2. Please tell Lucy that we're meeting at Dino's house before the concert. Could you ask her not to forget the tickets?
3. Could you tell Christopher that the beach party starts at noon. Please ask him not to be late.

Exercise 10
SECRETARY: I'm sorry. She's not in. Can I take a message?
MS. CURTIS: Yes, please. This is Ms. Curtis. Would you tell her that I'm staying at the Plaza Hotel? The number is 735-9001, Room 605. Could you tell her to call me?
SECRETARY: OK, Ms. Curtis. I'll give her the message.
MS. CURTIS: Thank you very much. Good-bye.

Exercise 11
2. Could I ask her to call you back?
   Yes. My number is 669-3241.
3. Who's calling?
   My name's Graham. Graham Lock.
4. Can I take a message?
   Yes, please. Could you tell him Ros called?
5. Could I speak to Paul, please?
   Let me see if he's in.
6. I'm sorry. She's busy at the moment.
   That's OK. I'll call back.

A change for the better!

Exercise 1

2. A: I haven't seen you for ages.
   B: <u>I know. How have you been?</u>
3. A: You know, I have three kids now.
   B: <u>That's terrific.</u>
4. A: How are you?
   B: <u>I'm doing really well.</u>

Exercise 2

2. Kim and Anna <u>have stopped eating out in
   restaurants</u>. Now they cook dinner at home every
   evening. It's much cheaper.
3. Alex<u>'s started going to the gym</u>. He looks healthier,
   and he has more energy.
4. Jerry<u>'s spent a lot of money on clothes</u>. He needs to
   dress up for his new job.

Exercise 3

Answers will vary. Possible answers:

2. Susan doesn't smoke anymore. *or* Susan smoked
   a lot.
3. Elena doesn't wear glasses now. She looks better
   than before. *or* Elena wore glasses before.

Exercise 4

Possible answers:

2. James was heavier before.
3. Mary has changed schools.
4. Tess is divorced.
5. My hair is longer.
6. We quit smoking.

Exercise 5

A

Answers will vary.

B

1. Aki   <u>c</u>
   Now I actually look forward to getting up early.
   I dress up now.
   My hair is shorter.
2. Luis   <u>a</u>
   I got married!
   My wife and I often have friends for dinner.
   We're taking evening classes.
3. Rosie   <u>b</u>
   Now I work as a computer programmer.
   I've gained several kilos.
   I feel much happier and healthier.

Exercise 6

2. Marie lost her job. Now she's <u>broke</u>, and she can't pay
   her rent.
3. Now that I'm going to college, I want to be more
   <u>responsible</u> about doing my classwork.
4. Lucy wants to pay off her student <u>loan</u> before she
   buys a car.
5. Philip plans to <u>retire</u> at an early age. He's almost 55
   now.
6. I'd like to be <u>successful</u> in my first job. Then I can get
   a better job and a raise.

Exercise 7

LEO: I <u>want to get</u> a summer job.
   <u>I'd like to save</u> money for a vacation.
MELISSA: Really? <u>Where would you like to go?</u>
LEO: Well, I<u>'d love to travel</u> to Latin America.
   What about you, Melissa?
MELISSA: I<u>'m not going to get</u> a job right away.
   I <u>want to go</u> to Spain and Portugal.
LEO: Sounds great, but how <u>are you going to pay</u> for it?
MELISSA: I <u>hope to borrow</u> some money from my brother.
   I have a good excuse. I <u>plan to take</u> courses in Spanish
   and Portuguese.
LEO: Oh, I'm tired of studying!
MELISSA: So am I. But I also <u>hope to take</u> people on tours
   to Latin America. Why don't you come on my first
   tour?

Exercise 8

Answers will vary. Possible answers:

1. I hope to find a new job.
   I want to make more money.
   I plan to take a computer class.
2. I'm going to go to a gym.
   I'd like to stop smoking.
   I'd love to find a new job.
3. I'm going to join a singles club.
   I want to meet new people.
   I plan to move into town.

Exercise 9

2. Heather's salary is much <u>lower than</u> before. She
   had to take a pay cut.
3. I dress up for my new job, and I'm always on time
   now. I'm <u>more responsible</u> these days.
4. After graduation, Jack plans <u>to work</u> for an
   international company.
5. This job is <u>more stressful than</u> my last job.
6. Mel hopes <u>to move</u> to a small town.

Exercise 10

Answers will vary.